The Age of Electronic Messages

New Liberal Arts Series

Light, Wind, and Structure: The Mystery of the Master Builders
Robert Mark

The Age of Electronic Messages
John G. Truxal

Medical Technology and Society: An Interdisciplinary Perspective
Joseph D. Bronzino, Vincent H. Smith, and Maurice L. Wade

Understanding Quantitative History
Lauren Haskins and Kirk Jeffrey

This book is published as part of an Alfred P. Sloan Foundation program.

The Age of Electronic Messages

John G. Truxal

The MIT Press
Cambridge, Massachusetts
London, England

Third printing, 1991

© 1990 Massachusetts Institute of Technology

This book was set in Galliard and Univers by The MIT Press using disks provided by the author, and was printed and bound in the United States of America.

Library of Congress Cataloging-in-Publication Data

Truxal, John G.
  The age of electronic messages / John G. Truxal.
    p. cm. — (New liberal arts series)
  ISBN 0-262-20074-0
  1. Telecommunication. 2. Electronics. I. Title. II. Series.
TK5101.T79 1990
621.382—dc20   89-12669
                                                           CIP

To
Keith, Leila, Steven T, David, and Steven F.—
a wonderful group of grandchildren who
will live in the age of electronic messages.

Contents

12   Broadcasting and Narrowcasting   457

Series Foreword

The Alfred P. Sloan Foundation's New Liberal Arts (NLA) Program stems from the belief that a liberal education for our time should involve undergraduates in meaningful experiences with technology and with quantitative approaches to problem solving in a wide range of subjects and fields. Students should understand not only the fundamental concepts of technology and how structures and machines function, but also the scientific and cultural settings within which engineers work, and the impacts (positive and negative) of technology on individuals and society. They should be much more comfortable than they are with making calculations, reasoning with numbers and symbols, and applying mathematical and physical models. These methods of learning about nature are increasingly important in more and more fields. They also underlie the process by which engineers create the technologies that exercise such vast influence over all our lives.

The program is closely associated with the names of Stephen White and James D. Koerner, both vice-presidents (retired) of the foundation. Mr. White wrote an internal memorandum in 1980 that led to the launching of the program two years later. In it he argued for quantitative reasoning and technology as "new" liberal arts, not as replacements for the liberal arts as customarily identified, but as liberating modes of thought needed for understanding the technological world in which we now live. Mr. Koerner administered the program for the foundation, successfully leading it through its crucial first four years.

The foundation's grants to 36 undergraduate colleges and 12 universities have supported a large number of seminars, workshops, and symposia on topics in technology and applied mathematics. Many new courses have been developed and existing courses modified at these colleges. Some minors or concentrations in technology studies have been organized. A Resource Center for the NLA Program, located at Stony Brook, publishes and distributes a monthly newsletter, collects and disseminates syllabi, teaching modules, and other materials prepared at the colleges and universities taking part in the program, and serves in a variety of ways to bring news of NLA activities to all who express interest and request information.

As the program progressed, faculty members who had developed successful new liberal arts courses began to prepare textbooks. Also, a number of the foundation's grants to universities were used to support writing projects of professors—often from engineering departments—who had taught well-attended courses in technology and applied mathematics that had been designed to be accessible to liberal arts undergraduates. It seemed appropriate not only to encourage the preparation of books for such courses, but also to find a way to publish and thereby make available to the widest possible audience the best products of these teaching experiences and writing projects. This is the background with which the foundation approached The MIT Press and the McGraw-Hill Publishing Company about publishing a series of books on the new liberal arts. Their enthusiastic response led to the launching of the New Liberal Arts Series.

The publishers and the Alfred P. Sloan Foundation express their appreciation to the members of the Editorial Advisory Board for the New Liberal Arts Series: John G. Truxal, Distinguished Teaching Professor, Department of Technology and Society, State University of New York, Stony Brook, Chairman; Joseph Bordogna, Alfred Fitler Moore Professor and Dean, School of Engineering and Applied Science, University of Pennsylvania; Robert W. Mann, Whitaker Professor of Biomedical Engineering, Massachusetts Institute of Technology; Merritt Roe Smith, Professor of the History of Technology, Massachusetts Institute of Technology; J. Ronald Spencer, Associate Academic Dean and Lecturer in History, Trinity College; and Allen B. Tucker, Jr., Professor of Computer Science, Bowdoin College. In developing this new publication program, The MIT Press has been represented by Frank P. Satlow and the McGraw-Hill Publishing Company by Eric M. Munson.

Samuel Goldberg
Program Officer
Alfred P. Sloan Foundation

Preface

As the twentieth century draws to a close, the study of technology has emerged as a critically important discipline. Active participation in many public decisions requires that we learn the capabilities and limitations of the technologies involved. In addition, understanding technology allows us to function more effectively at work and to enjoy more fully our leisure activities.

Technology covers many different topics—structures, energy, materials, and so on. To achieve any depth of understanding, we have to concentrate on one area of technology. The technology of communications seems especially appropriate for concentrated study. Many people have an appreciable general familiarity with and a considerable interest in audio and television systems, communications satellites, radar, and computer speech. In addition, many students perceive the subject as directly relevant to their careers and their future leisure activities. The technology of communications is easily demonstrated, and is changing rapidly, and it illustrates well the characteristics, limitations, and capabilities of modern technology in general.

The course from which this book evolved has been offered since 1979 at the State University of New York at Stony Brook. About 5,000 students have taken the course, and they have provided valuable feedback. The course is usually taught with the help of undergraduate teaching assistants ("alumni" from the preceding year), who have contributed to its development.

I also want to recognize the contributions made by my colleagues on the Stony Brook faculty—notably my frequent adviser and close friend Marian Visich, Jr., and my friend Thomas Liao. The comments of J. Ronald Spencer (Trinity College), Allan Mazur (Syracuse University), and many others have also been helpful. The enormous task of putting my materials into presentable form has been handled beautifully in every way by my associate Mrs. Carol Galdi, with major contributions by Mrs. Linda Erickson. After 17 years at Stony Brook, I still find it a stimulating place to work. The Alfred P. Sloan Foundation has supported my work in the New Liberal Arts Program and many of the activities that culminated in this book.

I now come to the most important contributor, my wife Doris. She has patiently sat through three offerings of the course and has provided essential feedback, rewriting, and substantive suggestions. She clearly should be considered a co-author of the book.

The Age of Electronic Messages

Chapter 1
The Technology of Communications

The elaborate ability to communicate distinguishes us from other animals. Today we communicate either by speech and the written word or by the vast technology of radio, light, and sound. In the electronic arena, an explosion is underway. Never before have we been able to transfer information in such great quantities, so accurately, so rapidly, and to and from such remote parts of the world.

We can send messages to submarines deep underwater, monitor the blood pressure of astronauts in space, take television pictures inside the human body, and transmit 5,000 simultaneous telephone conversations on a single cable across thousands of miles. The "information age" is made possible by the new capability to communicate electronically and to process information with computers.

This book focuses on the ideas underlying the technology of communications. By understanding the scientific principles behind it, the reader will hopefully be better able to recognize its capabilities, limitations, and dangers.

The industrial revolution drastically changed the lives of people in the nineteenth century. The water-powered factories of Lowell, Massachusetts, for example, attracted farm girls from northern New England, and then immigrants from Europe, to an urban life unknown early in the century. The transcontinental railroad ended the wagon trains west and quickly led to statehood for the American territories.

The information revolution we are witnessing today is having an even greater impact on the way people think and act. Let us look at some of the reasons why this technology is so important; in the course of doing so, we will define what we mean by the term *communications technology*.

1.1 Social Changes

The average home has the television set on at least seven hours a day. This means that the typical high school student has spent more hours watching TV than sitting in classrooms. Consequently, the knowledge possessed by an 18-year-old American has been determined to a great extent by television. Students are likely to be much more familiar with international events than their parents were at the same age, but also less able to do routine math calculations or to write reasonably well.

The ability of the TV camera to show us what is happening in other parts of the world can greatly change our attitudes. During the Vietnam war, television brought pictures of dying men, homeless people, and starving children into our living rooms daily. No amount of flag waving or flashy parades could counter the effects of this.

In addition, television both reflects and influences the place of women in society. Seeing women depicted as lawyers, scientists, doctors, and business leaders, the public begins to accept these roles as suitable for women. Similarly, television has given the population around the country more common attitudes and experiences; it has diminished regional differences.

The adverse effects of TV are familiar. We worry that children will copy the violent behavior they see or the reckless driving habits of TV heros. The unrealistic picture of the "supermom" who holds a responsible job, runs a busy household, and continually keeps herself beautiful, energetic, and in good humor may contribute to the increase in depression among young women. Periodically there is a rash of airplane hijackings, each one receiving extensive coverage. Extremists quickly learn to use television to further their political objectives; consequently, in a sense the TV coverage of one hijacking causes another. In a similar vein, political assassinations are probably encouraged by the publicity they receive.

1.2 Political Effects

Franklin Delano Roosevelt, Adolf Hitler, and Winston Churchill were the first great masters in the use of radio to gain political objectives. All three were persuasive orators who sensed the effectiveness of this new means of mass communications. Hitler's meteoric rise to absolute power stemmed from economic and social conditions in Germany, but was possible only because of his ability to reach into every home through radio. Today, TV and radio play a central role in information control in dictatorships, and are of major importance as the Third World nations try to move toward developed status.

In our own country, we see how charismatic politicians can make use of the media.

1.3 Transportation

The worldwide air and ship transportation systems and the management of the taxi, railroad, and trucking systems, depend on rapid, accurate relaying of information by means of radar, sonar, and radio. Electronic technology makes possible the most sophisticated navigational system (Navstar) as well as the auto dashboard display that presents an ongoing record of fuel economy.

Within the next few years, communications will have a major impact on the flow of automobile traffic in urban areas. Sensors will measure traffic density and speed at many points, computers will determine optimum routes, and the system will communicate to you (the driver) how best to move toward your desired destination. You will be a part of this automated communication system.

1.4 Manufacturing

Today communication and transportation technologies mean we are living in a small world. Our manufacturing industries must compete with those of countries (such as Korea) that provide much lower wages and poorer fringe benefits. We must emphasize productivity and quality control—in other words, we must lead in automation. This essentially involves two technologies: communications and robotics.

An automobile assembly plant is one example. Here, because of options available in color and accessories, the plant makes thousands of different cars (in one year, no two cars may be identical). As the parts are assembled step by step, a central computer sends appropriate instructions to each section along the assembly line. For example, when welding is to be done, a robot must be told exactly where to weld. Furthermore, at many locations, tests are made to ensure quality; the results are communicated to the computer, which then decides on the next step. The success of such automation depends critically on the communications technology—in many cases, in an environment of excessive noise, vibration, and electromagnetic interference.

1.5 Service Industries

Communication is also central to the improved productivity and performance of the service industries (government, criminal justice, insurance, health care, the mails, and so on). Today's banking is possible only because of electronic communications and data processing. Experts have estimated that if the methods of 1950 were still in use, the Bank of America alone would now be employing more than half of the workers in the state of California.

1.6 Entertainment

Over 100 million people watch the Super Bowl on TV. The popularity of TV news shows has unquestionably been a major factor in the sharp drop in the number of daily newspapers. Our reliance on TV, radio, and recorded music as our primary sources of entertainment affects not only our way of life, but the economy of the country as well.

These few examples illustrate how communications technology dominates our lives. I have not even mentioned such diverse applications as the use of automation in our criminal justice system, in medicine, in the military, or in helping the physically handicapped.

1.7 Factors in Decisions about a New Technology

As we consider communications systems in the following chapters, we will encounter three major factors that arise again and again in the study of technology. Besides making the work of engineers difficult and challenging, these factors must be considered by all of us when we are faced with decisions about whether to allow or encourage a new technology.

1. The technology should be matched to the characteristics and capabilities of the human users so that they will be able to use it without making major changes in their behavior. This requirement means that the engineer must be familiar with physiology and psychology. The telephone system does not attempt to reproduce all sounds made by the person speaking; that would be unnecessary and too expensive. Instead, we determine scientifically which parts of the sound are necessary in order for the message to seem natural and intelligible to the listener. For this, we need to know how human hearing works.

2. A system employing a new technology should be well-designed, because once the technology is in use changes are likely to be difficult or impossible. For example, the doctor's stethoscope—first used in the early nineteenth century—distorts chest sounds badly; nonetheless, physicians are accustomed to diagnosing from these poorly communicated sounds, and a well-engineered stethoscope with accurate reproduction of chest sounds finds no market.

3. Perhaps most important, we must anticipate the possible consequences of the new technology. While we all accept risk as a daily part of our lives, we need to weigh the risks posed by a new technology against the benefits to be derived from it.

Studying the effects of technology on human health is usually difficult, at least if we seek solid, scientific evidence. What has been the effect of radiation from citizen's band radios on truck drivers and motorists? Unfortunately, even major epidemiological studies may be unable to answer such a question, since environmental effects often appear only decades later, and since the causes may be synergistic (for example, drivers who use CB radios may have other habits whose effects combine with the radiation and make it hazardous).

The risks of a new technology may be economic or social as well as medical. For example, more and more states are authorizing "home arrests." The convicted criminal is allowed to live at home, but must wear an ankle bracelet containing a radio transmitter to allow continuous monitoring of his location. Such a system clearly reduces the crowding of our prisons, but it raises the specter of invasion of privacy.

A new technology is often watched closely only until it becomes commonplace; then the monitoring is relaxed or disappears.

1.8 Measuring Information—A Central Concept

As we consider the various aspects of communications technology, we will find one concept appearing again and again—a concept which is the heart of engineering. A technology is designed on the basis of measurement of the information that is to be transmitted. In other words, how complex is the signal? If one computer is "talking" to another, relatively simple messages are sent and received—perhaps just a long sequence of zeros and ones. The information sent to create a changing television picture is much more complicated; for each point in the picture, both the brightness and the color must be communicated.

The idea of measuring information is crucial when a new technology interacts with people. When you receive new information (for example, by sight), you first store this information in your brain's short-term memory. If you will want to remember this much later, you then transfer it to your long-term memory. Suppose you look up a telephone number in the directory, then walk across the room to the phone. Unfortunately, by the time you start dialing, you have forgotten the number. The trouble is that you have not transferred the number to your long-term memory, and your short-term memory is able to store only about four chunks of information.

1.9 The Plan of the Book

The main topics of this book are the scientific principles that underlie the design of modern communications systems, the capabilities of these systems, their danger, and their impact on our lives. We are interested in electronic communication from person to person (both between two people and from one to many); from person to machine, and vice versa; and from machine to machine, as between computers.

Our interest is restricted to messages and information we can measure. When two people carry on a face-to-face conversation, probably more than half the information is conveyed by facial expressions and body language—aspects we still cannot measure well and hence cannot enhance or reproduce with technology. While we struggle to produce satisfactory computer-generated speech, we do not worry about giving the computer a capability for body language.

The underlying goal of the book is to show that modern technology is understandable by the layperson. I want to break down the barrier that separates the scientist-engineer from other concerned citizens. I want to convince you to become at least reasonably knowledgeable about technology, which so dominates our environment, so that you can assume a full role in today's world.

Chapter 2
Messages without Errors

We meet in a crowded supermarket where conversation is difficult, so I suggest that you call me when you are back home. You ask my phone number. I reply, "4236269," but the surrounding noise level is so high, neither of us is sure you have heard correctly. There are several ways we can check this:

1. I can simply repeat the number. If you hear the same set of seven digits, the chances are you have heard correctly.

2. You may say the number back to me. If I hear the correct number, again the odds suggest we're O.K.

3. I may tell you the *digital root* of the number—the remainder after dividing the number by 9. In this case, the digital root is 5. If you find the digital root of your number is also 5, we probably have communicated without an error. (See box 2.1.)

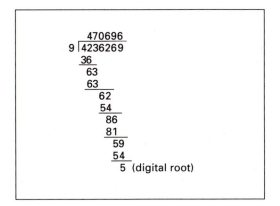

Box 2.1

In each case, we have used *redundancy* to improve the reliability of communication. In other words, to be sure you have understood my message, we have given and received more than the basic information. In case 1, we doubled the communication time by the repetition (I said the number twice); in case 2, we used feedback for checking (you repeated the number so I could be sure you heard it correctly); in case 3 we transmitted one additional check digit (5). If the environment is particularly noisy or if my pronunciation of the digits is not too clear, we might use even more elaborate schemes to make sure you heard the number correctly. In the following pages, we look at a few of the redundancy techniques that are used in modern communication systems.

2.1 Redundancy in Language

By nature, our language is very redundant. If we take an isolated sentence and omit 50 percent of the letters, we can usually understand the thought in the sentence. As an example, I have taken one clause from a paragraph (box 2.2) and have flipped a coin to decide which letters I will omit and which letters I will keep. If the coin came up with heads, the letter was discarded; if tails, the letter was retained.

From this example, we might deduce that our language is approximately 50 percent redundant: that is, information could be transmitted in half the letters. Actually, the redundancy of ordinary English is appreciably greater, since a full text (rather than a single sentence) tends to repeat and re-emphasize thoughts. If we read a novel, for example, we can skip significant sections without losing the details of the plot. As you read this chapter, you are aware of a great deal of redundancy.

National Geographic is a fine magazine—so fine in fact, that nobody ever throws it away. Issue after issue piles up in attics and basements and barns all over America gathering dust. There is no "recycling, just the horrible and relentless accumulation of this static vehicle of our doom!" Inexorably, -h-w-iht -f --e --gaz-n-- --ll tr-gg-r -a-thq--k-- -- C-l--o--i-, ---k c-a- min--g -owns, a-- prec-p--at- -ud s-id-s.

The sentence reads: Inexorably, the weight of the magazines will trigger earthquakes in California, sink coal mining towns, and preciptiate mud slides. This paragraph is taken from an article in Discover magazine about the humor magazine for scientists, Journal of Irreproducible Results. JIR printed an article entitled, National Geographic, the Doomsday Machine.

The result is on the verge of readability.

Box 2.2

2.2 Spelled Speech

When the background noise is excessive and the information must be transmitted with a high degree of accuracy, we can add enormous redundancy by switching to spelled speech: use of a word for each letter. The word "today", for example, is communicated by saying the words

Tango   Oscar   Delta   Alpha   Yankee

where the first letter of each word presents the message.

The International Civil Aviation Organization has agreed on a spelled speech alphabet for use in international communication among pilots and air traffic controllers. Because the communicators are of varying nationalities and have a wide range of native languages, words must be chosen which are easily understood regardless of accent. Box 2.3 shows the words that have been used. (The words in parentheses are the code used by the U.S. military before the international agreement on the ICAO alphabet.) A fascinating—and useless, unless you're a comedian—pastime is to search for a maximally incomprehensible alphabet—e.g., Aesthetic for A, Knight for K, Pneumonia for P, Oedipus for O, Tsar for T, Mnemonic for M, and so on.

Spelled speech represents an additional method of using redundancy to make sure our message is understood accurately. In contrast to the rote repetition or the feedback, spelled speech requires much more than the minimum time for communication; we effectively trade a great deal of time for vastly greater reliability.

2.3 Communicating Numbers

Sending messages by the use of language can be complex because each language has many set characteristics. For example, in English q is always followed by u except in proper names, and th starting a word is always followed by a vowel,

Alpha	(Able)	India	(Item)	Romeo	(Roger)
Bravo	(Baker)	Juliet	(Jig)	Sierra	(Sugar)
Charlie		Kilo	(King)	Tango	(Tare)
Delta	(Dog)	Lima	(Love)	Uniform	(Uncle)
Echo	(Easy)	Mike		Victor	
Foxtrot	(Fox)	November	(Nan)	Whiskey	(William)
Golf	(George)	Oscar	(Oboe)	Xray	
Hotel	(How)	Papa	(Peter)	Yankee	(Yoke)
		Quebec	(Queen	Zulu	(Zebra)

Box 2.3

r, or w. If we had a phone conversation and part of one sentence was garbled, the listener could surmise what the unclear words were because of the overall content of the conversation.

To understand different redundancy schemes, we will find it simpler to talk about numerical messages—that is, a sequence of separate digits like

5 1 6 4 2 3 6 2 6 9.

Here each number is an independent quantity: each digit can be anything from 0 through 9, and each is independent of the preceding or following digit.

Let us focus primarily on two number systems: binary numbers (to the base 2), such as

0 1 1 0 1 1 0 1,

where only two digits are used (0 and 1), and decimal numbers (to the base 10) such as

4 2 3 6 2 6 9,

where ten digits are used (0, 1, 2, 3, 4, 5, 6, 7, 8, 9).

The binary and decimal systems differ radically in the number of digits required to represent a quantity. The decimal number 115, for instance, is 1110011 in binary (box 2.5). In computers and communications, the increased length is offset by the advantage that only two symbols need be transmitted. If

---

Number systems can, of course, have any base, although historically only a few have been common:

Base 2   Certain aborigine cultures in Africa, Australia, and South
          America.

Base 3   One Brazilian tribe used the three joints of one finger

Base 4   Yuki Indians of California used the spaces between the fingers.

Base 5   Very common.

Base 10   Ancient China, Egypt, Greeks, Romans.

Base 20   Fairly common using fingers and toes to count. Mayan system
          was the most advanced. It survives today in French quatre-
          vingts for 80. This is where the term "score" meaning 20,
          originated.

Base 60   Babylonians (time and angle measurement still persists).

Box 2.4

Decimal number 115 in binary form:

(1)   The highest power of 2 less than 115 is 2^6 or 64. Hence the binary number starts with a 1 to be followed by six more digits (seven in all)

(2)   Subtracting 64 from 115 leaves 51. This is more than 32 (25) so the second digit is a 1.

(3)   Subtracting 32 from 51 leaves 19, more than 16 (24) so the third digit is a 1.

(4)   Subtracting 16 from 19 leaves 3, less than 8 so the fourth digit is a 0.

(5)   3 is also less than 4 (22) so the fifth digit is a zero.

(6)   3 is more than 2 so the sixth digit is a one, and the 1 left is represented by a 1 in the last digit.

Box 2.5

a 0 is represented by no pulse and a 1 by a pulse, the receiving equipment need only decide whether a pulse has been transmitted or not. There is no need to measure the size of the signal. For example, if a 1 is received as a 10-volt pulse and a 0 as no signal, any noise (which causes a pulse) less than 5 volts does not cause an error in communication.

2.4 Digital Root

For decimal numbers, the digital root of a number is *the remainder after division of that number by 9*. For example, the digital root of 24 is 6, and that of 427 is 4:

$$
\begin{array}{r}
2 \\
9\overline{)24} \\
18 \\
\hline
\end{array}
\quad \text{6 digital root}
\qquad
\begin{array}{r}
47 \\
9\overline{)427} \\
36 \\
\hline
67 \\
63 \\
\hline
\end{array}
\quad \text{4 digital root}
$$

The digital root of a number can be found without the tedious long division. We simply add the digits, then subtract as many nines as possible to leave the smallest possible positive integer (whole number). For example, to find the digital root of 427, we add digits $(4 + 2 + 7)$ and obtain the sum of 13; we then subtract 9 from the sum to obtain the digital root 4. Actually, since we are later going to subtract 9 as often as necessary, there is no point (when we add the digits) of including any sum equal to 9. Hence in adding

4 + 2 + 7

we omit the 2 + 7 and obtain the answer 4 immediately.

The proof that the digital root of a number is the same as the digital root of the sum of the digits is illustrated by the example

4281 (four thousand, two hundred, eighty-one).

This number is really

4(1000) + 2(100) + 8(10) + 1,

which can equally well be written

4(999 + 1) + 2(99 + 1) + 8(9 + 1) + 1

or

4 + 2 + 8 + 1 + 4(999) + 2(99) + 8(9) .

The part over the brace has no remainder when divided by 9. Hence, the remainder after dividing 4281 by 9 is the same as the remainder after dividing (4 + 2 + 8 + 1) by 9.

Thus, the digital root of 2713184 is found as follows. We first omit any digits adding to 9, as indicated by the underscoring below:

2 7 1 3 1 8 4

We are left with 1 + 3 + 4, or 8.

Thus, if we wish to communicate the phone number

4 2 3 6 2 6 9

we omit the 9, the 3, and the 6. Then we find the sum of the remaining integers: (4 + 2 + 2 + 6) = 14; we subtract 9, and the digital root is 5. After transmitting the complete phone number, we also send this digital root, so the message is

4 2 3 6 2 6 9 5 .

The 5 is a *redundant check digit*. The receiver knows the system being used, calculates the digital root for the first seven digits, and compares the result with the received 5. In this way, if any *single* digit is transmitted incorrectly, the receiver knows an incorrect message was received and can ask the sender to repeat the message.

This redundancy scheme is useful for *error detection*, but not for automatic *error correction*. In other words, the receiver knows there is an error, but has no idea which digit is incorrect. Furthermore, the redundancy catches with certainty only a single error. If the receiver above determined the message to be

4 2 1 6 4 6 9 5

there would be no indication of an error (the third digit is 2 less than it should be, the fifth 2 more, so the digital root of the first seven digits is still 5).

The study of numbers that are numerically congruent (that is, numbers with the same digital root or, more generally, with the same remainder after division by any number) was first emphasized by Carl Friedrich Gauss, a nineteenth-century genius called the "prince of mathematicians." At the age of 10, he entered his first arithmetic class, where the teacher kept the students busy for long periods by asking for some such sum as that of the 100 numbers in the arithmetic progression

81297, 81495, 81693, . . . 100899

(where each number is 198 more than the preceding one). Although he had never heard of such a problem, Gauss found the formula immediately and gave the correct answer in seconds. This so impressed the teacher that Gauss was excused from the regular studies and allowed to work with a mathematics tutor. Before the age of 20, Gauss was clearly on his way to being the greatest mathematician in Europe.

2.5 Casting Out Nines

The digital root is the basis for the checking technique of "casting out nines." When two numbers are added, subtracted, multiplied, or divided (with no remainder), the digital roots are related by the same operation.

Example 1:   <u>Addition</u>   Check (digital roots)

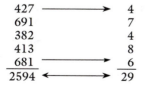

427	⟶	4
691		7
382		4
413		8
681	⟶	6
2594	⟷	29

Digital root of both 2594 and 29 is 2.

Example 2:   <u>Multiplication</u>   Digital roots

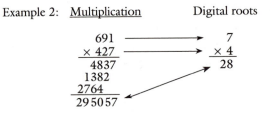

Digital root of both 295057 and 28 is 1.

The name "casting out nines" comes, of course, from our technique for finding digital roots: for each number, we simply throw out nines (or digits that add up to 9). This technique for checking arithmetic calculations (an approach that has also been used in computer circuitry) was discovered by the Arabs about 800 A.D. (As a result of the emphasis on the Greco-Roman heritage and the dominance of the Christian church in Europe during the Dark Ages, we tend to underrate the contributions made to our civilization by the Arabs. The Arabs contributed not only the number system, but also the algorithmic approach to problem-solving and important elements of algebra.)

2.6 Transmission with Error Correction

Now we want to look for *error correction* as well as *error detection*. That is, we not only want to know when an error has been transmitted, but we also want to know what the error is. We can do this by arranging the digits in a rectangular array (with zeros added, if necessary, to complete the rectangle). For example, we want to transmit the 12-digit number

4 7 2 9 3 6 8 2 1 7 4 3.

We first arrange the digits in a 3 × 4 array or matrix:

4 7 2 9
3 6 8 2
1 7 4 3

We sum each horizontal row and each vertical column and cast out tens. (This means we would use only the last digit of the sum—i.e., a 14 would be 4.) We place these digits to the right of and below the existing numbers.

```
4 7 2 9 | 2
3 6 8 2 | 9
1 7 4 3 | 5
8 0 4 4 | 6
```

worry about sending the item through backward. We are now down to sixteen possibilities for each half.

The last six, unnecessary possibilities disappear when two light and two dark regions are required—again a convenience for the machine, since a hair or a crack down the middle of a light space does not yield a false reading. (If a code is read that is not allowable, a buzzer sounds, the checker can then run the item through again and, if necessary, insert the number manually.)

Basically, the available redundancy has been used to increase the reliability of the machine's operation.

Pros and Cons

The development of this technology led to public arguments over the desirability of allowing supermarket automation. In an attempt to list the advantages and the disadvantages, a decision must be made as to the appropriate interest group: the customers, the store manager, or society as a whole (including the computer manufacturers and service personnel). Certain aspects may have disadvantages for one group, and advantages for another. Since this is not an attempt at a quantitative justification of the new technology, what follows is simply a list of the advantages and the problems.

Advantages

1. Checkout is much faster (the normal 50 items per minute   can rise to 100), and the extensive delay sometimes encountered when the checkout person doesn't know the price of an unmarked item is avoided. Actual experience indicates a 30 percent increase in productivity. This saving allows for more effective scheduling of store personnel and cuts the costs of store operation.

2. Errors in charging the customer are reduced by 75 percent in some tests. In many supermarkets, it is estimated that the total of undercharges approaches the total profit of the store. A significant loss arises from "sweetheart sales," where the checkout person intentionally undercharges a friend.

3. Store losses because of forgotten sales taxes are sharply reduced. Also, the customer can be confident that a sales tax is being charged only on taxable items.

4. The cost of handling coupons is reduced by perhaps 50 percent.

5. Each customer receives a clearer, more detailed sales receipt.

6. Inventory control is automated, and the cost of inventory can be significantly reduced.

7. Automated reordering helps to even the workload of warehouses and distributors. Saturdays are peak sales days, so, without a method of smoothing

the workload, orders tend to peak sharply on Monday. This is of particular importance to a chain of supermarkets.

8. The floor manager receives a signal automatically when a register requires change or cash pickup.

9. Detailed information is available to evaluate sales promotion campaigns or special offers.

10. Prices can be changed instantaneously from the computer terminal in the manager's office, so limited-time sales can be offered.

11. Records are easily completed at the end of each working day.

12. Prices need not be stamped on each item. Among consumer-interest groups, this feature is undoubtedly the most arguable. Several states have passed special legislation requiring prices on each item.

Disadvantages

1. The capital cost is high ($15,000 per checkout counter), and spares must be available. An immediate effect of widespread use will be the transfer of business from smaller stores to larger stores, which can afford the automation.

2. Maintenance and reliability problems are severe. System breakdown would be a disaster if a long period of repair were required.

3. Produce will increasingly be prepackaged with a reduction in customer choice. Produce can be handled by using scales that print appropriate gummed labels, but the trend toward prepackaging will undoubtedly grow.

4. If errors are made, they can be corrected, but only with some difficulty because of the equipment's complexity.

5. There will be less total employment, particularly of relatively unskilled people. In many cases of automation, this is a serious problem as more and more complex technology tends to demand workers with more education and specialized training.

6. Customers frequently mistrust technology, especially when it is new. A number of supermarket chains posted conspicuous signs promising that any item for which the machine overcharged would be given free to the purchaser. This mistrust symbolizes the kind of resistance that often characterizes techno-logical innovation.

Obviously a very convincing argument can be made either for or against supermarket automation from the viewpoint of the public. The basic question is whether the benefits from lower prices and improved service will outweigh the costs and risks of a more computerized living environment, less employ-ment of the relatively unskilled, and less freedom of personal choice.

These questions are not unique to supermarket automation; they often arise when automation of a service industry is considered (for example, the post office, library services, health care, or education). Unfortunately, there are never simple, obvious answers. In the supermarket case, the net public benefit depends on the extent to which cost savings are passed along to the customer and the amount by which service actually improves, both of which are really unpredictable.

As late as 1977, one candidate for supervisor in a populous county in New York ran on a platform which included the claim that he had kept supermarket automation out of the region—with the implied assumption that this was an accomplishment which the voters should praise. Such a political stand presumes that the average voter associates the term *automation* with unemployment and depersonalization. Yet any hope for greater productivity and better performance in the service industries demands the controlled introduction of automation—controlled in a way designed to prevent unemployment and to ensure a better quality of life.

Appendix 2.1
Telephone Numbers

Waiting at O'Hare Airport in Chicago, I decide to call my office and use my *calling card* (the phone company's name for its credit card). To carry out this operation, I have to dial the sequence of numbers

0 516 632 8760 P 516 423 6269 8233.

(The P above represents a pause, while I wait to hear either a tone or a recording which says, "Now dial 0 for an operator or your calling card number.")

Twenty-five digits to complete a telephone call! And I didn't even call a foreign country. Worse yet, there is a fair probability that after all this I'll hear only a busy signal, meaning that in five minutes I'll have to repeat the whole process—or decide that I really don't want to talk to the office.

If we look more closely at the different parts of this 25-digit number, we find impressive testimony of two aspects of modern technology:

1. The rapid spread of automation—the use of machines (especially computers) to replace human beings (here telephone operators) in decision-making tasks.

2. The remarkable extent to which modern technology is designed carefully to match the characteristics of the people using the technology.

In the following paragraphs, we will look at dialing procedures from these two viewpoints. This will reveal both why I am so impressed by modern technology as I dial all these digits and why I am awed by the science and the behavioral study that has gone into their selection.

Parts of the 25-Digit Number
The 25 digits serve the following functions:

0	signals the central office equipment that I am about to need an operator or will be using my calling card.
516	is the area code I am calling to.
632-8760	is the local, seven-digit telephone number of my office.
516-423-6269	is the area code plus local telephone number of my home—the address to which the cost of the call will be charged.
8233	is the four-digit number assigned me to identify my calling card. If just the ten digits of my home number were used, anyone who knows my home number would know my calling card number. Thus, 8233 is the identification number I must remember when I use the calling card.

The 25 digits then include an indication to the equipment that this will be a call to be charged, the number called. the number to which the call is to be charged, and a number verifying that I have the right to charge the call to that number (the equipment has to check this verification automatically). We will look at how each of these elements has been engineered.

The Seven-Digit Local Number
In the late 1950s in the United States, the decision was made to convert all local numbers to seven digits. Previously many towns had used only four digits, since four digits gave as many as 9,000 possible numbers even though the first digit could not be 0 (which would call the operator). Even in cities where seven digits were already used, the first two digits were described by letters representing the particular area. For example, in 1956 my number in the Hollis section of New York City was HO 4-4960 (the HO for Hollis), so I really had to remember only the five digits 44960.

When the telephone company decided to go to seven digits (all numbers), there were vehement public complaints about the inhumanity of forcing people to remember seven numbers. The first conversion was in San Francisco, where the protests were widely publicized by the media.

Most changes in technology that demand modification in human behavior seem to be opposed, often with remarkable spirit. Eight hundred years ago, when Western Europe moved to adopt Arabic numerals $(0, 1, 2, \ldots, 9)$, there were violent objections. The Arabic numerals were introduced into Western Europe in the twelfth century, largely through the efforts of the merchants. Even in the following century, the intellectuals were sharply divided; in 1299 Florence passed legislation forbidding the use of Arabic numerals. Those favoring the new digits were known as algorists (after al-Khevarizini, who also gave us the concept of the algorithm); those favoring the Roman numerals were abacists (presumably because the manufacturers and teachers of the abacus foresaw that that device would seldom be needed once Arabic numerals were widely used).

Fortunately, the opponents of change lost in the case of numerals, or we still might be manipulating Roman numerals (a real challenge for the designer of electronic chips or microcomputers).

In the 1970s we witnessed the same public resistance to change when the U.S. government announced a conversion to the metric system. School textbooks were rewritten, a few states changed highway signs to measure distances in kilometers as well as miles, and weather reporters gave temperature in degrees Celsius as well as Fahrenheit. But there was little public enthusiasm (to put it kindly), and even the federal government really did not convert. For example, in early 1974 the national maximum speed limit was mandated as 55 miles per hour, not 88 kilometers per hour. By 1988, we had essentially abandoned the conversion to the metric system. Even though the Omnibus Trading Act of 1988 includes a mandate that by 1992 federal agencies must use the metric system in their business, realistically we probably can look forward to moving into the twenty-first century with the five other nations that cling to the British system of units (industrial giants such as Brunei, Mali, and Upper Volta).

Actually, the seven-digit local phone number was chosen with careful attention to human capabilities. A number of eight or nine digits would have been preferable and would have avoided the problem that recently beset Los Angeles County and New York City (area codes 213 and 212) when the telephone companies ran out of seven-digit numbers. The only solution was to break each metropolitan region into two different area codes.

This step is already finished in Los Angeles County, where the area code 818 was introduced for half the region. During a six-month transition period, either area code works, but then the changeover is complete. In New York City, the phone company made a similar change. Again, community and political leaders protested, but there was no alternative. Seven digits just do not allow enough different numbers.

Human Short-Term Memory

When you look up a number in a directory or someone tells you a number, you store the information in your short-term memory. If you ask me the number of my license plate and I say "9246," you can repeat the number back to me without error a few seconds later. The number is simple enough that you have no trouble remembering it for a short period of time.

If I tell you my Social Security number,

032-85-1742

you probably will find it difficult to repeat it back without error. Four digits are easy to recall, nine digits are difficult. Yet I have no trouble remembering my Social Security number; I have transmitted this number to my long-term memory, where it is permanently stored (although I have to recall the number occasionally to be sure it remains easily retrieved). Transfer of a number to long-term memory requires a conscious effort and several seconds. Consequently, phone numbers must be simple enough so that they can be stored in short-term memory (and held available during the time from consulting the directory to completing the dialing).

How many digits can the average person hold in short-term memory? An experiment illustrates that the answer is not simple. Have someone read aloud the following numbers, one at a time:

9 2 4 3
8 1 5 7 3 0
4 2 3 6 2 6 9 1
6 0 7 4 4 9 8 2 3 5
2 7 3 7 4 6 8 8 1 0 9 5

Grouping the digits in familiar packages helps. For example,

1 4 9 2   1 7 7 6   1 9 8 4

is easy if the digits are grouped as indicated, but twelve random digits forming no patterns are impossible for most people.

The answer to the question above is that you can store in short-term memory about four *chunks* of information. There is no precise definition of a *chunk*, but it refers to a digit or a small set of digits which is remembered as a unit. In my home phone number,

423-6269,

the first three digits (423) constitute one chunk for anyone living in my area, where this is a local exchange number.

Thus, the seven-digit local number is near the limit of human short-term memory. Some numbers, which have no logical groupings, cause trouble, but usually you can remember a number from the time you see or hear it to the completion of dialing.

Area Codes

Area codes were introduced in the 1960s as an important step in automation. Previously, you made a long-distance call by having the operator first connect you to the distant local exchange. With each geographical area described by a distinct area code, you can now dial Los Angeles (213), then the local number there (444-7692); the entire call is completed without human intervention. (Just as in banking, this automation is essential for today's level of service; there just aren't enough people available to put through today's number of calls with yesterday's technology.)

The area codes are all three digits. Each state and the District of Columbia has at least one code. A heavily populated state such as California requires ten separate codes, and there are codes allocated to Canada, Mexico, Puerto Rico, etc. Approximately 130 area codes are needed—too many for two digits, so three digits must be used.

Once we have decided on three digits, there are

$$10 \times 10 \times 10, \text{ or } 1{,}000$$

possible area codes, and we need only 130. How do we reduce the number?

First, there are some constraints. The first digit can not be 0 (this signals the operator or equipment that the caller will need operator assistance or be using a calling card), and it cannot be 1 (in many areas, an initial 1 is used to signal that a long-distance call is being made; it calls the equipment for automated determination of the charges into play. Thus, we are left with

$$\underset{\substack{\text{not 0} \\ \text{or 1}}}{8} \times 10 \times 10, \text{ or } 800$$

possibilities—still far more than the 130 necessary.

There must be some way for the equipment to recognize as soon as possible that the numbers being dialed represent an area code, not the first three digits of a local number. In the early days of area codes, the seven-digit local numbers started off with two letters—for example, our HO 4 4960, with HO standing the Hollis. Thus, the first two digits of the local, seven-digit number were

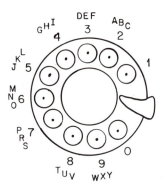

Figure 2.21
Typical rotary telephone dial.

originally *letters*. Consequently, the first two digits were never 0 or 1; there are no letters associated with these digits.

The digits 0 or 1 in the first location in the area code are already forbidden, as described above. But 0 and 1 can appear as the second digit in the area code, and in the 1960s neither appeared as the second digit of a local number. Consequently, the second digit of every area code is either 0 or 1. As you dial 51, the equipment knows that you are starting with an area code.

This restriction to either 0 or 1 as the second digit of the area code means that there are

8	×	2	×	10,	or 160
not 0		0 or 1		any	
or 1				digit	

three-digit numbers available for area codes—still a few more than needed. The three-digit numbers

211 311 411 511 611 711 811 911

are reserved for special functions (e.g., 411 for local directory assistance, 911 for emergency service), and numbers with the third digit zero are not used:

200 300 400 500 600 700 800 900
210 310 410 510 610 710 810 910

so we have left 136 allowable area codes—just the right number.

When Los Angeles and then New York ran out of seven-digit numbers (with each of the first two digits neither 0 nor 1) a few years ago, the first step to increase the number of local numbers was to allow the second digit to be 0 or 1. We then needed a way to indicate to the equipment that the first three digits were to be an area code. To handle this problem, any call to another area code has to be preceded by a 1. For example, from Los Angeles, 813-4269 is a local call, but 1-813-423-6269 is a call to the Tampa, Florida region (area code 813). This situation exists only in a few heavily populated areas; in most of the country, the second digit dialed 0 or 1 means that the first three digits constitute an area code.

Assigning Area Codes

Once the phone company decided to use three-digit area codes (with the second digit 0 or 1), the problem arose of how to assign the various area codes to the various regions. With a rotary dial, 1 is the number dialed most rapidly and with least chance of error. Next comes 2, then 3, and so on, with 0 requiring the longest time and most likely to cause an error.

Thus, it was decided that the "most important" region of the country should be assigned the area code 212, for the following reasons:

The first digit can not be 1, so 2 is simplest.

The second digit should be 1, not 0 (the alternative).

The third digit should be 2 (211 is a special, telephone company number).

This area code was assigned to New York City.

Next in "importance" are the regions with area codes 312 (Chicago) and 213 (Los Angeles). Then we have 412 (Pittsburgh), 313 (Detroit), 214 (Dallas), and so on until we reach the least "important" regions, including 906 (northern Michigan), 808 (Hawaii), 907 (Alaska), 709 (Newfoundland), and 809 (Virgin Islands, Puerto Rico, Bermuda).

Thus, you can generally tell the "importance" of a section of the country by the digits in the corresponding area code. Little wonder that people in Los Angeles County objected to a switch from 213 to 818, or that Brooklynites fought 718 replacing 212.

This ordering is, of course, significant only for phones with rotary (rather than push-button) dials. Using a rotary dial to signal the digit 5, for example, you rotate the hole at 5 clockwise around to the stop or end, then allow the rotating device to return back to its normal position. The number 5 is communicated to the telephone office during this return period, when there are five breaks in the electrical circuit (five pulses sent). The return occurs at the rate of ten breaks a second, so the number 5 requires ½ second on the return. (Some equipment operates at 20 breaks a second, but the normal rate is 10.)

Thus, the time it takes to dial 5 is the time it takes to insert your finger, plus the time needed to rotate the "5 hole" to the end, plus ½ second for the return.

The total time depends on the area code. For example, 212 Requires about 3½ seconds, 516 about 4½ seconds, 605 about 6 seconds, and 909 about 7½ seconds. To minimize the time the telephone-office equipment is tied up awaiting the completion of the area code, we want the area codes commonly used to be the ones requiring less time. (999, almost the hardest number to dial, is used in the United Kingdom for the emergency number; in the U. S., we use the much easier 911.)

Furthermore, with a rotary dial there is more likelihood of human error with the numbers that are more difficult to dial (9 and 0, for example). Errors may occur because the person dialing doesn't carry the hole all the way to the stop or allows the rotary section to move counterclockwise (slip backward) during the forward, clockwise motion. Once again, the area codes 212, 213, 312, etc. are the easiest to dial and the least susceptible to human errors.

With a push-button phone, all digits are handled similarly and require the same time. When you press a button, two different audio-frequency notes (two signals, each at its own pitch) are communicated along the wires to the telephone office. Each column in figure 2.22 is described by one frequency, each row by a different frequency. The office equipment measures the two frequencies, and can then identify the column and the row—hence identifying the digit that has been dialed.

Once all phones are converted to push-button dialing, all area codes will be *equal*. People living in northern Michigan (906) will no longer have any reason to complain.

Comparison with the United Kingdom
In the United States, we take for granted a technology that works as well as telephone dialing. The United States Postal Service serves as an impressive example of a communication organization that has not always used technology

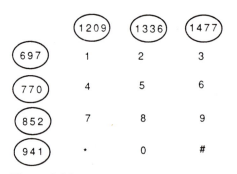

Figure 2.22
Representation of push-button telephone dial, showing frequencies.

to provide continuous improvement in service. But we don't normally compare the telephone and postal systems.

To understand the remarkable technology of our telephone dialing system, we might compare it with the system in the United Kingdom. The entire U.K. is serviced by British Telecom, a government-owned company. In the U.S., even before the 1984 breakup of AT&T, there were a large number of local telephone companies, which made arrangements to tie in with the AT&T system for calls out of or into the local region. Thus, we might assume that the U.K. system would involve simpler dialing arrangements.

In the U.K., dialling (the British spelling) also uses area codes, but there are over 3,000 and they vary in length from two to six digits. For example, to place a toll call from any rural area to one of the six major cities, you use the following area codes:

01	London
021	Birmingham
031	Edinburgh
041	Glasgow
051	Liverpool
061	Manchester

In each case, you follow the area code with the local telephone number of seven digits.

Calling any place other than these major cities is more complex. The U.K. is divided into local (L) areas. To call within your own L area, you use an area code for the town called; to call the same town from a different L area, the area code is different. For example, to call from Leeds to the town of Marston (in the same L area), the area code is 98; to call Marston from London, the area code is 0943.

Thus, when you want to place a call from Leeds to another town, you have to consult your directory to find the appropriate area code. This area code may have as many as six digits (Leeds to Deerness: 085674) or as few as four (Leeds to Dean: 0594). Finally, within your local (L) calling area, the area code depends on the town from which you are calling.

Consequently, when a business prints its phone number on stationery, it must give something like

Aberdeen (0224) 34344 .

Here 34344 is the local phone number (five digits in the case of Aberdeen); 0224 is the area code if you are calling from outside the local (L) area—for

---

Special Services of British Telecom

Telephone repair   151

"Directory inquires" (directory assistance)   192

Operator help on international calls   155, 156, 157, 158, 159
(depending on region)

SOS-Emergency Calls ("fire, police, ambulance, Coastguard")   999

Puffin Storyline (bedtime stories)   8071

Cricketline (cricket scores)   16

Other recorded services with obvious meanings:

Traveline, Raceline, Recipeline, Skiline, Timeline, Weatherline, Leisureline
(in three languages in London), and Wake-up or Alarm calls.

Box 2.6

example, from London; and Aberdeen is the exchange, given so that anyone calling from within the local (L) area can look up the four-, five-, or six-digit area code that is appropriate to that origination and destination.

British Telecom also provides a sizeable group of special numbers for particular services, as shown in box 2.6. The U.K.'s system differs from that of the U.S. in one other way: there, after you dial, the ringing tone and the busy signal ("engaged tone") have sounds of the same pitch or frequency. Long pauses between the tones indicate ringing; short pauses indicate a busy signal. (In the U.S., a low tone is used for ringing, one of medium pitch for a busy signal.)

Clearly, the U.K.'s system is not engineered to match the limitations of the human user. In contrast, if I want to call anywhere in New Hampshire from New York, I know that the area code is 603 and that the local telephone number has seven digits. With New Hampshire, to call Hanover from Concord (in the same area—both 603) I need dial only 1 followed by the seven-digit number; there is no necessity to consult my directory to find the area code.

Final Comments

In this appendix we have seen how a technology has been carefully designed to take into account the capabilities and limitations of the human beings who use that technology. Telephone numbers constitute a technology that we ordinarily take for granted.

The evolution of the American system over the past several decades is a beautiful example of the technological changes that are so critical in moving toward automation. Because the engineers of the telephone company planned

---

Calling Papua

To call a number in Papua, New Guinea, you dial

011 - 675 - 21 - local number - # button

011 is the area code which connects you to international lines. (After you dial the 0, you have only three seconds to dial the next 1 or the call will be switched to the local operator.)

675 is the code for the particular country, papua, New Guinea (occupies the eastern half of the island of New Guinea).

21 is the routing instructions for that country—essentially the area code. Actually, Papua, New Guinea, is small enough (1.5 million people) to have no area code, but most countries do, so we include this item here.

is the final signal if you have push-button dialing to indicate the end of the number. If you don't have push-button dialing or choose not to use this key, the local switching office has to wait to be sure you're done, since the area code and local number in other countries do not have a fixed number of digits.

Box 2.7

ahead, we can now dial directly throughout all the U.S. and, indeed, much of the world (see box 2.7). We can now make a calling-card call without help from a human operator; indeed, at some locations we can simply insert our calling card into the phone for automatic reading of the calling-card number, so we don't even have to dial these digits.

Indeed, the telephone-number system has been so well designed that there have been proposals that the U.S. Postal Service use the telephone number, instead of the zip code, for addressing envelopes. The area code would allow initial sorting of the mail for the proper region. At the post office of the recipient, the local seven-digit number would be read automatically. A computer memory would store all phone numbers and addresses so that the letters could be put in order for the appropriate mailman. One important advantage of such a postal addressing system is related to the remarkable mobility of the American people. In some urban areas, 20 percent of the people move during a calendar year. The telephone directory has to be computerized to stay up to date; we might as well use this directory for mail, instead of having the Postal Service try to maintain changes of address—often without the cooperation of the individuals who move so often.

Review Questions

R2-1. In "supermarket automation," what is automated? Explain briefly.

R2-2. What are the principal arguments for supermarket automation (the Universal Product Code)?

R2-3. Define redundancy in communications technology and give one example.

R2-4. People can type 80 words per minute—far beyond the capability of a human being to identify a letter, then move to strike the proper key. Explain briefly.

R2-5. What are the principal arguments against supermarket automation (the Universal Product Code)?

R2-6. In the Universal Product Code for supermarket automation, why are seven binary digits used to represent each decimal digit? Explain briefly.

R2-7. What are the advantages gained by converting a signal to digital form?

R2-8. "Technology should be designed to match the characteristics and capabilities of the human user." Discuss briefly, with one example.

R2-9. What is meant by "automatic error detection and correction"?

R2-10. What is meant by a check digit? Explain with a simple example.

R2-11. In supermarket automation, the laser scanners now use holography. Why?

R2-12. The Hamming Code gives automatic error detection and correction. What limits the number of message digits that can be handled by one set of check digits?

R2-13. What is the approximate limit of human short-term memory? Define any terms used.

R2-14. The Hamming Code with six correction digits would allow 57 message digits. Why is such a long packet seldom used?

R2-15. Why are telephone numbers seven digits (rather than eight or nine)?

R2-16. The Hamming Code uses four check digits for eleven message digits. What characteristic do we gain by using four (instead of one) check digits?

R2-17. The U. S. Postal Service uses a code that, in part, reads

00011-1 00110-3
00101-2 01001-4

Five binary digits are used, rather than the four necessary. What is gained by using the extra digit?

R2-18. The U.S. Postal Service uses a check digit that is the last digit of

50 – (sum of digits).

What happens if the person typing in the code interchanges two digits (11749 instead of 11794)? (This problem is avoided in the UPC code.)

R2-19. The Hamming Code automatically detects and corrects any error in the packet of information and check digits. What happens if there are two errors?

R2-20. Explain briefly why the British 999 (in contrast to the American 911) is an unfortunate choice for an emergency number.

R2-21. The check digit for the UPC (Universal Product Code) is the last digit of

210 - 3(a + c + e + g + i + k) – (b + d + f + h + j).

Why is the 3 used?

R2-22. The bar code for the U.S. Postal Service is a move toward automation. Does this represent complete automation of the mail routing operation? Discuss briefly.

R2-23. The bar code used by the U.S. Postal Service differs from the Universal Product Code used in supermarkets in several ways. What, briefly, are two of these differences?

R2-24. In the Universal Product Code, a 7 on the left is represented by 0111011 and a 7 on the right by 1000100. How does the equipment tell the direction in which it is reading the label?

Problems

P2-1. Working with a partner, demonstrate that human short-term memory can handle about four chunks of information. Carry this out with a series of numbers of varying length and with a series of names of familiar objects.

P2-2. Measure the time required to dial 212 and 909 on a rotary dial. (It is easiest to measure the time for 909 by dialing 909 909 909 and dividing the total by 3.) Two or three measurements of each time are useful to obtain an average. From these measurements, estimate how long it will take to dial 605, and check against an actual measurement. Note that there are three different activities: (1) locating the hole and inserting your finger, (2) forward or clockwise motion to the stop, and (3) automatic return counterclockwise at constant speed (10 numbers per second).

P2-3. How does the ranking of the area codes compare with the ranking of regions by population? What factors would cause differences?

P2-4. Only eight area codes are currently unused (719, 917, 407, 903, 409, 708, 908, and 909). What will these be used for in the near future? Once these are all used, what can be done when another area code is critically needed?

P2-5. Los Angeles and New York have now passed the point where the 213 and 212 area-code regions had to be divided. Each area-code region allows 8×10^6, or 8 million different numbers; neither region has this many residences. Why are the local numbers all used up?

P2-6. In general, the introduction of automation in an industry allows greater productivity—more output for the same number of workers. In addition, automation increases the demand for skilled workers and changes the jobs available. In the case of the telephone system, automation is essential as the number of calls increases simply because of a shortage of available workers. Describe other examples in which our present-day level of activity would be impossible without automation.

P2-7. In push-button dialing, two audio tones convey information on the digit dialed (figure. 2.22). If a 6 is dialed, the audio signal consists of two pure notes: one at 770 hertz (representing the second row), the other at 1477 hertz (for the right column). The telephone-office equipment measures the two frequencies and, hence, knows the 6 was dialed. To give you an idea of what these frequencies mean, we can note that in music middle C is 262 hertz, one octave above middle C is 524 hertz, two octaves above middle C is 1048 hertz, and three octaves above middle C is 2096 hertz. Thus, all seven notes lie in the second and third octaves above middle C, well within the range of notes on a piano.

If we compare the four row frequencies (697, 770, 852, and 941), we find that the numbers increase in steps of about 10 percent, corresponding to two notes on our musical scale. The three column frequencies (1209, 1336, and 1477) are related in the same way. Why was this separation chosen?

P2-8. The idea that human short-term memory stores *chunks* of information appears frequently in the study of performance. For example, a human being has a basic response time of about ¼ second. That is, if you receive a signal to press a lever or move your finger in a certain way, you don't respond at all until ¼ second has passed. If you are sleepy, inattentive, or intoxicated, the response time tends to be greater, but under the best of conditions it is ¼ second.

Typing is one task in which many people develop impressive skill. Let's look at this task. If a typist sees the next letter, then responds in ¼ second by moving his finger to the appropriate location and hitting the key, each letter must require *more* than ¼ second—¼ second to start the action, then some time to complete the act of hitting the key. Let's assume that the action is very fast and the whole operation takes only ⅓ second for each letter.

Then the typist should be able to hit 3 letters or keys per second—180 each minute. This corresponds to 36 words per minute, which should be the maximum possible typing speed. Yet a good typist can handle 70 words per minute. How can we explain this apparent contradiction?

Experiments have shown that about 36 words per minute is indeed the fastest possible speed if the typist is shown only the next symbol until the present symbol is completed. If the typist can see ahead, however, speed increases. Indeed, as the number of symbols ahead increases, the speed increases until, when the typist can see seven symbols, the speed reaches a maximum. Notice that seven is exactly the number of digits in the local telephone number and approximately the capacity of human short-term memory.

Psychologists are not sure how a typist takes advantage of this knowledge about future symbols. Apparently the typist uses a combination of chunking the information (for example, treating a common pair of letters such as "th" as a unit or chunk) and parallel mental processing (when the pair "rt" appears, the processing for the "t" starts well before the "r" is typed).

(a) The earliest psychological study of "chunking" was applied to expert telegraphers. Is the same concept applicable to reading? In reading, is such observation of chunks of information obviously present?

(b) Measurements have been made of the eye movements of expert typists. What would such an experiment show?

(c) Arguments for the parallel-processing explanation include the experimental results showing that the typist recognizes immediately when an error has been made and that typing speed does not diminish greatly when the letters are random rather than occurring in normal English words. Explain why both experimental results argue against the chunking concept as the only explanation for high typing speeds.

P2-9. The telephone serves as an example of many important characteristics of modern technology—including how hard it is to change technology once it is common, and how technology should be designed to match human characteristics and capabilities. The early history of the telephone also illustrates how very difficult it is to predict what the impact of a new technology will be.

The official invention of the telephone by Alexander Graham Bell occurred in 1876. Even though this was the time when Americans were awed by new technology and Thomas Edison was rapidly becoming a national hero, during the decade of the 1880s there was no agreement about the importance of the telephone—or even about how to use the telephone. In New York City, businesses still found it cheaper to send out messenger boys. In London, telephone transmitters were installed in theaters; you could call the theater and listen to a play. Edison, certain that phones would never be commonplace, invented the phonograph partly to record phone messages; the record or disc would then be delivered to the addressee's home. By the end of the decade, there finally was some use in the cities as both doctor and lawyer groups established exchanges for inter-communication. (I've always been awed by the early salesmen of telephones: imagine trying to sell a phone to someone with no friend who has one!). Even Western Union tried to impede acceptance when it lobbied for a regulation that phone calls must be charged according to the number of words spoken.

Around the turn of the century, the telephone was finally accepted by the wealthy. Thereafter, the technology expanded rapidly, and a phone soon became a necessity.

The telegraph, invented in 1845, spread over the country more rapidly than the telephone. Why was one of these two technologies more readily accepted than the other?

P2-10. The United States Postal Service (USPS) is now moving ahead with the nine-digit zip code (called "Zip plus 4"), first proposed in 1980. This is a step toward automation of mail sorting and routing.

The relevant characteristics of the present system are as follows:

The USPS handles 118 billion pieces of mail a year. (The U.S. generates nearly half of the world's mail—one indication of our standard of living.)

Of the mail, 83% is from businesses, or government, etc., 6% is personal correspondence, and 11% consists of replies to the business mail. Thus, there is no point in trying to convince the individual to use "Zip plus 4."

Currently 60–70% of the business mail can be sorted automatically, but at least 10% more is necessary to justify the cost.

Once the "Zip plus 4" system is in place, the USPS hopes to save $600 million per year, largely by reducing employment through normal attrition. (There are currently 650,000 employees—second only to the Department of Defense in numbers.) One-fourth of the saving will be passed on to businesses in the form of reduced rates; the rest will be used to hold down postal rates.

The system will work as follows. The USPS will buy 650 machines for optical character recognition (OCR) to read the city, state, and code, to check that the code is appropriate, and to translate the code into a bar code stamped on the bottom of the envelope. The USPS will also purchase 700 bar-code sorters (much cheaper machines) to sort five-digit codes to the destination post office, and nine-digit codes to the specific carrier. The total cost for the two kinds of equipment will be $740 million over the coming five years.

To convince businesses to use the nine digits voluntarily, the USPS will offer reduced prices. The 25-cent rate is already reduced by 3 cents if a batch of over 500 letters is presorted according to the five digits. An additional 0.5 cent per letter will be granted if the nine digits are used, and a reduction of 0.9 cent will be given for use of nine digits with non-presorted mail in batches over 250. These planned reductions are quite small, and it is not clear that businesses will rush to convert their mailing lists to the "Zip plus 4" system.

The OCR equipment is the technology that limits the automation of the sorting operation. To compare cities with codes, the OCR equipment must accept misspellings (e.g., one model includes 20 possible spellings of Philadelphia), poor contrast, abbreviations, extraneous printing, etc.

(a) Instead of check digits, the system uses redundancy by comparing the city and the state with the zip code. What are the severe limitations of this?

(b) To save $600 million per year when the equipment costs $740 million, estimate the corresponding reduction in the USPS workforce. The answer depends on the annual cost of the equipment, but we might assume that the equipment has a life of 5 years and that its annual maintenance cost is ⅕ the initial cost.

(c) The USPS is a quasi-public corporation which is controlled to an appreciable extent by the Congress (which usually has to appropriate enough money to offset the deficit). From the federal government's standpoint, what factors should be considered in a decision on whether to proceed with the automation described above? In other words, what considerations are unique to the federal government's viewpoint?

Chapter 3
Electrical Safety

Lightning fires can be extinguished only with milk.

This belief was widely held in both the United States and Europe during the last century. Though today we recognize it as ridiculous, lightning still has an aura of mystery and superstition about it. Flashes that light up the sky, crashes of thunder, howling wind and rain conjure up visions of ghosts and haunted houses. Even the telephone, in many rural areas, adds to this dramatic atmosphere by giving a short ring after every lightning bolt in the vicinity.

Lightning is an extreme example of the power and danger of electricity. At any one time, there are 1800 lightning strokes around the world. In the United States, over 100 deaths per year and the most serious forest fires are caused by lightning. Seeing this destructive force of nature, we might assume that people would be especially conscious of the risks involved in using electricity in their daily lives. Unfortunately, we are so accustomed to electrical energy for running home appliances, heating homes, starting the car, and sending or receiving information that we have become careless in handling electrical devices. As a consequence, electrical shock is now a major cause of personal injury and accidental death.

In the following sections, we look at the hazards inherent in the use of electrical energy and the basic aspects of electrical safety. What are the risks? How can they be minimized while we still have the benefits of electrical energy?

3.1 Basic Concepts of Electricity

Electrical current is the *flow* of electrons or particles carrying electrical charge. Every material consists of atoms, with each atom being a positively charged nucleus around which negatively charged electrons rotate. In a metal or any electrical conductor, the nuclei are in a rigid pattern, and many of the electrons are free to move.

These free electrons make the material a *conductor*. Ordinarily the electrons are moving about in all directions (the higher the temperature, the faster they move). When an electrical current flows in the wire, the electrons still move randomly in all directions (because of the temperature), but they also move *along* the wire—for example, from left to right in figure 3.1. Thus, a current adds a directional flow to the random motion of the charges.

Actually, no one electron moves very far in the wire. Since negative charges repel one another, motion of electrons to the right at A in figure 3.1 repels electrons at B to the right. Thus, current travels through the wire by a sequence of these repelling actions—just as a long chain of standing dominoes topples over when the first one is tipped.

To understand electrical devices, however, we can picture current flowing through a wire just like water flowing through a pipe. If the current flows from left to right, charge enters the wire at the left, flows down the wire, and leaves at the right end.

When we look at water flowing through a pipe, we measure the flow in gallons per minute. My garden hose puts out a maximum of 6 gallons per minute. Similarly, we measure electrical current in the charge per second passing a point along the wire. The basic unit of current is

1 ampere (usually written as 1 amp or 1 A).

(One ampere corresponds to almost 10,000,000,000,000,000,000 electrons passing the point each second—an enormous number, because atoms are so very small.)

The size of currents varies tremendously. For instance:

1/1000 A is the current we can just barely feel when we are shocked.

2 A is the current flowing through the bulb of a small flashlight.

100,000 A is about the largest current in a lightning stroke.

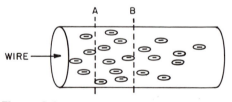

Figure 3.1
Wire with free electrons.

In the following discussion of electrical safety, we will be talking about currents over this full range. For example, why can a person die from $\frac{1}{10}$ A, yet someone else walk away after being hit by lightning?

Voltage

To be useful, electrical current must flow through something—a toaster, a TV set, or a light bulb. Figure 3.2 shows an electrical *circuit* in which current flows from a battery through a light bulb. (In electrical terminology, a current is indicated by the letter I.)

If we return to our analogy with water flow, the battery is similar to the pump raising the pressure and forcing the water through the pipe or hose. In electrical terms, the battery generates a voltage, or electrical "pressure." An automobile battery usually gives 12 volts; a lightning stroke may result from 100,000,000 volts.

In the circuit of figure 3.2, the battery uses chemical action to generate a voltage of 12 volts. This voltage (or pressure) causes current to flow through the light bulb and back to the battery. Current always flows in a closed or complete circuit, since the charge must return to the source. (If the current flowed only into the bulb, charge would build up there and oppose further current. Actually water also flows in a closed circuit. My water company takes water from wells, pumps up the pressure, and delivers the water to my house. I use the water and deliver it to the ground, where it works through the soil toward the underground water supply.)

Thus, electrical devices are described by the current and voltage—the flow and the pressure or force. We measure the current in amperes (A), the voltage in volts (V).

Ohm's Law

In our home water system, when I turn on the faucet just slightly, the water trickles out. As I open the faucet farther, the flow increases. The faucet valve

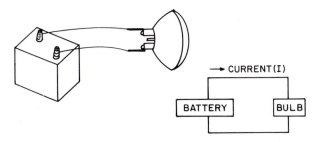

CURRENT(I)

BATTERY   BULB

Figure 3.2
Left: A circuit consisting of an auto battery and a headlight. The circuit diagram at right is the engineer's way of representing the system.

provides a *variable resistance* to the flow. Behind the valve, the water is under pressure (in my home, usually about 100 pounds per square inch). As the valve is opened more and more, the steady pressure results in greater and greater flow.

Similarly, the auto battery in figure 3.2 provides a constant voltage of 12 volts. The current that flows through the light bulb is determined by the electrical *resistance* of the bulb. This resistance (denoted by R) is a measure of how difficult it is to push current through the bulb. The higher the resistance, the less current flows. We measure a resistance in ohms, and we depict it in a circuit diagram as a zigzag line.

We can express this relationship among current, voltage, and resistance by the following equation, called Ohm's Law:

$$V = RI \quad (\text{voltage} = \text{resistance} \times \text{current}),$$

or

$$I = \frac{V}{R} .$$

The current that flows through a bulb is the voltage divided by the resistance. In our example, the battery provides a voltage of 12 volts and the resistance of the light is 6 ohms, so

$$I = \frac{12}{6} , \text{ or } I = 2 \text{ amps}.$$

That is,

$$\text{current} = \frac{12 \text{ volts}}{6 \text{ ohms}} , \text{ or } I = 2 \text{ amps}.$$

A light bulb is really nothing more than a filament, a very fine wire (as we can see by inspection). A normal wire (such as the cord of an appliance) has almost no resistance. There are so many free electrons in the metal wire that any desired current can flow with almost zero voltage (i.e., no pressure). As the wire is made smaller and smaller, the number of free electrons decreases and more voltage is required to cause a specific current to flow. Thus, in a light bulb, the resistance is determined by how fine the filament is and, also, by the particular metal (which determines the density of free electrons available to serve as a current).

Power

A batter in baseball swings; the ball soars out beyond the stands at the 425-foot mark; the TV announcer yells, "What *power*!"

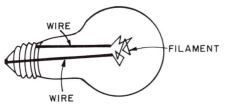

Figure 3.3
Electric light bulb.

You are asking your friend how she likes her new car. She replies, "It gets good mileage, but it doesn't have the *power* of my old Buick."

Lightning strikes a distribution tower of your local utility, and the town is blacked out. You turn on the transistor radio, and a utility spokesman says, "*Power* should be restored within an hour."

These three quotes all use the term *power* in an engineering way (in contrast to saying, "The President has lost his *power* during the last years of his administration"). As we consider radio and radar or the effects of radio signals on human beings, we will need a clear definition of this term, *power*. For example, in chapter 8 we will find that microwave ovens are "safe" if the power reaching you is less than a certain amount.

Engineering Definition of Power   In intuitive terms, power is the rate of doing work. An athletic young man can deliver about one horsepower for a very short interval of time (a few seconds), and about ⅛ horsepower over a period of minutes.

In scientific terms, power output is the rate at which energy can be delivered. Unfortunately, this definition depends on another concept: energy, which is itself difficult to explain.

Intuitively, we know what energy means. In the earlier baseball example, the batter hits the ball. The ball then starts out toward the stands with a certain energy imparted by the collision with the swinging bat. This energy, which we call kinetic energy or the energy of motion, is determined by the velocity of the ball as it leaves the bat. The greater the velocity, the more energy the ball has, and the farther it will go before it falls to the earth.

Analogously, when I am paddling a canoe, the greater the power I deliver to the paddle going through the water, the faster the canoe goes forward. If I increase the rate at which I stroke, likewise the power increases, and the canoe receives more kinetic energy.

Thus, power is the rate at which energy is delivered or transferred. This is an imprecise definition—we really have not defined energy—but we can focus on electrical power to go into more depth.

Electrical Power   My electrical room heater has a nameplate reading

120 VAC
1400 W.

The former number, 120 VAC, simply means that the heater runs from the normal wall outlet, where the utility provides 120 volts ac (alternating current or voltage as explained in section 3.3). The latter number, 1400 W, says that the heater provides 1400 watts of power—this is the rate at which electrical energy from the utility is converted to heat when the switch is on "High Heat."

The basic unit for measuring power is the watt. When I turn my hose on, water flows at a pressure of 100 pounds per square inch and a rate of 6 gallons per minute; if we calculate the power, we find that it is just under 500 watts. Thus, from the faucet we can draw this amount of water power.

The power of an electrical appliance is given by the equation

$$P = VI.$$

Thus, my heater is simply a resistor that allows a current of

$$\frac{1400}{120}, \text{ or } 11.7 \text{ amperes}$$

to flow when 120 volts is applied to it. This current raises the temperature of the heating element, then heat is radiated outward into the room.

In this appliance, essentially all the electrical energy drawn from the utility is converted into heat. (There is a small amount of energy converted to light, since the element does glow, but this energy is negligible.)

Here the electrical power is the *rate* at which heat energy is being delivered to the room by the utility. When the heater is on, I am using 1400 watts; the longer the heater is on, the more energy I use and, indeed, the greater the cost. At my home, I pay the utility 10 cents for each kilowatt-hour of energy I use. This heater, operating for an hour, uses

1400 watts × 1 hour, or 1.4 kilowatt-hours

and hence costs 14 cents per hour to operate.

How much power is 1400 watts? There are several ways we might try to understand the meaning of such a number, two of which are given below.

1. It turns out that 746 watts is the same as 1 horsepower. Thus, the heater is delivering almost 2 horsepower. For electrical energy, I pay about 7½ cents for each hour I use 1 horsepower.

2. While I am sitting in the room, my bodily functions go on with heat generated internally by the chemical and physical activities. If my internal body temperature stays at about 98°F, I have to get rid of heat energy at the rate of approximately 100 watts. Thus, the electric heater causes the same rise in room temperature as 14 people.

Other electrical appliances require, of course, very different powers. Light bulbs might be 60, 100, or 200 watts, a window air conditioner 2000 watts, a color television 200 watts. In each case, the power is measured in watts, named for James Watt.

James Watt was a technician and instrument maker at the university in Edinburgh. Trained by apprenticeship and without a university education, he invented a speed governor that allowed steam engines to run at a nearly constant speed—an invention which not only was essential for the arrival of the Industrial Revolution, but also was an early application of automation.

This governor used two heavy balls on extendable arms. When the engine started to rotate faster, the balls moved outward (just as the higher the velocity of a satellite, the greater the distance of the orbit from the earth). At the larger distance, the balls needed more power, so less power was available to rotate the engine. Thus, the balls (or governor) automatically prevented the engine from speeding up very much—the speed was held to very small changes.

This idea, which today we call feedback or (in popular terms) automation, was a remarkable breakthrough in engineering thought—an idea we now consider simple, but which had enormous economic and social implications. The origins of the Industrial Revolution are, of course, vastly more complex than just Watt's governor, but the product of his imagination holds an important place in the history of technology.

Indeed, that history is to an extraordinary extent based on a relatively small number of breakthroughs in thought—contributions by individuals able to think about a topic or problem in an entirely new way. Nearly all of us who are engineers tend to solve problems by slight advances. We probe just a little deeper than anyone before, understand just a little more. Occasionally, we innovate in a larger step by bringing an approach from one field over to our area. Rare, indeed, is the individual who looks at a problem in an entirely new way, but such people give us the great leaps forward.

James Watt is famous for another activity. He dropped a large bucket into a deep well, then had a horse pull the water up as fast as possible. The horse obviously was doing work—lifting the water. Watt found that the horse could lift the water at the rate of 550 foot-pounds per second. In other words, 55 pounds of water could be lifted 10 feet (that is 550 foot-pounds) in one second.

This was the maximum rate at which the horse could do work, so Watt called this one horsepower.

Electrical Energy and Power   We should emphasize the distinction between electrical energy and power. Power is the rate at which energy is delivered or used; as a utility customer, I pay for energy (10 cents for each 1000 watt-hours or 1 kilowatt-hour).

The average American watches television 7 hours a day (or at least this is one survey result, even though it's hard to believe). If a home television set, rated at a *power* of 200 watts, is turned on 10 hours a day, the homeowner pays for

200 watts × 10 hours, or 2000 watt-hours

of electrical *energy*. At a cost of 10 cents per kilowatt-hour, the family pays 20 cents a day or $73 a year just to operate the television set.

Small Power   The above examples of home appliances describe powers of hundreds or thousands of watts. When we turn to the biological and environmental effects of electrical signals (chapter 8), we will be interested in much smaller powers. For example, the allowable exposure of human beings to radar signals is measured in milliwatts or thousandths of a watt, and radio signals are often measured in microwatts, or millionths of a watt. These two prefixes—milli and micro—also appear later in this book when we talk about hearing and vision. The power involved in audible sound signals or visible light signals is very small—a class of 50 students screaming for 10 minutes doesn't generate enough sound energy to cook an egg.

Relations among I, V, R, and P
We now have finished our look at basic concepts of electrical devices. The operation of a device can be described in terms of four quantities:

current (I)—measured in amps (A)

voltage (V)—measured in volts (V)

resistance (R)—measured in ohms

power (P)—measured in watts (W)   (746 watts is one horsepower).

To talk about electrical safety, we need to understand these quantities and the two relations among them:

Ohm's Law—V = RI (voltage = resistance × current)

Power—P = VI (power = voltage × current).

Knowing any two of the four quantities, we can find the other two from these equations.

We can now understand the problem faced by Thomas Edison a hundred years ago as he struggled to invent an electric light bulb. If he assumed 100 volts to be available, and if he wanted a power of 50 watts, he needed a current of

$$I = \frac{P}{V} = \frac{50}{100} = \frac{1}{2} \text{ A}$$

or a filament with a resistance of

$$R = \frac{V}{I} = \frac{100 \text{ volts}}{\frac{1}{2} \text{ amp}} = 200 \text{ ohms} .$$

Thus, he had to look for a metallic wire (filament) with this resistance and simultaneously with two properties:

1. The filament should not be so fine that it would burn out (i.e., break) when subjected to 50 watts.

2. The heated filament should give off a reasonable amount of light, rather than just heat.

By trying many materials, Edison finally found that a carbonized cotton thread would do the job, although even today the standard incandescent lamp gives off only about 5 percent of its power in light. (The rest goes to heat. A 100-watt bulb gives off as much heat as a person sitting in a room. A well-lit classroom filled with students can become excessively warm by the end of the day.)

3.2 Lightning

With these basic concepts of electricity, we can now begin to understand the behavior of lightning, which is the rapid flow of electrical current between a cloud and the ground.

Under thunderstorm conditions, the gas in the cloud is ionized—the atoms divide into positively and negatively charged particles. The positive charges rise and the negatively charged electrons accumulate in the center of the cloud. We now have a very dense concentration of charge, which means a very high voltage, possible as much as 100 million volts. Down below, the conducting earth is at zero voltage. (We use the earth or ground as the basis of our voltage measurement.) Furthermore, since the earth is a reasonably good conductor, it has an ample supply of positive charges to attract the electrons from the clouds. If a conductor (for example, a very tall building) were connected to the earth at one end and were in the cloud at the other end, heavy current would flow between the cloud and the ground to neutralize the charge.

Air is nearly a perfect insulator, so no current flows between the cloud and the ground. A conducting path is needed before the negative charges in the clouds and the positive charges in the ground can combine. The lightning stroke creates this conductor from the cloud to the ground. About 150 feet below the high concentration of charge in the cloud, the gas is ionized (the negative charges in the atom are pushed away from the nuclei of the atoms) by the high voltage in the cloud. Thus, this strip of ionized air serves as a conductor and brings the high cloud voltage down to point B in figure 3.5. These negative charges (now at point B), in turn, cause a concentration of positive charges just below, ionizing the air to point C. This sequence of steps, each lasting perhaps a thousandth of a second, continues until the downward path eventually reaches the ground. Now there is an ionized, conducting path between the cloud and the ground.

In this ionized path we have a low-resistance strip (that is, a conductor) from the cloud to the earth. The 100 million volts then causes 100,000 amperes to rush through the path. This intense energy transfer (i.e., power flow) wildly excites atoms along the path to a temperature of about 30,000°C. As those atoms return to their normal state, the excited electrons lose the energy they acquired in the rush of current. This energy is lost partly through emission of visible light—the lightning flash.

The entire lightning stroke lasts only about ¼ second. During the stroke, the energy transfer also creates rapid pressure changes along the ionized path. The build up and collapse of these pressure changes then spreads outward as sound waves—the thunder.

As mentioned above, the current, the voltage, and the power in lightning can be awesome. To ionize dry air requires about 10,000 volts per centimeter, so

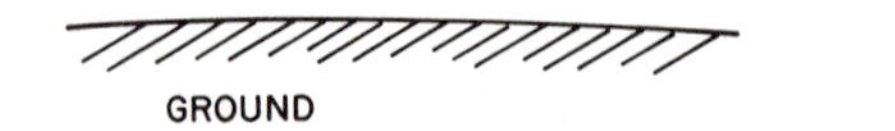

Figure 3.4
Condition before a lightning stroke.

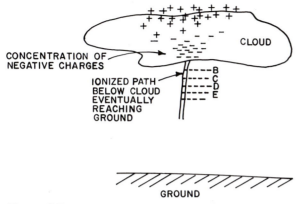

Figure 3.5
Ionization path to ground

very high voltages are required to initiate the air breakdown. This phenomenon is illustrated differently by our ability in a dry house to deliver an electrical shock to another person. As I rub across a woolen rug, I build up a charge on my body. If I reach out my hand toward another person, when my fingertip is perhaps ½ centimeter away my voltage is high enough to cause ionization of the air and a small arc between my fingertip and the other person. This is exactly the principle in a lightning stroke. The air is ionized by the high voltage, and a conducting path is created for the electricity.

The voltage just before a lightning stroke is so large that it is difficult to create the same conditions in an engineering laboratory. In the last few years, however, such studies have become a necessity in the design of automobiles. Until recently, lightning striking a car presented no problem: the metal frame conducts the voltage around the passengers, and a car is actually a safe haven in a thunderstorm.

Even today's metallic car, however, usually includes a computer to control the engine in order to obtain better fuel economy and lower emissions. Now we have to worry about the lightning causing such large currents that the computer malfunctions or is damaged. Consequently, manufacturers build laboratories to create 100,000-volt lightning strokes for testing.

With these tremendous voltages and currents, how do people survive being struck by lightning? Why did Benjamin Franklin live through his classic experiment proving lightning was electrical? (Actually, the experiment was ridiculous—the next scientist to try it was killed.)

A lightning stroke lasts for only a fraction of a second. Once the charge in the cloud is neutralized, the stroke is over. There is no utility company furnishing more current to the clouds. In direct contrast, if we touch a live wire, the current keeps flowing until we pull our hand away.

Ben Franklin lived through his experiment because during the split second of time he was hit by the lightning stroke, his heart was in the right part of its beating cycle, as we'll see in section 3.5.

The description above of the formation of the lightning stroke from the cloud to the ground explains why the stroke is along the path of *least electrical resistance*. Outside in a storm, you are in particular danger when you are part of that path. If you're standing under a tree, you can represent a better conductor than the tree—particularly if you're wet, and even more so if you're holding a metal golf club. There is folklore which says that, if you feel your hair standing on end in a thunderstorm, you should drop to the ground. While you seldom receive such generous warning, this is not entirely stupid. If *you* are the best conductor in the area, charges will flow through your body to your head (toward the cloud) just before the stroke.

Once Franklin discovered the electrical nature of lightning, he recognized the importance of the path of least resistance (although Ohm had not yet presented the concept of electrical resistance). Franklin then went on to design the first lightning rod: simply a metal rod reaching well above the house, with a pointed top to encourage electrical breakdown on one end and solidly imbedded in the ground at the other end. Experiments show that the rod protects reasonably everything within the angle shown in figure 3.6—a rule of thumb which indicates how high above the house to put the top of the rod.

3.3 Home Electrical Energy

For most of us, "electrical energy" simply refers to the energy available at the nearest wall outlet. The local utility generates the energy at some distant point,

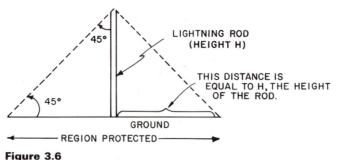

Figure 3.6
Protection from a lightning rod.

then distributes it to each home in the region through a complex grid of electric wires. Whenever I plug an appliance into a wall outlet, I am confident that 115 volts will be there, ready to drive current through the particular appliance.

The voltage that enters our house comes in on two wires. One of the wires is always at the voltage of the ground—we call this zero volt. The voltage of the other wire changes continually with time. Figure 3.7 shows how the voltage varies in a repeating pattern. At time A, the voltage is 80; at B, 163; at C, 40; and by D, –80.

What does negative voltage (for example, –80) mean? The voltage is positive half the time, negative the other half. If I plug a lamp into a wall outlet (figure 3.8), the current flows in the direction shown by the arrow half of the time, in the opposite direction the other half. Thus, a positive voltage on the top wire *pushes* current through the lamp in the arrow direction; a negative voltage on the top wire *pulls* current through the lamp in the opposite direction.

We call this voltage provided by the utility

115 volts ac 60 hertz.

What does this mean?

ac . This stands for "alternating current." Perhaps we should use "alternating voltage." But, as we saw in figure. 3.8, both the voltage and current alternate, so both are described by the adjective "alternating."

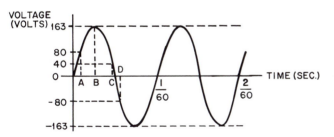

Figure 3.7
Voltage continually changes with time.

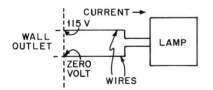

Figure 3.8
Lamp connected to wall outlet.

115 volts. Why not 163 volts, since that is the maximum value? The voltage changes continually: at times it's near zero, at other times near 163. To find the *effective* value of the voltage, we ask: if we apply this voltage to a light bulb or toaster, what light or heat will be generated? In particular, how large would a *constant* voltage have to be to generate the same light or heat? It turns out that the constant voltage would be 115 volts (71% of 163, or 163 divided by $\sqrt{2}$), so we say the effective value of the ac voltage of figure 3.8 is 115.

60 hertz. Here "hertz" is just the scientific term for cycles per second. 60 cycles per second is the frequency of this voltage signal: 60 times each second, the voltage varies through its full cycle. (We will study the sine signal—the voltage plotted in Fig. 3.7—much more in the next chapter. Here we should note, however, that this voltage signal has a very special way of traveling through one cycle. Indeed, it turns out that the specific voltage of figure 3.7 can be described by the mathematical equation

$$V = 163 \sin(377t).$$

The voltage varies as the sine in trigonometry. We really are not interested in the mathematics, however. This sine signal does have one remarkable characteristic: "persistence of waveform." This means that adding or subtracting two sine signals at the same frequency (here, 60 cycles per second) leaves a result that is also a sine at that frequency. The sine is the only signal that can make this claim. This feature is critically important for an electrical utility. The current I receive at home is the utility current minus that used by my neighbors. When the neighbors turn on their TV sets and suddenly use more current, my own current shape would change if this persistence of waveform were not valid. Thus, if the utility can keep the current (and the voltage) exactly sine signals, it can deliver a current to my house that does not change shape when my neighbors turn on appliances.)

Thus, home electrical voltage varies continuously. If we touch a wire for just a very short time (much less than $\frac{1}{60}$ second), the effect we feel depends strongly on the exact time in the cycle. If we happen to come in contact with the wire when the voltage is about zero, there is no effect at all. In most cases, of course, our contact lasts appreciably longer than $\frac{1}{60}$ second, and we receive the full, average effect of the shock.

A current (for example, the current drawn by a light bulb or a toaster) depends on the voltage according to Ohm's Law:

$$\text{current} = \frac{\text{voltage}}{\text{resistance}} .$$

Hence, as the voltage varies periodically, the current varies in exactly the same way: the current is ac, just like the voltage. The average power consumed by the appliance is

P = IV   (power = current x voltage).

For example, if V is 115 volts and P is 100 watts (our light bulb), the current I is 0.9 amperes. (Henceforth, we will refer to the voltage of figure 3.7 as 115 volts—its effective value when compared to a constant voltage. Likewise the current I is an effective value.)

A electric frying pan has the label

1250 watts   120 volts.

The voltage is listed as 120 volts, while we've been discussing 115 volts. Actually, the voltage from the utility can vary over a modest range—perhaps from 110 to 125 volts. Appliances are designed to work over this range, although of course the useful power will vary as the voltage changes (if the voltage of the frying pan drops from 120 to 110, the heat is reduced by 16 per cent, and food takes longer to cook). The power rating of 1250 watts indicates that the current is

$$I = \frac{1400}{120} = 10.4 \text{ amps.}$$

Why does the utility use an ac voltage, rather than the much simpler dc or constant voltage? (dc stands for direct current. If graphed, the dc voltage would simply have a constant value for all time.) Actually, in the early days of electric power dc was used; as late as the mid-1960s there were still sections of Boston and New York City where dc was distributed. The choice of ac traces back to the last years of the nineteenth century. In the rest of this section, we review this history, since the early arguments between advocates of dc and ac strongly involved safety.

History of ac
The electric power industry started in the United States in the 1880s. Thomas Edison had just invented the light bulb, and dc electric motors were developed to the point where they could do useful work. In 1882 the Edison Electric Light Company opened its first generating station in New York City and offered electrical energy for sale. Even recognizing the charisma of Edison's name in those days, we marvel at the rapid public acceptance: by 1887 there were 121 generating stations in or nearing operation to serve 325,000 lamps. The entire Edison system operated on dc.

Meanwhile, George Westinghouse, Jr., started selling dc power systems, but with little success in the competition with Edison. In 1885, Westinghouse bought the American rights to the European patents on ac generation, and his engineers rapidly improved the system and simplified manufacturing processes. The first ac system was in operation by the end of 1886, and within nine months generating stations able to light 135,000 lamps were nearing completion.

One of the bitterest battles in the history of technology now occurred as the Edison and Westinghouse forces argued the relative merits of dc and ac. At the beginning of the argument in 1886, it was not clear which system was best.

The ac system has one primary advantage: transformers can be used to change the ac voltage. A transformer cross-section is shown in figure 3.9. When an ac voltage is applied to the input side, a voltage appears at the output side. This output voltage is N times as large as the input, where N is the ratio of the number of turns on the output winding to the turns on the input. In other words, the transformer can step up (or step down) the voltage by any desired amount. The transformer acts like a lever: the output power is the same as the input, but the force or voltage can be very different.

This feature of ac is especially important when we want to transmit energy over long distances. There is an appreciable loss of power when a large current flows through a long wire, even if the resistance is very small. In a transmission line, the power wasted depends only on the current, not on the voltage (actually on the square of the current or I^2R). If we step up the voltage by a factor of 100, the current drops by the same amount (since power is the voltage times the current). An ac system lets the utility send power over long distances—indeed, today it is not unusual to step up the voltage to more than 500,000 volts before transmission to keep the loss of current (and, hence, the loss of power) very small. Then at the destination the voltage is stepped down again to a safe level for home and industrial use. There was no efficient way to change dc voltage similarly until very recently.

This disadvantage of dc meant that Edison could only distribute energy for a distance of about a mile. To serve New York City, consequently, generating stations had to be built throughout the city. When these were later converted

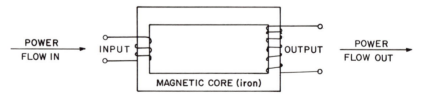

Figure 3.9
Transformer to change ac voltage. The output voltage is twice the input voltage, but the two powers are approximately the same.

to ac and brought together in one system, the name Consolidated Edison (or Con Ed) was appropriate.

Disadvantages of ac

At the beginning of the Edison-Westinghouse battle, there were two clear disadvantages of ac, both of which were removed within a few years:

1.There was no ac power meter. The result was that customers were charged a flat rate per lamp. As might be expected, customers then simply left the lights on. Westinghouse ended up providing 50 percent more power than Edison for the same number of customers. (Similar behavior occurs when people are charged a flat rate for water and there is no metering of use, as still is true in almost all of New York City. Metering seems to reduce water consumption by about 30 percent, but a decision on whether to meter has to weigh this benefit against the costs of installation, meter reading, and individualized billing.)

2.There was no practical ac motor, so the ac energy could not be used simultaneously for mechanical work.

In 1888, O. B. Shallenberger invented the ac watt-hour meter, and in the same year Nikola Tesla invented the practical ac motor. With these two roadblocks removed, all technical advantages were on the side of ac, and the battle was really over.

The dc forces refused to give up, however, and a bitter campaign was launched to convince the public that ac was much more dangerous than dc (actually there are no major differences in the hazards). In early 1888 the Edison Electric Light Company published a red pamphlet entitled "A Warning." The 83 pages included a description of all the dangers of ac and a list of everyone supposedly electrocuted by ac.

On December 18, 1888 a number of newspapers published a challenge by Harold Brown (working with Edison):

I . . . challenge Mr. Westinghouse to meet me in the presence of competent electrical experts and take through his body the alternating current while I take through mine a continuous current. The alternating current must have not less than 300 alternations per second (150 hertz)....We will begin with 100 volts and will gradually increase the pressure 50 volts at a time, I leading with each increase, each contact to be made for five seconds, until either one or the other has cried enough, and publicly admits his error. I will warn Mr. Westinghouse, however, that 160 volts alternating current for five seconds has proved fatal in my experiments, and that several men have been killed by the low-tension Jablochkoff (a type of arc light) alternating current.

In 1890, the Edison forces succeeded in convincing the State of New York to use an ac Westinghouse generator for the first legal electrocution, held August 6 at Auburn Prison—certainly one of the low points in public morality in the history of engineering.

Even though the wild publicity campaign and the public demonstrations electrocuting animals may have convinced some of the people that ac was the "killer current," dc had lost the battle. The transmission advantages of ac were emphasized when a French economic group cornered the market on copper and doubled the price to 20 cents a pound. The copper wires represent a major cost in a distribution system. Figure 3.10 shows the size of wire required for a 100-volt dc system feeding 500 lamps one mile away from the generator and for 1000-volt and 2000-volt ac systems with the same efficiency.

In 1892 the engineers for the largest hydroelectric plant ever built (at Niagara Falls) decided to generate ac, and in 1893 the Chicago World's Fair used ac for lighting. In 1892, the Edison General Electric Company merged with Thomson-Houston (the number two company in ac) to form the General Electric Company, and Thomas Edison lost influence in the electric power industry.

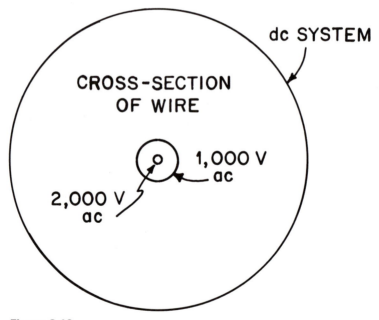

Figure 3.10
Sizes of wires needed for dc and ac power distribution.

The preceding description may paint an unfair picture of Thomas Edison. Biographers of Edison often emphasize his very deep concern with public safety as the basis for his personal opposition to the high voltages used in ac transmission, and the fact that he personally did not approve many of the actions of the dc adherents.

3.4 Shock from a Toaster

My pop-up toaster is always plugged in. To toast bread, I simply drop in the bread and push the lever down. As time passes, the lever gradually rises. After the toasting is completed, the lever springs up to its top position and the toasted bread rises so that I can easily grab the pieces. Many toasters have a thermostat that measures the temperature and moisture content of the toast to adjust the browning time. Also, the time is automatically reduced if the toaster is already hot from previous use. A toaster is much more complex than we might at first guess.

I put a bent piece of bread in my toaster; it sticks in the coils and prevents the toaster from popping up and shutting off. I decide to reach in with a fork and try to remove the toast. Why is this stupid and dangerous? (As will be pointed out below, I'm also stupid to reach in with a fork when the toast is done and the power off.)

The toaster operates as shown in figure 3.11. The 115 volts is available at the wall socket. One side of this line (one of the two wires) is grounded—always at the same voltage as the ground. The other wire varies from +163 volts to −163 volts, as we saw in the last section, so that effectively there is 115 volts between the two wires.

My toaster stays plugged into a wall socket. Thus 115 volts comes to the appliance, but the open switch on the toaster means that no current flows through it.

When I close the switch by pulling the toaster lever down, the 115 volts appears across the heating coil. This is a fine wire with enough resistance to give a current of 10 A. Thus, the resistance of the coil causes a power dissipation of

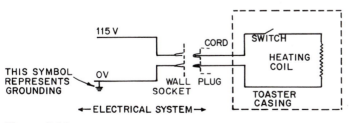

Figure 3.11
Toaster circuit.

115 V × 10 A,   or   1150 watts.

Almost all of this power goes into heat (although there is a very small amount of light as the coil glows). The hot wire radiates heat outward, some directly reaching the bread, some reflected off the toaster wall back to the bread. Most of the heat ends up in the bread, although some warms the air and the case of the appliance.

Voltage along Coil—Toaster Off

First, let's consider what happens if I stick my fork into the toaster when it is off (the lever fully up)—perhaps the small muffin I was toasting did not pop up far enough. We return to the electrical circuit of figure 3.11.

In the wall socket, one hole is 115 volts, the other is 0 volt (at ground)—we don't know which is which. When I insert the plug on the end of the toaster cord, I can hold this plug in either of two orientations; which one I use depends on how I happen to pick it up (figure 3.12).

One of the prongs is connected inside the plug to wire A, which goes directly to the switch; the other prong is attached to wire B, which goes directly to the heating coil (figure 3.13).

I have either of two different circuits, depending on which prong is inserted in the hole carrying 115 volts (the other prong goes to 0 volt). Figure 3.14 shows the two possible circuits. Recall that I don't know which is the correct description of the toaster (plugged in, but off—with the switch open). Half the time at random, circuit a is correct, half the time circuit b. That is, there is a 50 percent probability of either circuit, because when I put the plug into the wall outlet I simply don't know which prong is connected to the 115 V and which prong to the 0 V.

Today plugs for kitchen appliances and the wall outlets are "polarized": there is only one way I can insert the plug in the outlet. This is done to ensure that circuit a of figure 3.14 always is the arrangement. We continue, however, to consider the common, older system.

The voltage along the heating coil inside the toaster is different in these two cases. In both circuits, no current flows because the switch is open. In circuit a, prong B, wire B, and the heating coil are all at 0 volt—the same voltage as the ground or the plumbing fixtures. Prong A and wire A are at 115 volts. If I touch the heating coil, I receive no shock—it's just as though I touched the faucet.

In circuit b, the situation is dangerously different. Now prong B, wire B, and the heating coil are all connected to 115 volts at the wall outlet. Since no current flows (because the switch is open), there is no voltage change by Ohm's

Now we add 8 + 0 + 4 + 4, cast out tens, and get 6. Then we add 2 + 9 + 5, cast out tens, and get 6. (This is *not* a digital root. The digital root is found *only* by casting out nines.) The 6 is the same whether calculated from the vertical column or from the horizontal row.

We transmit the entire array of 20 digits in any sequence previously agreed upon with the receiver so that it can recreate the array. Any single error in the 20 digits can then be detected and automatically corrected. For example, the receiver believes the array to be

```
4 7 2 9 | 2
3 2 8 2 | 9 ←
1 7 4 3 | 5
8 0 4 4 | 6
    ↑
```

The receiver knows that the second row and the second column do not check. Hence, if we assume there is only one error, the entry common to this column and row must be wrong.

```
4 7 2 9 | 2
3 — 8 2 | 9
1 7 4 3 | 5
8 0 4 4 | 6
```

The missing entry must be a 6, determined from either the horizontal row or the vertical column.

This scheme is our first startling result of the use of redundancy: to transmit a message of twelve digits, we need send only twenty digits (twelve message digits and eight check digits) to achieve *automatic detection* and *correction* of any single error (or any number of errors up to three).

If we wanted to use a different method of finding these errors, we might simply send the message over and over again. We would have to transmit the twelve digits three times to get the same detection and correction we got by using the rectangular array. This means we would have to send 36 digits (3×12) instead of 20.

Even the rectangular array is not a particularly efficient scheme (we have eight check digits for twelve message digits), but it does illustrate the capability of redundancy and gives us some appreciation of the power of the very complex redundancy in language.

Exactly the same scheme can be used with binary signals. Here, if we cast out twos we get check digits that add up to an even number of ones in each horizontal row and each vertical column:

```
1 1 1 0 | 1
1 0 1 0 | 0
0 1 1 1 | 1
0 1 0 1 | 0
1 0 1 1 | 1
1 1 0 1 | 1
```

This form of redundancy, called *parity check* in computer science, is used frequently in the magnetic-tape storage systems of computers.

In both the decimal form and the binary form, we can positively detect and correct up to three errors occurring simultaneously.

2.7 Hamming Code

The Hamming Code is a more efficient use of redundancy to detect and correct any single error. The code, first presented by Richard Hamming at Bell Telephone Laboratories, is used in electronic switching systems and military computing equipment.

To explain the code, we consider a specific example in binary code:

1 0 1 1 0 1 0 1 1 1 0 1 0 1 0 0.

This sequence of ones and zeros, reading from left to right, carries the information of the signal. Electrically, this signal can be sent as shown in figure 2.1. A pulse is either transmitted or not transmitted at regular intervals of time. A pulse that is sent represents a one; when no pulse is sent we mean a zero.

When noise is added during transmission, the received signal has the appearance of figure 2.2. During the second pulse interval, the signal should be zero, but the noise happens to look like a pulse to the receiver. If these first six binary digits,

1 0 1 1 0 1,

represent the number 45 in the message, the error in the reception of the second digit means the receiver interprets the number as

1 1 1 1 0 1,

Figure 2.1
Series of pulses representing the binary signal.

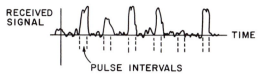

Figure 2.2
Received signal when noise is added. (Only the first six pulse intervals of figure. 2.1 are shown.)

or 61 in the decimal system. (We are assuming that the above are binary numbers, converted in the usual way to their decimal equivalents.)

In order to avoid this sort of occasional error, we can introduce redundancy as follows:

1. The signal to be transmitted is first grouped in sets of four digits. We initially consider the first four:

1   0   1   1.

2. Next we draw a set of three overlapping circles called A, B, and C (figure 2.3). In this figure, there are seven distinct, closed regions. Two such regions are g (common to all three circles) and f (common to A and C).

3. In place of d e f g we insert in *order* the four numbers of our message, 1 0 1 1 (figure 2.4).

4. We now fill in the numbers for a, b, and c by choosing each as either 0 or 1 in such a way that the total number of ones in each circle is even. In other words, in figure 2.4, circle A already includes three ones; hence, we must choose a = 1 to make the total number of ones even (here four). Similarly, b = 0 and c = 0 (figure. 2.5).

5. We now transmit the seven-digit sequence

a   b   c   d   e   f   g

or in our case

1   0   0   1   0   1   1
Extra   Original
digits   message

Each block of four digits in the original message is handled in this way. In other words, for every four message digits we actually transmit seven digits—three more than necessary.

These three redundant or extra digits permit *automatic correction* at the receiver of any single error in the seven-digit block. The receiver must, of course, be familiar with the *coding* used at the transmitter. Then at the receiver

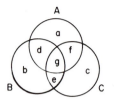

Figure 2.3
Three overlapping circles with the regions a through g defined.

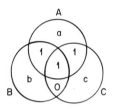

Figure 2.4
The digits of the signal are inserted.

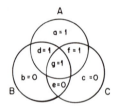

Figure 2.5
Determination of transmitted signal.

we reconstruct the three-circle diagram of figure 2.5. If any one digit is received incorrectly, one or more of the circles contains an odd number of ones.

As a specific example, we can return to our earlier problem and assume the second digit of the message is wrong. That is, the receiver obtains the following:

1 0 0   1 1 1 1
Redundant   Four digits
digits   of message

The receiver checks the validity of this message by constructing the diagram shown here as figure 2.6. We find that there is an odd number of ones in circle B and also in circle C. Therefore, if there is only one error, it must be the element common to circles B and C, or element e. Hence, the received signal can be automatically corrected to

1 0 0 1 0 1 1.

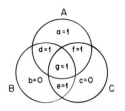

Figure 2.6
Received signal including error in e.

Of course, electronic equipment does not construct a diagram. Instead, the receiver is designed to measure $a + d + f + g$, $b + d + e + g$, and $c + e + f + g$. Each of these three sums should be even. In the case of our received signal, the three sums are 4, 3, and 3; the last two are odd; the error is in the element common to B and C but not to A or element E.

The Hamming Code uses three extra digits for each four message digits. The same procedure can be used if we draw four regions overlapping in all possible combinations (this is a complicated geometric construction). There are then four extra digits for each eleven message digits. Similarly, five extra digits compensate for 26 message digits. As the message block is made longer and longer, however, there is a growing possibility of two simultaneous errors—a situation the system cannot correct.

Because with even four regions the geometry is messy, it is easier to decide on the correction digits by a systematic procedure. We visualize (but don't draw) four regions (A, B, C, and D) that overlap in all possible combinations:

AB AC AD BC BD CD ABC ABD ACD BCD ABCD.

These eleven "regions" are assigned the eleven message digits. Then we determine the digits for regions

A B C D

so that each region has an even number of ones.

The Hamming Code is interesting because it is used in practical communications systems. It indicates the simple way in which technology uses redundancy to improve communication among men and machines. With the code described above, we can *automatically* correct any single error in each set of digits. With more complex codes, we can correct any one or two errors. Thus, we can build communications systems that are essentially error-free.

2.8 Bar Codes

Bar codes have become a common method for identifying particular products. The Universal Product Code was first used in supermarkets in the 1970s to allow for rapid checkout and better inventory control. Today factory automation demands that robots and other equipment be able to quickly and accurately identify an item moving along the production line, and bar codes are used for that. In 1981 the U.S. Department of Defense started requiring manufacturers to use bar codes to identify all items sold to the military.

Although the codes are different for various applications, there are several underlying principles that are common to all of them. The code is a sequence of white and black (or colored) bars, or bars of two different lengths. Consequently, the set of bars from left to right represents a sequence of zeros and ones (the choice between only two possibilities). This sequence of zeros and ones differs from item to item, so it can serve as an identification tag.

To determine what a particular item is, the identification equipment "looks at" the bars, usually from left to right. A focused light (often from a laser) shines on a single bar. If the bar is white (or very short), much of the light reflects back to a detector which measures electrically the amount of incoming light. If the bar is black (or very long), much less light is reflected. Thus, as the reader scans from left to right, the electrical output indicates the proper sequence of zeros and ones.

A major problem at supermarket checkouts arises with frozen food. A glaze of ice over the bar code reflects light even from the area of a black bar. The checkout clerk may have to scrape the ice off the bar code to obtain a measurement.

Coding Principles

A manufacturer assigns a sequence of decimal digits to each product he wants to label. For example, Snyder's of Hanover Corporation gives the number

Figure 2.7
Examples of bar codes we all encounter daily. Left: UPC. Center: mail code. Right: magazine code.

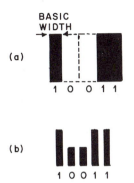

(a)

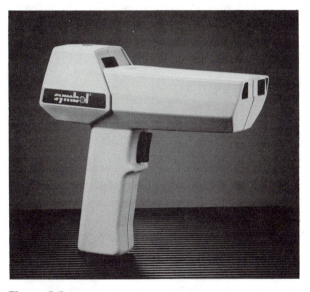

(b)

Figure 2.8
Two ways a set of bars can represent binary numbers. (a) Part of a bar code. The white bar represents 0, the darkened bar 1, so the partial symbol stands for 10011. (b) Code with the binary number indicated by the height of the bar (the taller bar represents 1, the shorter one 0).

Figure 2.9
Hand-held laser scanner. (Photograph from Symbol Technologies, Inc., of Bohemia, New York—a leading manufacturer of bar-code scanners.)

0 - 77975 - 02248

to its 9-oz. package of pretzel rods (figure 2.10).

Each of these decimal digits is first represented by a sequence of binary digits. Then the binary digits are displayed in bar-code form (a black bar for a one, a white bar for a zero). The next section explains how the decimal numbers are converted to a set of black and white bars.

Redundancy—Check Digit

In order to decrease errors in reading the bar code, a check digit—one extra digit at the end—is usually added. For example in figure 2.10 the bars on the far right (those that are a little below the principal group) represent the check digit, which in this case is a one.

The check digit is added to indicate whether the preceding numbers have been read correctly. The light detector measures the check digit and compares its reading with the computer calculation of what the check digit should be on the basis of the first 11 digits measured.

For example, suppose I want to communicate to you my home phone number, 226-4878. To find a check digit, I might just add up all the digits,

$$2 + 2 + 6 + 4 + 8 + 7 + 8 = 37,$$

and use as a check digit the last digit (7) of the sum. I would then say to you

226 4878 7.

Knowing the rule we are using, you calculate the check digit from the first seven. When you calculate 7 and you receive 7 from me, you know that there has not been any one error in the phone number you received. Any single error would have resulted in a different check digit.

The scheme for determining the check digit on a bar code is usually more complex. Because the most common error we make in repeating a number is to interchange two digits (for example, 262 4878 instead of 226 4878) the check digit calculated from the sum of the digits would not spot such an error.

Figure 2.10
Bar code identifying Snyder's pretzel rods.

To avoid this problem, I might multiply *every other* digit by 3 before finding the sum. For the example above, 226-4878, I would get

2 × 3 = 6
6 × 3 = 18
8 × 3 = 24
8 × 3 = 24.

I would then add these four to the digits I have skipped over,

6 + 2 + 18 + 4 + 24 + 7 + 24 = 85,

and use the last digit of the sum, or 5, as a check digit. If I interchanged two successive digits, I would be multiplying the wrong one by 3, and the check digit would be wrong.

This idea of using a check digit to verify that the identification number has been read correctly is an example of the intelligent use of redundancy. In the next section, we see how the code for supermarket automation works. (The problems at the end of this chapter give other examples of bar codes.)

2.9 Universal Product Code

Almost every prepackaged item sold in supermarkets today has a label with a bar code. This symbol, called the UPC or Universal Product Code, was selected in 1973 by a committee established by seven trade associations. The vertical bars on the code represent the digits below, which are printed for human recognition (figure 2.11) if the automatic reader should fail.

The checkout person moves the item across a small opening in the counter. Under the opening there is a helium-neon laser sending a light beam up toward the label. The dark regions absorb the light beam; the light areas reflect the beam downward, where a light-sensitive detector reads the pattern of light and dark bars by measuring the reflections.

This information is sent to a central computer, where the specific product is identified from the code. For example, 0-51000-02261 (figure 2.11) is the

Figure 2.11
Universal Product Code.

code for the 10¾-ounce can of Campbell's chicken alphabet soup. The computer then does two different things:

1. It orders the cash register to ring up 33 cents for the soup, displays this price on a small indicator the customer can watch, and prints on the sales slip the entry

GRO .33F SOUP

representing a grocery item, a charge of 33 cents with eligibility for food stamps (F), and a description of the product (figure 2.12).

2. It updates the inventory stored in the computer memory by subtracting one can of soup from the total number of cans still in the store.

The key to the technology is the laser scanner-reader that identifies the product. This form of supermarket automation was first proposed in 1932, but the laser and computer technologies were not available until the late 1960s. The laser is essential because the light beam must be very sharply focused to read accurately the widths of successive bars. Furthermore, with the laser emitting light at a single color or frequency, the detectors or sensors of the reflected light can be tuned to that same frequency so that ambient light does not cause reading errors. Finally, the reading of the code must be possible when the label is carried across the opening in the checkout counter in any direction and at varying speeds. The focused laser beam can be scanned rapidly across the product in the pattern of figure 2.13. The complete set of bars is always read on one of the four legs.

```
        THANK YOU FOR
      SHOPPING WALDBAUMS
         60 WALL ST
       HUNTINGTON  NY
    STORE #136  06/01/88


    MOT APPL SCE    .47F
    ROMAINE         .99F
    POL RIC CH     1.99F
    DELL SKIM      1.29F
    GR PARMESAN    3.05F
    POLLYO MOZZA   2.99F
    LL YOGURT      1.99F
    TURNIP/WHT.     .24F
      862    .40LB
         1LB/  .59
    ASPARAGUS       .80F
      812    .81LB
         1LB/  .99
    GARLIC         1.00F
      836    .59LB
         1LB/ 1.69
    GRFT./NM        .98F
           2/.98
    GRAPES/GRN.    2.83F
      930   1.78LB
         1LB/ 1.59

       TOTAL     18.62

       CASH      20.00

       CHANGE     1.38

    1270  147  1  4.26PM
```

Figure 2.12
Sales slip.

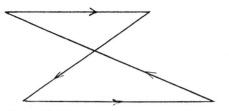

Figure 2.13
Direction of laser-beam scan.

How was the UPC symbol designed? First, the size of the symbol obviously has to be a compromise. The larger the symbol, the easier it is to read by machine. But a very large symbol means there is less room for the name of the product, an attractive picture to catch the consumer's attention, and the listing of ingredients, weight, etc. The final choice ensures that less than 1 percent of the items are unreadable by the equipment (in other words, the numbers have to be inserted manually for less than one product per 100). The choice of a particular code strongly influences this reject rate. The code was cleverly designed to avoid errors resulting from wrinkling and stray marks on the symbol, or even from intentional tampering by the consumer.

The symbol has two parts:

1. A series of numbers (in figure 2.14, 0-17800-51583), available to be recorded manually if necessary.

2. An array of vertical dark lines of various widths. These lines, representing the numbers, are readable by the laser and the optical system.

Set of Numbers
In the preceding example, there is a set of twelve numbers:

0-17800-51583-2.

The twelfth digit is not printed on the label; it is a *check digit* used to ensure that the system is working. First, consider the eleven digits that are printed on the label. What do these represent?

The first digit (0) describes the type of product: 0 for grocery-store items.

The next five digits (17800) describe the manufacturer, here the Ralston Purina Company. Thus, any Ralston Purina grocery-store product starts with 0-17800. The manufacturer is assigned its number by Distribution Codes Incorporated in Washington, an organization established with the agreement of the trade associations.

The next five digits represent the particular product (Tender Vittles) and are chosen by the manufacturer who affixes the label. Thus, there is room for

Figure 2.14
UPC for Tender Vittles.

100,000 manufacturers of grocery products and 100,000 items for each manufacturer.

The last number (the twelfth one, not printed) is the check digit, given by the following formula. If the first eleven digits are labelled a, b, c, … , k, the check digit is the last digit of

210 − 3(a + c + e + g + i + k) − (b + d + f + h + j).

In the Ralston Purina Tender Vittles example, the formula gives 2—the last digit of

210 − 3(0 + 7 + 0 + 5 + 5 + 3) − (1 + 8 + 0 + 1 + 8) = 132.

Pictorial Representation of a Number

The Universal Product Code represents each of these digits by a set of vertical lines so that the machine can read the number automatically. The first 1 can serve as an example. It is represented by a set of bars in the following sequence from left to right:

a light space twice the minimum width,

a dark or black space twice the minimum width,

a light space twice the minimum width,

a dark space the minimum width.

First, visualize a space divided into seven segments of the same width (figure 2.15). The first two vertical bar areas are left light, the next two are made dark, the next two are left light, and the last is made dark. This symbol now represents the number 1 (figure 2.16).

Since the bars are either light or dark, it is convenient to describe the representation by a binary number—a number made up of zeros and ones. With 0 representing a light bar of minimum width and 1 representing a dark bar, the code for the number 1 in figure 2.16 is

0 0 1 1 0 0 1.

Figure 2.15
Space divided into seven segments.

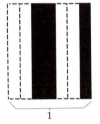

Figure 2.16
Graphical representation of 1. (The dashed lines do not appear on the label; they are included here only to show how the symbol is constructed.)

Two Consecutive Digits

The first two digits of the manufacturer's number in figure 2.14 are

1 7.

The graphical symbols for these are simply run together so that the 7 follows immediately after the 1 (figure 2.17). Thus the codes are as follows:

"1" 0011001
"7" 0111011.

Complete Graphical Symbol

Now it is time to consider the complete graphical symbol of the example illustrated in figure 2.18. At either end, the code starts with two dark bars separated by a light bar. These *guard bars* indicate the beginning and the end of the pattern. When the equipment detects both "start" and "finish" symbols, it knows that the complete pattern has been read on that part of the scan.

Next, starting from the left, a pattern of long bars represents the first zero (figure 2.19). Where the zero starts and stops cannot be determined unless the rules are known—indeed, the equipment itself must also understand these rules to be able to read the code.

Two rules are sufficient to understand the structure of the representation of the zero.

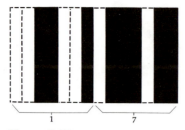

Figure 2.17
Graphical representation of 1 and 7.

Figure 2.18
UPC Symbol.

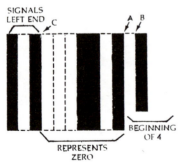

Figure 2.19

Rule 1: On the left half of the symbol each digit starts with a light bar (a zero) and ends with a dark bar (a one). The opposite is true on the right half.

   Now it becomes clear that the representation of the zero starts at C and must end at A (not B).

Rule 2: Each digit is represented by "seven" vertical bars (light or dark).

This rule suggests that the zero is represented by

light, light, light, dark, dark, light, dark.

The seven-digit, binary representation is

0001101.

The next five digits (42000) are again each represented by seven bars, the code always beginning with a zero and ending with a one. Two long bars denote when the center line has been reached. These are followed by the right half of the code, which represents the particular product.

   The complete code is an impressive engineering design. The left half always starts with a zero and ends with a one, so any possible representation of a digit has the form

0XXXXX1,

where the X can be 0 or 1. Thus, there are 32 possibilities (2^5), but only ten are required for the digits 0 through 9. The 32 possibilities are further narrowed by two additional rules.

Rule 3: Odd parity exists on the left half of the label—that is, there is always an odd number of ones in each allowable representation of a digit.

(Even parity exists on the right; hence the machine can tell at once whether the label is being read from left to right or from right to left.) As a consequence of this rule, half of the 32 possibilities for the digits on the left half are eliminated, leaving

0000001	0011001
0000111	0101001
0001011	0110001
0010011	0011111
0100011	0101111
0001101	0110111
0010101	0111011
0100101	0111101

The last rule selects ten of these sixteen seven-digit, binary numbers:

Rule 4: Each allowable representation has two light regions and two dark regions.

For example, the representation 0101001 is disallowed because there would be three light and three dark bands. Elimination of all seven-digit representations with two or six total regions gives the final list of allowable numbers:

0001011-9   0110001-5
0010011-2   0101111-6
0100011-4   0110111-8
0001101-0   0111011-7
0011001-1   0111101-3

Also shown is the decimal digit associated with each of these representations. On the right half, the complement in each case is used, replacing each zero with a one and vice versa in the binary representation. Thus, the number 9 is represented on the right half by

1110100.

In binary form then, the code

0-41219-00008-5

is represented by a sequence of light and dark bars corresponding to figure 2.20.

The four rules on which the code is based were chosen to simplify machine reading through intelligent use of redundancy. The code starts with seven bars, or $2^7 = 128$ possibilities. By requiring that the code always start and end the same way (each representation starting with 0 and ending with 1, whether reading right-to-left or left-to-right), machine uncertainty about where a digit starts and ends is reduced, but three-quarters of our 128 possibilities are sacrificed.

Requiring odd parity on the left and even parity on the right allows the machine to determine its direction of reading. The checkout person need not

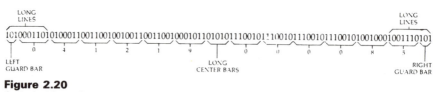

Figure 2.20
Code in binary form.

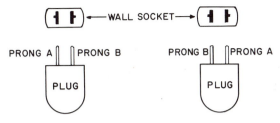

Figure 3.12
Plug can be inserted into wall outlet in either of two ways: prong B on the right or prong B on the left.

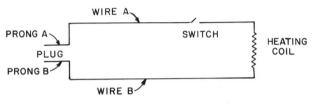

Figure 3.13
Circuit for the toaster.

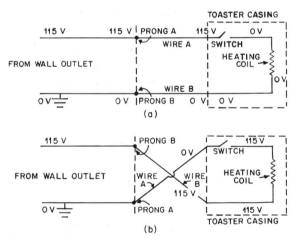

Figure 3.14
Two possible circuits for toaster plugged in but turned off (switch open).

Law—this whole section is at 115 volts. Touching *any* part of the heating coil exposes me to a shock from the 115 volts.

Thus, even when the toaster switch is open, there is a 50 percent change that the heating coil is at a dangerous voltage. I can be electrocuted if I use a metal fork to reach in for my muffin, even though I know the toaster is off and I *think* everything is "safe."

Voltage along Coil—Toaster On

When the toaster switch is closed and full voltage is applied to the heating coil, the risk is now quite different. As is shown in figure 3.15, one end of the coil is at 115 volts, the other end at 0 volt—which is which depends on the way the plug is inserted in the wall outlet. Current flows down through the resistance of the coil.

One quarter of the way down (¾ of the way up), the voltage is ¾ of 115, or 86 volts; halfway down, it is 57 volts; and so forth. As we go down the coil, the voltage drops steadily from 115 to 0.

When I insert the fork, the voltage coming to my body depends on where the fork touches along the coil. Of course, just looking at the coil, I can't tell where the voltage is high or low, since all parts of the coil heat up equally because they carry the same current.

It is surprising that inserting my fork may be riskier if the toaster is off than if it is on. As we'll see in the next section, how large the voltage must be to give a bad shock depends on many factors. Suppose, just as an example, that 100 volts is needed to shock severely. What is the probability of my receiving a bad shock when I insert the fork?

If the toaster is *off*, the probability is 0.5—half the time the plug will be in the socket in the dangerous direction.

If the toaster is *on*, the probability is 0.13—only 15/115 of the coil length has a voltage of 100 or greater (100/115 has a smaller voltage).

In this case, I am four times as likely to be hurt if the toaster is off!

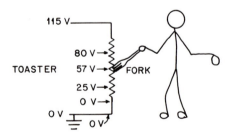

Figure 3.15
Voltage along toaster coil as my fork makes contact.

About 1100 people die each year in the U.S. from electrical shock; the great majority are young people. Furthermore, 30,000 are seriously injured. Thus, electrical shock ranks well below auto accidents as a serious problem, so it is difficult to generate interest in better public education.

3.5 Electrical Effects on People

When I insert my fork into the toaster and accidentally touch the coil, the metallic, conducting fork brings to my hand a voltage, which can be of any size from 0 to 115 volts. What will happen? Can we answer if we know the voltage?

Might I be killed? Could I be burned severely? May I receive such a strong shock that I fall and sustain other injuries? Might I feel nothing? The answer to each question is *Yes*. Determining what is likely to happen to me turns out to be very difficult, even if we know the voltage at the point my fork touches the coil.

Why is this such a hard problem? There are two answers:

1. Finding the current that flows into my body is essentially impossible without doing the actual "experiment."

2. If we could find the current, we could not predict what the effect on me would be.

These two difficulties illustrate the problems of determining the effects of technology on human beings very broadly. We will consider both of them in more detail in this section. Similar difficulties occur when engineers try to estimate the effects of particular kinds of auto accidents, levels of air pollution, intensities of noise, and so on.

Finding the Current
In figure 3.16, we suppose the fork touches the coil where the voltage is 80 volts. The fork is a perfect conductor, so this voltage reaches the end of the fork, which is in contact with my hand. Current now flows from the fork into my

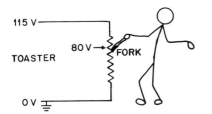

Figure 3.16
Fork touches the coil where the voltage is 80 volts.

hand, through my body, and somehow back to the ground, whence it can return to the generating station.

The current flowing through my body is given by Ohm's Law:

$$I = \frac{V}{R} \quad .$$

Here, the voltage V is 80, so the current depends on the resistance R from the fork handle through my body to ground. Unfortunately, we have no way to calculate this resistance except with very crude approximations.

If I am standing on a good insulator (very high resistance) and not touching anything else, R is essentially infinite and no current flows—I don't even feel a shock (figure 3.17). At the other extreme, if my other hand is grasping firmly the faucet (which is at ground voltage because the metallic plumbing goes through the ground), the current can flow to my hand, up my arm, across my chest, down the other arm, and to the faucet (figure 3.18). Now the resistance from the fork to ground might be as low as 1000 ohms, and the current could be large enough to kill me.

Even if we know exactly what I'm touching, however, we still can only estimate the resistance roughly. This resistance depends on the contact between my hand and the fork; how tightly I'm holding it, how moist my hand

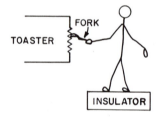

Figure 3.17
Standing on an insulator while touching the coil with a fork. An insulator is a material with almost no free electrons, so no current can flow through it.

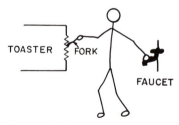

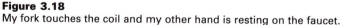

Figure 3.18
My fork touches the coil and my other hand is resting on the faucet.

is, the resistance provided by my skin. It also depends on the resistance of my arms and torso. What are the dimensions? What is the material through which current flows?

Finding the Effect of the Current

Engineers in a safety laboratory might do an experiment as follows. One stands in the proper position, reaches out with a fork, and touches 0.8 volts (rather than 80), and they measure the current as 0.8 milliamp. They then infer that a voltage 100 times as great would cause an equal increase in current. In this way, they experimentally determine the total resistance. The experiment will have to be repeated with many different people if we want a valid number for the average risk involved in inserting a fork into the toaster.

Now we know the current will be 80 milliamperes (mA). Unfortunately, we still don't know the effect such a current will have on a person. There are various possible results of a current flowing through the body. For example:

1. At the skin the current may cause a burn. The power converted to heat is I^2R, where R is the resistance of the contact between the fork and my hand.

2. The muscles are energized by electrical currents in normal body operations. Thus, the muscle current may cause muscles to contract suddenly.

3. The central nervous system is electrical—nerve signals are sent to the brain by electrical pulses. The current may cause abnormal pulses or may destroy certain nerve cells.

4. The beating of the heart is controlled by an electrical pulse generated within the heart, then traveling around to cause valves to close and open in sequence. A strong electrical current through the heart may disrupt this beating operation.

Which of these occur and the severity of each vary greatly from person to person. There is no hope of doing an experiment with a small current and trying to use the results to predict what happens with larger currents; for example, the heartbeat is not affected at all by a very small current. (The *Guinness Book of Records* says that the highest-voltage shock that has ever been survived was 230,000 volts, survived by a young man on the tower of a power line in Los Angeles in 1967. Presumably this is true, but we don't know where the current flowed in the body or even what the current was. The resistance may have been so large that the current was small. High voltage alone is significant only when resistance is low.)

Thus, all we can do is observe a few effects with small currents and analyze as carefully as possible what may have happened in actual cases of shock. We can do some experiments on animals, but the results are very limited and we never can be sure that the effects also appear in human beings.

From these studies, we can deduce only general statements—for instance, statistical averages applicable to "most people" under "most circumstances." Furthermore, we find it impossible to determine *threshold levels*. For example, we know that 100 mA often causes death and that 80 mA may cause death in some cases. Is there a value of current (say 20 mA) below which death never occurs—a "safe" threshold? Possibly there is, but we never can find this. Our theory is too incomplete, and we cannot do the required experiments on many people.

This inability to establish a *safe threshold* arises again and again in environmental problems. In air-pollution studies, how much lead in the air is safe? Knowing that lead poisoning is extremely serious and common among children in the cities, the United States early in the 1970s required that new cars use only unleaded gas. Western Europe did not follow suit (unleaded gas was not available there). Some epidemiological studies indicated that there may be no human effects of airborne lead particles from auto emissions, because they are not retained in the body. Subsequent studies showed these conclusions were wrong, and Europe is now moving toward unleaded gas. What engineers need is a threshold level below which lead particles are not harmful; without such knowledge, we can only guess at the benefits from requiring unleaded gas, and we have no intelligent way to compare the benefits with the costs.

Our Best Estimates

Even though there are no simple answers to the question of human effects of electrical currents, we do need some rules of thumb for safety studies and testing of appliances. The following data are based on the limited experiments that can be performed.

Awareness Current   We are aware of currents of about 1 mA (one milliampere, or 1/1000 ampere). When this amount of current flows, we can usually feel a slight tingling. The actual level depends on the sensitivity of the part of the body.

Two flashlight batteries give 3 volts. If we moisten two fingers on the same hand to cut down skin resistance and touch the two terminals, we can feel the current of about 1 mA.

Occasionally I touch the casing of an appliance (e.g., a hair dryer or a toaster) and feel this tingling. This is often the first sign that something is wrong, and it should alert me to either discard the device or have it repaired.

What is happening inside an appliance if I feel a slight shock (or tingling) when I touch the casing? Let's return to the toaster. When the device is new and operating properly, the incoming wires and the coil are carefully insulated from the metal casing (the housing). Where the wires enter the casing, they are wrapped in heavy insulation and they may enter through a hole in which the metal is separated from the wire by rubber. Inside, the coil is built so that it never comes close to the casing.

In use, the toaster may fall to the floor or be hit by a solid object that either dents the casing or moves the coil from its normal position. Perhaps the last person who inserted a fork caught the coil and twisted it. Possibly the coil overheated in one region and became distorted in shape. For any of these reasons, a point along the coil is now close to the casing.

The electrical result is shown in figure 3.19. There is a relatively small resistance introduced from the coil to the casing—a resistance we call R_{defect} to emphasize that it comes from a defect in the appliance. Now I touch the casing. The resistance through my body to ground is R.

The current that flows through my body is

$$\frac{V}{R_{defect} + R},$$

where V is the voltage at the critical point along the coil. When the device is new, R_{defect} is almost infinite, and there is no current. As R_{defect} becomes smaller and smaller because the defect gradually gets worse, the current increases until it exceeds 1 mA and I just sense the tingling.

Something is wrong. No appliance should give you a perceptible shock when you touch the casing. If I do nothing, the defect may continue to worsen, the current increase, and eventually I will receive a serious shock.

The problem is especially serious with hair dryers. First, they are often used in the bathroom, where the user may be touching the plumbing. Plumbing is grounded, so the resistance through the body to the ground is low. (Any

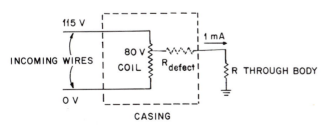

Figure 3.19
Circuit diagram for a defective toaster.

electrical appliance in the bathroom is potentially dangerous.) Second, the hair dryer contains both a coil to heat the air and a motor to drive the fan. Hair inside the device can cause the motor to overheat with a subsequent movement of the internal parts or breakdown of the insulation, especially with rough handling.

Let-Go Current   As the current increases beyond the tingling value, we soon reach sizes of currents that affect the muscles. If the muscles contract, the grip of your hand on the appliance can tighten (thereby decreasing the resistance), and you may be unable to let go. Thus, the current will *continue to flow* through your body until someone shuts off the electricity to your house. An electrician uses the back of his hand, or only his fingers, as much as possible to avoid this effect.

The "let-go current," the value at which you cannot let go, varies widely from person to person; typical values are 15 mA for men, 10 mA for women, and as low as $\frac{1}{3}$ of the adult levels for children. A value of 5 mA protects 99.5 percent of the population.

Even at these relatively low currents, we are limited in the experiments we can do on people, since we're not sure about any long-term effects of repeated shocks and abnormal muscle stimulation. Animal experiments are often used, with primates the best subjects but very costly, sheep quite comparable to people, and dogs relatively inexpensive. The extrapolation of animal results to people, however, is always open to question.

The let-go current is the largest value at which we can do experiments to measure the effects of frequency. As was pointed out in section 3.3, the dc-ac argument around 1890 raised the question of which type of voltage is more dangerous. Recent research has led to the curve of figure 3.20, which shows that 60 cycles per second is actually the worst frequency we could select. The let-go current at dc (zero frequency) is more than 6 times that at 60 cycles per second.

We do not know if Edison was right. The evidence is really not clear, since the lethal current may well not vary with frequency in the same way as the let-go current. Perhaps the low value at 60 cycles per second arises from the nature of muscle action.

As the current increases to the let-go value, we are also into the range where shock may cause serious injury because of the surprise and the unpredictable human reaction. Trying to jump away, a person can fall; fear may even bring on a heart attack. The problem is especially serious with battery-operated children's toys. A young child may use a toy in a way totally unanticipated by the manufacturer—for example, as something to chew. (Imaginative use of electri-

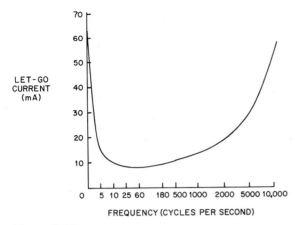

Figure 3.20
Let-go current for adult males as it depends on frequency. Note that the horizontal scale is distorted to show frequencies at which measurements have been made. (The worst frequency for fibrillation seems to be 250 cycles per second, so there is nothing uniquely bad about 60.)

cal devices is not restricted to children. A hair dryer is often used to defrost a refrigerator, dry a dog that's been out in the rain, or dry the ignition wires of a car while the person is standing on a wet driveway.)

Serious Injury When the current increases to 50 mA, we are in the realm of serious injury. Pain, fainting, exhaustion, and serious injury to the muscles are common, and contraction of the chest muscles may make breathing difficult.

Ventricular Fibrillation A current of 100 mA is *roughly* the body current at which enough current reaches the heart to cause ventricular fibrillation. Ventricular fibrillation means that the heart muscle fibers are contracting out of synchronism; the uncoordinated contractions result in a failure to pump blood through the lungs and the body.

The body current required to cause fibrillation depends on what fraction of the current goes through the heart. (To minimize current flow across the chest, you should keep one hand in a pocket when working on live electrical devices.) For example, in a two-year-old child, fibrillation may occur with only ⅓ the body current needed for an adult. When the individual has a pacemaker, with wires leading directly into the right ventricle, very little external current is needed to cause fibrillation.

When we talk about a current of 100 mA going into the body from a source of only 115 volts, the body resistance *plus* the resistance from the body to the ground has to be 1150 ohms. This low value means that we probably have to be in a bathtub or a swimming pool, or at the very least in good electrical contact with both the 115-volt supply and the ground. Of course, if I work inside an operating television set, I can be exposed to several thousand volts.

Severe Burns   Currents of 3 amperes can cause severe burns and physical damage.

The above numbers for let-go current, fibrillation current, and so forth have to be recognized as only estimates and average values. Much lower currents can, under the right circumstances, cause these problem. For example, 30 mA is likely to cause fibrillation in a two-year-old, but we have to go down to 5 mA to ensure safety. The problem of electrical safety in the house is a compromise. We need as high a voltage as possible to obtain efficiency in appliances, but we want to limit the voltage to minimize severe shocks. In the United States, probably because of the emphasis in the ac-dc controversy on danger, we chose 115 volts for the standard wall outlet. Europe uses the more efficient but more dangerous 230 volts.

Importance of Timing in a Brief Shock

An electrocardiogram shows the electrical activity during one cycle of the heart's beating. For a normal individual, the electrocardiogram has the shape shown in figure 3.22. The different parts of the signal are called the Q, R, S, T, and P waves, as shown.

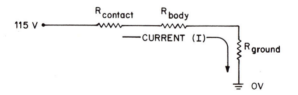

Figure 3.21
When I touch a hot (115-volt) spot on the toaster or other appliance, the current I that flows is determined by three resistances: $R_{contact}$ (the resistance between the conductor carrying 115 volts and my hand), R_{body} (the resistance through my body), and R_{ground} (resistance from my body to ground). By Ohm's law, the current is

$$I = \frac{115}{R_{contact} + R_{body} + R_{ground}}$$

To obtain 100 mA, the sum of the three resistances must be 1150 ohms. Since R_{body} is usually nearly this value, the contact and ground resistances must be very small.

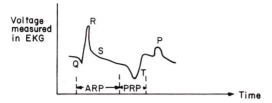

Figure 3.22
One cycle of an EKG.

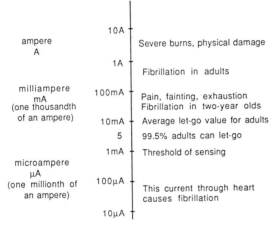

Figure 3.23
Summary of electric shock effects with current at 60 hertz (60 cycles per second).
The vertical scale is logarithmic—that is, each division up corresponds to multiplication by 10.

The time around the T wave (that is, the T pulse) is called the partial refractory phase (PRP). This is about 20 percent of the total time, and it occurs just after the longer absolute refractory phase (ARP).

During the ARP, electrical current has no effect on the heart because the muscles are fully stressed—that is, the muscles are fully driven electrically, and additional current does nothing. As this stress is released, a current from external sources can have an effect, especially near the peak of the T wave.

Thus, fibrillation is likely only if the shock occurs near the middle of the PRP, especially if the shock lasts less than ¹/₁₀ second. This fact is important for two reasons:

1. It explains why short shocks so often are not lethal.

2. It tells us that protective equipment to terminate a shock in less than ¹/₁₀ second can cut fatalities sharply.

Appendix 3.1
Scientific Notation

Since we often use very large or very small numbers in science, we need a way to express these numbers in a shortened form. This abbreviated form also makes calculations much simpler.

Basically, what we do is express decimal places as powers of 10. This method of expressing numerals is called *scientific notation.*

To write any large number, move the decimal point until only one digit appears to the *left* of the decimal point. Count the number of places you moved the decimal point and use that number as the exponent of the power of 10.

Examples:

1,000,000 is the same as 1×10^6,

which is $1 \times (10 \times 10 \times 10 \times 10 \times 10 \times 10)$.

96,000 is the same as 9.6×10^4.

365 is the same as 3.65×10^2.

For numbers *less* than 1, move the decimal point to the *right* until only one *nonzero* digit appears to the *left* of the decimal point. Count the number of places you moved the decimal point to the right and use that number as a *negative* exponent of the power of 10.

Examples:

0.00063 is the same as 6.3×10^{-4} , or $\dfrac{6.3}{10^4}$.

0.007 is the same as 7×10^{-3}.

Thousands, Millions, etc.
The above "scientific notation" can often be simplified even more. When we talk about frequencies in hertz, we will have such numbers as

18,000 Hz, or 1.8×10^4 Hz.

We can also consider this 18 thousand hertz, written as 18 kHz (where k stands for kilo, a prefix meaning thousands). Similarly, 87,000,000 Hz is written as 87 MHz (M for million). For numbers less than 1, m stands for thousandths, and μ for millionths. Thus, 0.002 amperes, or 0.002 A, is written 2 mA (2 milliamperes), and 2×10^{-6} A is written 2 μA (2 microamperes, or 2 millionths of an ampere).

Appendix 3.2
One Problem in Human Experimentation

Whenever current flows, there is a magnetic field in the vicinity. Thus, standing near any electrical appliance or under the power lines leading into your house, you are unconsciously exposed to an artificial magnetic field. Does this artificial environment have any long-term, harmful effects—or, indeed, any effect at all?

Superficially, this might seem like an easy question to answer. We could simply enclose test subjects in a room with an artificial magnetic field and measure any physiological or psychological changes. Difficulties would arise immediately, even if we used a control group. We are interested in *long-term* effects, but it isn't practical to pay people to spend years or even months in a small test room. The psychological effects of this are likely to be so great that we would need large test and control groups to obtain meaningful results. The experiment is likely to be unethical.

Perhaps we can first ask a simpler, although different question: Can human beings detect the presence of a moderate magnetic field? In the 1970s, one of the nation's leading biomedical engineers, Otto Schmitt, and a colleague, R. O. Tucker, found an amazing result. Certain subjects apparently could detect the presence of a moderate magnetic field with startling accuracy.

Unfortunately, current flowing through a large coil surrounding the test room creates effects in addition to a magnetic field. The magnetic field from one current exerts a force on a nearby wire carrying current as the two magnetic fields interact (this is why a motor turns). The result is some vibration and also a small sound signal at 60 Hz. Perhaps the test subject feels the vibration or hears the sound.

The following paragraphs describe briefly the tedious, expensive, and time-consuming experiments Schmitt and Tucker had to go through before finally establishing that the test subjects could not detect the magnetic field.

This example illustrates two serious difficulties in experimentation involving environmental effects on people.

1. Ensuring that only one phenomenon or signal is present is very demanding. Most experimenters have neither the patience nor the resources to continue the study until results are conclusive.

2. Scientists usually hope for positive results; we start an experiment with the anticipation that effects will be found. After several tedious refinements of the experimental equipment, we are tempted to accept the positive results we hoped for.

The work of Schmitt and Tucker is remarkable in both respects.

Case History on the Difficulty of Eliminating False Clues from Acoustical or Vibrational Noise

In 1973, Schmitt and Tucker published an article dealing with the possibility of human perception of moderate strength, low frequency magnetic fields. It was concluded that, for the test setup which they employed, certain subjects had uncannily accurate abilities to perceive the field to a high degree of statistical reliability. This occurred despite the experimenters' best efforts to isolate possible clues (vibration or acoustical noise, for example). These subjects, which were capable of sensing the fields, or at least the "field on" condition, reported with great certainty that they were sensing the field, although they could not state whether it was something they heard, felt, or otherwise perceived.

Apparently, as a sequel to this interesting pilot study, Tucker and Schmitt conducted additional tests regarding human perception of 60-Hz moderate strength magnetic fields under the auspices of the National Academy of Sciences. The first step in these tests was to produce an improved acoustically padded cabinet to house the experimental subject, and to isolate him from sound and vibration. Significant efforts were made to silence the coils by clamping them on air pocket packing material. Oddly enough, even with these improved precautions, including the isolation cabinet, sensitive subjects still reported that they thought they were faintly hearing hum and were producing extremely high scores to identify the "field on" condition.

To remedy this situation, a special cabinet was fabricated with four layers of 0.5-in plywood, full contact epoxy glued and surface coated into a reinforced monolithic structure to make a very rigid heavy structure weighing, in total, about 300 kg. The structure was made without the use of ferrous metal fastenings (to avoid magnetostriction vibration), and only a few slender brass screws were used. The door was of similar epoxy four-ply construction but faced with a thin bonded melamine plastic sheet, and the door was hung on two multitongued bakelite hinges with thin brass pins. The door was sealed against a thin closed cell foam rubber gasket, and was pressure sealed with over a metric ton of force by pumping a mild vacuum inside the chamber, such that the "cabin altitude" was approximately 2500 ft above the ambient altitude so that no serious health hazard was included.

Even with these precautions, while most scores dropped dramatically, a few individuals still made impressively significant high scores to detect the "field on" condition.

To remedy this, an extreme effort was made to improve even further the already good isolation. This was done by suspending the cabinet from the ceiling via aircraft shock cord supports to the roof timbers. The cabinet was ingeniously prevented from swinging as a pendulum by four small non-load-bearing lightly inflated automotive inner tubes placed between the floor and the cabinet base. The magnetic field exciting coils were firmly reclamped, the cabinet draped inside with a sound-absorbing material, and the chair for the subject shockmounted with respect to the cabinet. With this super isolation, final experiments indicated minimal perception.

While recounting this series of experiments might well make an interesting anecdote, the difficulties reported in achieving complete isolation from acoustical and vibrational problems are of great importance. Experimenters hoping to eliminate all influences other than electric fields, and also in interpreting the literature, would do well to read completely the results of this study. With the exception of the above reported test, none of the studies or ongoing research reviewed to date revealed this attention to detail to eliminate the possibility of acoustical or vibrational influences. This strongly suggests that, in a number of behavioral experiments wherein some positive effect has been reported, some strange simulation could have alerted the animal to achieve faster test scores; and this might well have arisen from almost imperceptible acoustic noise or direct vibration conducted into the test area.

From J. E. Bridges and M. Preache, "Biological Influences of Power Frequency Electrical Fields—A Tutorial Review from a Physical and Experimental Viewpoint," *Proc. IEEE*, Sept. 1981, p. 1116 (© 1981 IEEE).

Review Questions

R3-1. The Windmere Products hand-held hair dryer has the following warning on the casing:

Danger—Electrocution possible if used or dropped in tub. Unplug after using.

Explain this warning. Why is electrocution possible if the hair dryer is used in the bathtub?

R3-2. On most appliances you see the Underwriters Laboratories label on the casing. What does this tell you about the product?

Underwriters Laboratories, Inc., is an independent, not-for-profit organization established to test products for public safety. After developing a new product, the manufacturer contracts with and pays UL for the testing. UL then buys randomly chosen samples and puts them through an extensive series of safety tests, including probable careless handling and as many imaginative uses as the UL engineers can think of. When a product is approved, it can carry the UL label—an indication to the consumer that the manufacturer cares enough to have his product tested, and that UL engineers have found it as safe as reasonably possible.

To guide the manufacturers, UL establishes standards governing both the engineering of the device and the content of the instruction manual included when the device is bought. There is no convenient way, of course, to ensure that the user actually reads the manual.

In the case of a hair dryer, UL requires that safety precautions precede operating instructions. The following is a partial list of the safety commands that must be included:

Do not immerse in water or other liquids.

Do not use while bathing.

Unplug the appliance from outlet when not in use.

Do not operate after it has been dropped or damaged in any manner.

Use appliance only for intended use.

Do not use outdoors or operate where aerosol (spray) products are being used, or where oxygen is being administered.

Do not drop or insert any object into any opening.

Do not block air openings.

Do not use while sleeping.

Do not direct hot air flow toward eyes or other heat sensitive areas.

Save these instructions.

R3-3. A toaster oven has a label with this information:

1500 W   120 V   50 - 60 Hz   ac only

What does each of these notations mean?

R3-4. I have two appliances that I use to make breakfast. My toaster is 120 volts, 1100 watts; my coffee maker is 120 volts, 1000 watts. This is a normal home with each circuit breaker set to open at a current of 15 amps. My kitchen has one wall outlet with two sockets. Can I make toast while the coffee is perking?

R3-5. If you live on a street with above-ground telephone lines and power lines, the power lines are always higher on the pole than the telephone lines. Why?

R3-6. While doing electrical repairs, Joe accidentally touches the hot electrical line and a current of ½ A flows. What is the physiological cause of Joe's death?

R3-7. Electrical toys for children pose an especially difficult safety problem. Why is the problem of serious electrical shock more difficult than for appliances used by adults?

R3-8. Nikola Tesla, inventor of the ac motor, should receive major credit for our modern system for distributing electrical energy. Explain briefly.

R3-9. Why does the electrical utility go to such great pains to be sure the voltage (or current) waveform is sinusoidal?

R3-10. Home electrical energy in the United States is supplied at 60 Hz, while in Europe it is at 50 Hz. What are the advantages of the U.S. system?

R3-11. What is meant by the "let-go" current?

R3-12. When a person receives an electrical shock, does the severity depend primarily on the voltage, the current, the power, the energy, or the resistance?

R3-13. After the invention of the electric light bulb, how much time passed before this invention was actually used to light homes and offices: 3 weeks, 3 years, 30 years or 300 years?

R3-14. What is the primary reason we now use ac rather than dc for electric energy distribution?

Problems

P3-1. What electrical characteristics make it possible for one utility company in the United States to buy energy from a utility in a different part of the country?

P3-2. Consider one kitchen appliance and discuss the characteristics of the device that are matched to the human user. What features of the appliance are poorly matched to the user?

P3-3. When you walk across a woolen carpet on a dry winter day, you acquire static electricity. Your body may reach a voltage as high as 10,000 volts. Electrical charge builds up in your body because you are so well insulated by the dry air. When you come close to another person, an arc forms and current flows between you. The question immediately arises: With such a high voltage, why aren't you both electrocuted? The answer: The human effect of electrical shock depends only on the *current* that flows, not on the voltage. In this case, the current only lasts for ½ second and is less than 25 mA. This is larger than the let-go current, but there is almost no danger to anyone. Why?

P3-4. Your local electric utility provides energy to your home or residence in the form of a 60 hertz, 115-volt source. Your residence probably receives 230 volts also, and industrial and commercial places can obtain higher voltages. In this problem we will focus on just the 115-volt supply.

While the frequency is held very close to 60 Hz by the utility, the voltage may be quite different from 115 V. At your house alone, the voltage may change from day to day by a few volts. There are likely to be similar differences in the voltages at homes in different parts of the region served by the utility.

Manufacturers of appliances such as TV sets and air conditioners need to know the voltage coming into the device, at least within 5 percent. Furthermore, the voltages should be about the same everywhere in the United States, since no manufacturer wants to make different models for different parts of the country. Consequently, we must have national *standards,* to which all utilities must conform.

National standards are essential in many technical areas, and convenient in others. For example, all AM radio stations must broadcast the same kind of radio signal so a single receiver can be used anywhere. An example of a convenient standard is the law allowing vehicles to turn right after a stop at a red light. A few years ago the U.S. Department of Transportation finally coerced all states into going along with this practice; now interstate drivers no longer have to try to remember the rule for the state they're in.

Both of these standards were established by the federal government, which has this responsibility when the welfare of the people is concerned. Typically, the appropriate government agency drafts a standard, publishes it in the Federal Register, holds hearings for comments, revises it, and then issues the final, legal version.

Voluntary standards are preferable when they are possible. The American National Standards Institute (ANSI) in New York City is an organization established to develop such voluntary standards. When an important problem (such as utility voltage) is identified, ANSI sets up a working committee with representatives from equipment manufacturers, utilities, the public, and the government. This group attempts to develop a standard to which all parties agree. Then the government has to take over only when agreement cannot be reached or when Congress deems the issue so important to the public welfare that special legislation is needed.

In 1977, ANSI made the latest revision in the standards for the voltage that utilities deliver to the customer. This has two separate parts, since the critical voltage is at the appliance but the utility is responsible for the system only up to the entrance to the house. The voltage at B in figure 3.24 is less than at A because current for the appliance flows through the house wiring. When this wiring is old or cheap, it is often too small and the resistance is too high. By

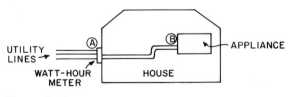

Figure 3.24
Home wiring.

Ohm's Law, we lose too much voltage by the time the energy reaches the appliance.

Thus, the standard sets allowable voltages at both A and B.

At A: This is called the "service voltage," the voltage at the point where the utility transfers energy to the customer. This voltage must be between 114 and 126 V.

At B: This is called the "utilization voltage," the voltage at the appliance or device. The allowable range is 108 to 125 V (with the exception that for lights the minimum is 110 V).

Thus, the service-voltage standard tells the utility the limits within which it can operate; the utilization-voltage standard restricts the wiring within the house and tells the manufacturer how the appliances should be designed.

For most appliances, trouble occurs when the voltage drops too low—below the 108 V "guaranteed" minimum (or 110 V for lights). Then for lamps, the light output falls sharply—a 10 percent drop in voltage may result in 20 percent less light. For window air conditioners, refrigerators, and freezers, a drop in voltage below 108 may mean that the compressor motor does not start, and serious damage is likely to result. This is the reason you should immediately turn off air conditioners when you hear on the radio that the utility has dropped the voltage 6 percent on a hot summer afternoon to avoid total loss of service (i.e., when there is a "brownout"). The cautious customer will also unplug the freezer and refrigerator.

The high voltages that may exist (for example, 125 V) ordinarily do no harm to appliances, but in some cases energy is wasted. In an electric range, there is very little change in the energy used to cook a given food as the voltage varies, although the time needed for cooking may vary considerably. Dishwashers operate satisfactorily down to about 108 volts; below that, they may not wash or dry well. Below about 108 volts, the performance of a TV set deteriorates.

Thus, we would like to drop the maximum voltage, but not change the minimum voltage.

In the late 1970s the California Public Utility Commission ordered all utilities to drop the maximum voltage from 126 to 120 whenever this can be done without unjustified capital costs. The commission predicted that this change would save the equivalent of almost 4 million barrels of oil a year.

(a) Why have other states not adopted the same rules? (Presumably the U.S. could then save 40 million barrels of oil a year with essentially no inconvenience to anyone.)

(b) California and the Sun Belt states have more new housing than the Northeast. Why would it be much riskier to adopt this policy in New York than in California?

(c) No one really knows what the effects of such a policy will be. In the light of all the scientific research sponsored by the federal government since the late 1950s, why has essentially no research been done on this problem by either government or industry?

P3-5. Frank Oppenheimer was the leader and inspiration behind the Exploratorium, the successful science museum and center in San Francisco. He quoted the following questions from a young visitor to the electricity display.

Question 1: Why do you have to attach two wires to the electrical outlet?

Answer: Because the current goes in one and out the other.

Question 2: The same current?

Answer: Yes.

Question 3: If we don't use any current, why do we have to pay for it?

Answer the last question to satisfy our young visitor.

P3-6. The *ground-fault interrupter* (GFI) is a device that automatically detects the existence of an electrical shock and then turns off the power before the victim is seriously injured.

To understand the operation of a GFI, return to our basic circuit for an appliance (figure 3.25). One wire of the incoming circuit is at 115 volts, the other at ground or zero voltage. The resistance indicated by the zigzag line represents the energy consumption of the device; in a hair dryer, this energy would be consumed by the heater and the motor-fan combination.

Usually a shock occurs when a person provides an alternate path to the ground. The voltage now causes two separate currents: one flowing through the heater and the motor, the other through the person being shocked. The currents that exist in the system are shown in figure 3.26.

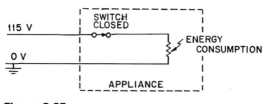

Figure 3.25
Appliance operated by 115 volts

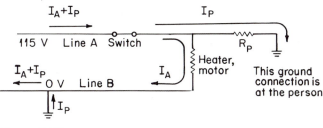

Figure 3.26
Circuit during shock.

The total current drawn from the utility is $I_A + I_P$, all flowing in on line A. Of this total, I_A (the normal current drawn by the appliance) flows back on line B, but I_P (the shock current to the person) flows through the person to ground, through the ground, and back to the service box.

Thus, the difference in the currents in line A and line B is a direct measure of the shock current — the current leaking out of the system. The GFI measures this difference in current; when the difference exceeds 5 mA, the circuit is opened within $\frac{1}{40}$ second — fast enough to avoid a serious shock in most cases.

National regulations now require GFIs in new outlets in bathrooms and garages, as well as outside, or in outlets supplying swimming pools and fountains. There is a group arguing that GFIs should be required on all circuits. Actually, there is also a serious question whether the device should be *required* anywhere. Is this just another example of unnecessary government regulation overprotecting the people without concern for costs?

The argument arises from a study of the costs and benefits associated with such national regulations. If we include the equipment, installation, and operating costs, we find that the regulation costs the public about $3,000,000 per life saved, even if we use the most conservative numbers. If we have a reasonable amount of money to invest in reducing personal risk, GFIs look much less attractive than smoke detectors, mandatory seat belts, and many other devices—perhaps even less attractive than allocating the same dollars for better public understanding of the principles of electrical safety.

Outline briefly how you would make a decision on a government regulation to protect people from such an electrical-shock hazard. You can assume that the description above is all that you have available.

P3-7. In the United States electrical energy is distributed at 60 Hz (60 cycles per second), while in Europe the frequency is 50 Hz. Once the technology is in place and customers have appliances designed for 60 Hz, the advantages of changing frequency have to be overwhelming. Thus, for the last 90 years new generating stations have been built to generate 60 Hz voltage even though we now have the technological know-how to use 200 or 400 Hz, with the associated advantage of much smaller motors.

(a) The U.S. Navy uses 400 Hz for electrical energy on its ships. Discuss briefly the reasons this standard is practical and the implications.

(b) The largest hydroelectric generating station now operating is the Itaipu system on the border of Paraguay and Brazil. Unfortunately these two countries use different frequencies (50 and 60 Hz, respectively), so separate generators are needed and the energy cannot be switched from one country to the other as the demand changes. Why have the two nations adopted different standards?

P3-8. American hair dryers and shavers do not work in Europe because both the frequency and the voltage amplitude differ from U.S. standards. The Europeans normally deliver energy to the home at a much higher voltage (230 rather than our 115). Why did the United States adopt the less efficient, lower voltage at the end of the last century?

Chapter 4
The Building Blocks of Signals

A telephone company, Northern Electric of Canada, decided to change the sound of the telephone ring. They wanted a more pleasant sound than the present harsh ring, but at the same time the sound had to be heard even in a very noisy atmosphere.

The engineers and social psychologists selected a group of possible telephone rings which seemed attractive and easily done technically. They then tested each of these possibilities by asking a sample group of customers to indicate which of a large number of adjectives were appropriate to describe each sound. After an analysis of the results, they selected the tone shown in figure 4.1—a tone that had been described by all subjects as "different," "modern," and "progressive." In addition, the women thought it was "cunning" and "mysterious," the men "bold" and "youthful."

The new telephone ring was chosen much more scientifically than the above anecdote implies. All the sounds tested on the customers were chosen to match the known characteristics of human hearing. For example, the engineers did not even consider sounds that could be heard by only half of the elderly people in the population, or sounds that would be masked by the typical noise from an operating dishwasher.

Thus, a minor change in technology made life a little more pleasant for the customers of Northern Electric of Canada. Now when their phone rings, they hear a cunning, youthful sound. Although this technological development is certainly not earth-shaking, and we can justifiably wonder what makes a sound "cunning," the story does illustrate an important aspect of modern technology: good engineering means that a new device should be carefully matched to the person using it.

Overtones

♩ = 120

Figure 4.1
New telephone ring of Northern Electric of Canada telephone company.

The same matching of technology to the human being underlies not only the design of hi-fi systems, electric guitars, alarm clocks, and a wide range of sound and audio technology, but the design of *all* communication systems.

This is one of the most important principles of good engineering. Radios, televisions, satellites, automatic reading machines for the deaf, and the hundreds of other devices and systems that we use to send and receive messages all require a knowledge of how the human being senses the world around him. Only then can the engineer make a design that is properly matched to these human characteristics.

Before learning to read and write, a child must know the alphabet and some rules of the language. In a similar manner, before we can understand how communication systems are designed and operated, we need to be familiar with the building blocks of science and engineering—the topics of this chapter.

4.1 Sine Signals

Figure 4.2 shows a simple pendulum hanging from the ceiling. The heavy ball at the bottom is initially pulled to position A and released. Thereafter, the ball swings back and forth from A to B to C to B to A to B, and so on.

To describe the motion of the ball, we can plot the way the angle θ (Greek theta) changes as time progresses (figure 4.3). At time $t = 0$, the ball is at A. Three seconds later the ball is at B; after another 3 seconds, it is at C, where the angle θ is negative.

Over a long period of time, our pendulum *slows down*, and ultimately it will stop (figure 4.4). Because of air friction, the pendulum loses a small amount of energy each cycle. To keep it going indefinitely, we have to give it a slight push regularly—just as a child on a swing needs to pump occasionally to keep swinging.

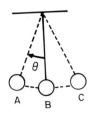

Figure 4.2
A simple pendulum. The ball swings from A to B to C to B to A and so on. We want
to plot the way the angle θ changes as time progresses.

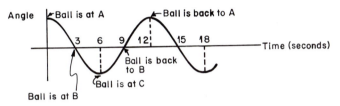

Figure 4.3
Sine signal showing the motion of the pendulum in figure 4.2..

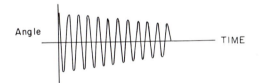

Figure 4.4
Plot showing how the pendulum in figure 4.2 loses a small amount of energy each
cycle.

For our purposes, we can neglect this tendency to slow down and concentrate in more detail on the regular, repeating wave pattern or oscillation of
figure 4.3. This curve is basic in our discussion of modern communications: the
same plot describes the simplest sound, radio, or television signals. It is the
fundamental building block for understanding of very complex systems.

The curve is called a sine signal or a sinusoid. This title comes from the
mathematical formula for the plot of figure 4.3 (see box 4.1).

We are not interested in the mathematics, however. Instead, let's focus on
the characteristics of a sine signal as shown in figure 4.5.

1. The signal changes very slowly near the peaks, more rapidly near zero. Our
pendulum moves fastest as the ball passes through the bottom position (B in
figure 4.2). Similarly, the hours of daylight change slowly in December and
June, more rapidly during September and March (figure 4.6).

Sine Signal

Mathematically,

Angle = A sin(bt + c).

Here, a, b, and c are just constants. At any particular time (for example, t = 12), we can simply replace t by 12 in the formula and find the angle from the trigonometric value of the sine of (12b + c).

Box 4.1

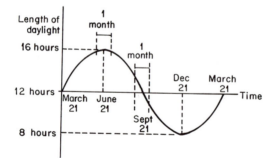

Figure 4.5
Characteristics of a sine signal. The signal changes very slowly at the peaks and more rapidly at the zero crossings.

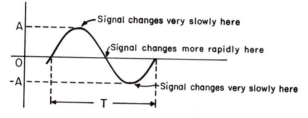

Figure 4.6
Plot of the daylight hours during the year. (The curve is approximately a sinusoid.) This curve is for a location in the United States where the longest daylight is 16 hours. The sine signal changes very slowly around the peaks, and rapidly near the zeros. As a result, near June 21 and December 21 the times of sunset and sunrise change very little each day. Around March 21 and September 21, the changes are much greater.

2. The sine signal has a certain *amplitude* (A in figure 4.7). The signal varies between +A and –A. Thus, the term *amplitude* refers to the maximum swing from the rest or zero position. The total motion is twice the amplitude (figure 4.8).

3. The signal is also described by its *period* T—the length of time for one complete cycle. In figure 4.3, the period is 12 seconds: every 12 seconds, the motion is repeated. For figure 4.6, showing the variation of daylight hours, the period is one year.

4. The *frequency* f is the number of complete cycles in a given period of time. The frequency of our pendulum is $\frac{1}{12}$ cycle per second (a full cycle every 12 seconds; see figure 4.10. The frequency of daylight hours is 1 cycle per year (see figure 4.6).

Usually in communications we are working with many cycles each second, so frequency is normally given in cycles per second. This unit is given the name hertz, abbreviated Hz, so we would say the pendulum has a frequency of $\frac{1}{12}$ Hz. Similarly, your principal brain wave when you are awake is called the alpha rhythm and has a frequency around 10 Hz (figure 4.11).

Thus the sine signal or sinusoid is a simple oscillation or pattern of motion or change. The sine signal is described by two numbers: the amplitude (A) and the frequency (f). The period T of the sine signal is just the reciprocal of the

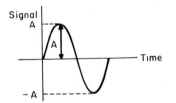

Figure 4.7
Amplitude of a sine signal.

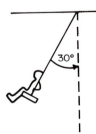

Figure 4.8
Child on swing going 30° in amplitude.

Figure 4.9
The tides vary in a sinusoidal fashion at any one location. They are partially caused by the gravitational pull of the moon and sun. They are influenced, however, by the earth's motion and by the motion of the water. There is no theory that allows prediction of how big the tides will be at a particular location, or the time when high tide will occur. The picture shows Mont St. Michel in France, which is famous for the speed with which the tide changes. High tides rise as high as 50 feet, and low tides recede to as far as 11 miles from shore. High tide travels into shore at a rate of 20 miles per hour. The top photo shows high tide; the bottom photo shows low tide. *(French Government Tourist Office)*

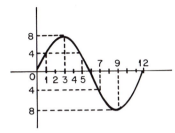

Figure 4.10
Proportions of a sinusoid. The peaks (maxima and minima) occur at regular
intervals. The zero values occur midway between peaks. During the positive half
cycle, for example, the sinusoid has half its peak value at moments one-third of the
time from the zero to the peak in either direction. This particular sinusoid is drawn
for an amplitude of 8 and for a period (cycle duration) of 12.

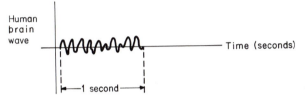

Figure 4.11
The EEG or brain wave signal—the electrical voltage measured across the scalp.
This is not exactly a sine signal, since each cycle is not a perfect repetition, but it is
close.

frequency: a frequency of 10 cycles per second (or 10 Hz) means the period is
$\frac{1}{10}$ second (figures. 4.12, 4.13, 4.14).

The next five chapters use sine signals to explain how human speech, sound,
radio, and television work. Technological communication systems are designed using sine signals.

As we have already seen, the pattern of motion or change represented by sine
signals is often seen in familiar situations. Even more importantly, in section 4.8
we will see how *any* signal can be viewed as a sum of simple sine signals, each
described by its own amplitude and frequency.

4.2 Concept of Frequency

The voltage between the two poles of an electrical wall socket varies as time
progresses (figure 4.15). The voltage reaches a maximum of +163 volts, a
minimum of −163. We call this 115 volts because it has the same heating effect
as a constant voltage of +115.

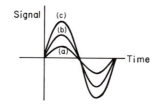

Figure 4.12
Sinusoids differing in amplitude or size.

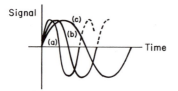

Figure 4.13
Sinusoids of different frequencies but the same amplitude. Curve a has the highest frequency, curve c the lowest.

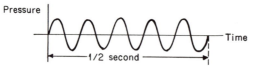

Figure 4.14
Sine signal with frequency of 10 Hz (10 cycles per second, or 5 cycles in ½ second.)

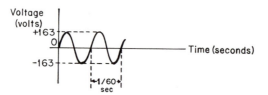

Figure 4.15
Voltage supplied by electric utility company.

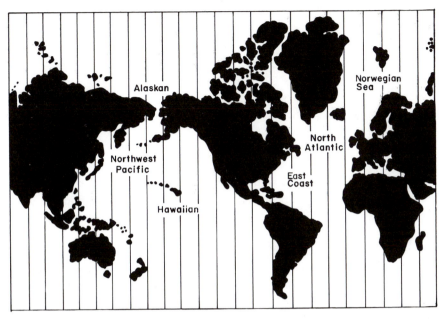

Figure 4.16
Time zones of the world. One of the problems in picking time zones is the difference in daylight hours between the eastern and western ends of the zone. Furthermore, some people (farmers) are primarily interested in the time of sunrise, while others are most concerned about the time of sunset. In addition, the earliest sunrise does not come the same day as the latest sunset. Before 1883, each U.S. city set its own time by calling the time when the sun was directly overhead "noon". Thus, when it was noon in Washington, DC, it was 12:24 P.M.. in Boston, and 11:00 A.M. in Savannah, Georgia. All these cities are now in the same time zone.

The voltage is *periodic*; every cycle of the oscillation is exactly the same (figure 4.17).

One extremely important feature of this voltage signal is the *frequency*—how many times a second the voltage goes through a complete cycle. In home electrical voltage, the frequency is

60 cycles per second, called 60 hertz or 60 Hz.

Thus, the period or duration of one cycle is $\frac{1}{60}$ second; every $\frac{1}{60}$ second, the voltage repeats itself.

Electrical appliances tend to hum at 60 Hz. As the electrical voltage changes at this frequency (between +163 volts and −163 volts), the appliance vibrates slightly in synchronism with the voltage. This vibration pushes the neighboring air molecules back and forth to generate a sound wave, which you then hear as a hum.

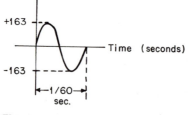

Figure 4.17
One cycle of the voltage of figure 4.15.

When we discuss sound signals, we will see that 60 Hz is quite a low frequency (musically, about two octaves below middle C), so the hum is a quiet, steady background which you easily become accustomed to and disregard.

Frequencies and Musical Notes

A tuning fork generates a sound wave which is a pure note at the particular frequency at which the fork vibrates when the tines are struck by a rubber hammer. The smaller the fork, the higher the frequency generated. Thus, a sound signal is created in which the frequency is determined by the dimensions of the tuning fork (figure 4.18).

A few years ago, there was international agreement that the musical note A above middle C corresponds to 440 Hz. Once this one number is chosen, the frequencies of all other notes are determined.

Moving up one octave doubles the frequency: if we start from 440 Hz, one octave higher is 880 Hz, an additional octave brings us to 1760 Hz, then 3520 Hz, and so forth. Each drop in frequency by an octave halves the frequency. Thus, the A notes on a home piano or any musical instrument are

28 Hz 55 Hz 110 Hz 220 Hz 440 Hz 880 Hz 1760 Hz 3520 Hz.

On the Western musical scale there are twelve distinct notes in each octave:

A A# B C C# D D# E F F# G G#.

In other words, as we go in frequency from A at 440 to A at 880 (an octave higher), there are twelve intervals or jumps in frequency. If A is 440, what is A#?

The twelve notes divide the octave in such a way that the frequency is *multiplied* by the same amount in each step. To double the frequency in 12 steps, the frequency of each note is

1.05946 × the frequency of the preceding note.

This means that the frequency of each note is about 6 percent higher than the frequency of the preceding note (figure 4.19).

Figure 4.18
A tuning fork is used to produce a pure note; that is, one single frequency. The smaller the fork, the higher the frequency generated.

C	262	523	1046	2093	4186
C#	277	554	1109	2217	4435
D	294	587	1175	2349	4699
D#	311	622	1244	2489	4978
E	330	659	1318	2637	5274
F	349	698	1397	2794	5588
F#	370	740	1480	2960	5920
G	392	784	1568	3136	6272
G#	415	831	1661	3322	6645
A	440	880	1760	3520	7040
A#	466	932	1865	3729	7459
B	494	988	1976	3951	7902

Figure 4.19
Frequencies of notes five octaves about middle C.

Pitch and Frequency

The *frequency* of a musical note is a scientific term that can be precisely defined. If A above middle C is set at 440 Hz, middle C comes out to be 261.6256 Hz, or about 262 Hz.

In music, however, the goal is enjoyment and emotional impact, not scientific accuracy. Hence, a musician tunes his instrument so that middle C is at a pleasing frequency; exactly what the frequency is may be irrelevant (although it of course will be in the vicinity of 262 Hz). Regardless of the choice, we say that note has a *pitch* of middle C. Thus, pitch is the human *perception* of the sound; it is a term corresponding to the scientific characteristic called frequency.

We have now introduced the concept of frequency—basically the rate at which the electrical or sound signal oscillates. The frequency is measured in cycles per second, which are called hertz.

4.3 Sound Signals

When the tuning fork vibrates at 400 Hz, the tines are moving back and forth at this rate. Immediately adjacent to the tine, the air molecules are pushed to the right, to the left, to the right again, and so on. As a result of this disturbance, a small air pressure oscillation is established near the tine: the air pressure varies as shown in figure 4.20. In other words, the air is compressed, then expanded, then compressed, then expanded, and so forth.

At time t there is a peak of pressure, a half cycle later there is a minimum, and so on. This pressure variation travels out from the tuning fork in all directions, exactly as a wave travels outward in a pond from the point at which a rock was dropped in. As these pressure variations of the air hit our ears, they produce what we interpret as sound.

As the tuning fork continues to vibrate, the outgoing sound wave continues. At one instant of time shortly after the beginning of the vibration, we have the picture shown in figure 4.21. The start of the signal has reached point A. Up to this time, the tuning fork has gone through just over three cycles of vibration.

Let us again stop the action and take a look at the pressure variation a half cycle (or $1/800$ second) later (figure 4.22). The front of the wave has moved outward.

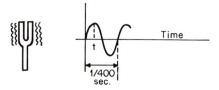

Figure 4.20
When the tuning fork vibrates at 400 Hz, an air-pressure oscillation occurs near the tine.

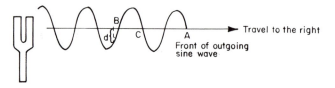

Figure 4.21
Sound wave traveling out from the tuning fork.

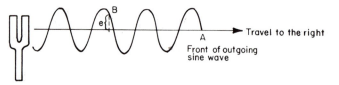

Figure 4.22
Sound wave of figure 4.21 a half-cycle later.

In other words, each of these two plots is a sketch of the way the wave varies in space at one moment of time. If we could photograph sine waves, these two plots are the snapshots we would get.

Now let us look at what is happening at one point. Suppose we are standing at B in figure 4.21 and measuring the pressure as the wave passes by us. At the instant of time of figure 4.21, we are measuring distance d—the amount of pressure at that particular point. At the later time described by figure 4.22, the pressure at point B has changed; it is now e. During the time between the two snapshots, the pressure varied as in figure 4.23, as the wave went by us.

Velocity of Sound

In air at sea level, sound travels at a velocity (or speed) of about 1120 feet per second, or 760 miles per hour. This means that almost 5 seconds are needed for sound to travel a mile. If the thunder is heard 5 seconds after a lightning flash is seen, the lightning hit about a mile away (since light travels at a *much* higher velocity).

The velocity of sound decreases as the temperature falls—hence sound travels more slowly as we go up in altitude in an airplane. At the normal cruising altitude of transcontinental airlines, the speed of sound is about 670 miles per hour. In metals and solids, on the other hand, sound travels as much as 10 times faster than in air.

Wavelength

Let us return to our picture of a sound wave traveling outward from a source, Figure 4.21 shows the stop-action picture when the front of the wave reaches point A. At *this instant of time*, the pressure varies in space as shown. There is a zero at A and a similar zero at point C. If we were to travel very rapidly from A to C, we would find the pressure along the way going through a complete cycle in space. This distance from A to C is called the *wavelength* of the signal: as the signal travels, it is the distance between similar points along the sinusoidal pressure variation at one moment in time.

Figure 4.24 reveals that this wavelength (usually given by the symbol λ, the Greek letter lambda) is related to the velocity and the frequency. In the last cycle

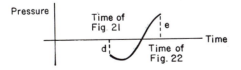

Figure 4.23
The pressure at B as the wave passes by that one particular point.

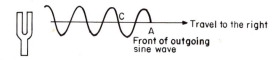

Figure 4.24
The wavelength is the distance between two similar points on the sine signal in space. Here the wavelength is the distance from A to C.

or period, the front of the wave has traveled from C to A with the velocity of sound. Hence,

$$\text{Velocity} = \frac{\text{Distance}}{\text{Time}}, \text{ or}$$

$$v = \frac{\lambda}{\text{Time}}.$$

What is the time? Exactly one cycle of the signal, or 1/frequency. Thus, $v = \lambda f$—that is, the velocity of a wave is the wavelength times the frequency.

Because $v = \lambda f$, we can describe a signal in terms of its frequency *or* its wavelength: the two are equivalent; from one, we can find the other. For example, a signal at 440 Hz has a wavelength of

$$\frac{v}{f}, \text{ or } \frac{1120 \text{ ft/sec}}{440/\text{sec}}, \text{ or } 2.5 \text{ feet}.$$

Since wavelength and frequency have the same information, why do we introduce yet another term (wavelength)? The answer is that wavelength is a particularly valuable idea when we want to talk about radiating energy or generating sound waves. The ability of a loudspeaker to get energy out into the air (i.e., into sound waves) depends on the size of the loudspeaker relative to the wavelength. In general, the efficiency of an antenna depends on the ratio

$$\frac{\text{Length of diameter of antenna}}{\text{Wavelength}}.$$

For a sound signal at 44 Hz, the wavelength is 25 feet. The speaker for such a low frequency should have a diameter of perhaps $\lambda/10$, or 2.5 feet, to be efficient. The nearer we can approach this value, the more energy we will get out into the air. This is the reason for the woofers, or large, low-frequency speakers in a hi-fi system.

Waves

This section has introduced the concept of a sound wave traveling outward from the source. The wave moves with the velocity of sound, 1120 feet per second in sea-level air at room temperature. We have restricted ourselves to sounds of a single frequency—the "pure notes" of music. Such a sound signal can be described either by a frequency (f, in hertz) or a wavelength (λ, in feet or any other measure of distance). The frequency and the wavelength are related, since their product is the velocity of the sound wave.

This idea of a wave described by its frequency or wavelength carries over directly to light, radio, and radar. Our central theme throughout these notes is communication, whether we consider a conversation you and I may have, or the radio transmission of Home Box Office movies from Time's home station to an orbiting satellite and thence to my home TV set. In both cases, the signal is a wave traveling through space.

4.4 Human Communication

The last two sections lay the groundwork for our study of communication. We are interested in all forms of communication:

person to person

person to machine, and the reverse

machine to machine.

It is easiest to start with communication between people.

Even in this case, we have to simplify. Language is our primary basis for communication, but we use language for a lot of different purposes:

conveying ideas or facts

self-expression

entertainment

ritual

record-keeping

prayer

reasoning.

Many of these roles of language are very difficult to study scientifically. They certainly lie outside the realm of the engineer—and in this book we are primarily interested in the engineer's approach to communication.

Even if we restrict our study to conveying ideas, the engineer worries about only a small part of person-to-person communication. When two people are talking to one another, they communicate ideas in four different ways:

1. Verbal sounds—words, phrases, and sentences which use the language.

2. Nonverbal sounds—the length of pauses, the grunts and hisses, and the emphases placed on certain words.

3. Body actions—not only hand gestures, but also movements of the eyes and head, facial expressions, and body attitudes. This whole subject, called kinesics, was first studied by Darwin. To see how important it is, try having an extended conversation with someone in a totally dark room.

4. Use of space—the changing of the space between the speaker and the listener. This topic is called proxemics in psychology. In some countries, people conversing stand much closer together than is usual in the United States.

In our studies of sound waves and speech, we focus on item 1 and, to a lesser extent, on item 2. Yet psychologists tell us that these aspects, which can be measured easily, account for less than half of the information flow when two people are talking together.

When we turn to the study of communication back and forth between people and machines, engineering is much better at describing the situation. At least so far, we are having enough trouble building computers that talk and recognize speech, so we are not anxious for the machine to nod, grimace, or frown.

Engineers can analyze and design equipment only when the signals are measurable. With a microphone, we can record and then measure verbal sounds—the words you say as you are talking. We can design a telephone system to convey these words to someone across the country. At much greater expense, we can send a picture of you while you talk, but we have to send the entire picture. We do not know which gestures or body movements are important. We cannot even answer such simple questions as: What is the significance of the other person looking directly at you rather than off to the side while he or she talks?

Thus, our study of human communication is severely narrow. When we consider conversation or speech, for example, we consider only the actual sounds traveling from the speaker to the listener.

Within this narrow limitation, we can begin our study. In the preceding sections, we looked at sine signals—that is, sounds that are pure notes at single frequencies. Intuitively, we know that these signals are too simple to be interesting. I call you on the phone; when you answer, I start singing middle C, and I continue indefinitely. After a while, you certainly stop listening. Almost no information is conveyed by such a single-frequency signal.

To send information, I have to use more complex signals (more than one frequency) and change the frequencies often. Indeed, in chapter 7 we will find that the information sent increases with the unexpectedness (or unpredictability) of the signal. To receive lots of information, you must be unable to predict the signal.

Thus, real signals are necessarily more complex than a single sinusoid. In the next two sections, we turn to signals that are complex combinations of sine signals.

4.5 More Complex Signals

Information is conveyed when we have more complex signals; that is, when we change the frequencies unexpectedly.

Let us return to the first example of this chapter: the telephone ring developed by Northern Electric of Canada (figure 4.25). Here the machine wants to communicate—to tell the customer it's time to pick up the phone. To attract attention, the machine suddenly emits a sound signal.

During the first time interval, the signal consists of three notes played at the same time:

	C at 523 Hz
Sound I	G at 1568 Hz
	E at 2637 Hz.

In the musical notation, each space or line represents another note in the key of C—that is, C, D, E, F, G, A, and B. The lowest of the first three notes is C an octave above middle C. To find the other two, we simply move upward one note for each space or line.

During the second time interval, immediately thereafter, the sound signal switches to the second group of three notes played together:

	E at 659 Hz
Sound II	B at 1976 Hz
	G# at 3322 Hz.

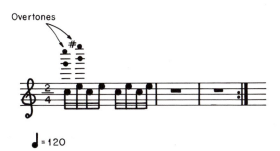

Figure 4.25
New telephone ring of Northern Electric of Canada.

The total ringing consists of the sounds in the sequence

I II I II Break I II I II Pause.

The musical notation is a convenient way to summarize this relatively complicated description. The engineer has a different graphical presentation of exactly the same information (figure 4.26). Before interval a, there is no sound. During the first interval, the sound is the sum of three different sinusoids—those at 523, 1568, and 2637 Hz. The graph shows that these three frequencies are present during this interval, and again in intervals c, f, and h.

In interval b (and d, g, and i), we have three different frequencies: 659, 1976, and 3322 Hz. During the short pause (e) and the long pause (j), there is no sound transmitted at all, so the graph is blank.

Thus, this type of plot, called a *spectrogram*, shows the frequencies being transmitted at every instant of time and the way the frequencies change to convey the information of the message. The spectrogram also shows clearly the length of time each part of the signal lasts.

If we compare the musical presentation of figure 4.25 and the engineering spectrogram of figure 4.26, the differences in approach of the two fields are apparent. The engineer works in terms of numbers, the musician in human impressions:

1. The engineer specifies frequency (e.g., 523 Hz), the musician is interested in the pitch (C above middle C), not in the exact frequency.

2. The engineer shows the duration on the time scale of each sound; the musician merely indicates sixteenth notes, and leaves to the performer the determination of the exact timing.

One graph is not better than the other; instead, they serve different purposes, and each is tailored to the special needs of the corresponding profession.

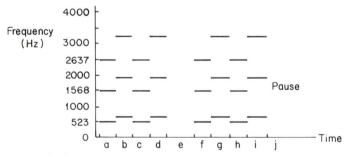

Figure 4.26
Graphical picture of frequencies involved in the telephone ring.

Overtones and Harmonics

Both graphs show that the two higher notes in an interval are approximate overtones or harmonics of the lowest note.

For example, if we play a note at 400 Hz on a musical instrument, the following frequencies describe the harmonics:

fundamental frequency (basic note)	400 Hz
2nd harmonic	2×400 or 800 Hz
3rd harmonic	3×400 or 1200 Hz
7th harmonic	7×400 or 2800 Hz
13th harmonic	13×400 or 5200 Hz.

We can have an infinite number of harmonics; the frequency of each harmonic is an integer (whole number) multiplied by the fundamental frequency.

Other than the notes from a tuning fork, there are almost no pure-frequency sounds (although an ocarina is close). Instead each sound includes harmonics of the basic sound. This applies to *all* sounds, not just notes played on a musical instrument. In speech, however, there may be many different fundamental frequencies at the same time. Thus the numerous fundamental frequencies, added to the harmonics of each, result in a very complex sound signal.

In the first sound of the telephone ring, the three frequencies involved are the following:

	C	G	E
Frequency	523	1568	2637
Third harmonic of the C		1569	
Fifth harmonic of the C			2615

Thus, the sound consists of a fundamental frequency (523 Hz) and two other notes, approximately the third and fifth harmonics of C. (Since the electronic equipment generates the three notes separately, we actually use exactly the third and fifth harmonics—approximately G and E.)

Why not use three totally unrelated frequencies, such as 523, 1200, and 2000 Hz? Generally, three notes harmonically related are more pleasant to the person listening; obviously, the engineers wanted the telephone ring to be a pleasing sound.

Musical Instruments

No listener would confuse a tuning fork and a flute, both playing the note middle A. Among the many reasons for this difference, the most important is that the flute causes a pressure signal that is nearly periodic (repeats over and over) but not sinusoidal (not a sine wave). The note from the flute includes the second, third, fourth, and fifth harmonics, and even a little of the sixth and the seventh. That is, the sound of middle A on the flute includes the frequencies 440, 880, 1320, 1760, 2200, 2640, and 3080. The sound includes not only the 440 Hz of middle A, but also 2, 3, 4, 5, 6, and 7 times this frequency—the second through seventh harmonics.

Each musical instrument produces a different set of harmonics. The clarinet does not show the second; in the oboe the fourth is very strong or of large amplitude; the violin includes sixteen or more. Thus, each instrument has a unique sound even though they may all be playing the same note.

We can show these differences by spectrograms, as illustrated in figure 4.27. The spectrogram primarily shows the frequencies present during the time the note is being played. Usually in a spectrogram, we also try to give a rough picture of the amplitude (or strength) of each frequency by the darkness of the corresponding lines. For the flute, the sixth and seventh harmonics are small or weak in comparison with the lower harmonics and the fundamental (440 Hz).

Thus, different musical instruments have different harmonic components. Actually, there are also other major differences when a note is played on a flute versus an oboe. The impression you obtain depends not only on the harmonics present, but also on the exact way the sound builds up at the start, how the amplitude varies during the middle, and how the sound fades out at the end. When engineers try to program a computer to sound exactly like a flute, for instance, they first measure many detailed characteristics of the sound from an

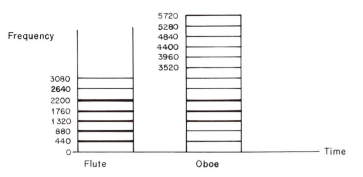

Figure 4.27
Spectrograms of flute and oboe, each playing middle A (440 Hz). The heavy lines indicate a large amplitude (louder) for those particular frequencies.

actual flute. The frequencies present (that is, the spectrogram) are just part of the complete picture—although they are the most important part for human hearing.

In this section, we have moved from pure notes (or single-frequency sounds) to signals consisting of a small number of different frequencies—often harmonics of the fundamental. Of most importance, we have introduced the idea of a spectrogram—a graph for showing these frequencies. In the next section, we look at a few other uses of spectrograms.

4.6 Uses of Spectrograms

A spectrogram shows the frequencies present in a signal during a short interval of time. Consequently, spectrograms are useful when we need to know the frequencies when a person says a specific sound or a bird gives a particular call. This emphasis on the short-time characteristics runs through this section as we consider a few applications of spectrograms.

Infant Cries

Spectrograms have been used to analyze the cries of infants. Apparently there are distinct characteristics associated with certain physiological problems that are otherwise difficult to diagnose (certain brain disorders and genetic anomalies). Distress cries of normal infants have fundamental frequencies from 400 to 500 Hz; those of abnormal infants are as high as 1100 Hz. In one reported case, the high frequencies came from a child who much later was found to have defective blood circulation between the heart and the lungs.

Musical Instrument Simulated by a Computer

The analysis of musical notes by spectrograms suggests the following questions:

1. What are the important characteristics of a note played by a single instrument?

2. Can computer-generated music, based on analysis of sounds from an actual instrument, come close enough to the original sound to be indistinguishable by a musician?

The spectrogram, alone, is not sufficient to characterize the note from an instrument. Playing back a taped piano note by running the tape in the opposite direction gives a very different sound, even though the spectrogram is unchanged by the reversal of time. In other words, if an actual musical note is analyzed with a spectrogram and all significant frequencies are measured, then a new sound is synthesized by adding together sine signals at these frequencies. Anyone can readily distinguish between the real and the artificial sounds.

Spectral Display   [piano]   forte, @238, Num 65, Hor .01

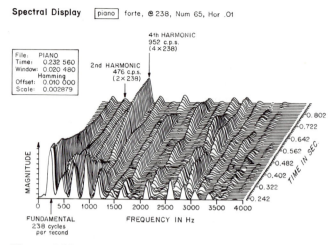

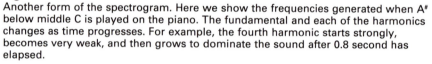

Figure 4.28
Another form of the spectrogram. Here we show the frequencies generated when A#
below middle C is played on the piano. The fundamental and each of the harmonics
changes as time progresses. For example, the fourth harmonic starts strongly,
becomes very weak, and then grows to dominate the sound after 0.8 second has
elapsed.

The problem is that the usual spectrogram shows the frequency content of
the sound over a short period of time. The nature of the sound (for example,
the identification of the instrument) depends strongly on how the sound builds
up and on the subtle changes in the frequency content during the note. Such
small changes in the spectrogram are not observable in the usual analysis.

By making a detailed computer analysis of several notes, including information on how each harmonic builds up at the beginning, Max Mathews and Jean-
Claude Risset have succeeded in generating artificial sounds which musicians
cannot differentiate from notes from a real trumpet. The violin turns out to be
a much more complicated instrument to analyze and simulate, but partial success has been achieved there as well.

In all cases, however, the problem is complicated by the fact that the same
notes are quite different when played by different musicians, or by any one
musician in differing contexts.

Analysis of a Musical Instrument
Musicians often have strong preferences about the materials their instruments
are made of. For example, brass instruments are usually covered with a lacquer
to prevent corrosion, and players continually argue that the lacquer ruins the
"tone."

In 1981, experiments at Bolt, Beranek and Newman, in Cambridge, Massachusetts, showed that the coating does indeed have a measurable effect. Spectrograms demonstrated that the lacquer decreases the amplitudes of the higher harmonics.

This experiment is a nice demonstration of the use of spectrograms, and it also shows how engineers can often find answers even when the science is unknown. Here, the effect of the lacquer was measured, even though scientists have no idea why it has any effect. The experiment also shows how keen human sensing is: musicians were aware of the effect long before it was actually measured. Finally, even though the effect is small, it may have significant impact when the technology is considered with the human being: the musician, aware the sound is poorer, plays with less spirit, and the negative effect is amplified.

Teaching the Deaf

Spectrograms are used in teaching a deaf child to speak in a natural tone. We record the voice of a normal child saying a desired word. We then make a spectrogram of that word and display it on a screen. As the deaf child attempts to say the same word, the spectrogram is displayed next to the "normal" spectrogram. Now the deaf child can compare the two visually, and by changing pronunciation, can try to make the two spectrograms match.

Speaker Identification

The most publicized use of spectrograms has been in speaker identification. When there are bomb threats to an airline, for example, the voice of the telephone caller is recorded and a spectrogram is made. If we want to know whether a particular suspect was the caller, another spectrogram is made. From the two tapes (one of the unknown caller, the other of the suspect), as many as ten simple words or syllables are selected (such words as "the," "and," "are," and "for"). For each word, we compare the spectrograms derived from the two tapes.

Generally, a person's spectrogram for a particular syllable is unique, even when the speaker tries to disguise his or her voice. If so, this spectrogram (also called a *voiceprint*) identifies the individual in the same way as a set of fingerprints.

Though great reliability may be claimed by companies selling the speaker-identification service, scientific tests have shown that improper identification is by no means unlikely. Spectrograms are recorded for 100 known people, for example, and then one of these is selected secretly to make a recording. Attempts to determine which one of the 100 was the speaker lead to errors about 10 percent of the time. Consequently, voiceprints cannot be used for positive identification of a suspect. However, this equipment is increasingly used by police departments as a guide in investigations and as a means of ruling out innocent people.

Other Uses

Spectrograms are the basis of the current work in developing computer-generated speech and computer programs to understand spoken speech—two applications discussed in more detail in the next chapter.

Ornithologists use spectrograms to identify different species of birds (figure 4.29). Utility companies pull microphones through underground gas lines and make recordings of the sound; then a spectrogram can identify the size and nature of a gas leak. Finally, spectrograms allow us to study the effects of a noisy environment on human beings.

4.7 Personal Verification

Scene A: Students, with trays loaded, wait in a cafeteria line. Half the students on campus are on the meal plan, so they need not pay cash. The cashier must

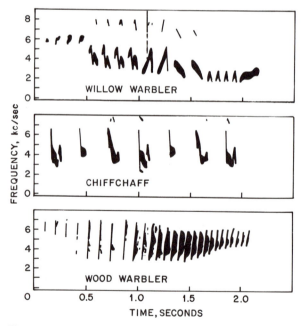

Figure 4.29
Spectrograms for three types of European warblers. Such recordings have been used (in this case by Gilbert White) as a basis for distinguishing different species. The willow warbler and the chiffchaff, for example, are otherwise very similar birds.

inspect each student's ID card with photograph, then determine whether the student is a paid-up member of the meal plan.

Scene B: I have just decided on the new car I want to buy, and I am anxious to transfer $5000 from my savings account to my checking account. I must take delivery of the car by this evening to take advantage of the current incentive program. I call my bank, but they can authorize the funds transfer only if they are sure that I am the person I claim to be.

Scene C: The Air Force has just discovered how to make a bomber completely invisible to enemy radar (no one said these scenes have to be true to life) and is holding a briefing at the Pentagon for chief engineers from four aircraft manufacturers. At the door, one individual has an ID card (the picture looks moderately like the man) and personal identification papers, but all these credentials might have been stolen from the rightful owner. Is the man the person he claims to be?

These three scenes represent a common problem: *personal verification*, or confirming that an individual is the person he or she claims to be. As so much of life becomes dominated by information technology, more and more situations arise in which personal verification is important. If we are to be confident that data stored in a computer are available only to those with a justifiable right to know, we must have some way of verifying the identities of people who want access.

Up to the present time, personal verification has been done in most cases by a human being. If you want to enter a room with secret information, a guard at the door decides if you are authorized. Human beings are fantastic in pattern recognition. At the mall, you may run into an acquaintance you haven't seen for months, but you will recognize her at once. When we try to program equipment to identify one person from a group of only 30 by looking at a television picture of the face, we encounter enormous difficulties and many errors (even though we may design the equipment to measure more than 20 facial features, such as distance between the eyes, width of each eye, and so on).

In spite of these shortcomings, machine personal verification is often a necessity. Human beings are not reliable in matching a person to an ID photo. Human identification of the telephone voice is not dependable. People become tired, bored, and careless when they have to perform the same task again and again. Finally, we may have to go to a machine to hold down the time required for verification or the cost. Thus, personal verification is essentially a decision-making task; replacement of people by machines is, therefore, automation, and we can expect to find all the customary arguments for automation. In this section, we want to consider various techniques for automation of personal verification.

An Inexpensive System

One relatively simple system (Identimat, made by Stellar Systems, Inc.) requires the applicant to insert the fingers of one hand in four slots. Photoelectric devices then measure the lengths and curvatures of the fingers and the webbing between the fingers. Thus, we obtain a set of numbers describing certain features of the hand shape. Because these devices measure biological or physiological characteristics, the topic is also known by the name of *biometrics*.

The verification process is essentially the same in all the automated schemes mentioned below. When a new person (Janet) is to be added to the authorized group, the equipment must be "trained." Janet comes to the equipment for the training session. Human operators first verify the identity of Janet. She then places her fingers in the machine, which is in the training mode of operation. The measurements taken are stored in a computer as a *reference* to later identify Janet. Usually at least two sets of measurements are taken; if these training measurements are approximately the same, the averages are stored in the computer memory to characterize Janet—to serve as the reference.

Possibly days later, an applicant arrives and wants admission; she claims to be Janet. Measurements are made and compared against Janet's known reference. If the differences are below a predetermined *threshold*, the equipment confirms that the applicant is indeed Janet, and she is admitted. If the differences are above the threshold, so the applicant would be rejected, she is allowed to repeat the test once in case there was a malfunction (perhaps she did not insert her finger properly, or the equipment was subject to temporary vibration or noise).

Evaluation of Performance

Such equipment obviously does not work perfectly, even though it may be a marked improvement on human verification (at the University of Georgia, the Identimat system has cut cafeteria costs by detecting more cheaters than human attendants checking ID cards). There are two types of errors.

Type 1 error: The system rejects an authorized person.

Type 2 error: The system admits an imposter.

When a doctor tests patients for a particular disease, there are similarly two types of errors. If we draw the analogy that having the disease is similar to being an imposter, Type 1 errors are false positives (the healthy or authorized individual is not OK).

At what level (called the *bias*) do we set the distinction between acceptance and rejection? Figure 4.30 shows the way each type of error changes as we vary the bias. (A small value of bias means that the measurements must agree very closely with the reference for the applicant to be approved.) As we ease up on

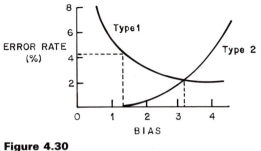

Figure 4.30
Testing errors.

the requirement and move to the right, the Type 1 errors fall steadily, but the
Type 2 errors grow. If we set the bias at 1.3, almost no imposters are admitted,
but 4.2 percent of the legitimate applicants are rejected. With the bias at 3.2,
both errors occur at a 2.2 percent rate.

The system operator has to compromise—to find the bias at which the system
operation is satisfactory and economical. For the Identimat equipment, the
manufacturer claims that, if Type 2 errors are allowed at 1 percent, the Type 1
errors are 1.5 percent.

Choice of a System

In the next subsection, we look briefly at the various technologies available for
personal verification. The choice of a particular piece of equipment clearly
depends on the application. If the University of Georgia wants to deter
poachers from a cafeteria line, occasional Type 2 errors (letting a cheater in) are
not catastrophic. Furthermore, would-be poachers are not going to put major
efforts into cheating the system (for example, by making a glove to match
closely the hand of an authorized person). In contrast, control of access to large
bank accounts or military secrets may call for personal verification equipment
where Type 2 errors are zero and cost is not a serious constraint. Also, in such
cases we may need systems that are very difficult to deceive.

Types of Systems

The Identimat equipment described above is one of the simplest and least
expensive systems. What other personal characteristics are unique to the
individual and readily measured by electronic equipment? A variety of different
technologies are available to respond to the widely different market needs. Brief
descriptions follow.

1. One of the most expensive systems is EyeDentify made by EyeDentify, Inc.
The equipment uses infrared light to scan the blood vessels of the applicant's

retina (the pattern is unique to each individual and, indeed, is the most distinguishable trait, even between identical twins). The pattern does change with time for diabetics, but most of the techniques require continual updating of the reference. The manufacturer claims less than one Type 1 error in 1000 tests, and less than one Type 2 error in a million tests.

2. Automated fingerprint reading uses the "minutiae points" of a fingerprint— the locations where ridges end or split or merge. The error rates are slightly higher than for EyeDentify, but the equipment is less expensive and may be less objectionable to the applicants. Fingerprint methods have the advantage that the data can be stored in "smart cards" (a credit card containing an electronic chip storing data), which the applicant can bring to the test site.

3. You sign your name in a distinctive way. For example, when I write a capital J (figure 4.31), I move upward slowly on the a portion, come down very rapidly in b, pause at the bottom, and gradually build up speed on the c portion. If we plot the vertical velocity against time, we have a curve such as that shown in figure 4.32. Furthermore, I follow essentially the same pattern whether I'm using chalk, pen, or pencil. Even a forger who can copy my signature with remarkable accuracy cannot reproduce the velocity profile of figure 4.32. Personal-verification equipment is available that measures the forces, velocities, and accelerations involved as the applicant signs the name of the authorized person. This relatively inexpensive equipment has error rates claimed to be in the 1 percent range.

4. The last approach is the one directly relevant to this chapter: voice analysis, for example over the telephone. Here the applicant speaks passwords or a phrase of about seven syllables. The equipment finds the beginning and the end of the

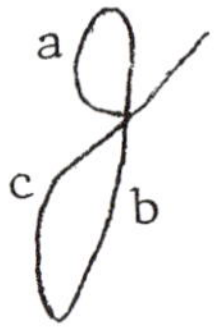

Figure 4.31
The J as I write my name.

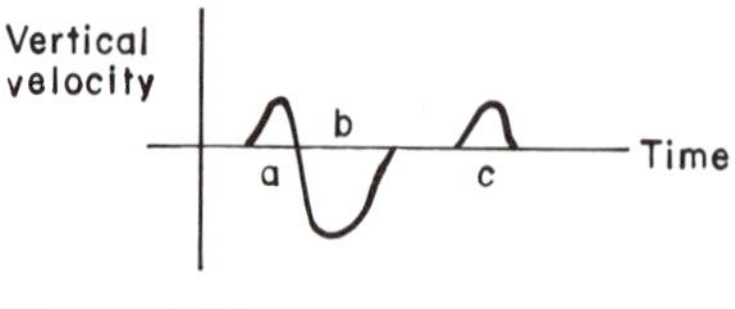

Figure 4.32
Vertical velocity profile.

speech, then looks at each frame (15/1000 second) to measure the energy and the spectrogram. The frames are automatically shrunk or expanded in time until the best match to the reference is found. The system yields Type 1 errors of 1.4 percent and Type 2 errors of 0.4 percent. (No system can give zero Type 1 errors, since people's voices do change with variations in nasal congestion, etc.).

These four approaches, plus the physiological measurements of fingers as described earlier, are the most common techniques for automation of personal verification. Completely different approaches are possible. We might, for example, use a polygraph or a lie detector. Unfortunately, polygraph tests are so subject to both types of errors that the technology is of little value for personal verification (in spite of the claims of some polygraphers and government officials); impartial studies of lie detection have indicated that up to 50 percent of truth-tellers can be classified as liars.

Final Comment

In this section, we have digressed from our study of the spectrogram to consider the specific technological problem of personal verification. The voiceprint or the spectrogram as an individual speaks a specific phrase is one of several techniques for personal verification. Like all these methods, spectrogram analysis is *not* always correct. To develop an intelligent opinion about whether we should allow a particular technological innovation, we must be aware of the limitations of the technology so that we can weigh the benefits against the risks to personal freedom.

4.8 Sound Signals of All Types

During a conversation, the sound signal might have the form indicated by figure 4.33. Over the course of a minute, the person talking would say perhaps 60 words (the maximum rate for reading aloud is about 150 words per minute).

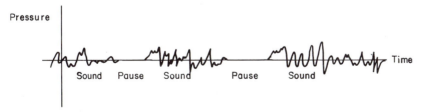

Figure 4.33
A picture of the air pressure during a conversation. In actuality, the various intervals of sounds and pauses are much longer than shown here. That is, during each sound interval there are hundreds of cycles of oscillation.

Most words consist of several different phonemes or distinct sounds, some of which run directly from one to the next with no pause in between. A minute of speech might consist of 100 intervals of sound and the same number of pauses—some very short between syllables, other long as the speaker decides what to say next. (Phonemes are basic sounds from which we construct meaningful speech. Each language has between 20 and 60 phonemes. In English, the p sound in "pit" is a phoneme—a sound made in a certain way by the mouth, tongue, etc., of the speaker.)

Thus, a typical speech signal is enormously more complicated than the telephone ring discussed earlier. Speech is never simply the addition of a few tones or pure notes of different frequencies. The complexity of speech is essential if it is to carry large amounts of information. The more the listener is unable to anticipate what the speaker will say next, the more information the speech can carry. The telephone ring, which is so completely predictable after it starts, is not something you want to hear for a long period of time even if it is melodious.

So our discussion of simple sine signals may seem useless when we turn to speech or most other sounds from the real world. The signal of figure 4.33 is obviously not a simple combination of pure-frequency sine waves at different amplitudes. Fortunately, there is a remarkable theorem in mathematics that shows us how even the most complex sounds can be analyzed by breaking the signal down into simple sine signals.

Fourier Theorem

A brilliant French mathematician, Jean Baptiste Joseph Fourier, provided us with a theorem that proved to be the keystone for a large fraction of today's communication engineering:

Any signal can be described as a sum of sinusoids of different frequencies.

In other words, the sine signal is a building block: any signal, even the one shown in figure 4.33, can be constructed exactly by adding up different sine signals.

Fourier   Jean Baptiste Joseph Fourier (1768-1830), orphaned at eight, was a child genius. By the age of fourteen he was ghost-writing sermons for one of France's leading clergymen. At sixteen he was a math teacher. In 1798 Napoleon took him on his Egyptian campaign as the first science advisor to a ruler. The role of science advisor was established at the outset: when Napoleon rushed home to reorganize his army, he forgot Fourier, who remained in Egypt for several years. His experience there convinced him that desert heat was healthy; in later years, he always dressed in heavy clothes and kept his Paris apartment at 90°F. Perhaps the fact that visitors seldom stayed very long accounts for his great scientific productivity, primarily in the matter of heat flow.

Meaning of Theorem   The Fourier Theorem is an astonishing idea. Look at the two signals of figure 4.34. Both are given over the same time interval. Signal A looks a little like a sinusoid already. It's not hard to imagine that this signal might actually be the sum of separate sinusoids, each with its own frequency and amplitude.

Signal B doesn't look at all like a sinusoid. There are even intervals where the signal is zero. Can we add sine components, as in figure 4.35, and obtain a sum that is zero over certain intervals, and is a given signal at other times? The Fourier theorem says "yes."

The Fourier Theorem simply tells us that decomposition (breaking a signal down into various frequencies) is possible. If we studied the mathematics, we would find that it also gives the formula for calculating the components (figure 4.35). Signal B is likely to require thousands of sine signals to obtain a reasonably accurate picture of the original signal: the more sine signals we use, the closer the sum comes to the actual signal.

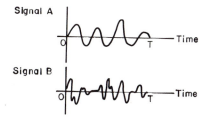

Figure 4.34
Two different signals existing over the same time interval.

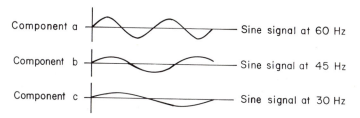

Figure 4.35
A few Fourier components of signal B in figure 4.34.

Spectrum

Once we make the Fourier decomposition (that is, once we find all the different frequencies in the signal), we can make a plot that shows the amplitude of each sine signal of a different frequency. This plot is called the *spectrum* of the signal.

A specific example illustrates the meaning of the spectrum. Figure 4.36 shows a given signal lasting 0.01 second. We carry out the Fourier decomposition and find that this signal is exactly equivalent to three sine components (figure 4.37). We are, of course, very lucky that there are only three components, rather than perhaps 30,000. (It really isn't luck; I cheated by picking the three components first, then adding them to obtain the signal.)

What do we mean when we say that the signal has these three components? At *each* instant of time, each sinusoid has a value we can read from the graph. Adding these three values gives the value of the original signal at that same time. For example, at a time of 0.0073 second, figure 4.38 shows that the three components are as follows.

Component A: −1.95

Component B: +1.80

Component C: −0.70.

The sum of these three is −0.85, which is also the original signal at the same time. An identical check can be made at any time during the total interval the signal lasts.

Thus, figure 4.37 shows the three Fourier components of the original signal:

Sine signal	Frequency	Amplitude
A	100	2
B	160	2
C	356	1

The spectrum (figure 4.39) is simply a plot that shows each of these components and saves us the trouble of writing out the table. Because we were so "lucky" and the Fourier decomposition gives only three components, the spectrum is just three vertical lines.

Usually there are thousands of Fourier components; a speech signal for an interval of 5 minutes might give the spectrum of figure 4.40. Instead of drawing all these vertical lines, we just draw the envelope (the outer shape of the plot as in figure 4.41), and call this the spectrum. Thus, the spectrum shows the amplitudes of the various sinusoids, which, when added together, give the original signal.

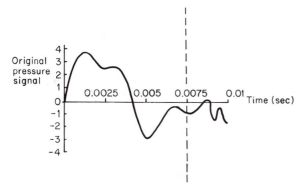

Figure 4.36
Signal lasting 0.01 second. This signal is exactly equivalent to three sine components of figure 4.37.

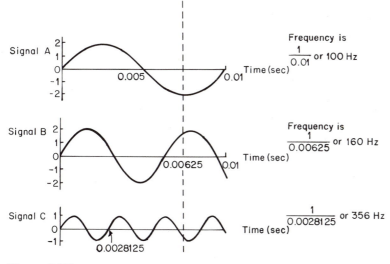

Figure 4.37
Three sine signals that added together give the signal of figure 4.36.

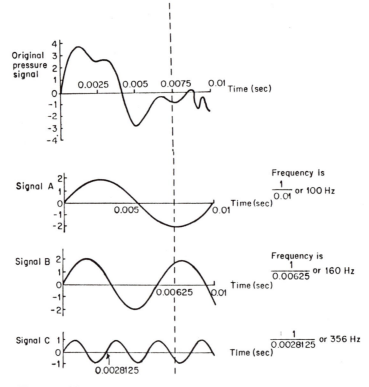

Figure 4.38
At a time of 0.0073 second, component A is –1.95, component B is +1.80, and component C is -0.70. The sum of these three is -0.85, which is also the original signal at the same time.

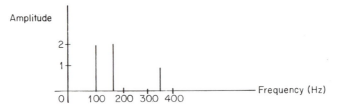

Figure 4.39
Spectrum for signal of figure 4.36. Each line shows the frequency and the amplitude for a component of the original signal.

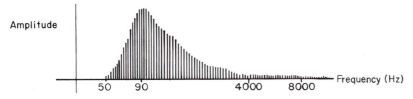

Figure 4.40
Spectrum of speech. Actually, there are thousands of components, although only a few are shown here.

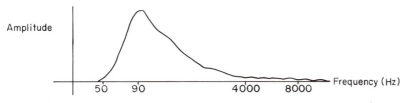

Figure 4.41
Spectrum as it is normally drawn. For simplicity, we draw only the shape of the plot, rather than all the individual vertical lines showing the frequency and amplitude of each component of the signal.

In this section, we have not discussed how the Fourier decomposition is actually done—how we find the components for a given signal. The procedure is described in the next chapter, but the crucial idea here is that the decomposition is possible: the sine signal is a fundamental building block for all signals, natural and engineering. Speech, television, earthquake pressure waves, and aircraft wing vibrations can all be described by their *spectra* (the plural of spectrum).

Once engineers know the spectrum of a particular signal, they have a better idea of the characteristics of that signal. This, then, is the basis on which modern communication technology is designed.

For example, measurements of speech from many people show that the spectra have the general appearance shown in Figs. 4.40 and 4.41. Most of the important components of human speech are at frequencies less than 4000 Hz; components above 10,000 Hz are negligible.

The communications engineer knows that to get good intelligibility the equipment should faithfully reproduce all frequencies out to 4000 Hz. This is the basis on which the telephone system is designed, and the reason we can recognize familiar voices calling long distance but we cannot clearly hear the sibilants. For high-fidelity speech communication, the equipment must reproduce faithfully all components at frequencies out to 8000 Hz (FM radio actually goes to 15,000 Hz to accommodate high musical notes). By using the

Fourier Theorem to find what frequencies exist in a signal, we can then design equipment that will reproduce or transmit those frequencies; the spectrum thus guides the design of communication equipment.

4.9 Spectrum and Spectrogram

In the use of the Fourier Theorem in communications engineering, there are two concepts: the spectrum and the spectrogram. As we have seen, these are quite different, and we need to distinguish carefully between them. Let us briefly review the two terms.

The Fourier Theorem states that *any* signal can be represented as a sum of sinusoids (pure, single-frequency components). The signal can be very short or can last over a long period of time—the *duration* determines whether we represent the Fourier decomposition by a spectrogram or by a spectrum.

Spectrum

A half-hour tape recording of your speech might look like figure 4.42. At time 0, you start talking. From A to B (and again from C to D), you pause between separate sounds. Of course, in a half-hour, you pause hundreds of times.

This half-hour is a long enough sample to represent an *average* of all the speech signals you will use in conversation. Consequently, this half-hour sample includes all the important characteristics of your speech. Within this half-hour, we can expect to find all the sounds you normally use in saying words and sentences.

We will apply the Fourier decomposition to this tape description of your speech: we will find all the sinusoids which, when added together, are identical with the signal of figure 4.42.

This analysis will require thousands of sinusoids. For example, we will have one component at 90 Hz, another at 200 Hz, and so forth. *Each of these components lasts the full 30 minutes*, even during the pauses in figure 4.42. During these pauses, the thousands of components add up to zero, but the components *still* exist (figure 4.43).

Obviously we are working here with a mathematical or theoretical idea. From A to B, the actual speech signal is zero—there is no signal. There are no reverberations or any such phenomena. When we look at the full 30 minutes, we need each of the thousands of components to describe the total signal. We are breaking down the speech signal into separate parts—parts which, that added together, give the total.

Thus, when we say that a signal has various Fourier components, we mean that each of these components exists over all the time. We do *not* mean that the speech is described for a while by one frequency, then by another, and so on.

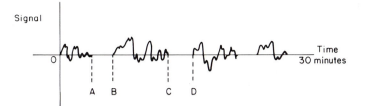

Figure 4.42
Speech signal (simplified).

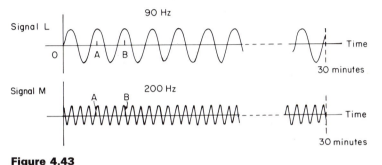

Figure 4.43
Two components of the speech signal of figure 4.42, one at 90 Hz and the other at 200 Hz.

There are other examples of the same idea of decomposition. If I push on a table with a force that is the signal of part A of figure 4.44, , I can find out how the table moves by saying the force is made up of three components: a constant force of 2 (figure 4.44, part B); a second component that is always zero except from 4 to 5, when it is –2 (figure 4.44, part C); and a third component that is always zero except from 10 to 11, when it is –1 (figure 4.44, part D). During the time from 4 to 5, the two components add up to zero. In other words, I take the signal apart so I can understand how the various components make up the signal, and so I can work with a set of simple signals.

Spectrogram
We can also apply the Fourier Theorem to a *very short* segment of a speech signal—for instance, a segment representing less than one phoneme. Ïf we do such a Fourier decomposition, we find that the Fourier components change rapidly as time passes—for example, as you say the word "shot". You have the sh sound, with its high-frequency components; you end with the t sound, with primarily low-frequency components.

Since this analysis determines the rapid changes in frequency components as time passes, the information is conveniently displayed by a plot of frequencies versus time: a *spectrogram* (figure 4.45).

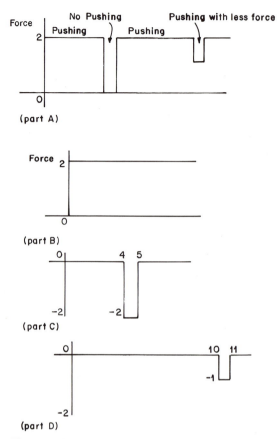

(part A)

(part B)

(part C)

(part D)

Figure 4.44
Different decomposition into simple components. (part A) I push on a table with a certain force. I can find out how the table moves by saying the force is made up of the following three components: (part B) a constant force of 2; (part C) a second component that is always zero except from 4 to 5 when it is –2. (part D) A third component always zero except from 10 to 11, when it is –1.

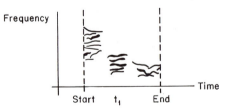

Figure 4.45
Spectrogram. The heavier line shows a larger amplitude.

At any instant of time (for example, t_1, when the speaker is in the middle of the vowel sound of "shot"), the spectrogram shows the different frequencies in a short segment of the sound wave around that time. The amplitude of each component is indicated by the heaviness or darkness of that marking on the graph, but this is only very vague; the spectrogram does not try to show the amplitudes accurately.

Thus, the spectrogram is a "running" Fourier decomposition: the computer continually looks at small pieces of the speech signal and makes a new decomposition. When the speaker pauses for breath, there is no sound signal, and the spectrogram shows nothing (in figure 4.45, these are the times before the start and after the end of the spoken work "shot"). The spectrogram portrays how the particular speaker says a word or phoneme; a female speaker usually has a higher-pitched voice than a male, so the spectrogram would show higher frequencies.

We want to tape a speech, then listen to it at a faster rate than when it was recorded. However, if we try to accelerate speech simply by tape recording, then playing back the tape at a higher speed, the voice will sound very high-pitched and unnatural (somewhat like Donald Duck), because all the frequency components are multiplied by the same factor as the tape speedup (figure 4.46). The Fourier decomposition serves as one basis for changing the rate without distorting the original speech.

For example, we want to double the speech rate without changing pitch. We tape the speech and perform the Fourier analysis. At one particular time, the signal is described by certain frequency components, say

100 Hz at amplitude 3

140 Hz at amplitude 2

160 Hz at amplitude 5.

We divide each frequency by 2, and generate a new signal by adding the three sinusoids

50 Hz at amplitude 3

70 Hz at amplitude 2

80 Hz at amplitude 5.

This signal is tape recorded; then when the tape is played back at twice the recording speed, the result is a signal identical with the speech in sine components, but occurs over an interval half as long as the original (figure 4.47).

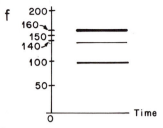

Spectrogram of original sound

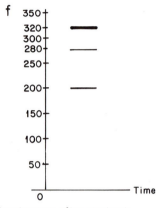

Spectrogram after playback

Figure 4.46
Accelerated speech with the Donald Duck effect. The original sound has only three
components (100, 140, and 160 Hz). This sound is recorded, and the tape is played
back at twice the recording speed.

When this process is carried out for every interval in succession, the speech
appears at the correct pitch, but at twice the original rate. The acceleration
factor of 2 was used here merely for illustration; any desired acceleration factor
can be obtained.

There have been two primary applications of speech acceleration so far:
"talking books" for the blind (where a sighted person reads the book onto tape)
and the recording of classroom or convention lectures. In both cases, it has been
found that the allowable acceleration rate depends on the individual talking
(not only the natural rate of speech, but also how clearly he or she enunciates),
the complexity and unfamiliarity of the ideas expressed, and the attentiveness
of the listener. Usually, 50 percent acceleration presents no problems, but 100
percent makes the result difficult to understand.

The Fourier decomposition is the ideal way to accelerate speech, but it is
expensive: a computer is needed to find the spectrogram. There are commercially available speech accelerators that operate more simply, though with less

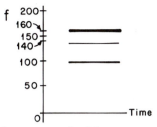

(a) Spectrogram of original sound

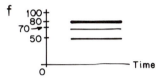

(b) Spectrogram of artificial sound

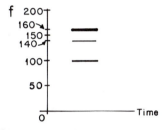

(c) Spectrogram after playback

Figure 4.47
Speech acceleration at natural pitch. We first find the frequencies present in the original sound. We then generate a new, artificial sound with each frequency half the original. After taping, we play back the tape at twice the speed. The result is the same, original sound, but lasting only half as long.

fidelity. For example, one machine simply cuts out pauses and then clips syllables.

Comparison of the Two Concepts
Both graphs, spectrum and spectrogram, depict the result of Fourier decomposition. The spectrum shows the *frequency content* of the signal over a long time; the spectrogram shows the frequency content as it changes with the different sounds.

4.10 Many Signals through One System

To a great extent, modern communication systems are explained in terms of the spectra of the signals. Thus, the following chapters use spectra to consider human hearing, radio, television, and even the search for messages from other civilizations. In the rest of this chapter, we mention two of the uses of the concept of a spectrum to show the wealth of ideas that flow from the characterizing of a signal by its Fourier or single-frequency components.

During its first 30 years, the telegraph system profoundly changed American economic and social life. By the 1870s when industries were growing throughout the United States and communication across long distances became a necessity, the nationwide system was severely strained because only one message could be sent over a wire at one time. Exactly the same situation arose 35 years later in the telephone system; industrial expansion created the need for more telephone capability.

Today we can send thousands of messages simultaneously over one system, and long-distance telephony is cheap, reliable, and convenient. To appreciate the U.S. telephone system, we only have to travel to many countries of South America, where it is not unusual to wait two days to place a long-distance call.

The possibility of sending many conversations through one system can be understood through the spectrum concept. A long-distance coaxial cable (a cable with a metallic outer conductor and another conductor down the center, as shown in figure 4.48) can transmit faithfully sine signals from 0 Hz to 6 million Hz.

If each telephone channel needs 4000 Hz (to cover the speech spectrum), then we can send 1500 conversations simultaneously over the one cable (6 million Hz divided by 4000 Hz—see figure 4.49). We cannot send 1500 con-

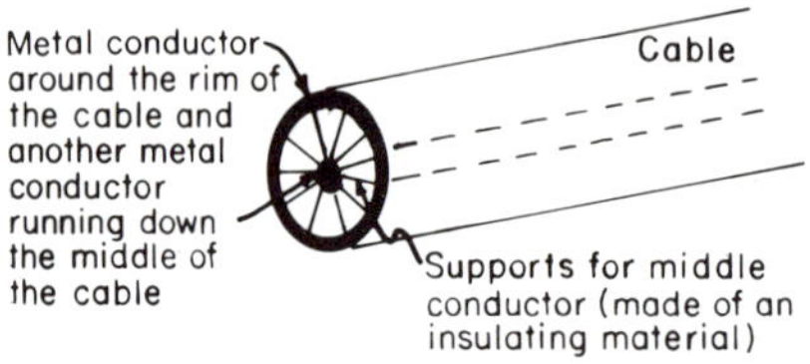

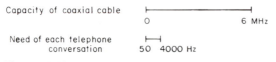

Figure 4.48
Coaxial cable. A long-distance coaxial cable can transmit faithfully sine signals from 0 Hz to 6 MHz. The current goes down the middle conductor and back up the outside conductor or vice versa (since the current is ac).

Capacity of coaxial cable |———————————————|
                                  0   6 MHz

Need of each telephone |—|
            conversation   50   4000 Hz

Figure 4.49
Capability of coaxial cable relative to the need of each telephone conversation. (Not drawn to scale.)

versations at the same time if we transmit each speech signal using the natural spectrum of speech for each conversation. So what we must do is change the frequency *range* used by each of the conversations. For example, one conversation is sent in its normal place, 50–4000 Hz. The second is modified so all its frequencies are shifted upward by 4000 Hz; it now covers 4050–8000 Hz. The third is moved up to 8050–12,000 Hz. And so on. The information of the original speech signal is unchanged, but all its frequencies are higher.

This process of changing the frequencies carrying the information, called *modulation*, turns out to be very easy electronically. It can be done by a simple electronic circuit.

Let's look at the Chicago-Denver long-distance telephone system. In Chicago, three people want to make a phone call at the same time. These three electrical speech signals come in from the homes or offices to the central telephone office. There they are prepared for long-distance transmission as shown in figure 4.50. After signal C is moved up to the range 8000–12,000 Hz, it is no longer a signal that would make any sense to anyone listening, but it carries all the information of the original speech.

The sum of the three signals, covering the band 0–12,000 Hz, is sent along the cable (or microwave relay or satellite system) to Denver. There we have electronic resonant circuits (as described in the next chapter), each of which selects one of the speech signals which is then shifted down to the normal 0–4000 Hz range.

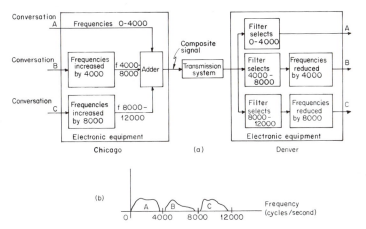

Figure 4.50
Multiplexing—the sharing of a communication system. (a) Three conversations (A, B, and C) are fed into the electronic equipment at the same time. Two of the conversations are shifted up in frequency, added to the other, and transmitted. When it arrives at the city of its destination, this combined signal is again fed into electronic equipment, which separates the three speech signals and returns them to their original frequency range. (b) Conversations B and C shifted up in frequency.

The complex arrangement shown in figure 4.50 is called *multiplexing* (the word "multiplex" means "many folds"). Actually it is the same idea as many AM radio stations and TV channels sharing the same air space: the information to be sent out by each station is shifted to a different band of frequencies.

The concept of the *spectrum* shows how we can accomplish this simultaneous transmission of many signals. Each signal has only a measurable spectrum width—in telephony, from 50 to 4000 Hz. The cable or satellite system can transmit a much wider band of frequencies, hence many conversations.

Figure 4.50 emphasizes that this system for long-distance communication essentially makes a trade. To cut way back on the expensive long-distance cables or radio relay systems, we increase the complexity of the electronic equipment at the two ends (Denver and Chicago). This equipment has two separate roles:

1. Shift the spectrum to a different set of frequencies. This is the process called modulation.

2. Separate the incoming signals. This is done with a filter or a resonant circuit.

Thus, in this section we have met a new operation on the spectrum: a sideways shift along the frequency axis (figure 4.51).

In the case of the transatlantic cable, where the cost is very high for laying a cable with amplifiers which will operate 20 years without failure, an even more elaborate scheme is used to maximize the number of conversations carried simultaneously. Studies have shown that people pause more than half the time when they speak (between words, syllables, and sentences). During these periods when no sound appears, the channel is unused. Consequently, it is possible to send six conversations over three channels.

Three conversations are multiplexed in the usual way. As soon as a pause occurs in any conversation, the fourth is put on that channel; for the next pause,

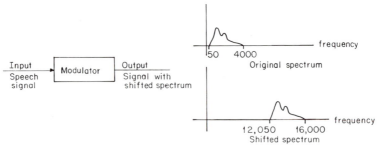

Figure 4.51
The modulation or frequency-shifting process. In this example, the spectrum is shifted up by 12,000 Hz.

the fifth; and the next pause, the conversation that has been waiting longest. On any one conversation, occasionally we lose short parts of syllables or sounds, but there is no real loss in intelligibility. The intricate switching is all done electronically, since a human operator could not respond fast enough.

4.11 Testing Automobile Engines

In the manufacturing of automobiles, the engine is made in a separate plant. The engine is built along a production line which travels back and forth across the plant floor. A number of pre-made parts are fed in as the engine proceeds through the assembly line. At the end, good engines go to a truck headed for the auto assembly plant, and faulty engines go to the repair shop.

The last station along the line is the "hot test" facility. Here each engine undergoes a test where it is fed gasoline and run for five minutes. This test allows "breaking in" of the engine, final adjustment, and diagnosis of any problem or malfunctioning.

The production line typically turns out an engine every minute. Since the hot test takes five minutes, there must be at least five parallel test stands. Usually seven stands are available to allow for maintenance of the test equipment or occasional delays in the testing operation.

For the hot test, an engine is first warmed up, then engine speed is increased to correspond to an auto speed of about 50 mph, and finally the engine is stopped. The test should show any malfunctioning of the various parts and also indicate (at least approximately) whether the engine will ultimately meet federal standards on emissions (hydrocarbons, carbon monoxide, and nitrogen oxides) and on fuel economy. This 5-minute test gives results which are closely correlated to the performance of the engine in a later federal auto test, which takes over an hour.

During the hot test, several signals are measured to decide whether the engine is working properly: engine speed, oil pressure, exhaust pressure, and

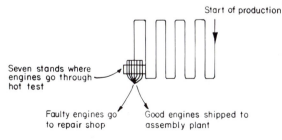

Figure 4.52
Diagram of manufacturing facility for engines.

various exhaust emissions. Each of these signals changes as time progresses over the 5 minutes. There now is the problem of deciding whether the engine is satisfactory; if not, there should be a printed diagnosis (insofar as possible) to be attached to the engine before it is transferred to the repair shop, where it will be fixed if the trouble is minor or junked for parts if there is a major difficulty. The diagnosis will also be used to monitor the total operation of the production line continually and decide on necessary changes to improve the percentage of good engines manufactured.

This matter of quality control is of fundamental importance in manufacturing—and an area in which the Japanese tend to outperform the Americans. It is not unusual for 20 percent of the engines to be rejected by the hot test. If half of these have to be junked, the cost per engine manufactured is increased more than 10 percent. Repair of the others is also an expensive operation since it requires individualized work. Thus, obtaining only a 2 or 3 percent increase in the number of engines passing the hot test results in a significant drop in the cost of manufacturing a car. Furthermore, the more engines passing the hot test, probably the fewer undetected problems that will show up after the car is in the customer's hands.

If we return to the hot test, we now have measurements of various signals. It turns out that interpretation of these signals is very difficult: looking at the signal of engine speed plotted against time does not easily indicate whether the engine is performing satisfactorily. If we find the *spectrum* of the signal, however, interpretation is much simpler—the spectrum shows clearly the various frequencies at which the engine oscillates or vibrates. Comparison of

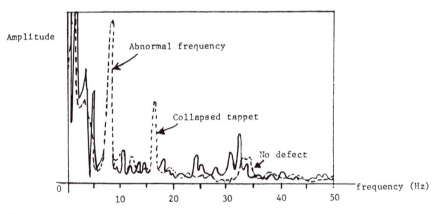

Figure 4.53
Comparison of the spectrum for an engine under test with the spectrum of a normal engine. The normal performance of the engine is shown by the solid line. The dashed line is the response of the engine under test.

the spectrum for the engine under test with the spectrum of a normal engine shows deviations from correct behavior (figure 4.53).

Furthermore, we can purposely test an engine for each of the common problems, and we can build up a dictionary for diagnosis. For example, the sharp peak in the spectrum of figure 4.53 at about 17 Hz corresponds to a malfunction called a "collapsed tappet." The computer which is fed the signals and calculates the spectra can automatically detect this abnormal peak, then print a diagnosis to be taped to the engine before it is sent to the repair shop.

Before the recent development of inexpensive computers or electronic filters, there was no way to find the spectrum sufficiently rapidly and inexpensively to allow such automated testing. A person had to stand at the hot-test station, observe the engine speed versus time, listen for particular frequency components (particular peaks in the spectrum), and then decide whether the engine passed or failed. The electronic equipment is much more reliable than people in detecting faulty signals.

The Fourier decomposition (or the spectrum) is the key to this automated testing facility. The computer does several things better than a human:

1. A human has to look at the time signal; the computer can calculate the spectrum.

2. The human operator can measure the spectrum only by listening to the sound made by the engine, but most of the sounds are at frequencies too low for human hearing (that is, below 25 Hz).

3. The automated system is not subject to fatigue, boredom, and distraction, so it produces far fewer false positives (decisions that an engine passes when it really is not working properly).

This example also illustrates the fundamental social problem of automation: the introduction of the automated equipment requires workers with different skills. In this case, workers need more computer and electronic training.

Review Questions

R4-1. What does the Fourier Theorem state?

R4-2. What feature of the speech spectrum makes it possible for a telephone company to send many conversations concurrently on a long-distance line?

R4-3. Describe how spectrograms can be used to explain why the same notes played on different musical instruments sound different.

R4-4. On the musical scale, what is the difference between octaves and harmonics?

R4-5. Explain how speech spectrograms can be used by police departments only as a means of ruling out innocent people in an investigation.

R4-6. The telephone company throws away all speech frequencies above 4000 Hz. How do the designers know that this simplification is permissible?

R4-7. Explain why two octaves above the 440-Hz musical note is 1760 Hz and the fourth harmonic of the 440 Hz musical note is also 1760 Hz.

R4-8. What is meant by the term "multiplexing"?

R4-9. A spectrogram is a plot of what vertically versus what horizontally?

R4-10. I play on a musical instrument a note A (a frequency of 440 Hz). What is the frequency of the third harmonic?

R4-11. Playing a single note on the oboe gives rise to not only the fundamental, but also every harmonic up to the thirteenth (that is, the second, the third, and so on). If the fundamental is C, which of the harmonics are also C?

R4-12. Explain briefly the difference between a spectrum and a spectrogram.

R4-13. A spectrum is a plot of what vertically versus what horizontally?

R4-14. I have a tuning fork at A, or 440 Hz. What is the frequency of the A two octaves higher?

R4-15. People with normal hearing perceive that friends talking to them on the phone sound different from the same friend face-to-face. Explain briefly.

R4-16. A telephone ring includes the frequencies 523, 1568, and 2637 Hz. Draw a spectrogram carefully to show this total sound signal.

R4-17. We play middle C (262 Hz) on a piano. The sound signal includes the tenth harmonic. What frequency is this harmonic?

R4-18. What sounds are missing in a phone conversation to Chicago?

R4-19. Sketch a typical spectrum for human speech.

R4-20. A bird call often has a fundamental frequency near 7000 Hz. Why is the frequency not 2000 Hz?

R4-21. What contribution did Jean Baptiste Joseph Fourier make to our field of communication technology?

R4-22. When A above middle C is properly set at 440 Hz, middle C is about 262 Hz. If the orchestra conductor sets A at 445, what will be the frequency for middle C?

R4-23. To build an electronic device to sound just like a piano, would we use the spectrum or the spectrogram of the piano output? Explain *briefly*.

R4-24. Describe briefly how spectrograms are used to teach a deaf child to speak normally.

R4-25. Joe can hear all frequencies from 31 Hz to 16,000 Hz. How many octaves are covered by Joe's hearing sense?

Problems

P4-1. A few years ago, a report claimed that the measurement of the voltage difference between the cornea and the retina of a person's eye (a measurement called an electronystagmograph, or ENG) indicates drug use by the characteristics of the waveform, as shown in figure 4.54. The argument was that the device actually measures impairment of the person's capabilities, which the blood-alcohol level (for example) does not do. Furthermore, the test is non-invasive (only a disposable headband is needed to measure the brain-wave "fingerprint").

If the spectra were determined for each signal, which would have strong high-frequency components? Which would have strong low-frequency components? Explain briefly.

P4-2. Figure 4.55 describes the heart rate of an individual engaging, at time t, in an exciting activity (for example, an astronaut stepping out onto the surface of the moon).

We want to estimate the highest frequency present in the spectrum of this signal. One way to do this is to look at the region where the change is most rapid (figure 4.56) and assume this segment is a half period of the component with the highest frequency.

What is the maximum frequency in Hz?

P4-3. In the nineteenth century, a good telegraph operator could send or receive as many as 50 words per minute (the signal was sent by key and received by ear). In 1914, automatic transmission was introduced and the maximum rate doubled. In 1936, the first coaxial cable was placed in service, from New York to Philadelphia, and the telephone company realizied transmission for a band of frequencies from 0 to 7.5 MHz. By 1951, coaxial cable was available from coast to coast.

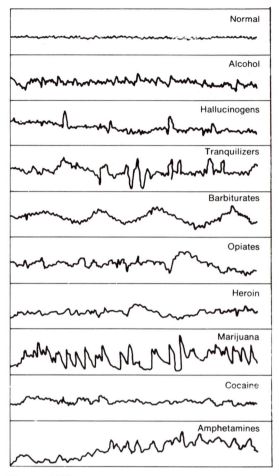

Figure 4.54

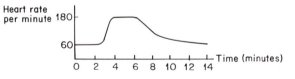

Figure 4.55

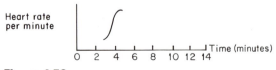

Figure 4.56

If each telephone conversation is equivalent to 18 multiplexed telegraph circuits, how many telegraph messages could be carried simultaneously on the NY-Philadelphia cable? Since a normal rate of human speech is about 100 words per minute, compare the communication capabilities when the cable is used for telegraph and for telephone.

P4-4. The graphs of figure 4.57 show the fundamental frequency plots over time for the cry of a normal baby (left) and a baby with brain damage (right). How do these plots relate to the spectrograms or spectra discussed in this chapter?

P4-5. In southern California and other earthquake-prone regions, protection of the electrical generating and distribution equipment is critically important. After a major earthquake, the long-term loss of electrical energy severely complicates rescue and recovery operations.

Until the 1971 San Fernando Valley earthquake, the utility facilities were designed to withstand a constant force (actually ⅛ the weight of the object). After the 1971 experience, California utilities changed to *dynamic* criteria: the forces were assumed to vary from 0.1 to 30 Hz, with the amplitude of the spectrum dependent on the expected vibration at the exact location of the equipment. In addition, all facilities were equipped with seismometers to measure action during subsequent earthquakes.

Explain why the change from static to dynamic criteria is so important.

P4-6. The cellular phone system (for car and portable telephones) is an elaborate example of multiplexing or sharing of the frequencies available in the

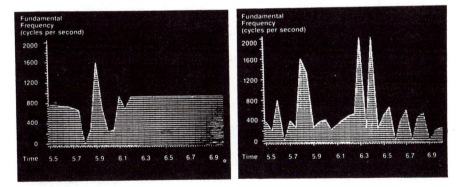

Figure 4.57
These figures are taken from the article "The Telltale Cry," by Steve Nadis (*Technology Review*, May/June 1988). This article describes the research of Dr. Howard Golub, who is attempting to use an infant's cry as a basis for predicting sudden infant death syndrome (SIDS) and developmental delay.

technology (in this case, radio). Until the mid-1980s, car and mobile phone service was severely limited in U.S. cities because only one person could use a given group of frequencies.

By 1971 AT&T had developed the concept of a *cellular* system. Each city is divided into many cells or small areas. A caller in one cell communicates with a radio receiver for that cell, and the phone conversation goes into the regular, wired telephone system and on to its destination. As the caller drives from one cell into an adjacent cell, the call is automatically switched to frequencies allocated to this new cell. In this way, many non-adjacent cells in the city can use the same frequencies.

Furthermore, in 1974 the FCC (Federal Communications Commission) allocated many more frequencies for cellular phones, partly by converting all television channels above 69. As a result, a major metropolitan region can now serve as many as 400,000 mobile phones.

Thus, the technology was available by 1971, the regulatory rulings by 1974. In 1978 a trial in Chicago started. In 1982 the FCC accepted applications for the 30 largest markets (major cities). In 1984 the FCC began granting licenses, and today the system is growing rapidly (by 1989 there were over 200,000 phones in the New York City area).

a. Cellular telephones were widely used in Europe and Japan by 1980, but in the United States (where the technology was initially developed) they were not until about seven years later. Why was the United States so slow to take advantage of the technology?

b. It is difficult to conceive of so many people wanting car and mobile phones. Why has the technology proved so popular, even though the cost is not small (typically $1000 for the equipment and $74 per month as a user's charge, although both figures vary enormously)?

c. The FCC was swamped by applications. The licenses to the 30 largest markets were awarded by evaluation of all proposals (with each region awarded two licenses—one for a regular phone or telecommunications company, the other for a corporation new to the field). In 1984 the FCC decided to use a lottery to determine winners of the licenses for all other markets. As a consequence, many corporations with no serious intention of ever providing phone service submitted bids. If they were lucky enough to win, they sold their licenses to the highest bidders. If you were a U. S. Representative or staff member, how would you evaluate this FCC decision to use a lottery?

Chapter 5
Resonance

In the late 1960s, officials at the U.S. embassy in Moscow suddenly learned that the Russians had been using ingenious technology to listen to conversations in the ambassador's office. On the office wall there was a plaque representing the American eagle. The Russians had secretly hollowed out a cavity in the plaque and covered the front of the cavity with a membrane in such a way that it would not be noticed from inside the room.

Across the street, the Russians had a high-frequency radio with the beam focused on the cavity in the eagle. Using the principle of *resonance*, they were able to listen to conversations with no "bug" or microphone in the ambassador's office, and indeed, no obvious way for the Americans to discover that the eavesdropping was going on.

Before trying to explain this clever bit of espionage, we need to discuss the technological concept of resonance.

5.1 Free Response

The rear shock absorbers on my car are not in very good condition. If I press down hard on the rear bumper, then let go, the bumper and the back of the car oscillate as shown in figure 5.1. The oscillation dies out in about three cycles; each cycle lasts about a second.

We have here a *resonant system* or *resonant device*; the car exhibits the phenomenon of *resonance*. What do we mean by these statements? Simply that the system, initially disturbed or displaced from its normal position at rest, returns to that normal position with an oscillatory motion—moving up and down, with each cycle smaller than the preceding one.

Figure 5.1
After release, my car's bumper oscillates through three cycles before coming to rest.

Figure 5.2 shows a second example of resonance. The swing oscillates back and forth and eventually comes to rest. In this case, there are seven cycles before rest, and each cycle lasts 4 seconds.

Meaning of Free Response

Both these examples are what we term "free response." This simply means that after the response starts (at zero time), we let the system move naturally; we apply no additional forces. In other words, we do not push again on the car bumper, and the child does not pump the swing.

Thus, *free response* means that we get the system or device started, then we allow it to oscillate *freely* thereafter.

If we throw a rock into a small pond, the initial impact of the rock causes waves, which then travel outward. If we hit a tuning fork (figure 5.3), the tines vibrate back and forth; then the oscillation dies out after thousands of cycles.

Resonance Defined

A system is *resonant* if, when initially excited and then allowed to behave freely, it exhibits an oscillation which gradually dies out.

The oscillation can be described by two numbers:

1. The *resonant frequency*, usually called f_r. This is the frequency of the oscillation in hertz or cycles per second. The rear of my car has a resonant frequency of 1 Hz, the swing an f_r of ¼ Hz. The f_r of the tuning fork depends on the length of the tines: the bigger the tines, the lower the resonant frequency, so we can buy tuning forks for musical notes in the low audio range (for example, 262 Hz or middle C).

2. The *quality factor*, called Q. This is the number of cycles before the oscillation dies out. For the rear of my car, Q = 3; for the swing, Q = 7.

If a tuning fork vibrates for 10 seconds at 262 Hz, the Q must be 2620—that is, 262 oscillations every second for 10 seconds. (Engineers have a much more precise and elaborate definition of Q; ours is obviously subjective. Exactly when

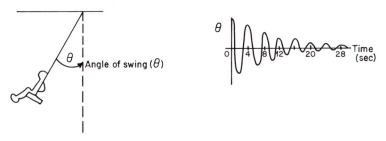

Figure 5.2
A swing is moved to the position shown, then is released at time 0. The angle θ
follows the pattern of a decaying oscillation; after seven cycles, the swing is at rest.

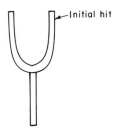

Figure 5.3
A tuning fork is a highly resonant system; it goes through many cycles before it
returns to rest.

does the swing stop oscillating? For our purposes, however, this simple
definition is satisfactory, since we are not looking for exact values). A resonant
system always has a Q of at least 1—otherwise there would be no oscillatory
behavior and we would not describe the system as resonant.

Notice that knowing the values of f_r and Q allows us to sketch the response
of any resonant system. We do not know exactly where in a cycle the response
starts, but we can sketch the general shape. See box 5.1.

5.2 Forced or Driven Response

Resonance shows up in a different way when a system is driven—that is, when
we continually apply a force or a signal to cause the system to respond.

Let us return to our swing example. A child climbs onto the swing and asks
you to push. You give a push, then push again, and so on. In other words, you
drive the system with the pushes shown in figure 5.4. We want to look at what
happens when you deliver these pushes at various rates.

Measurement of f_r and Q

Attach any object of moderate weight (a box of chalk, for example) to the end of a string about 4 feet long. Start the simple pendulum oscillating and measure the period; you can use a watch with a second hand or have someone else tap as rapidly as possible with a pencil on a piece of paper. The human being can tap close to six times a second.

Repeat the measurement while holding the string at a lower point (the pendulum length less). For the same reason (to shorten the period), we bend our legs in running.

Resonance causes a serious problem when a tall crane is trying to move a heavy load close to a building. The motion of the top of the crane excites the load, which wants to oscillate as a pendulum and crash into the building.

Box 5.1

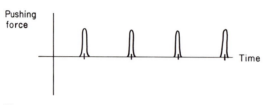

Figure 5.4
You deliver a push to the swing at regular intervals of time.

First, you push at a very low frequency—say one push every minute. As figure 5.5 shows, after each push the swing oscillates and comes to rest.

We now increase the rate or frequency of the pushes. When we push every 4 seconds, we are pushing at the same time each cycle (say right at the top of the angular motion). Each push gives more energy to the swing than is lost during the last cycle. Consequently, the motion of the swing builds up rapidly to a very large back-and-forth amplitude (figure 5.6). You are driving the system (the swing) at its resonant frequency; the system responds very strongly, and the child gets a great ride.

When you *drive* a system (that is, apply a force to the swing), the system shows a *response* (the swing moves). When you change the frequency of the drive (the rate at which you're applying pushes to the swing), the amplitude or amount of response is different. Resonance means that

there is a frequency of the drive at which the response is exceptionally large.

This frequency is called the *resonant frequency*. In the case of our swing, the resonant frequency is 15 cycles per minute, or one cycle every 4 seconds.

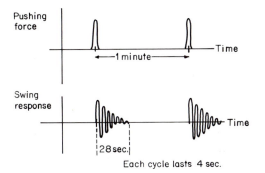

Figure 5.5
When the drive is at a very low frequency, the swing responds to each drive pulse separately.

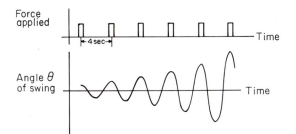

Figure 5.6
When you push the swing every 4 seconds, the motion of the swing builds up rapidly to a large back-and-forth amplitude. You are driving the system at its resonant frequency of 15 cycles per minute.

System Input and Output

Figure 5.7 is a representation of any of the systems we are discussing in this chapter. A drive or input is applied to the system, and a response or output results. An untold number of systems fit into this category. For example, if we were considering the national economic system, the input could be a tax cut and the response the number of unemployed workers. Thus, this picture of a system simply shows that the system accepts the input and generates a resulting output. The diagram just shows a cause-effect relationship.

Naturally we are interested in a special group of systems—those that are resonant. Three examples are given in table 5.1.

Driving with a Sinusoidal Signal

Your pushing on a swing, the wind force on a bridge, or the motion given to a violin string by the bow is never a sine signal. You don't push as shown in figure 5.8, where a negative pushing force would mean that you are pulling.

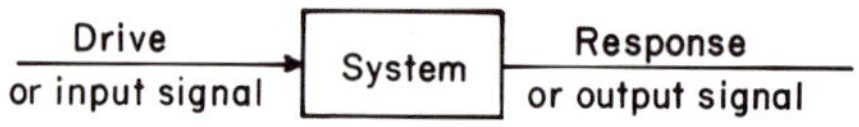

Figure 5.7
A "causal" system: the drive, or input, acts on the system and causes a response, or output.

Table 5.1

System	Drive or Input	Response or output
Swing	Your pushing force	Oscillation of the swing back and forth
Bridge	Wind force	Vibration of the structure
Violin	Motion of the string as the bow moves across	Sound signal caused by the vibrating string

The Fourier Theorem (chapter 4) tells us that any signal can be broken down into a sum of sine signals at different frequencies. Consequently, to study the behavior of a resonant system, let us first look at how the system would respond if we should decide to drive it with one sine. In particular, how does the response or output change as we change the frequency of the sinusoidal drive?

Figure 5.9 shows the kind of results we obtain when the system is resonant. In each of the four parts, the drive signal has the same amplitude; we change only the frequency as we move from one part of the figure to the next. At very low or high frequencies, the response is small. At one frequency (part c of the figure), the response is very large—this is the resonant frequency, and the existence of this large response means that the system possesses *resonance*.

Gain Characteristic or Plot
Drawing a figure like figure 5.9 to describe a system is terribly tedious, especially since we really should have many more parts to show the system's behavior at many other frequencies. If we inspect figure 5.9 carefully, we notice that in every case both the drive and the response are sinusoidal at the same frequency. The only features of interest are the amplitudes of the drive and the response.

Even further, the behavior of the system at any one frequency is described by the ratio

$$\frac{\text{Amplitude of response}}{\text{Amplitude of drive}},$$

a ratio which is called the *gain* of the system. A gain of 5 means that the output or response is five times as large as the input; a gain of $7/10$ means the output is

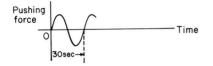

Figure 5.8
Sinusoidal force applied to a swing at a frequency of 2 cycles per minute. You never push a swing this way, since a negative pushing force would mean that you were pulling.

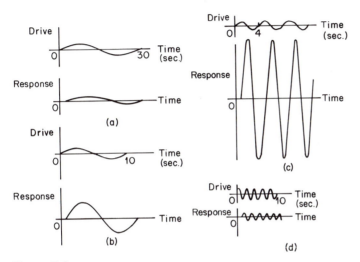

Figure 5.9
System response for four different frequencies of the sinusoidal drive.

$7/10$ of the input. The gain describes the system since the actual size of the drive is not important: if we double the drive, we double the response, so the ratio is the key characteristic. (This property, that multiplying the input by any number results in the output being multiplied by the same number, means the system is what engineers call "linear." The examples we consider all fall into this category.)

Figure 5.9 now reveals that that entire set of drawings can be replaced by the simple table 5.2. In other words, when the drive is a sinusoid at 6 cycles per minute, the gain is 1.5: the response is a sinusoid at the same frequency, but 1.5 times as large.

We mentioned above that, to describe the system, we really need the gain at many more frequencies than these four. Usually, instead of a table listing frequencies and gains, we simply draw a graph, called the gain characteristic.

Figure 5.10 shows the gain characteristic of a different system (not our swing). The graph is really a complete picture; table 5.3 is included here only

Table 5.2

Frequency (cycles per minute)	Gain	Part of figure 5.9
2	0.8	a
6	1.5	b
15	10	c
30	0.8	d

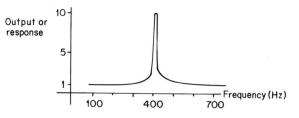

Figure 5.10
The gain characteristic of a typical resonant system. The system is resonant at 400 Hz. In the immediate vicinity of this frequency, the system responds much more strongly than at other frequencies.

Table 5.3

Drive-signal frequency	Amplitude of drive	Amplitude of response	Gain
100 Hz	1	0.8	0.8
200 Hz	1	1.0	1
300 Hz	1	1.2	1.2
398 Hz	1	4	4
400 Hz	1	10	10
402 Hz	1	4	4
500 Hz	1	1.3	1.3
600 Hz	1	1.1	1.1
700 Hz	1	1.0	1.0

to indicate where the plot comes from: the measurements we would make on the system to determine the graph.

Definition of Resonance

A system is resonant if the gain characteristic shows a sharp peak. The frequency of the peak is the resonant frequency.

Furthermore, the sharpness of the peak is measured by a quantity we call the quality factor, or Q—the same Q we met in section 5.1. In figure 5.11, which illustrates the gain characteristic for a system with a resonant frequency f_r, the gain is maximum at f_r. As we move in either direction away from f_r, the gain falls.

We define the bandwidth B as the frequency range around the resonant frequency over which the gain is high—at least 71 percent of the maximum.

With this definition, it turns out that

$$Q = \frac{f_r}{B} .$$

In other words, the smaller B is, the higher the Q. A large Q means a very *selective* system that only amplifies signals at frequencies very close to f_r (figure 5.12).

In this section, we have seen a second manifestation of resonance. In section. 5.1, we saw that resonance means oscillatory behavior of a free, undriven

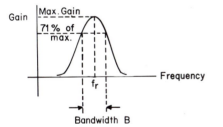

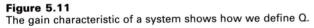

Figure 5.11
The gain characteristic of a system shows how we define Q.

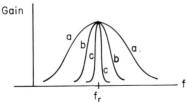

Figure 5.12
Three different systems, each with the resonant frequency f_r. System a has low Q, system c a very high Q.

system. Here we have seen that resonance means very strong response at or very close to a particular frequency.

5.3 Systems with Multiple Resonances

A system may have more than one resonance, as is illustrated by the gain characteristic of figure 5.13. Here there are resonances at the following four frequencies:

100 Hz   200 Hz   260 Hz   380 Hz.

Such phenomena are common in structures such as bridges or airplane wings, where each resonance corresponds to vibration in a different way (up and down, sideways, twisting, etc.) so that there may be 100 different resonances. A string on a violin has numerous resonant frequencies (in this case, harmonics of the fundamental or primary frequency), as we saw in chapter 4, where we looked at the spectrogram of a violin when a specific note is played.

Driving a Resonant System with a Realistic Signal

So far, we have discussed what happens when we drive a resonant system with a sinusoidal signal. In the real world, most signals are not sinusoidal. Instead, signals look like random variations and may even have pauses during which the actual signal is zero. Figure 5.14 shows typical signals driving the three systems we used previously as examples. Obviously, none of these is sinusoidal. How does a resonant system respond to such a signal?

The Fourier Theorem answers the question. Any input signal is the sum of a number of sinusoidal components, each at a different frequency. We can find how each of these components "goes through" the system—that is, the output resulting from each separate input component. The total output is then the sum of these different contributions.

As a specific example, let us consider the resonant system with the gain characteristic shown in figure 5.15. The system has a single resonance at 160

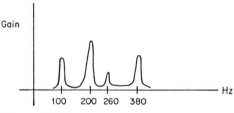

Figure 5.13
System with four resonances.

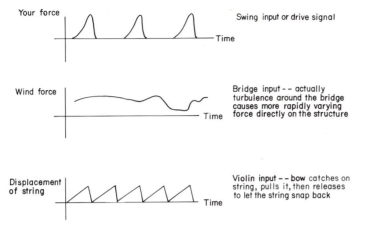

Figure 5.14
Real input or drive signals for the three systems previously used as examples.

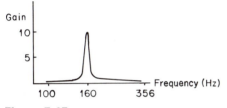

Figure 5.15
Gain characteristic of a system resonant at 160 Hz.

Hz. What happens when we drive this system with the signal shown in part a of figure 5.16?

This drive signal has the Fourier or sinusoidal components shown in part b of figure 5.16: components at 100, 160, and 356 Hz. We can consider each of these sinusoidal drive signals separately as in table 5.4.

Figure 5.17 shows the output or response of the system. The output still has three components (at 100, 160, and 356 Hz), but the output is primarily the component at 160 Hz. Only this component is strongly amplified because it matches the system's resonant frequency. Thus, the output looks almost sinusoidal at 160 Hz.

Thus, *resonance allows us to select one signal from a combination of many different signals.*

General Input or Drive Signals
The Fourier Theorem tells us that the drive signal normally includes components at essentially all frequencies covered by the spectrum. For example, as a

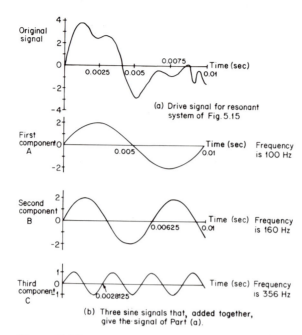

Figure 5.16
Drive signal for our example.

Table 5.4

| Drive component | Drive | | Gain | Response | |
	Amplitude	Frequency		Amplitude	Frequency
A	2	100	0.3	0.6	100
B	2	160	10	20	160
C	1	356	0.2	0.2	356

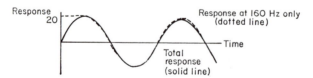

Figure 5.17
Response when the drive signal of figure 5.16 is applied to the resonant system of figure 5.15. The components at 100 and 356 Hz are so small that they are hardly noticed.

violin bow moves across the string, the string position at the point of contact changes as shown in figure 5.18a. The corresponding spectrum is shown in part b of the figure.

The string and the rest of the instrument have a gain characteristic as shown in figure 5.19. There are many resonances at the harmonics of the note being played.

With the input the signal shown in figure 5.18, the violin picks out or selects only those frequencies at which there are resonances. Consequently, the sound signal coming from the violin (that is, the system output) contains components only at these resonant frequencies. The result is the spectrogram shown in figure 5.20.

Similarly, the signal representing your pushing on the swing or the wind force on a bridge contains thousands of frequency components. The swing with a single resonance picks out one; the bridge may show several different types of vibration simultaneously, since it has many resonances.

We have now reached a basic concept: a resonant system can be used to select one (or a few) Fourier components of the drive or input signal.

American Eagle in Moscow
Let us return to the opening paragraph of this chapter, where we mentioned the American eagle in the ambassador's office of the U.S. embassy in Moscow. How did that system use resonance?

Figure 5.21 shows that the important parts were the cavity and the diaphragm. The cavity was simply an empty space lined with metal. This cavity was resonant for radio signals beamed at it. The *longer* the distance D from the front of the cavity to the back, the *lower* the resonant frequency.

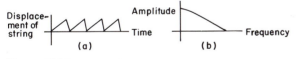

Figure 5.18
(a) Violin input—the bow catches on a string, pulls it, and then releases to let the string snap back. (b) The corresponding spectrum.

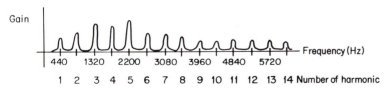

Figure 5.19
Gain characteristic of a violin playing A above middle C.

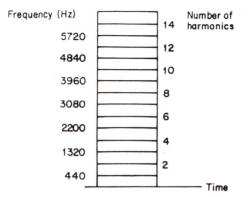

Figure 5.20
Spectrogram when A above middle C is played on violin.

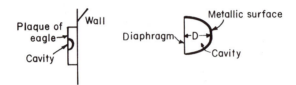

Figure 5.21
Resonant cavity made in wall plaque of eagle.

This resonance depending on size is just like sound signals resonating in organ pipes. The long pipes resonate at low frequencies, the short at high frequencies. A crystal glass partly filled with water acts the same way: the more water, the smaller the air cavity above the water, and the higher the frequency. Thus, the cavity in the eagle was a resonant system, with the resonant frequency measuring D.

From across the street, the Russians beamed toward the eagle a radio signal with many different frequency components. The echo coming back to them was strongest at the resonant frequency of the cavity.

During conversation in the ambassador's office, the speech sounds are really changes in air pressure. When

1. air pressure rose, then

2. the diaphragm in figure 5.21 was pushed to the right, and

3. the resonant frequency of the cavity increased (smaller D), and

4. the radio echo that the Russians picked up across the street was at a higher frequency.

Thus, the frequency of the echo received across the street directly measured the changes in air pressure or sound in the room. The Russians could listen to the conversation, but the only indication that the Americans had of this very elegant bugging was an extra, very weak radio signal, which probably could not be easily detected unless the frequency was known.

5.4 Uses of Resonance

Resonance allows a system to select only one component of the total input signal, the component at the resonant frequency. Actually the system selects all components at frequencies close to f_r. In this section we consider a few applications of resonance; in the last part of the chapter, we will look at a few other applications in more depth.

Resonance is a remarkable phenomenon with major implications in engineering, science, medicine, and the social and behavioral sciences.

Selecting One Radio or TV Station

AM, FM, and TV all operate on the same principle: each broadcasting station is allocated a narrow range of frequencies around its primary frequency. For example, AM radio station WCBS operates at 880 kHz (usually described as "88 on your AM dial") and has an allocation from the FCC of all frequencies from 875,000 to 885,000 Hz.

When I tune my AM radio to WCBS, the receiver is essentially a resonant electrical system with

$f_r = 880,000$ Hz

and

$B = 10,000$ Hz.

Hence, for the resonant system

$Q = 88$.

Now the receiver amplifies strongly only signals with frequencies between 875 and 885 kHz.

The electrons in the receiver antenna move in response to all the radio or TV broadcasts in the region, but the resonance means that the output loudspeaker receives only the audio being broadcast by WCBS. The gain characteristic of a resonant system (section 5.2) shows there is a little gain just below 875 kHz and above 885 kHz, so the FCC forbids any AM station in my area to use these adjacent channels.

Thus, resonance makes possible the frequency multiplexing discussed at the end of chapter 4—the use of the same space for simultaneous radio broadcasting by many different stations. If I want to listen instead to radio station WOR, I simply tune my receiver—I change the resonant frequency to 710 kHz and maintain the same bandwidth.

Stopping Shoplifting

Drug stores and other retail outlets are now tagging items with a device that can be detected by a radio signal as the customer moves through the exit. The device is an electronic resonant circuit.

The tag on the drug-store product shows the Universal Product Code or bar code denoting the particular item. Under this bar code is a resonant circuit (figure 5.22). As a shoplifter leaves the store with the item, he or she passes through a radio beam in which the frequency is changing over a range including the frequency the resonant circuit is tuned to. When the resonant circuit is in the beam, it absorbs energy from the radio signal. At the receiver, the signal varies with frequency in a dip which indicates that an item is passing through the beam and an alarm sounds to identify the shoplifter.

Figure 5.22
Resonant circuit used in store surveillance system.

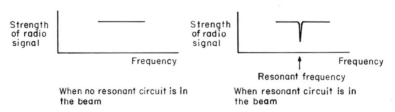

Figure 5.23
Frequency continually changes so as to pass through the device's resonant frequency.

Theoretically, we could build the transmitter to operate at just the tag's resonant frequency, rather than sweeping in frequency as described above. Then, however, the received signal could vary as a customer walked through the beam. Furthermore, the tag must be inexpensive (a penny or two), so we do not want to place overly rigid specifications on the precision of manufacture.

To deactivate the resonant circuit, the sales clerk pastes a metallized sticker over the bar code—a sticker typically reading "Paid. Thank you." The metal in this sticker prevents the radio signal from reaching the resonant circuit. The thief can, of course, do the same thing with his or her own sticker or a piece of aluminum foil, or can cut the resonant circuit, but such technological literacy is not anticipated from most shoplifters.

This technology raises some important issues. Certainly there will be a fair number of false alarms as salespersons forget to attach the sticker over the bar code. This situation is particularly likely since sales jobs are low-paying and turnover is high. Will the false alarms constitute a serious infringement on the rights of shoppers? Or is this disadvantage minor compared to the drop in theft? (If the profit of the store is only 2 percent of gross sales and 1 percent is lost in theft, stopping theft is significant economically.) Is the use of such tags another example of surveillance threatening individual privacy?

Measurement of Spectrum or Spectrogram

We have seen how a resonant system allows us to select just one component of the input or drive signal. The input can be very complex. This is exactly what we want to do when we measure the spectrum of a signal.

Suppose we have a speech signal, with components from 50 to 8000 Hz. We want to measure the component at 600 Hz (figure 5.24). We simply build a resonant system tuned to 600 Hz. The output of the resonant system measures the amplitude of the input component at that frequency.

By tuning the resonant system (or changing the resonant frequency), we can measure the spectrum at each frequency from 50 to 8000; we then have the spectrum.

To measure the spectrogram, we use a parallel arrangement of resonant systems (figure 5.25). Now over each short interval of time, the output meters show the amplitudes of each of the frequency components.

Other Examples

Examples of resonance in nature include the following:

1. Insect wings may vibrate as fast as 120 cycles per second, although nerve impulses driving the wings arrive only three times a second. This train of pulses

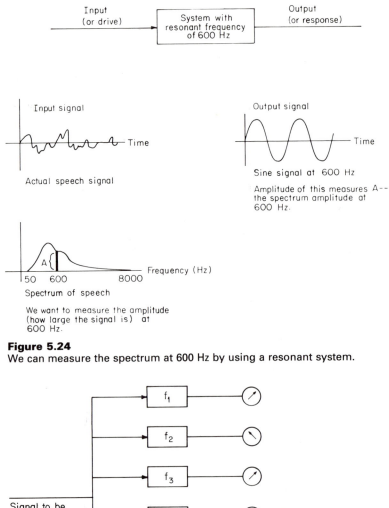

Figure 5.24
We can measure the spectrum at 600 Hz by using a resonant system.

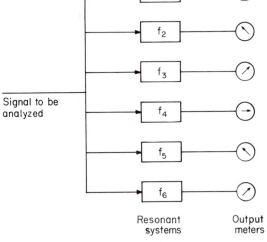

Figure 5.25
Measurement of spectrogram. This figure shows six resonant systems. (In practice, many more would be used.) Each output meter indicates the amplitude of the frequency components within the band of that particular resonant system.

every ⅓ second has a Fourier decomposition including a component at 120 Hz, the resonant frequency.

2. Canada's Bay of Fundy has astonishing tides, with the water rising as much as 35 feet. The water sloshing back and forth in the Bay has a resonant frequency of 1 cycle per 13 hours, very close to the frequency of the tides (1 per 12.4 hours). If a dam were built as was originally proposed in the 1930s to use this tidal energy for generating electricity, the resonant frequency would be modified slightly—probably toward the tidal frequency, so the tides would be even larger.

Resonance is also used in medicine. For example, nuclear magnetic resonance (NMR) or magnetic resonance imaging (MRI) allows remarkable imaging of the internal human body by capitalizing on the differences of resonant frequencies of various atoms or the resonance changes for the same atom in different molecules.

The classic example of a resonance disaster is the 1940 collapse of the Tacoma Narrows Bridge in the state of Washington. A strong, steady wind forced the bridge to oscillate with increasing amplitude until collapse occurred.

5.5 An Application of Resonance

Let us return to the discussion of personal verification (section 4-7) to illustrate an application of resonance.

Texas Instruments uses personal-verification technology to limit entrance to its corporate computing center.

To gain access, a person enters a testing booth. He inserts his I.D. card into a machine. The machine then "speaks" a four-word phrase, with each word chosen at random from one of these four columns:

Good	Ben	Swam	Near
Proud	Bruce	Called	Hard
Strong	Jean	Serve	High
Young	Joyce	Came	North

For example, the machine might say "Strong Joyce Called High." (The four words are chosen randomly, so it is difficult for an imposter to bring a pre-recorded tape of a valid speaker.)

The applicant then speaks the four words. This sound signal is fed into fourteen resonant circuits spaced in frequency from 300 to 3000 Hz to measure the spectrogram in each interval throughout the speech. The equipment automatically stretches and compresses parts of the speech until the spectrogram has the best possible match to the reference for the applicant.

If the spectrogram of the spoken phrase is not sufficiently close to the reference in the machine's memory, the equipment asks the applicant for a second phrase, then if necessary a third, and so on up to seven.

The system operates with an overall rejection rate of just less than 1/100 and an imposter-acceptance rate of 1/140. Actually the rejection rate is much lower under ideal conditions: only one person in the booth at a time, the test during daytime hours, etc. Furthermore, the rejection rate is much lower for people who have used the system often (so that the reference template incorporates normal changes in voice characteristics) and, indeed, for the vast majority of users. (A few legitimate applicants have abnormally high rejection rates.)

This application of resonance (or spectrograms) involves personal verification under carefully controlled conditions. The acoustical system (booth and microphone) can be designed to introduce very little distortion of the sound (in contrast to the problem when the applicant speaks over a telephone line). The sixteen words listed above have been chosen to give easily measured spectrogram characteristics. The machine first speaks the four-word phrase to indicate to the applicant the pronunciation and emphasis desired. The phrase is short enough that the equipment can automatically compensate for variations in speaking rate. If there is still uncertainty, additional phrases can be used.

In spite of these carefully controlled conditions, both types of errors are present at a level that would be troublesome in many applications. The basic difficulty is that the spectrogram varies so much even for a single person speaking under very different conditions. Indeed, the variation for one speaker may be as much as the variation among different speakers. Thus, the "voiceprint" (or spectrogram of an individual saying a particular word) does not have the uniqueness of the "fingerprint" in spite of the similarity in terms.

This difficulty with using the "voiceprint" for speaker identification in the criminal justice system is clear from a variety of objective or scientific studies. For example, one test used a population of 24 people and the goal was to identify which of the 24 was the speaker. Speech samples were collected from the 24, and another group was then added to listen to and identify one speaker of the 24. Even with the impressive capabilities of human perception, the error rate was 12 percent (one error in eight tests). With technology to measure spectrograms or other speech characteristics, error rates are at least twice as great.

Thus, speaker identification and personal verification technology are really useful only when the test conditions can be carefully controlled and when the applicant is anxious to cooperate.

5.6 Computer Speech

The human voice tract is a fascinating example of our use of resonance. To create different sounds as you speak, you vary the position of your tongue, lips, teeth, and so forth to change the resonant frequencies of this system. Analogously, we can use the concept of resonance to understand the current technology of *computer speech*.

There are two quite different aspects of computer speech:

1. Computer-generated speech (CGS), for communication from machines to people. Here the technology generates sound signals to convey information to human beings.

2. Automated speech recognition (ASR), where the machine listens to and interprets human speech.

The former is relatively easy technologically, at least if we are not too fussy about the quality of the sounds; many toys on the market today talk to the child. ASR, in contrast, is a very difficult technological challenge, primarily because of the great complexity of our spoken language. If engineers and linguists can develop ASR, however, the social and economic implications will be enormous. In the remainder of this chapter, we will consider briefly some of the characteristics and challenges of this technology, which is now developing rapidly.

Applications of CGS

We are familiar with a variety of applications of computer-generated speech. The toys of a few years ago have been followed by cars that talk to the driver when the trunk is open or the shoulder harness unattached, and by supermarket checkout equipment that verbally describes each item recognized by the laser reading the bar codes. It is interesting that neither of these examples has proved popular with the public; people apparently just do not like the car talking to them.

There are more significant examples. For some years an artificial larynx has been available at under $100 for the 40,000 people in the United States who have had the larynx removed surgically. Though the device is not a computer, the technology is in the category of artificial speech.

CGS is also used when production workers have a complex, detailed task, such as wiring an electronic system. The step-by-step instructions can be given verbally, with the pace controlled by the worker. The equipment frees the worker's hands and eyes for the task and is also useful when the worker is unable to read instructions.

When I call Directory Assistance for a telephone number, the operator who answers types in the name and address, then turns the response task over to the electronic equipment.

The Kurzweil Reading Machine for the blind is one of the truly remarkable technological achievements of the 1980s. The blind person holds the book or magazine to be read on the machine. An electronic device (like a TV camera) scans each letter by running around the exterior and measuring the horizontal and vertical maxima and minima. After the letters are identified, the equipment generates the corresponding sounds from a "dictionary" of how letters convert to sounds and, for English, a list of over 10,000 exceptions. (The four letters ough, for example, lead to quite different sounds in words such as ought, dough, cough, bough, and enough

Applications of ASR

There are already some applications of automated speech recognition. As so often happens, some of the early uses are frivolous, designed to capitalize on the public's love of new technology. I can buy equipment that lets me lie on the living room sofa and, with speech, control the TV set across the room—turn the power on and off, change the channel, or adjust the audio volume. A similar device is available to start my car from a location 50 feet away—on a summer morning I can start the car's engine and its air conditioning, so the car will be cool when I am ready to go.

Other applications are more significant. Section 5.5 describes the ASR for personal verification. The Digital Equipment Corporation markets a system for a radiologist to prepare routine reports to referring physicians after x-rays are analyzed. The Air Force has used ASR equipment for pilot control of an airplane, and NASA is planning to use it in the space station. ASR can also simplify the tedious task of taking inventory.

ASR research and development is aiming toward loftier goals. There is promise of early use in voice dialing of a telephone, and in well-defined tasks such as booking airline reservations. A major hope is for dictation directly to word-processing equipment. IBM is testing a system with a 5000-word vocabulary, and Kurzweil is considering 10,000 words. The complexity of the Japanese written language gives this kind of work a high priority in Japan.

Farther into the future is the hope for automated, real-time translation. The Moscow-Washington "hot line" is in reality fax equipment for the communication of written messages. Perhaps some day there will be electronic equipment that allows the U.S. President and the Soviet General Secretary to talk to one another, each speaking and hearing in his or her own language.

Automated dictation may well be common by the end of this century. This new technology will have major economic and social impacts. For example, many of the enormous number of typists and secretaries now employed by industry and government will no longer be needed unless the structure of business changes significantly.

5.7 Problems of ASR

Automated speech recognition is the part of computer speech that has the greatest implications for the quality of work and life. In this section, we will consider very briefly some of the major problems that occur as engineers try to build ASR equipment (for example, for automated dictation).

1. Spoken English contains an enormous number of ambiguities. The phrase

To be or not to be

contains four different words; each, when spoken, might correspond to several written possibilities:

To	to, too, two
Be	B, be, bee, Bea
Or	oar, or, oer, ore
Not	Not, naught, naut, knot

There are $3 \times 4 \times 4 \times 4 \times 3 \times 4$, or 2304 different ways to convert these spoken words to written form. Most of these make no sense at all, but this conclusion requires an understanding of the meaning and context of the language.

2. Spoken English has about 60 distinct sounds or *phonemes*. The word "science," for example, contains five phonemes: s, ay, uh, n, and s (in non-technical notation). We talk at a maximum rate of about 150 words per minute or 1050 phonemes per minute (18 phonemes per second)—appreciably too fast to allow full articulation. Consequently, in normal speech the phonemes roll into one another. Furthermore, the exact pronunciation of a phoneme depends on the preceding and following phonemes. For example, f is always pronounced in English as "eff" except in the word "of".

3. Our speech characteristics depend on our state of mind and many external characteristics. One challenge to ASR engineers has been to design a system with which a paraplegic individual can control his or her wheelchair, lights, window shades, telephone, etc. The wheelchair alone is a difficult challenge. We can build ASR equipment that recognizes a command such as "Stop". When the wheelchair is moving close to a descending stair, however, the customer is likely to yell "Stop" with quite unusual intonation and emphasis.

4. ASR is enormously simplified if the speaker clearly pauses between words (that is, uses interrupted speech rather than continuous speech). This is unnatural and very difficult, even when the speaker wants to cooperate. If the speaker does not carefully pause between words, the equipment cannot distinguish between two phrases such as "recognize speech" and "wreck a nice speech".

5. The enormous speech variation from one person to another means that it is relatively simple to build *speaker-dependent* ASR equipment—a system which is trained to recognize one particular speaker. The first step after the equipment is working involves "training": the speaker says each allowable word to the equipment, then types in what that word was. Thus, the equipment learns how the specific speaker says each word.

6. The vocabulary of a professional person is enormous—perhaps 20,000 words even if we do not count separately plurals, possessives, etc. Fortunately, a relatively small number of short words are used most of the time (the 100 most common words in written English have five or fewer letters, and almost all have four or fewer). In speech our working vocabulary tends to be relatively small. In designing its ASR automated-dictation system, IBM analyzed thousands of memoranda and found that 5000 words were sufficient to cover almost all situations.

These problems and difficulties mean that it is exceedingly difficult to build a system that makes an error very seldom. Fortunately, even in as complex an application as automated dictation, occasional errors are tolerable. The ASR equipment displays its interpretation on a video display terminal; the person dictating can then easily make corrections (and probably will want to make changes, in any case).

5.8 Generation of Human Speech

Both to understand ASR and to appreciate the problems of generating computer speech, we need to know a little about the generation and the resulting characteristics of human speech.

You normally speak while you are exhaling. As the air travels from the lungs through the vocal tract and out the mouth, you create the air-pressure signal that represents the desired speech. There are three quite different types of sounds in speech.

Voiced Speech

During these sounds air flows continuously through the larynx, where mechanical (muscular) vibrations cause the air flow to vary regularly. Figure 5.26 shows this signal; the fundamental frequency varies from 50 to 400 Hz for an adult. A specific person can change this fundamental frequency by less than one octave as he or she consciously tries to control the pitch. (A trained singer may vary the frequency by more than two octaves.)

The signal of figure 5.26 enters the vocal tract (throat, mouth, nose, etc.). If we made a Fourier decomposition of the signal of figure 5.26, we would find that the spectrum has the shape shown in figure 5.27. Here the fundamental frequency has been arbitrarily picked as 90 Hz. The higher frequencies have smaller amplitudes. Indeed, actual analysis shows that the spectrum falls off at the rate of 12 decibels per octave (that is, the amplitude at 360 Hz is one-fourth that at 180 Hz). Thus, most of the signal energy is at frequencies below 1000 Hz.

This signal now passes through the vocal tract, with an output which is the spoken sound. The vocal tract is a resonant system with many different resonant frequencies. Furthermore, the person speaking can change these resonant frequencies by varying the positions of the jaw and tongue, the curvature of the tongue, the opening of the mouth, the position of the teeth, and the amount of air through the nose.

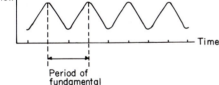

Figure 5.26
The air flow through the larynx varies regularly during voiced speech.

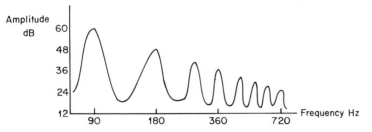

Figure 5.27
Spectrum of air flow signal entering the vocal tract during voiced speech.

Only the lowest three or four of these resonant frequencies are important: at higher frequencies, there is too little energy in the incoming air signal (figure 5.27). These resonances are called *formant frequencies*. Typically, they are as follows:

Formant 1   250–700 Hz
Formant 2   700–2500 Hz
Formant 3   2000–3500 Hz

Formants 1 and 2 are particularly important.

Figure 5.28 shows one example of the way the formant frequencies characterize the sound. We consider seven different words:

Heed   Hid   Head   Had   Hod   Hood   Who'd.

These differ primarily in the vowel sounds—the voiced speech. The figure shows that the first two formants change markedly over the range of these sounds; actually, "who'd and "hood" are quite similar sounds, so they appear very close together in the figure.

Figure 5.29 is a spectrogram for the spoken word "about". The word takes about 0.6 second. The bottom graph shows the energy or amplitude of the speech signal. During the first 0.05 second, the "a" is spoken—a vowel sound with modest energy. The bulk of the energy is during the emphasized vowel sound for "ou".

The top part of figure 5.29 shows the spectrogram. During the "ou" sound, there are four formant frequencies (the two lowest merge together in the figure). The voiced signal lasts relatively unchanged for almost 0.2 second.

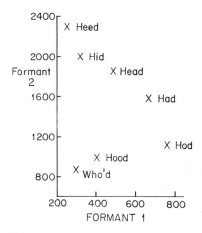

Figure 5.28
Formants 1 and 2 for various vowel sounds. (Formant 1: 250–750 Hz; formant 2: 700–2500 Hz.)

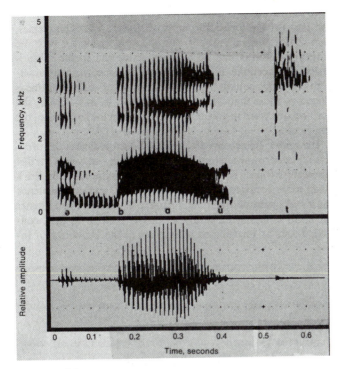

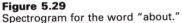

Figure 5.29
Spectrogram for the word "about."

The frequencies listed above are for normal speech. Professional singers develop much greater control and range. Sopranos, for example, have a "singing formant" in the range between 2500 and 3500 Hz to be heard above the orchestra, where the sound energy peaks well below 1000 Hz.

Unvoiced Sounds

These sounds include *fricatives* (s, sh, ge, f) and *stop consonants* (p, t, k). In the case of a fricative, there is friction as the air is pushed through a constriction. In the s sound, for example, we push the air through our teeth.

In both these cases, the speaker continuously exhales, but the air flow is turbulent because of a contraction. The spectrogram now displays no strong resonances, since the air turbulence results in a spectrum like that for noise, with many different frequencies for a short period of time.

Plosive Sounds

The third type of sound is an "explosion" of air. There is complete closure of the air path, pressure builds up behind the closure, and then the air is suddenly released. The consonants are b, d, g, p, t, and k. (p appears in both unvoiced and plosive sounds, corresponding to "spin" and "pin", respectively).

Thus, voiced speech (primarily made up of vowel sounds) is relatively easy to identify in ASR, since the signal during a vowel sound is generally strong and it lasts for many cycles of the formant frequencies. The consonants are more difficult to identify correctly. This is the reason that, even with a vocabulary limited to the ten single digits, the ASR equipment frequently confuses "nine" and "five"—the vowel sounds are similar.

5.9 Example of ASR

Credit card calling from rotary telephones would be significantly simplified if equipment were available to recognize reliably the credit card number spoken by the person calling. In the present state of the technology there are several major problems:

1. The speaker should use isolated speech, clearly pausing after each number— not the normal way of speaking, and not easily achieved even if the equipment reminds the speaker.

2. The telephone line may be noisy so it confuses the listening equipment. (Even the pause between words may not be easily measured.)

3. Most people speak too rapidly. The 14-digit number should be spread over at least 5.6 seconds, but typical times are less:

Louisville	5.33
Milwaukee	5.16
Boston	5.09

4. The zero causes problems because of the different words used:

"Zero"	29%
"Oh"	51%
Both "oh" and "zero"	9%
Other words	11%

In the last category are "double oh" for 00 and "hundred" for the terminal 00. "Zero" is preferable because there is so little energy in "oh".

5. "Five" and "nine" are frequently confused, as was mentioned above.

Thus, this ASR task, which seems so simple because we only have to recognize a vocabulary of ten words, actually pushes the technology beyond its current capability if we demand a very low error rate.

Review Questions

R5-1. What is a phoneme?

R5-2. The vocal tract with one position of the tongue, lips, teeth, and palate has several different resonances. Explain what the preceding statement means and what the sound effects are.

R5-3. After being struck, a tuning fork at 400 Hz oscillates for 20 seconds. What is the Q of this resonant device?

R5-4. An aircraft wing may have 200 different resonances. Explain this statement briefly.

R5-5. The formant frequencies describe voiced speech (for example, vowel sounds). How are these formant frequencies changed as the speaker changes vowel sounds?

R5-6. A particular device has resonances at 2, 4, and 5 Hz, each with a Q of 10. As the input is varied in frequency from 1 to 8 Hz but kept constant in amplitude, sketch the way the response changes (the amplitude of the response versus frequency).

R5-7. Each of two systems has a resonant frequency of 1000 Hz. System A has a Q of 10, system B a Q of 1000. What can be said about the selectivity of each—that is, what range of frequencies is selected?

R5-8. Current equipment for automated speech recognition requires the speaker to pause between words. Why?

R5-9. Experiments to allow phone customers to use spoken digits for "dialing" have had difficulty handling the digit 0. Why?

R5-10. There are two ways to show that an actual system (such as a tower) is resonant. Explain.

R5-11. The Q (or quality factor) of a resonant system measures what?

R5-12. Automated speech recognition has difficulty distinguishing "five" and "nine". Why?

R5-13. In automated speech recognition, what is meant by a *speaker-dependent* system?

R5-14. In automated speech recognition, what is meant by *interrupted* speech?

R5-15. "The lowest two formant frequencies are critically important." What are "formant frequencies"?

R5-16. How is Q, the quality factor of a resonant system, defined in terms of free response?

R5-17. How is Q, the quality factor of a resonant system, defined in terms of forced response?

Problems

P5-1. My car has a particularly annoying resonance in vertical vibration. If I give a hard downward push to the rear bumper, the car then oscillates at about 2 cycles per second. (This vibration dies out after a few cycles—my shock absorbers are obviously not good.) This behavior indicates a resonant frequency of about 2 Hz.

When I drive at 55 mph on the concrete expressway, the slabs of the roadway are about 45 feet long. This means that either set of wheels hits a slight bump at the divider between slabs every half-second. Thus, there is a vertical force on the front of the car as shown in figure 5.30. We have here a system that is naturally oscillatory at 2 Hz, and we are driving it with two hits per second— right at the resonant frequency. The result is that the oscillations become large: I can feel the car vibrating or shaking. At a slightly lower or higher speed, the frequency of the applied force is different. Thus, as I accelerate, I feel the uncomfortable vibration as I pass through 55 mph.

The frequency at which a car resonates changes as we go from one type of car to another. What are some of the characteristics that determine this resonant frequency?

P5-2. Artificial speech (now computer generated speech) has a long history. In 1791 Wolfgang von Kempelen in Hungary built a mechanical analog of the human vocal tract to create speech sounds. A bellows provided the air flow, reeds simulated the vocal chords, and resonant cavities substituted for the vocal tract.

Although this device more or less worked, von Kempelen suffered from a poor reputation. Earlier he had "built" an automaton to play chess. It was

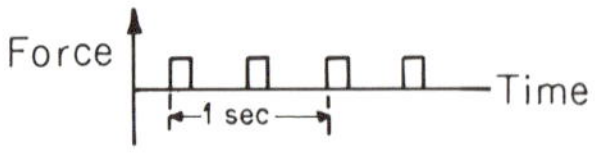

Figure 5.30
Force applied vertically to car.

subsequently discovered that the box contained a legless Polish army officer who was a chess master.

In 1820 Joseph Faber in Vienna built a machine similar to von Kempelen's and operable by a highly skilled person. At a performance in London, the machine "sang" a recognizable version of *God Save The Queen*.

At the 1939 New York World's Fair, Bell Labs demonstrated the VODER (Voice Operation DEmonstrateR). Electrical signal sources, representing buzzes and hisses, passed through resonant circuits for six formant frequencies. Operation of this machine required extensive training, since a keyboard, wrist switches, and foot pedals had to be coordinated.

Today much more elaborate systems can be realized with solid state electronics and special-purpose computers.

This brief history is another example of a the technological idea preceding by many decades the existence of the technology making the device feasible. In other cases the availability of a technology suggested an application for the first time. Discuss briefly these two avenues to technological innovation, with examples of each.

P5-3. The technology of speech synthesis (CGS) is becoming more and more common. The engineer designing the speaking equipment has to decide whether to use a male or a female voice. The male voice is cheaper—the lower frequencies permit the storage of fewer samples.

If we look at various applications, we find that male voices are used for communication to car drivers about malfunctions (such as "low oil pressure" or "trunk open"), in video games (especially involving shooting or sports), in TI Speak and Spell for teaching spelling, and in many products developed and tested in Japan. Female voices are used in supermarket checkouts, vending machines, telephone directory assistance, and department stores' order processing.

In the light of these characteristics, is this technology sexist? Does it strengthen our all-too-frequent prejudices about careers appropriate for women or men? Is this situation sufficiently serious to warrant concern?

P5-4. The following story is taken from Health Technology Case Study 26, Assistive Devices for Severe Speech Impairments, Congress of the United States Office of Technology Assessment, Washington, D. C. 20510, Dec. 1983.

When their first child was born in 1962, it wasn't obvious to the Hoyts that anything was wrong. But Ricky didn't develop as most babies do, and within a year the Hoyts—who live in Westfield, Mass.—were to learn of a disorder they had never heard of. Pediatricians told them that Ricky had a very serious case of cerebral palsy. He would never walk or be able to feed himself and was mentally retarded. "Put him in an institution," the pediatricians advised the Hoyts, "he will always be a vegetable."

Two decades later, it is true, as predicted, that Ricky cannot walk or feed himself. The Hoyts felt intuitively, however, that their son was bright. So when their minister told them they had a choice between really going to bat for him or feeling sorry for themselves forever, they decided to seek out the best professional help available.

Because the Hoyts live in Massachusetts, they took the child to the cerebral palsy unit at Children's Hospital in Boston soon after they were told of his prognosis. There, he was seen periodically by a team of rehabilitation experts, and Judy Hoyt, his mother, was instructed in how to provide the little boy with daily therapy sessions at home.

"In those days," she recalls, "a technique called 'brushing and icing' was part of the standard treatment for cerebral palsy kids like Ricky," who, in addition to their other problems, were seriously speech-impaired. The idea was that cracked ice regularly applied to their mouths and throats with a toothbrush would reduce the flaccidity of the speech-producing muscles and eventually enable these children to talk.

"Ricky and I did all his physical therapy sessions together and enjoyed most of them, but both of us hated this," she recalls. "Besides, it became very evident that we weren't getting anywhere. Ricky was 7 or 8 when the speech therapist at Children's finally had the guts to say 'Hey, this child is really never going to speak and we need to be looking for other ways for him to communicate.' To hear him say it, at last, came as a relief."

Meanwhile, Ricky had long since begun to do such things as look at the refrigerator when he was hungry or thirsty, or at the window when he wanted to go out. So Judy, more confident than ever that the child was not stupid, had already begun her own program to give Ricky a foundation for language skills.

A psychologist at Children's Hospital in Boston had suggested to her that, since Ricky couldn't even crawl, she bring the material world to him by rubbing his body with a variety of objects—some hard, soft soft, some smooth, some rough—so that he could explore these sensory realities for himself. Eventually, she hit on cutting letters out of sandpaper to enable him to learn the alphabet and begin to learn to spell. As it happened, the psychologist was a wheelchair user. This further convinced the Hoyts that handicapped people could succeed. And it was a bonus that they drew the courage from their counseling sessions with him to have another baby. Their second son, Robby, was born to the couple when Ricky was 2, and a third son, Russell, when Ricky was 6.

But, the arrival of Russell is getting ahead of the story. It is characteristic of Judy that, when Ricky was 4, she arranged to enroll him in a church-sponsored nursery school and kindergarten in exchange for her caring for the teachers' children and the children of several women who agreed to fulfill his special needs of toileting, feeding, and play during the hours he was away from home.

Judy also taught her disabled son to swim (and has since taught other disabled youngsters to swim as well). The head control Ricky gained in the process is probably largely responsible for his being able to operate both the switches that control his electric wheelchair and those for what the Hoyts call "the hope machine."

The "hope machine" is more formally known as the Tufts Interactive Communicator—the TIC for short. This machine, developed at Tufts University, uses a lighted letter display board and paper strip printer to enable nonvocal people, otherwise incapable of writing, to communicate. Had it not been for Ricky, this device might not exist.

In addition to being seen by therapists at the Children's Hospital in Boston, Ricky was also regularly seen by an occupational therapist at a cerebral palsy clinic closer to his home. One day, Judy went to a conference there, where she met Richard Foulds, then a graduate student in rehabilitation engineering at Tufts. Foulds had been toying with building a communication system for severely physically handicapped nonvocal people, and once the occupational therapist introduced him to Ricky, he agreed to make the concept a reality.

First, however, there was a major obstacle to overcome. The parts to build prototypes and a production model would cost about $5000, and at that point neither Foulds nor his university had the funds. Through a dinner dance their church sponsored and a series of bake sales, yard sales, and other activities, the Hoyts and their neighbors raised the money. Foulds began to design the machine in earnest when Ricky was 8. When Ricky was 10, the first TIC ever made for practical use became his for keeps.

The Hoyts were, of course, elated. Only one hurdle remained: except for a special education program described by Judy as "not very systematic," they had never been able to get Ricky into public school. They had succeeded in pressuring the authorities to move the special education program from space in an old age hospital into the back room of an actual school. But every time they attempted to have Ricky go to classes with able-bodied youngsters of normal intelligence, school officials adamantly refused.

Still undaunted, the Hoyts resorted to a kind of "back door" approach. They hired tutors, among them some youngsters who were proficient at science and arithmetic. These children came to like Ricky and to realize that he was as capable of learning as they were. "He doesn't need to be in a special class," they told their teachers. And so even before Ricky was 12—when the law in Massachusetts changed to make "mainstreaming" his right and he was admitted to fifth grade—he was allowed to attend regular classes in science and arithmetic. With the change in the law and Ricky's TIC, the schools could also no longer believe that his parents might be answering for him when he was tested. The answers Ricky programed the device to produce were unmistakably his own.

Ricky is 21 now. He graduated from high school with the class of 1983, is taking two courses at Westfield State College in Westfield, Mass., and has been admitted to Boston University. He plans a major in computer programing and will enter the University in January 1984. Meanwhile, he has been supplied with new communication equipment, designed and assembled by Richard Foulds and his colleagues at Tufts University, largely from Radio Shack components, which has both synthetic voice and print-out capabilities.

There are probably about one million people in the United States who are unable to speak because of congenital impairments, severe illness including stroke and trauma, or progressive disorders of the central nervous system. The OTA report describes the technology available to help these individuals communicate.

The development of such "prosthetic" devices has moved slowly. Discuss briefly the social, economic, and political factors that have led to this very slow progress.

P5-5. The exchange below is from a Bell Laboratories system for making airline reservations.

Machine: This is the Bell Laboratories flight information system. May I help you?
User: I want one first-class seat on flight number three one to Denver on Sunday.
Machine: I am sorry the flight is not available on Sunday.
User: I would like to leave on Saturday.
Machine: Flight number three one leaves New York at nine forty-five A.M.; arrives in Denver at one ten P.M.
User: What is the flight time?
Machine: The flight time is five hours and twenty-five minutes.
User: How many stops are there on the flight?
Machine: This flight makes one stop.
User: I want a nonstop flight.

To understand better how the system works, consider one line: the user's question "What is the flight time?" The ASR equipment first determines that there are five separate words. (The user must pause between words.) Then it tries to identify each word:

Candidates for word no. 1			20 frames
What	1 .	.180	

Candidates for word no. 2			29 frames
Is	1	.270	

Candidates for word no. 3			24 frames
Nine	1	.343	
One	1	.278	
Six	1	.370	
Seven	1	.242	
The(alt)	1	.314	

Candidates for word no. 4		24 frames
Some	1	.296
Flight	1	.341
One	1	.414
Three	1	.390

Candidates for word no. 5		28 frames
Nine	1	.378
Oh	1	.390
Time	1	.291
One	1	.411
Seven	1	.396
Times	1	.315

There is only one candidate ("what") for word 1. This is quite close (only 0.180 away) from the machine's analysis of the word "what". For word 3, there are five promising candidates; the best is "seven".

After this analysis, the machines decides the sentence was

What is seven some time?

This sentence makes no sense, so the equipment looks for the next most likely sentence. In this fashion, the first sentence that makes sense is

What is the flight time?

After the ASR equipment interprets each statement or question of the user, it responds. What is the dominant characteristic of each response? If this description represents the current state of the technology, are we close to a system useful for making airline reservations?

Chapter 6
The Engineer Looks at Hearing

You are driving in very heavy traffic when suddenly you hear the sound of a siren. It is obviously coming from an ambulance, fire truck, or police car. Your immediate reaction is to move your car out of the way. You listen intently to determine the direction of the sound. One moment the siren's wail seems to come from behind you; perhaps you should go through the approaching intersection where there is room to pull aside. However, if it is coming from the side street, you should stop where you are. As you sit there trying to make a decision, you wonder, "Why aren't sirens designed so it is easy to know the direction from which the sound is coming?"

Unfortunately, the design of such a siren presents problems. The choice of the particular sound transmitted from a siren has to satisfy several conflicting requirements:

1. The sound should be markedly different from the sounds people normally hear, so that the siren alerts the listener to the emergency situation. However, it is more difficult to recognize the source direction for an unfamiliar sound than a familiar one.

2. The sound should be relatively high in frequency (for example, 2000 Hz and up) to attract attention. On the other hand, the sound must be clearly heard by most people, and many elderly people hear poorly when sound frequencies are as high as 4000 Hz.

3. The horn sending out the sound signal can not be too directional (pointed in one specific direction). While we are primarily interested in alerting cars directly ahead of the emergency vehicle, the sound should also warn motorists moving on the cross streets. To do this, the siren must send out a signal over nearly an arc of 180° ahead of the ambulance (figure 6.1). The sound will then

travel down side streets. However, the sound from the siren will hit the buildings on the sides of the street, bounce off the buildings, and go ricocheting in many directions. Thus, even the driver of a car directly ahead of the ambulance may be confused by the direction of the source of the siren (figure 6.2).

4. Most of the sound will reach the driver through an open window of the car. If a window on the left side of the car is open, the driver will think the sound comes from the left. If a window on the right is open, he will believe the sound comes from the right.

5. The sounds must be loud enough to catch the driver's attention even if the car windows are all closed and the radio is on. This creates additional problems for some people who find sound discrimination difficult when it is too loud.

This seemingly trivial design of a siren is actually an example of a problem with no good engineering solution. The propagation characteristics of sound vary so much from one location to another that it is difficult to determine general guidelines. As a result, several, very different sirens are used in different cities, and there is no simple way to decide which one is best.

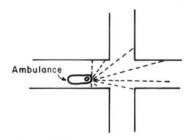

Figure 6.1
A siren sends out a signal in an arc of 180° ahead of an ambulance.

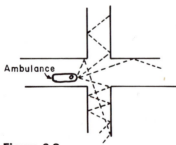

Figure 6.2
Sound bounces off buildings on both sides of the street.

Furthermore, the design problem is complicated by our incomplete understanding of how a human being hears—how sound direction is determined,
which signals are best to catch attention, how hearing capabilities vary over the
population, and so on. This chapter considers what is known about human
hearing and how audio or sound technology can be designed to match those
human capabilities.

6.1 The "Black Box" Approach to Hearing

A baby learns to speak by mimicking the sounds made by older people. A small
child learns to make words from these sounds, then phrases from the words, and
finally sentences from the phrases. By the age of three, most children have
learned many of the intricacies of the language—all by listening to the
conversations around them. Thus, without our sense of hearing, we would lose
the primary way we communicate with other people.

The engineer's interest in hearing arises from the need to design a wide range
of sound and acoustical systems so that they match the characteristics of the
human ear. An understanding of hearing is essential for intelligent design of the
telephone, radio, hi-fi, and orthotic devices (hearing aids) for those who have
serious hearing deficiencies. In addition, to protect the public against noise
pollution, we need an understanding of what is harmful to our ears and nervous
system.

Thus, the engineer looks at hearing quite differently from the physician:

1. The engineer is primarily interested in *normal* hearing, the physician in the
malfunctioning of the hearing system.

2. The engineer looks at the *external characteristics*: that is, what type of sound,
how loud a sound, how high pitched a sound, etc., a person can hear. The
engineer wants to know when a sound is painful, what sounds are pleasant. His
only interest in the physical structure and functioning of each separate part of
the ear is in relation to the general characteristics of hearing.

This second point is particularly important. To design a telephone, for
example, the engineer must know when the user will be able to understand
spoken speech. How strong must the sound signal be coming into the ear?
What fidelity is necessary to allow the listener complete understanding of the
conversation and even recognition of the person talking?

To attempt to answer these questions, the engineer looks at hearing as a
"black box"—a device with a certain input and a response (figure 6.3). In this
case, the input is the sound signal arriving at the ear; the response (the output)

is the listener's understanding of the sound—that is, the brain's interpretation. For the design of audio equipment (a telephone, for example), the engineer does not need to know the details of what goes on inside the "black box" (figure 6.4); he or she needs to know only what hearing input signal is necessary to give the desired output, or what is the input-output relationship.

This "black box" approach means that we can describe a system (in this case, hearing) by its input-output relationship rather than by the details of how it is constructed. Furthermore, we can focus on only those characteristics which are important to us. For example, we may describe a car's engine performance by stating the car can accelerate from a stop to 60 mph in 10 seconds. This is an input-output relationship that omits entirely any description of how the engine and car are built; we focus on only the acceleration capability and are not concerned at all with noise, air pollution, driver comfort, etc. The description represents the car as a device that has

Input—full throttle
Output—acceleration to 60 mph in 10 seconds.

The term "black box" means simply that we do not need to see inside, or that we do not need to understand the role of each of the hundreds of separate parts. Instead, we are describing hearing by the performance capabilities of the system.

Why is the concept of the "black box" approach so important in engineering? It seems to be a trivial idea—we simply describe a system by the way it performs and don't worry about the detailed interplay of the separate parts. The answer is that the "black box" viewpoint allows us to design devices to change the operation of the system without waiting for scientists to learn why the system operates as it does. In the hearing example, we can have hearing aids without knowing why the patient has a deficiency. Technology can move ahead without

Figure 6.3
The engineer views hearing as a complete system, with an input and an output.

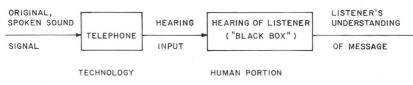

Figure 6.4
The complete telephone-hearing system.

waiting for science; indeed, technology can drive the science by indicating to the scientist what should be studied.

Medicine provides many examples of the "black box" approach. A drug has a desired, known effect and is used, even though the biologist may have no real understanding of why it works. In this sense, the doctor is like the engineer: the physician has to make decisions and solve problems in the real world, even though scientific knowledge is lacking.

The medical example also illustrates the point that the "black box" viewpoint is useful only until science catches up with the technology. Drugs have unanticipated, long-term side effects because we don't understand what is going on biologically. Similarly, better hearing aids will be designed when we know in greater detail how human hearing works. Thus, the "black box" approach is a substitute for good but missing science.

6.2 Frequency Response of Human Hearing

The Fourier Theorem states that any sound signal can be decomposed into pure-frequency components. Therefore, we first ask: What frequencies can be detected by human hearing (figure 6.5)?

Minimum Frequency
The minimum frequency which the normal person can recognize as a tone is about 15 Hz. Sound signals are air-pressure variations arriving at the ear; if the sound is loud enough (the signal strong enough), our tactile sensors also respond—we "feel" the pressure variation against our bodies. In this sense, we can detect sound signals at frequencies down to zero, but these are sensed as forces rather than sound or musical tones.

Many animals can hear sounds at frequencies much lower than 15 Hz. Some scientists believe that farm animals may be able to hear the extremely low-frequency sounds and vibrations that precede an earthquake; perhaps this explains the erratic behavior of animals that is frequently reported before a quake. Pigeons far surpass people in low-frequency hearing; perhaps they navigate by listening to the winds whistling through distant mountains (figure 6.6).

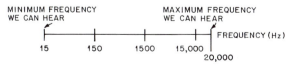

Figure 6.5
Frequencies we can hear.

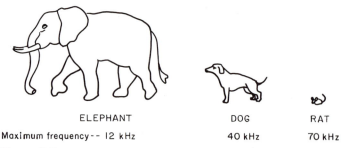

ELEPHANT   DOG   RAT

Maximum frequency-- 12 kHz   40 kHz   70 kHz

Figure 6.6
For mammals, the highest frequency of hearing increases as the size of the animal decreases. The best correlation seems to be with the distance between the ears. The elephant measures about 42 inches between the ears and has a maximum frequency of 12 kHz, dogs go to 40 kHz, rats to about 70 kHz. Consequently, a dog whistle at 22 kHz does not disturb people, but is perceived by the dog. Whales and dolphins are exceptions to this general principle; they have a response up to 100 kHz, since the very high frequencies are necessary for precise echolocation. As another example of the matching of hearing capabilities to the needs for survival, moths can go as high as 240 kHz in order to hear the sonar signals emitted by their predators, the bats. Mosquitos, in contrast, hear only in the narrow range from 150 to 550 Hz.

Maximum Frequency

The maximum frequency that a human can hear varies strongly from person to person. Young people with excellent hearing can detect tones up to 20,000 Hz (20 kHz); infants may be able to detect even higher tones. The maximum typically falls off with age for two reasons:

1. The tissues in the inner ear lose their resiliency with age, just as skin tissue does. (Pinch the skin on the back of your hand and observe how long it takes to return to normal. This time will be markedly longer for a senior citizen.)

2. The nerves deteriorate, especially as a result of loud noises, certain drugs, and inflammation from disease.

Frequency Discrimination

One of the remarkable capabilities of the human being is the ability to discriminate between two frequencies that are very close together. For low frequencies (below 2000 Hz) we can distinguish two notes differing in frequency by 3 or 4 Hz. For example, if you hear two notes, one at 120 Hz and the other at 124 Hz, you will realize one is at a higher frequency than the other. If you hear two notes, one at 120 Hz and the other at 122 Hz, they will sound the same to you. Thus, we are able to detect about 600 different frequencies in the low range between 20 and 2000 Hz (figure 6.7).

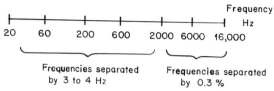

Figure 6.7
Human ability to discriminate between frequencies close to one another.

When we come to the high frequency range (over 2000 Hz), the ear behaves differently. Now, when we hear two notes that are just distinguishable from each other, the upper frequency is 0.3 percent higher than the lower (that is, the upper is the lower plus 0.003 times the lower).

In other words, at 10,000 Hz, we can detect a change of

10,000 × 0.003, or 30 Hz.

Thus we can distinguish among notes at 9,970, 10,000, and 10,030 Hz.

Each different frequency is 0.3 percent higher than the next lower. Hence, the rule of 72 (box 6.1) tells us there are

$$\frac{7.2}{0.3} \text{, or } 240$$

distinguishable frequencies per octave (for each doubling). Hence, from 2 kHz to 16 kHz, where there are three octaves, we can distinguish 3 × 240, or 720, different frequencies.

Thus, the human being can detect about 1320 different frequencies (600 from the low part, 720 from the high portion)—a truly astounding achievement with a device as small as the inner ear. This capability indicates generally how we are able to communicate so much information through speech and sound.

In this section, we have looked at the frequency capabilities of human hearing. All of our information came from *external* measurements: we generate sound signals of various frequencies to determine what people can hear. We have never asked what goes on *inside* the ear or brain, how hearing is accomplished, or what physiological trait makes it impossible for us to hear a dog whistle. Yet from this "black box" approach, we know, for example, that an ideal hi-fi system should reproduce faithfully all frequencies from 15 Hz to 20 kHz (the range of frequencies that we can hear). From a study of the external or input-output characteristics of hearing, we have begun to define the desirable characteristics of the technology which is to match the human user.

> **Rule of 72**
>
> The rule of 72 describes compound interest or exponential growth. If a sum of money is invested with P percent interest per year compounded, the investment doubles in about 72/P years.
>
> Thus, if the population of Mexico City, 15 million in 1980, grows at 3.6 percent per year, it will double in 72/3.6 or 20 years—it will be 30 million by the year 2000. In our example of frequency discrimination, P is 0.3 percent: each frequency is 0.3 percent higher than the preceding one.

Box 6.1

6.3 Sensitivity of Human Hearing

Put your forefingers in your ears to block the transmission of sounds arriving through the air. The noise you hear is the movement of the muscles of your fingers and arms.

This dramatic demonstration shows the remarkable sensitivity of human hearing—that is, the ability to detect very weak sounds. Indeed, if your hearing were slightly more sensitive, you would hear the vibrations of your head as you walk and the noise of your body and muscle movements. Thus, hearing is as sensitive as feasible with the constraint that we don't want to be bothered by irrelevant noises.

To discuss sensitivity further, we first must recognize that the weakest signal we can hear depends on the frequency of that sound. As the last section indicates, people can hear frequencies from about 20 Hz to 16,000 Hz. At each end of this range, our hearing sensitivity gradually disappears. For example, we can detect a signal of 30 Hz only if it is very loud (figure 6.8), but we can hear a note at 960 Hz that is very soft.

Decibels, or dB

In figure 6.8, the amplitude or strength of the sound signal is plotted vertically in dB or *decibels*—the customary way to measure the loudness or amplitude of sound. What does this term mean?

Normally at sea level the atmospheric pressure is about 14.7 pounds per square inch. If we have a container covered by a membrane (figure 6.9) and we pump all the air out from under the membrane, the atmosphere presses down on this membrane with a force of 14.7 pounds on every square inch. This is the air pressure that exists because of the atmosphere above us; the pressure is present even when there is no sound.

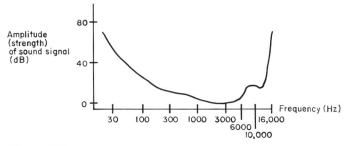

Figure 6.8
Sensitivity of an average person with good hearing. The plot shows the minimum or weakest signal the average person can hear at each frequency.

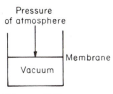

Figure 6.9
The atmosphere presses down on a membrane with a force of 14.7 pounds per square inch.

Now suppose a sound starts at the time t_1 (figure 6.10). Then the pressure in the air starts to vary a *very small* amount around 14.7. If the sound is *very* loud, the pressure may rise to 14.71, and it may drop later to 14.69. Usually the pressure variation is very much less than this amount.

The weakest signal detectable by a person occurs when the frequency is just above 2000 Hz; we call the amplitude or size of this weakest noticeable pressure variation 0 dB (figure 6.11). Actually, the pressure then varies sinusoidally with an amplitude which is 0.2×10^{-9} (0.2 billionths) of atmospheric pressure. As the sound wave passes through the air, the pressure (normally 14.7 pounds per square inch) is varying *very, very* slightly. (If in a small volume there are 1 trillion molecules with no sound, there are a few extra molecules when the peak of the sound wave passes through.)

Let us consider a simple sound signal—a pure note at 2000 Hz. The weakest signal we can hear is a very small pressure variation, which we call 0 dB. Now let's make the signal bigger or louder. When it is 100 times the minimum, we have 40 dB; 1000 times the minimum, 60 dB. Each time we *multiply* the pressure amplitude by 10, we add 20 dB.

The maximum signal the human can hear corresponds to the point at which severe pain and physical damage occur; this is approximately 140 dB, which is

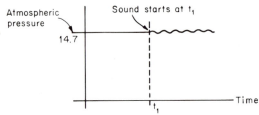

Figure 6.10
A sound, starting at t₁, causes a pressure variation.

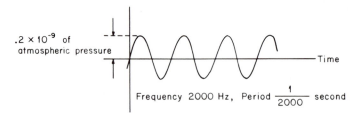

Figure 6.11
The weakest sound signal detectable. A sound signal this size is called 0 dB.

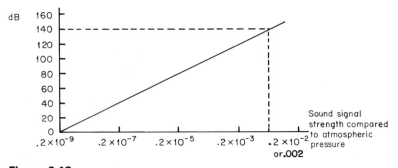

Figure 6.12
Meaning of dB sound level.

0.002 of atmospheric pressure, or about 0.03 pounds per square inch. (If the sound signal hits the front of me and I present an area of 700 square inches, I feel a force of 21 pounds spread over my body.)

Thus, the ear has an astonishing "dynamic range." We can hear sounds varying in amplitude so that the strongest sound is 10 million times the weakest. To avoid the large numbers (10,000,000 for example) required to describe this tremendous range of amplitudes, we describe the sound intensity in terms of dB. The range then corresponds to 140 dB—each additional 20 dB means that the actual pressure variation is multiplied by 10.

Weber-Fechner Law

There is another, more important reason for using dB instead of the amplitude of the pressure signal. Regardless of the existing level of sound, people are able to detect an increase of about 3 dB (which is equivalent to a 40 percent increase in amplitude). In other words, if I am talking to you at a sound level of 70 dB (typical of conversation), you notice I have raised my voice if the level goes up to 73 dB. If I'm using a power mower and the noise level rises perceptibly, it has increased perhaps from 115 to 118 dB. In both cases, the increase in pressure variation is 40 percent, although in the latter case the actual increase is much greater since we started from a much stronger sound signal.

Thus, when we say that a human being can detect a 3 dB increase in sound level, we are stating that a 40 percent increase in amplitude is just noticeable. This means that

$$\frac{\text{Change in intensity}}{\text{Intensity}} \text{ is } 0.40 \, .$$

Engineers call this type of response "logarithmic." We respond to a *particular percentage* change—the louder the noise, the more it must change to be detectable.

This characteristic of the human senses was first noted by Weber in 1834, and Fechner shortly thereafter pointed out that mathematically it is a logarithmic response. The Weber-Fechner law says that our senses (sight, touch, hearing, and so on) generally respond in this logarithmic way. If I press on your wrist with a certain force, you feel it. Perhaps I have to press with 25 percent more force for you to realize the force has increased. In the next step, I'll have to press with 25 percent more force than the last time I pressed your wrist. Again, if I start with 1 unit for force, successive amounts are

1   1.25   1.56   1.95   2.44   3.05.

Each number is 25 percent higher than the preceding number (figure 6.13). According to the Weber-Fechner Law, this same behavior describes vision, heat sensing, pain, smell, taste, and so on, although in each case the percentage increase (40 percent for hearing) may be different.

As measurements of hearing, vision, smell, and the tactile senses have become more precise, it has become apparent that the Weber-Fechner Law is only an approximation, and that there are exceptions. However, the law does generally describe our response to sounds of different amplitudes.

Loudness

Loudness refers to our *perception* of the amplitude of the sound. Thus, the amplitude is actually the size of the pressure wave or the corresponding measure in dB; the loudness is the resulting human interpretation. (Pitch and frequency have comparable meanings. Frequency is the scientific, measurable term; pitch is the human perception of the sound. The musical note middle A is set by world agreement at 440 Hz. A conductor can have his orchestra members tune their instruments to a few cycles higher if he wishes, with the pitch still middle A.)

When do people judge one sound twice as loud as another? The answer of course varies with the individual, but usually the two sounds are about 10 dB apart: a sound at 100 dB seems about twice as loud as a similar sound at 90 dB.

Frequency of Peak Sensitivity

Peak hearing sensitivity occurs in human beings at 2000 Hz or a slightly higher frequency, as shown in figure 6.8. This means we can hear the softest tone when it is at about 2000 Hz. This high a frequency is confusing, since we might guess hearing would be reasonably well matched to speech. The strongest components in the speech spectrum are at a much lower frequency, typically a few hundred hertz. Thus, hearing is most effective in a range where speech (or even music) has relatively little energy.

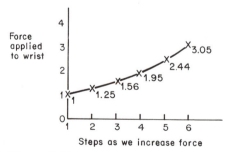

Figure 6.13
Force is increased 25 percent more each time. This is a logarithmic response.

Now we can begin to think rationally about the siren question with which the chapter began. Obviously the siren should emit a sound signal with a lot of energy from 1 kHz to 4 kHz—the region where hearing is most sensitive and also where the sounds are markedly different from those of speech.

6.4 Audiometry

When you go to an ear specialist to have your hearing measured, he or she uses an audiometer—a device to measure hearing. You listen to a sound at 2000 Hz; the loudness is reduced until you are on the border between hearing and not hearing it. This measurement is repeated at frequencies, usually from about 20 Hz to 8000 Hz.

The physician then has a record of two plots (called audiograms), one for each ear, which show how sensitive your hearing is (figure 6.14). Zero dB is the normal peak sensitivity; –20 dB means that your hearing at that frequency is down 20 dB; that is, the sound has to be 20 dB larger for you to notice it. Thus, the audiogram shows the ear's sensitivity as the frequency changes.

Audiometry is a relatively young technology. Until 1850, the tester simply whispered as he moved away from the patient, and the patient then indicated when the whisper no longer could be heard. Such a crude test, in which results were rarely repeatable, was still extensively used in testing school children until the last few decades.

By 1850 tuning forks were available to generate pure-frequency signals and permit the sketching of an audiogram. By 1900 the tuning fork signal entered a telephone, and reached the patient's ear through a telephone receiver. By 1920, electronic audio oscillators replaced the tuning fork and permitted detailed audiograms over the full range of frequencies. Seven years later Western Electric came out with an audiometer using phonograph recordings; an electronic buzzer masked the sound entering the ear not being tested. The

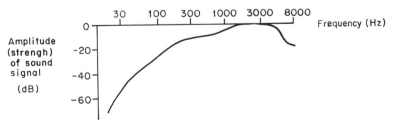

Figure 6.14
An audiogram measuring sensitivity of the ear. This audiogram shows that the person's hearing ability is less at low and high frequencies. The curve is just figure 6.8 inverted.

extensive hearing damage suffered by veterans of World War II and the concurrent, rapid development of electronics led to the wide range of excellent audiometers available during the last thirty years.

Bone Conduction

So far in this chapter, we have emphasized the primary hearing channel: the entrance of the airborne sound wave into the ear through the protruding outer ear. Sound signals can also reach the inner ear through the bones of the head.

Take a pencil and hold it between your lips (not your teeth). Tap the outside part of the pencil, and you'll hear a faint sound. Now grasp the pencil with your teeth and repeat the tapping. The sound is loud and clear—the pencil vibration is tightly coupled by your teeth to the bones which send the vibration into the inner ear.

Bone conduction provides an alternate path to the inner ear—a path which is particularly effective in transmitting the low frequencies. When you talk, the sound reaches your inner ear both through bone conduction and through the air. When you record your voice and then listen to the recording, you do not have the strong low frequencies that you normally hear through bone conduction; hence, your recorded voice seems to be unnatural to you, and missing the soothing low frequencies.

To avoid the military draft, some young men claimed air-conduction deafness in one ear. This can be checked with simple electronic equipment. As the man speaks, his voice is recorded, then played back through a loudspeaker with a time delay of perhaps one second. The good ear is blocked, but the deaf ear is open. If the man is actually deaf, he will hear his own speech only through bone conduction and will have no difficulty speaking. If the deaf ear hears, he will hear his speech delayed by a second and will soon be babbling incoherently.

Thomas Edison had air-conduction deafness as a result of a childhood accident. In his laboratory in Fort Myers, Florida, visitors can see the table on which the experimental phonograph rotated. The edge of the table is filled with tooth marks where Edison bit tightly to improve the bone conduction as he listened to the phonograph playing.

6.5 Other "Black Box" Characteristics

The previous sections focus on the frequency and amplitude characteristics of human hearing—the two features which are simple to measure. Throughout this chapter, we have discussed the response to sound signals at a *single frequency*. These pure notes (or sinusoids) arise only when we are listening to a tuning fork. Actual sounds are a *combination* of many different frequencies.

In speech, the frequency content changes with different phonemes and syllables.

When the sound signal is complex, several other external phenomena are observed, some of which are not at all understood. To show the complexity of human hearing, we will mention only a few of these characteristics.

Masking

One sound can be made completely inaudible by the presence of a second sound. A lower-frequency sound tends to mask one of a high frequency. One sound can mask another arriving later, and, strangely, the later one may mask the earlier sound. The difficulty in explaining such phenomena arises because they are probably the result of the brain processing the information arriving on the auditory nerve, and we have a very inadequate understanding of how the brain operates.

Interrupted Speech

The human listener can fill in interruptions of the incoming sound signal. Here we refer to very brief intervals when no sound arrives. The young, normal person unconsciously fills in these breaks or interruptions in the sound and doesn't notice their existence. One sign of hearing deterioration with age is a diminished ability to interpret such interrupted speech.

Direction-Finding

Standing in an open field and watching a soccer game, you hear your name called. You turn your eyes toward the direction of the sound to identify the speaker. Obviously, our hearing has direction-finding capability (although not with the accuracy of the vision sense).

How do we then measure the arrival angle of the sound? Apparently there are four different ways; three of these have been known for many years:

1. If the sound has a clear start (for example, if it is a click), and if it is coming from your right side, it reaches the right ear before the left—the sound has farther to travel to your left ear. The farther to the right the sound is, the greater the delay before it reaches the left ear (figure 6.16).

Figure 6.15
A listener can estimate the direction or angle a sound is coming from.

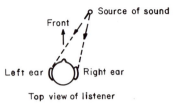

Figure 6.16
If the sound is coming from the right side, it reaches the right ear before the left—it has farther to travel to the left ear.

2. If the signal is a pure note (a sine wave) or close to it, the peaks and zero crossings occur later at the ear farther from the source. In figure 6.17, the signal at the left ear has its "phase delayed" in comparison to the signal at the right ear. Just as in case 1, this difference results from the different travel distances to the left and right ears.

3. The head creates sound shadows just like light shadows. The head blocks some of the sound, hence the sound is stronger at the ear toward the source. There is some bending of the sound around the head, so the shadow is not complete (figure 6.18).

Until the 1960s, scientists believed that these three methods were the only way we could determine the direction of a sound. A simple experiment illustrates that there must also be another method. You sit quietly and blindfolded in a chair facing person A (figure 6.19). There are three people helping with the experiment. Person A is directly in front and person B is directly behind you. One of the two claps his hands. You have no difficulty deciding which of the two clapped. If a similar noise is generated over your head by person C, you recognize that direction as well.

From any of these three source positions, the sound reaches your two ears simultaneously, the signals at the ears are exactly in phase, and the amplitudes are identical at your two ears. Yet you can determine the direction. How?

One explanation might be that you wobble your head slightly during the sound (just as a radar antenna is wobbled to find echo direction), so that the sound doesn't come from directly in front. However, you still have the same capability even if your head is rigidly clamped, so wobbling is not the answer.

There is another clue: when the sound is totally unfamiliar, you lose the direction-finding ability. This observation suggests that the sound reaching your eardrum may be changed according to the direction it comes from. Careful measurements at the eardrum have shown this is true.

Figure 6.20 is a grossly simplified picture of the external ear up to the eardrum. Here we show two different ways a single sound signal can reach the

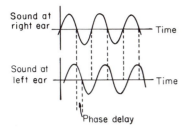

Figure 6.17
Sound at left ear is delayed because of greater distance traveled, so at left ear zero crossings and peaks occur later than at right ear. This picture is for sound originating on the right side of the listener.

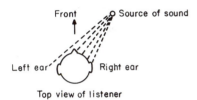

Figure 6.18
The head creates sound shadows just as any solid object creates light shadows. Some of the sound is blocked by the head.

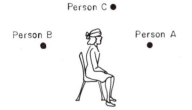

Figure 6.19
Direction-finding test.

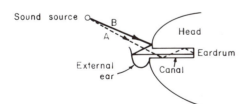

Figure 6.20
Two different ways a sound signal can reach the eardrum.

eardrum. There are actually many different paths, since the sound does bend around obstructions. The signal at the eardrum is the combination of all these different signals.

What these different paths are depends on the direction of the source. When the source is directly behind the listener, the paths tend to give signals which add cumulatively when the frequency is around 1000 Hz. Thus, when the source is behind you, you hear the familiar sound, but with the spectrum amplified or enhanced around 1000 Hz. When the source is overhead, high frequencies (over 8000 Hz) are boosted; when the sound comes from the front, frequencies below 500 Hz and above 3000 Hz are accentuated.

Thus, the sound is distorted (or changed) in different ways, depending on the direction of the source. When you listen to a *familiar* sound, you unconsciously measure this distortion and thereby estimate direction.

To build a superb stereo hi-fi system, engineers can intentionally distort the signal to give the listener the impression that each source (for example, each instrument in an orchestra) is coming from a desired direction. The only trouble is that the electronics are then extremely expensive.

Cocktail-Party Effect

One last external characteristic of hearing emphasizes the complexity of this sense and our relatively poor scientific understanding of it. When you are engrossed in conversation with another person, you can hear his words with reasonable accuracy even though the total sound level in the room may be much greater than the amplitude of his speech sounds. In other words, you can selectively pick out his words even in a very noisy background. This phenomenon is called the "cocktail-party effect," from the 1950s when cocktail parties were common social gatherings; if it were discovered today, it probably would be termed the "disco effect."

How human hearing achieves this capability is not known at the present time; the cocktail-party effect is a capability engineers are unable to duplicate with even elaborate electronic equipment. The astonishing feature is that the noise (the unwanted sound from other people talking) has essentially the same spectrum as the particular speech sound you are listening to.

In this section, we have looked at a few "black box" or external characteristics of human hearing—features which are interesting and important, but which together give us only a very partial picture of how we hear.

There are really two major difficulties in trying to develop an input-output model or description of hearing:

1. The output is the person's perception or interpretation of the arriving sound signal. In response to sound, the ear and the auditory nerve feed electrical

signals into the brain; there these signals are processed in a way we really don't understand at all. Before we can hope to understand the cocktail-party effect (or even direction-finding), we probably need to know how the brain recognizes particular spoken words and sounds.

2. There is enormous variation in hearing characteristics from person to person. Whenever we study human or social systems, we can only derive descriptions in terms of average or maximum or minimum capabilities—at best in very general terms.

In spite of these limitations, a large amount of technology has been developed over the past few decades for sound, music, and speech. To a great extent this technology is designed on the basis of the "black box" description of hearing discussed in this chapter. Section 6.6 considers one example of this technology, the stethoscope.

A Retrospective View
After considering the capabilities of human hearing, we can begin to understand the importance of the Fourier Theorem and the spectrum. At this point, we pause to consider once again the meaning of the Fourier Theorem.

The Fourier Theorem This theorem simply states that any signal can be represented by a sum of sinusoids. For example, suppose I plot the distance I travel by car when I go from my office parking lot to my home 20 miles away. The plot might have the shape shown in figure 6.21.

The first minute, I am warming up the car and backing out of my parking space. From minute 8 to minute 11, I am caught in a traffic jam and don't move. Thus, the plot shows the total distance traveled at any moment during the 32 minutes it takes me to reach my home.

This distance traveled as time progresses is a signal. Since it is a signal, the Fourier Theorem says that this signal is equivalent to a sum of sinusoids. We

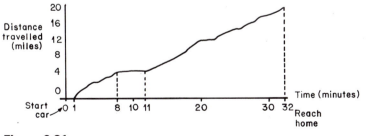

Figure 6.21
Distance traveled.

would need thousands or millions of sinusoids to add up to the signal shown in the graph above, but we could find these. Each sine component would have a *frequency* and an *amplitude*—that is, the above signal has a spectrum.

Sound Signals   Sound signals are pressure variations. In the air, the signals travel outward from the source of the sound at a velocity of about 1120 feet per second.

What frequencies are present in sound signals? If I slam a book down on the top of my desk, a sound results which has components at many different frequencies. In general, sound signals may have frequencies from zero to millions of hertz. Figure 6.22 shows this range of frequencies.

The sound from a book hitting a desk includes components having frequencies in this entire range, but many of these components are very small.

Human Hearing   Even the healthiest human beings hear only sounds from about 12 Hz to 18,000 Hz. Below this lower limit, we have sounds of earthquakes or the wind roaring through the mountains. At much higher frequencies (1 MHz and up), there are the sound signals used by an obstetrician to take pictures of a fetus.

Thus, we hear only a small portion of the sound signals existing around us. What we actually hear may differ markedly from the actual sound. And since your hearing and mine differ, we perceive the same sounds quite differently.

When familiar sounds occur, what each of us hears is unique to the individual. As will be shown in the next section, a physician is accustomed to the sounds heard through a conventional stethoscope, and hence has little interest in an improved stethoscope that gives much clearer but very different transmittal of a patient's chest sounds.

Figure 6.22
Range of frequencies in sound.

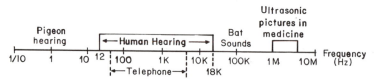

Figure 6.23
Uses of sound frequencies.

The Fourier Theorem (that is, the spectrum of the sound signal) permits us to understand which parts of the sound are perceived by human hearing. Therefore, the frequency characterization of hearing permits the design of technology matched to the characteristics of the human user. Indeed, as we will see later in this chapter, the ear analyzes the incoming sound wave partly by determining the frequency (or Fourier) components. Thus, the Fourier Theorem is essential for the understanding of sound communications.

6.6 The Stethoscope

Engineering, or new technology, occasionally has an amazingly strong impact on a particular profession. For example, the invention of the stethoscope profoundly changed the practice of medicine.

In the mid-1700s, the physician diagnosed almost entirely from visual observation and by listening to the patient's complaints. The standards of modesty did not allow physical contact, so the doctor could not touch the patient or manually probe to find the exact location of the pain. Since there were very few effective medicines anyway, errors in diagnosis often made little difference.

In 1761 Leopold Avenbrugger of Vienna described the technique of percussion for diagnosing chest problems. Here the doctor taps sharply on the patient's chest or back, then listens for echoes. Unfortunately, Avenbrugger's technique did not win general acceptance for two principal reasons:

1. He did not describe accurately the sounds corresponding to different illnesses.

2. He did not confirm his diagnoses with autopsies, so there was no indication the technique really worked.

Occasionally a doctor did use percussion or was even bold enough to place his ear on the patient's chest (auscultation, or listening for lung and heart sounds).

In Paris in 1819 Rene-Theophile-Hyacinthe Laennec published a report entitled "On Mediate Auscultation" in which he described the stethoscope. (He chose the title as follows: *auscultation* is the listening process; *mediate* refers to the fact he used an object to capture and amplify the sounds he heard.)

The idea for the stethoscope came to him when he had a fat female patient. Her weight made percussion useless, and Laennec was too proper to put his ear on her chest. He solved the problem by rolling up a pad of paper, holding one end on her chest and the other at his ear. Experimentation then lead to a wooden stethoscope (figure 6.24) with a hollow tube down the middle. At the

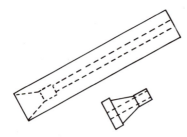
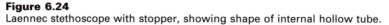

Figure 6.24
Laennec stethoscope with stopper, showing shape of internal hollow tube.

end placed on the patient's chest, the tube would pick up the breathing sounds spread over the lungs.

When the physician wanted to listen to heart sounds, he inserted a stopper to decrease the size of the opening. The stethoscope placed directly over the heart would then pick up fewer breathing sounds.

Within ten years, the stethoscope had become a common tool for the physician. Eventually flexible rubber tubing and a binaural design replaced the old model. The rapid acceptance of the stethoscope within the medical profession came for several reasons:

1. Laennec carefully described different sounds and documented their meaning accurately, so other doctors found it easy to learn to use the device.

2. Laennec carefully confirmed his diagnoses with autopsy studies.

3. Modest patients were not embarrassed by the use of the device.

4. Laennec and his associates were ardent advocates of the stethoscope.

5. Medical results were significant. Previously, it was difficult to distinguish between pleurisy and tuberculosis.

These features were sufficiently important to overcome the tendency of any profession to oppose change.

The stethoscope ushered in the modern age of medicine: use of instruments and technology for measurements of the patient. The stethoscope is basically a *qualitative* measuring device: there are no numbers resulting from the measurement. Instead, the physician has to interpret the sounds he hears.

In this century, this "scientific" approach has moved into *quantitative* measurements. Now the physician can obtain a wide array of numbers describing different characteristics of the patient. For example, chemical analysis of a blood sample can give a score of different measurements making diagnosis more scientific.

Figure 6.25
Modern binaural stethoscope.

The stethoscope is an interesting technological device for several reasons:

1. The modern stethoscope is not appreciably better than the early Laennec model. Ideally, the sounds reaching the physician's ear should be exactly the same as the original chest sounds: the stethoscope should not cause any change in the spectrum of the sound signal. In this sense, the ideal instrument is like a superb hi-fi set: over the range of frequencies we are interested in, the output should be the same as the input. If we achieve the characteristic of figure 6.26, we say the instrument has perfect fidelity.

Figure 6.27 shows that the actual stethoscope certainly does not have perfect fidelity. The modern stethoscope has a response greater than one around 100 Hz—in other words, sounds at these frequencies are stronger at the physician's ear than at the patient's chest. Components at frequencies above 200 Hz are weaker. The stethoscope gives a total sound quite different from that actually present at the patient's chest.

The interesting feature of figure 6.27 is that the modern stethoscope is different from Laennec's, but not too much better. The modern device seems to introduce even more distortion than the original, wooden version.

2. The stethoscope does not really give any significant amplification: the doctor hears about what he would if he placed his ear against the patient's body. The principal effect of the stethoscope is to block from the ear sounds coming from the room or the environment.

3. Engineers can easily build a stethoscope with perfect fidelity: a microphone picks up the sound, which is then amplified to any desired level and sent to the doctor's ear with no distortion. Such electronic stethoscopes have been manufactured inexpensively, but have not been widely adopted by physicians. Why?

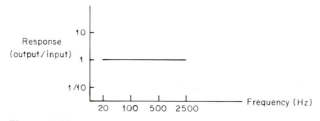

Figure 6.26
Response of the ideal stethoscope. There is no distortion of the signal, because at each frequency the output equals the input.

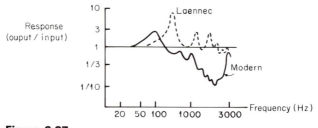

Figure 6.27
Characteristics of the stethoscope.

The answer is that once a reasonably satisfactory technology is widely used, it is difficult to replace this with an improved version. Doctors have learned to interpret the sounds coming from the traditional stethoscope; use of the electronic model would require retraining with only negligible gain. One company marketing a new electronic stethoscope found that this conflict with the familiar even included behavior patterns. Some doctors were accustomed to throwing their stethoscopes on a desk or table—treatment the electronic product could not tolerate over a long period of time.

Thus, new technology, requiring an adaption or re-learning by the user, must present significant, demonstrable advantages.

6.7 Parts of the Ear

Although the "black box" approach to hearing guides us in the study of stethoscopes, hearing aids, and other sound technologies, we could do even better engineering work with a detailed understanding of how the ear and the brain work—what is normal processing of the incoming sound waves, and how the individual actually interprets the air-pressure variations to understand speech or other sound signals. For example, this information might indicate what features of the sound wave must be faithfully reproduced to ensure optimum comprehension by the listener.

As a teacher talks in a classroom, the student receives the sound signal along a variety of paths: one direct from the speaker to the listener's ears, others bouncing off the walls, floor, ceiling, and furnishings. Thus, the total sound signal reaching the listener is a complex addition of many copies of the original speech, copies with varying time delays and different distortions of the spectrum. If we understood how the ear and brain accept this confused signal so that the listener can interpret the original speech signal, we would know what acoustical features are important in a lecture hall.

Unfortunately, the science of hearing is still pretty much a mystery. We do know generally how each part of the ear functions, but our knowledge is at best skimpy.

Furthermore, hearing is a very complicated phenomenon, at least in terms of the models and mathematics we customarily use. Part of this complexity is a consequence of the important role played by the brain as it interprets and processes the electrical signals arriving along the auditory nerves from the two ears. In this section, we focus on the operation of the ear alone and consider the question: how does the ear convert the incoming sound waves into electrical signals leading to the brain?

In very general terms, the ear works as follows. Sound is rapid and *very small* changes in the pressure of the air. These pressure changes travel through the air to the eardrum. The changing pressure on the eardrum causes that thin membrane to vibrate or move mechanically, just as a window pane vibrates when it is hit by the sound of a loud clap of thunder.

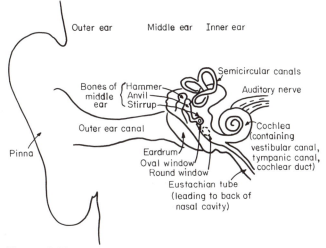

Figure 6.28
The human hearing system.

The middle ear consists of a set of levers which carry this eardrum vibration to the inner ear's canals, which are filled with fluid. The sound now travels down these canals and causes the fluid to move back and forth. Within this fluid there are hairs attached to nerve cells. As these hairs vibrate, the nerve cells generate electrical pulses, which travel along the auditory nerves to the brain.

Thus, the ear converts the sound signal in stages to

mechanical motion,

fluid motion,

and voltage or electrical signals.

6.8 Outer Ear

The outer ear has only two parts:

1. the pinna, or the part protruding from the head, and

2. the outer ear canal (the tubular passageway into the eardrum, where the middle ear begins).

The pinna serves as some physical protection for the ear, but primarily collects sound energy and directs it into the canal. In this way, the pinna acts like an ear trumpet which was a familiar sight in the days before hearing aids. An ear trumpet like that in figure 6.29 may have a gain as high as 10: that is, the sound signal at the eardrum is 10 times what it would be with the ear alone.

Most birds have no pinnas, since such protuberances would ruin the *streamlining* and require much more energy for flying. Bats depend so critically on their hearing to navigate and to detect food (insects) that they have very large pinnas in spite of the severe aerodynamic disadvantages.

The canal (about one inch long) also serves to partially isolate the eardrum from the external world. Not only is the eardrum protected, but the tempera-

Figure 6.29
An ear trumpet.

ture and humidity at the eardrum are held approximately constant even when external conditions vary radically. (The elasticity of the membrane changes with temperature and humidity; in the absence of the outer ear canal, hearing capability would change noticeably with environmental conditions.) This insulation from the environment is one reason hearing is such an important sense for animals. Vision depends on the availability of light; smell is easily overwhelmed by an extraneous signal. Furthermore, we continue to hear while we are doing other things. We hear even when we are asleep. One remarkable characteristic is our capability to sleep through the sounds of sirens or thunder, but to be awakened by a quiet tone from an alarm clock. Finally, sound signals go around obstructions—we hear the siren on the side street, even though our vision is blocked by the corner building.

The outer ear canal carries the sound signal to the eardrum. This tube acts as a resonant pipe and tends to accentuate the sound frequencies around 2000–4000 Hz—the principal reason that human hearing has maximum sensitivity in this high frequency range.

This resonance property may be particularly troublesome when we wear earphones to listen to music. The earphone emits sound waves, which travel down the canal, reflect back off the eardrum, and return to the earphone. If the earphone is a cheap or poorly designed model that reflects (rather than absorbs) these returning waves, the reflection sends the waves down the canal again toward the eardrum (figure 6.30). This doubly reflected wave adds to the signal being sent out by the earphone. If the two components are in phase, they simply add together to produce an even louder sound. Thus, the sound waves bouncing back and forth inside the outer ear canal can cause a sharp increase in sound, especially at the resonant frequencies where each doubly reflected signal simply adds to the original signal.

Furthermore, we saw in section 6.5 that the changes in the spectrum tell us the direction the sound is coming from (particularly when the sound originates in front, in back, or overhead). This boosting of certain frequencies and cutting down of others depends very strongly on the pinna and canal of the outer ear. The simplified picture in figure 6.31 shows that the sound can reach point 0 at

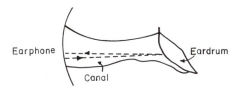

Figure 6.30
Resonance in outer ear canal. A sound wave travels down the canal and reflects back off the eardrum.

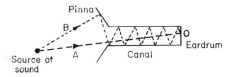

Figure 6.31
A very simplified pinna and canal, showing only two paths of sound.

the eardrum by different paths (only two of which are shown). Path B is obviously much longer than path A. If the frequency is such that path B is half a wavelength longer than A, the two signals will tend to cancel at 0; this frequency will seem much weaker.

In actuality, the pinna, the canal, and the eardrum are all irregularly shaped, so that even detailed analysis cannot predict which frequencies are boosted or which decreased. We need a variety of experimental measurements, because there is significant variation from person to person. Even the simplified sketch of figure 6.31 shows why we can use this spectrum change to determine the direction of unfamiliar sounds. This crude analysis also explains why music heard on cheap earphones sounds like it's coming from the middle of your head: the reflecting earphones accentuate all frequencies.

Thus, the outer ear (the pinna and the outer ear canal) isolates the critical parts of the middle and inner ear from the external environment, transmits the sound signal to the eardrum, and even does a small amount of frequency change to help determine the direction of the sound source.

6.9 Middle Ear

The eardrum (or tympanic membrane), separating the outer ear from the middle ear, vibrates in response to the incoming sound or air-pressure variations. The middle ear converts the vibration of the eardrum to a corresponding vibration of the oval window, another membrane located at the beginning of the inner ear. If the middle-ear input is a membrane vibration and the output is a similar membrane vibration, what is the purpose of the middle ear?

Because the air pressure is changed such a small amount by an incoming sound signal, the pressure on the eardrum causes a very minute vibration. Indeed, the eardrum may move less than the diameter of a hydrogen atom. If there were no middle ear, and the eardrum came between the outer ear canal and the inner ear, the fluid in the inner ear would not move enough to cause the hair motion to generate electrical signals.

The bones of the middle ear serve as a mechanism to increase the force on the oval window leading to the inner ear (figure 6.32). Three small bones create a lever action:

hammer (or malleus)

anvil (or incus)

stirrup (or stapes).

Ideally, the total effect of these three bones should be a lever ratio of 300 to 1. This means that the motion of the oval window should be 300 times that of the eardrum. Actually, the ratio is appreciably less, but the effect is still that the oval window moves much more than the eardrum.

The middle ear thus matches the external air to the inner-ear fluid. It is not surprising that animals living only in water have no middle ear; no matching is necessary in such cases since the sound energy is already moving through a liquid.

Other Functions of Middle Ear

The middle ear also contains two muscles which allow a change of this lever ratio. When you anticipate a loud sound, these muscles act to reduce the power transfer to the inner ear and thereby protect your delicate hearing system. As a result, a sudden, *unexpected* sound seems much louder than the same sound when we expect it.

The middle ear contains the opening to the Eustachian tube leading to the back of the nasal cavity. Inside the tube is a valve which opens occasionally to allow the average air pressure in the middle ear to equal the pressure on the valve in the outer ear. When descending rapidly in an airplane, the difference in pressure between the outer and middle ears causes a discomfort which usually can be cleared by swallowing. This eases the air flow through the Eustachian

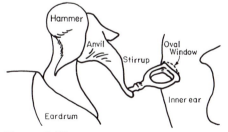

Figure 6.32
The bones of the middle ear.

tube, which helps to equalize the pressure between the outer and middle ears (figure 6.33).

The middle and outer ears together largely account for the frequency characteristics of hearing. The impedance matching obtained in the middle ear varies markedly with frequency because the two membranes and the three bones possess a large number of resonances (just as an airplane wing has hundreds of resonances or different ways in which it can vibrate).

6.10 Inner Ear

The inner ear is by far the most complex part of the hearing system. The critical part is the cochlea, a snail-like structure or helix with about two and a half turns. It contains the vestibular canal and the tympanic canal which are separated (most of the way) by the cochlea duct. Figure 6.34 shows the spiral unwound.

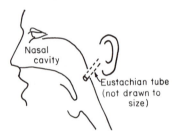

Figure 6.33
Rough diagram of Eustachian tube as it enters the nasal cavity.

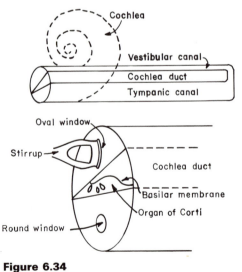

Figure 6.34
The inner ear.

The sound signal enters through the oval window, travels down the two canals, and ends up at the round window facing the middle ear.

The cochlea duct is partitioned by the basilar membrane, which also holds the organ of Corti: the hair cells that convert mechanical or sound signals to electrical signals for nervous-system transmission to the brain. There are about 15,000 hair cells in each ear, and these cells which respond electrically when the basilar membrane is mechanically moved by the sound or pressure signal traveling down the canals.

How these hair cells respond electrically to incoming sound signals is not really understood. The theories postulated by scientists have turned out to be too simple:

1843	Ohm (famous for Ohm's Law) proposed that the ear used Fourier decomposition—that is, the ear measured frequency components present in the arriving sound signal.
1863	Helmholz proposed the *place theory* of hearing—that different frequencies excite different portions of the organ of Corti.
1930–1950	Von Bekesy (Nobel laureate in 1961 for his work) showed that sound waves travel down the canals, and that the higher frequencies give peak motion near the oval window, the lower frequencies farther down the canal away from the oval window.
1949	Wever suggested that the place theory explained the ear's response to high frequencies (above 2000 Hz), but that the detection of low frequencies could be explained by a *time theory* of the neurons firing in response to changes in the sound signal.
1970	Nordinark postulated that the ear recognizes various time patterns just as the eye recognizes visual patterns.

Thus, scientists still seek an explanation of the relation between the electrical signals in the auditory nerve and the characteristics of the incoming sound wave. As so often happens in attempts to explain the behavior of a complex physiological system, simple hypotheses explain some properties (some of the "black box" characteristics). As measurements become more refined and as new "black box" behavior is observed, we find that the simple explanations are inadequate; the more we learn scientifically, the more unanswered questions there are.

Unfortunately, more knowledge is essential if we are to build technology to help those who are totally deaf. The hearing aid is an *orthotic* device—that is, it supplements an existing human capability. A hearing aid is of no value if there is no sound transmission through the middle ear or if the inner ear is completely non-functioning. All a hearing aid can do is amplify the sound signal at the ear-drum: the hearing aid uses a microphone to convert the sound signal to an electrical form, amplifies this signal with an electronic amplifier, and then converts the signal back to a sound wave by means of a "loudspeaker" (figure 6.35).

For people totally deaf but with an intact auditory nerve and normal brain function, we would like to use a microphone to detect incoming sounds, then determine from this sound signal the appropriate electrical signal to send on the auditory nerve to the brain. Success requires that we know the coding scheme used by the normal ear: what electrical pulses are generated for a given sound signal? The answer to this question is very difficult for several reasons:

1. Scientists cannot experiment on normal people except in a most elementary, non-traumatic way.

2. Scientists inevitably look for explanations and models in familiar forms—for example, since Fourier decomposition has proved so useful in engineering, we think of sound signals in terms of spectra. Human sensors may well behave in entirely different ways. Engineering systems are inevitably simple, since they are designed by human beings and they must be comprehensible by the designer; human or physiological systems have no such restriction.

3. Human characteristics vary enormously from person to person and even from time to time.

4. The ear and the brain *combine* to give us our hearing capability. Since scientists know so little about the brain's operation, there are very few guides as to how the ear may work.

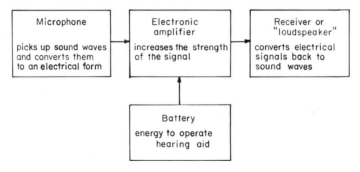

Figure 6.35
Diagram of hearing aid.

Review Questions

R6-1. When we describe a system by its input-output relationship rather than by the details of construction and operation, we say we are using what approach?

R6-2. An unexpected loud sound is more dangerous to hearing and seems much louder than the same sound when it is anticipated. Why does this difference exist?

R6-3. What is the difference between the "black box" characteristics of frequency range and frequency discrimination of the human ear?

R6-4. The human ear has a varying sensitivity at different frequencies. Sketch the graph, with amplitude (dB) on the y axis and frequency on the x axis, for this "black box" characteristic of the human ear.

R6-5. Give two reasons why we use dB to indicate the amplitude of sound signals.

R6-6. The human being can hear changes in sound level of 3 dB, regardless of the ambient sound level. Explain briefly what this means.

R6-7. The human ear has a huge *dynamic range*. What does this statement tell us about our ability to hear sounds of different loudness? (Explain in terms of dB and sound pressure.)

R6-8. The use of dB to indicate sound levels matches human hearing characteristics. Explain briefly this statement.

R6-9. The lowest frequency people can hear is about 15 Hz. Why is it an advantage not to be able to hear much lower frequencies?

R6-10. A study showed that portable audio equipment (like the Walkman) can deliver sound at a level over 120 dB. Why is this a worrisome finding?

R6-11. What are three ways the human listener estimates the direction of an incoming sound?

R6-12. Edison was deaf but still developed the phonograph. Explain briefly.

R6-13. What normally happens to human hearing capability as one approaches senior-citizen age?

R6-14. Why should we require licensing of sellers of hearing aids? (See problem 6-8.)

R6-15. The sensitivity of the human ear is determined by audiometry tests. Sketch the amplitude vs. frequency graph for the sensitivity profile for normal hearing.

R6-16. Why has the electronic stethoscope been a commercial failure even though it works very well technologically?

R6-17. Explain why my voice sounds so different to me when I talk than when I tape my speaking and listen to the tape.

R6-18. For a sound coming from directly behind you, how do you tell the direction?

R6-19. Technology for the deaf, the blind, and the paraplegic is often not very advanced. Explain briefly.

R6-20. Why does human hearing sensitivity peak at about 2000 Hz?

R6-21. What is meant by the term "cocktail-party effect"?

R6-22. We test the hearing of a specific man and find he can hear reasonably well from 20 Hz to 5000 Hz. How many octaves is this range?

R6-23. 0 dB could be defined as any specific sound amplitude. How is it defined?

R6-24. "Human hearing is as sensitive as we would want." Explain briefly.

R6-25. "Human beings can detect changes of 3 dB in sound amplitude." What does this term "3 dB" mean?

Problems

P6-1. After a new city airport is built, we sometimes find that housing suddenly appears near the end of the runway (figure 6.36). Occupants then complain loudly about the intolerable noise levels as planes take off. In our example, the noise level in the house reaches 110 dB; residents state that they are unable to bring food on a fork to their mouths because of the air-vibration forces.

After a few years, the airport is so busy that a second runway is needed. To take advantage of the prevailing winds, the runway is built parallel to the first, and the homeowner now faces the situation shown in figure 6.37.

If two similar planes take off simultaneously, is the noise level in the home now

(a) 220 dB,

(b) 116 dB,

(c) 113 dB,

or

(d) 110 dB?

Hint: Two planes do not generate twice the noise of one. As figure 6.38 shows, the two sound signals are not related. Consequently, part of the time the two signals tend to cancel one another.

P6-2. The retired RCA engineer Edward W. Herold has emphasized the problems the normal elderly have with modern audio equipment. There are

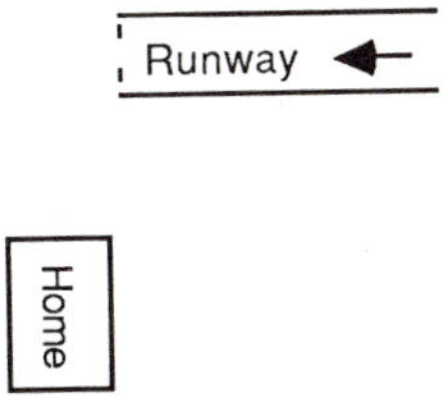

Figure 6.36

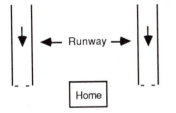

Figure 6.37

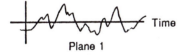

Plane 1

Plane 2

Figure 6.38

three primary changes in hearing as one ages:

1. Sensitivity to the high frequencies (above 500 Hz) decreases.

2. The dynamic range (from the weakest signal perceived to the threshold of discomfort) decreases.

3. The individual's comprehension falls rapidly as extraneous background noise or sound increases.

Unfortunately, it is often young engineers who design audio equipment, and the primary market is young people. Perhaps as a result, the tone control decreases high-frequency response, the CD raises the dynamic range from 76 to 96 dB (whereas the over-65 listener would prefer 40 dB), and TV and movie producers frequently use background music or street noise when the actors are speaking important lines.

Is this a sufficiently important problem for the federal government to be involved? What options exist for a congressional committee cognizant of the problem and anxious to respond to the needs of this growing group of voters?

P6-3. Many musicians consider a few concert halls to have especially good acoustics:

Carnegie Hall, New York   Musikvereinssaal, Vienna
Symphony Hall, Boston   Tonhallesaal, Zurich
Concertgebouw, Amsterdam

All these were built during the nineteenth century, without the "advantage" of modern construction materials. All have thick plastered walls, very high ceilings, and wooden furniture and paneling. All have sharply elevated seating to give good visibility and, hence, direct lines for the sound to reach the audience. Furthermore, these architects did not have to worry about building and safety codes, use noisy heating and air-conditioning systems, or consider excessive street sounds (or even subway noise).

In the 1986 renovation of Carnegie Hall, seats, walls, floors, carpets, and ceilings were removed and tested acoustically to determine absorption and reflection of sound signals as a function of frequency—all in order to ensure that the remodeling would not damage the acoustic characteristics.

In spite of the large amounts of money spent on modern concert halls, the newer structures are often criticized severely by performers. What are some of the economic constraints which increase the difficulties of building such structures?

P6-4. Figure 6.39 shows the allowable noise environment under federal regulations. These levels have been set from past medical histories, which show

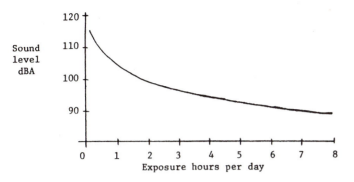

Figure 6.39
Allowable noise exposure in industry. If there are two or more exposures at different levels, the limiting value is determined by the fraction of the allowable time at each level. This total of these fractions should not exceed 1. For example, 5 hours at 92 dBA (where 6 are allowed) contributes 0.83; 1 hour at 95 dBA (when 4 are allowed) contributes 0.25. The sum is 1.08, which exceeds the allowable value of 1.

that $\frac{1}{6}$ of the people working in an environment at this level will have severe hearing problems in later life (the fraction is $\frac{1}{14}$ for the general population). Figure 6.40 gives the typical noise levels from a few common sources.

(a) Estimate the noise of a power lawn mower. (If you have never used one, ask someone who has to make the estimate with the help of figure 6.40.) Then determine how many hours a day a high school student should be allowed to cut lawns.

(b) The basis for setting federal noise standards is given above. This criterion certainly does not lead to a "safe" environment. Discuss the value and the ethics of this criterion.

(c) The effects of noise depend on the background noise level. The impact of a noisy truck is much greater in a quieter residential area at night than when merely added to the drone of a busy freeway. In an attempt to take this situation into account, engineers use a *noise susceptibility index*. How would you define such an index (or, alternatively, a measure of the annoyance of a particular noise)?

P6-5. The degree of *annoyance* caused by any noise depends upon the background noise level. For example, when the background noise level is 70 dB(A) a sound of 80 dB(A) can be disturbing and therefore considered as noise. Many people commute in vehicles (autos, trains, buses) in which the interior noise level is well above 85 dB(A) and do not recognize an 80 dB(A) sound as noise. From figure 6.41 and your experience, describe a few situations that would probably result in community complaints.

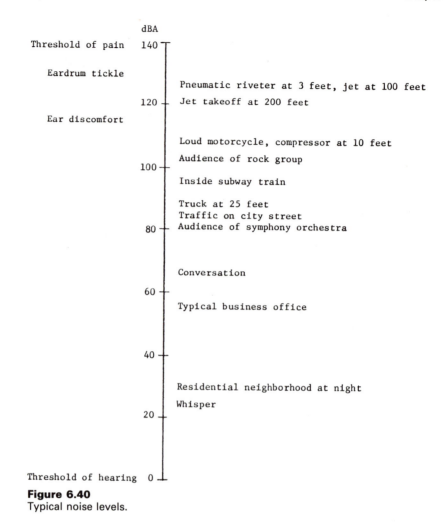

Figure 6.40
Typical noise levels.

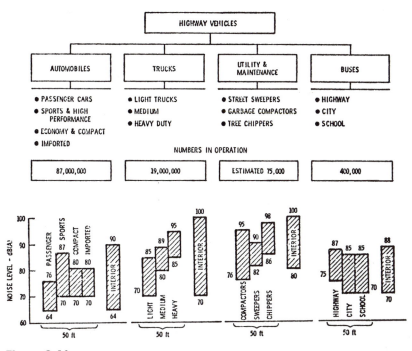

Figure 6.41
Noise characteristics of motor vehicles.

P6-6. The following description is taken from an advertisement by Telesensory Systems, Inc., an innovative high-technology concern.

The **Crib-O-Gram** is a portable device providing a completely automated method for screening profound hearing loss in newborn infants in either the well-baby or ICU nursery. The importance of neonatal auditory screening is generally recognized insofar as early treatment markedly improves prognosis. Developed by Dr. F. Blair Simmons at Stanford University School of Medicine, the **Crib-O-Gram** now provides a practical and reliable procedure for the mass screening of newborns' hearing at a very low cost per child.

The basic element of the **Crib-O-Gram** is a motion-sensing transducer which lies beneath the mattress of an isolette or bassinet. The output of the transducer is automatically tabulated as a baby's activity is monitored for 10 seconds before and 1½ seconds after the introduction of a one-second-long filtered white noise stimulus of about 92 dB. The transducer is so sensitive that it can detect virtually any motion stronger than an eye-blink, including respiration and heartbeat.

Hearing responses are scored by comparing the baby's motor activity during the pre-stimulus, or baseline period, with the activity immediately after the sound is introduced. The entire screening process is computer controlled including the monitoring of the pre-test state, the administration of the sound stimulus, the recording of the infant's response, and the scoring of the results obtained according to precise pass/fail criteria (periodic silent tests help check scoring criteria being used).

The **Crib-O-Gram** has several advantages over other screening tests, either conventional behavioral testing or application of the High Risk Register:

- It is capable of detecting babies having severe hearing loss with a low level of false positives and a very low level of false negatives, as validated in exhaustive field evaluations
- It can be realistically applied within the framework of current medical practice, and without disrupting nursery operations
- Reliability of tests is assured by repeated testing of each child in each screening cycle
  - Rapid and accurate data analysis; objectivity
  - Practical on a mass scale
  - Modest unit cost; operationally, less than $3.00 per infant
  - Safety; no infant contact with any part of the device
  - Little personnel time required
  - Applicability to any nursery setting.

"White noise," mentioned in the report, is a sound consisting of equal amplitudes of all frequencies sounded simultaneously.

a. Is such a system necessary? Why can't the same results be obtained by just having a person clap his hands and observe the infant?

b. The Environmental Protection Agency (EPA) has indicated that exposure to sounds above 90 dB can be harmful. Why is such a loud sound used in this system?

c. Why is "white noise" used rather than a series of individual tests at specific frequencies?

P6-7. One essential characteristic for every hearing aid is a device that keeps the amplitude (loudness) from exceeding a certain size. This device is called a limiter. Why is this feature so important?

The normal human ear does not have a limiter, but there is some protection against loud noises that are anticipated. Explain.

P6-8. The hearing aid is an electronic development that represents a major contribution of technology to the "quality of life" for one segment of the population. Even this simple device, however, has a recent history that raises serious questions about the role that the federal government should play in controlling the use of technology.

When electronic devices became inexpensive after World War II, large profits were made by hearing-aid manufacturers. By the 1960s, transistors and then integrated circuits made small hearing aids possible and sharply reduced the size of the batteries required. Many companies entered the field, and the prospective customer had a wide variety of competitive models from which to choose.

Most purchasers did not seek advice from physicians who were hearing specialists. Hearing aids were available across the counter; many people made their selections on the basis of physical appearance and cost. The customer had no way of evaluating competitive models; indeed, the usual customer had no understanding of the many different forms that hearing deficiency can take and the capabilities and limitations of different hearing aids. For example, some of the devices gave poor amplification above 1000 Hz, others had extremely poor fidelity, others introduced serious distortion, and so forth.

By the mid-1970s, the situation represented a serious problem for consumers, particularly the culturally disadvantaged who did not regularly use physicians. The public then learned that the Veterans' Administration had made an extensive evaluation of hearing aids, but that the results of this study were confidential. The VA did not want to be accused of favoritism toward certain manufacturers or to engage in lengthy legal disputes over the validity of its testing procedures. A public-interest lawsuit was entered under the Freedom of Information Act—an act which states that information obtained with public funds by a federal agency must be available to the public (unless that information is classified for security purposes). The VA finally published a booklet summarizing its evaluations, although in such general terms that it is of limited value.

The problem of protection of the public is complicated by the fact that some states do not regulate sale of hearing aids or license salespeople. There is a general desire in this country to minimize the amount of governmental regulation of small retail businesses.

a. What should we know about the customer's hearing before selecting a hearing aid? To what extent can we make hearing-aid selection "scientific"?

b. State briefly the arguments for and against the enactment of federal controls over the sale of hearing aids. Why has this been essentially left to the states for regulation?

P6-9. In the 1987 World Series, the Minnesota Twins won all four games played in their domed stadium and lost all three in St. Louis, where the Cardinals play in an outdoor environment. The question arose whether familiarity with the high noise level in Minneapolis helped the Twins.

Bill Clark, a Cardinal fan and a scientist with the Central Institute for the Deaf in St. Louis, measured noise levels at the two sites. He found 92 dB during relatively quiet periods in Minneapolis, 83 dB in St. Louis. This means that the noise seemed about twice as loud in Minneapolis.

Why would this greater noise level be an advantage for the home team? What would the Twins have learned from their earlier experiences in this noisy environment?

Chapter 7
Digital Signals

In recent years, both audio and video entertainment electronics have "gone digital." In audio this started with the compact disc (CD), which was followed by digital audio tape (DAT). Digital television provides the home viewer with a better picture, freedom to stop action and zoom, and the chance to divide the screen to show two channels simultaneously.

This move toward digital technology emphasizes that there are two quite different ways in which the engineer describes signals (speech, music, pictures, heart rate, temperature, and so on):

1. Spectrum or frequency description. Here we decompose the signal into its component frequencies and show the results in a spectrum or spectrogram. Chapters 4–6 have focused on this approach.

2. Digital description. We represent a signal by a sequence of numbers showing the value or size of the signal at regular instants of time (in a CD, for example, every 1/44,000 of a second).

Both the spectrum and the number sequence represent the signal precisely.

The digital description requires an enormous set of numbers (an hour of audio on a CD needs 158 million numbers). To store and recover these numbers, we need very small electronic devices. Consequently, the recent technological advances in semiconductor or computer electronics have been essential to the emergence of digital consumer equipment. We are entering an era when the cost of the digital devices themselves is almost zero; the cost of digital audio or video is in the design or programming and in the display (the conversion to a form the human being can understand).

The magnitude of this technological change is indicated by a simple analogy. In the late 1950s, digital computers were becoming available in industry and colleges. In the intervening 30 years, the cost of computing power has dropped rapidly and steadily. If the cost of an automobile had fallen at the same rate, we would be able today to buy a Mercury Sable for eight cents.

This chapter introduces the basic ideas of digital signals—the second half of the concepts underlying modern communications technology. It leads up to a description of the compact disc as an example of a familiar digital system.

7.1 A Tactile Communication System

We start with a simple example of *digital signals*. You and I are together in a noisy and dark environment, and I want to send you a message. If I speak, you cannot hear me because of the noise; if I move my hands to signal, you cannot see in the darkness. We decide to use the sense of touch—tactile communication. We agree ahead of time on a code, and I touch you at pre-selected points to indicate the message.

Now let's turn to a simple tactile communication system. As in figure 7.1, I stand behind you and face your back. I want to communicate to you three numbers:

4   2   7.

We agree ahead of time that I will touch you on an imaginary line across your back, with the far left end representing a 0, the far right a 9, and the other digits at appropriate intermediate points (figure 7.2).

This is not a good communication system. The chances are that you will decide the numbers I sent were

4 2 6,   or   4 3 8,   or   3 2 9.

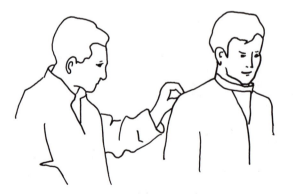

Figure 7.1
A simple tactile (touch) communication system.

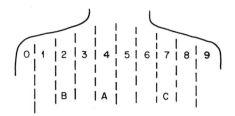

Figure 7.2
The code or arrangement we agree on for our tactile communication system. To send you the information 4 2 7, I touch you, in turn, at points A, B, and C.

You will seldom receive the correct message. Even if I repeat the sequence of three digits several times, the reliability is not good.

The trouble is that each time I touch you, there are too many possible locations (ten), from which you must decide on one. We are trying to send too much information with each touch.

Let's try a different scheme. First, we'll convert each digit (4, 2, and 7) to binary form according to the conventional binary numbers (table 7.1). You and I agree on this code ahead of time.

Now to send you the number 427, I will send the following twelve binary digits.

0100   0010   0111.

For a 0, I'll touch you on the left side of your back, for a 1 on the right side. Thus, I'll touch you twelve times in sequence:

LRLL   LLRL   LRRR.

Communication is slower, but the reliability is great! All you have to decide is whether I touched you on the left or the right side each time. As long as I stay well away from the middle of your back, there is really no chance of error. We have a communication system which is slow, but which *hardly ever has an error*.

If we are worried that there might be a single error occasionally, we can even send a *check digit*. You and I agree ahead of time that after I've sent twelve binary digits, I will count the number of ones. If this number is even, I'll send a zero (to make the total number of ones stay even). If the first twelve digits have an odd number of ones, I'll send a one to leave an even number of ones:

0100   0010   0111   1.

When you receive this thirteen-digit message, you count the number of ones. If your total is even, you know that a single error has not occurred. (There might

Table 7.1

Decimal number	Binary number
0	0000
1	0001
2	0010
3	0011
4	0100
5	0101
6	0110
7	0111
8	1000
9	1001

be two errors, but we assume that the probability of that is negligible.) You know that the message you have is correct.

We have a communication system that is, in practice, essentially perfect. There is almost no chance of an error; if there should be one error, you will recognize this right away.

Comments on Our Tactile Communication System

We have devised a remarkably reliable tactile communication system. (The word *tactile* simply means we are using touch.) Why is the system so free of errors? Primarily because the receiver (you) need determine only which of *two* signals was sent. For each binary digit (0 or 1, left or right), you don't care exactly how far to the left or the right the signal is, but rather only if it is to the left or the right.

If you turn slightly as I am about to touch your back, there still is no error, as long as your turning does not move my contact from the left half to the right. *Noise is any unwanted disturbance (or signal) added to the signal carrying the information.* In our system, noise can be your turning slightly, the wind moving my arm, or my inadvertently jerking sideways. In our digital system, a small amount of *noise* does not cause an error.

The system has a second important feature: we can easily add an extra digit or a few extra digits to check the accuracy of the communication. We call this use of extra check digits *redundancy*, as was discussed in chapter 2. After we send a block of information or message digits (twelve in the example above), we stop the message for a check digit (the redundant or extra digit). This concept was first proposed during World War II by H.C.A. van Duuren; since then, the use of redundancy to improve accuracy has become almost universal in communications.

Finally, there is a third advantage of the binary communication system: the transmitting and receiving equipment is simple. In our human system, I need only move my hand well into the left or right half of your back; the exact location is immaterial, so I do not need precise operation of my nervous and muscular systems. In an electronic system, the devices can be quite crude and still operate satisfactorily.

Thus, there are three major advantages of the binary communication system:

1. There are very few errors.

2. It is easy to insert redundancy for detection of errors.

3. The equipment can be simple.

What do we pay for these advantages? A longer message. Instead of three decimal digits (427), we have to send at least twelve binary digits (010000100111). This disadvantage diminishes when we study machine systems, since electronic equipment often can send a 0 or a 1 much more rapidly than a precise decimal value. Even with this feature, however, we do need more time to send binary signals.

The advantages of digital signals are so overwhelming that essentially all communication technologies are changing to this form. As we will see in section 7.8, compact discs use digital signals to record music. Digital television is about to take over home TV. Even our well-established telephone system is changing rapidly. Finally, more and more of our telecommunication capability is used by computers "talking" to computers, and computer information is always digital.

7.2 Morse Code

The Morse Code is an example of a signal which is basically digital. There were operating telegraph systems well before Samuel F.B. Morse's 1840 demonstration. Morse's contribution was the simplification and accuracy achieved by using a system of dots and dashes to represent each letter.

In the Morse system, an electrical current flows from the transmitter through wires to the receiver. When the current flows for only one interval of time, we are sending a dot; a dash lasts three intervals of time. The letter A is represented by a dot and a dash, with one interval of time between the two symbols. In terms of binary numbers, the signal is

$$\underbrace{1 \quad 0}_{\text{Dot}} \qquad \underbrace{1 \quad 1 \quad 1.}_{\text{Dash}}$$

Thus, the system has the advantages inherent in digital signals: in each time interval, the receiver need determine only whether there is a current or no current.

The Morse Code represents a major technological advance for another reason: the code is quite "efficient." That is, the more frequently the letter appears in written English, the faster it can be sent. For example, E is by far the most common letter (box 7.1), so Morse chose a single dot to represent an E. The second most common letter is T, which is represented by a single dash (requiring three times as long to send as a dot). Thus, a minimum amount of time is required to send a long message—the code is efficient (box 7.2).

Actually, today's telegraph equipment almost never uses the Morse code. With machines to transmit and receive, the number of symbols sent per second is much less important than the accuracy; consequently, we go to a digital message (a set of ones and zeros) with redundancy to allow automatic determination of an error. Each letter is represented by seven binary digits—for example,

0100011   or   1000110.

With seven digits available, there are 2^7 ($2\times2\times2\times2\times2\times2\times2$) or 128 different possibilities—far more than we need. To allow automatic recognition of any single error, we use only the seven-digit binary numbers *with three ones*. Now how many different, allowable numbers are there? We might simply list these and find there are 35—plenty to cover all the letters in our alphabet.

The telegraph really ushered in modern communications. Messages traveled over wires at nearly the speed of light. Never again would we have a major battle fought after the war was over (the Battle of New Orleans, in the War of 1812, occurred between the signing of the peace treaty in London and the arrival by ship of the news in this country). Digital signals were, of course, used before the telegraph (the Braille alphabet is one example), but the telegraph had a major impact on our culture.

7.3 Sampling

When we listen to music or to someone talking, what is the sound? How does the sound reach our ears?

When there is no sound, the air pressure around us is about 14.7 pounds per square inch—the "atmospheric pressure" resulting from the atmosphere over

Frequency of letters in written English. In each 1000 letters, E appears 132 times, T 104 times, and so on.

E	132	R	68	L	34	G	20	V	9
T	104	I	63	F	29	Y	20	K	4
A	82	S	61	C	27	P	20	X	1
O	80	H	53	M	25	W	19	J	1
N	71	D	38	U	24	B	14	Q	1
								Z	1

Box 7.1

Modern Morse Code, with letters ordered according to time for transmission. Comparison with box 7.1 shows that the only common letter with an inappropriately long sequence is O. (Actually Morse's original code was slightly different: O, for example, was represented by dot - double space - dot.) The similarity between the letter sequences in boxes 7.1 and 7.2 indicates the remarkable efficiency of the Morse Code. Indeed, the best possible code would save only 6 percent of the time required to send messages.

E ·	S ···	U ··−	B −···	P ·−−·
T −	R ·−·	L ·−··	V ···−	X −··−
I ··	H ····	F ··−·	K −·−	Z −−··
A ·−	D −··	G −−·	O −−−	Y −·−−
N −·	M −−	W ·−−	C −·−·	J ·−−−
				Q −−·−

Box 7.2

The van Duuren code which uses seven binary digits for each letter, always with three ones. If the received signal has one error in each packet of seven digits, the error is immediately recognized (there will be either two or four ones). H.C.A. van Duuren invented the code during World War II; by 1956 it was an international standard under the title ARQ for Automatic Repeat Request—when the receiver sees other than three ones in a packet of seven digits, it automatically requests a repeat of the packet. The system is not common in satellite communications since a relay from a geosynchronous satellite involves a delay of at least $1/4$ second each way. The ARQ would arrive at the sender more than a half second after the original signal.

A	0011010	G	1100001	M	1010001	S	0101010
B	0011001	H	1010010	N	1010100	T	1000101
C	1001100	I	1110000	O	1000110	U	0110010
D	0011100	J	0100011	P	1001010	V	1001001
E	0111000	K	0001011	Q	0001101	W	0100101
F	0010011	L	1100010	R	1100100	X	0010110
						Y	0010101
						Z	0110001

Box 7.3

our heads. We live in this environment of air pressure, which varies slightly from day to day.

A sound signal from a loudspeaker or a person talking causes this air pressure to change very, very slightly (air is compressed, then expanded). Figure 7.3 shows the way the air pressure midway between the loudspeaker and our ears might change with sound present. Up to time t_1, there is sound, and the pressure varies above and below its normal value. From t_1 until t_2, there is no sound, and the pressure stays at its normal value. At t_2, the sound starts again.

This pressure or sound signal travels from the loudspeaker to our ears, where the human hearing system involves the brain's interpretation of the sound signal. For our purposes here, however, only the sound signal is of interest—the way air pressure changes with time.

The signal shown in figure 7.3 is an *analog signal*. That is, the signal exists at every instant of time and changes smoothly from one value to the next. Many signals we encounter in real life have this analog characteristic: for example, the speed we are traveling in a car, or the outside temperature or wind velocity.

We want to describe this signal in digital form—by a sequence of zeros and ones. How can we possibly represent a sound signal like that shown in figure 7.3 by a sequence of numbers?

Fortunately, we do not need to describe the signal at every instant of time. Any real-world signal never changes instantaneously from one value to a very

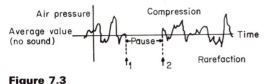

Figure 7.3
A possible sound signal.

different value. Changes are always smooth and are limited in how fast they occur. Thus, if we look at a small piece of the sound signal in figure 7.3, we find the gradual changes shown in figure 7.4—even if we pick a time interval when the signal is changing most rapidly.

When any signal is limited in how fast it can change, we can describe that signal by *sampling*—looking at the signal frequently for a very short period of time. Thus, the sound signal of figure 7.5 is entirely equivalent to the sequence of samples shown at the bottom of the figure. From the actual sound signal, we can find these samples. If the samples are given, we can reconstruct the original, smooth sound signal.

Actually the idea of sampling is nothing especially novel in human experience. We sample frequently in the course of our normal activity. As I sit here writing, it is January on Long Island and there is a threat of snow tonight. Every once in a while I glance out the window to see whether the snow has started: my decision on when to leave the office will depend on when the snow starts. I am sampling the weather-condition signal by occasionally glancing out the window.

Driving home, my eyes will frequently focus on the road in front of my car. I also sample the signal from behind through the rear-view and side mirrors, look right and left to observe cars approaching on side streets, and so on. Indeed, engineers have used a TV camera directed toward the driver's eyes to determine that a normal driver is looking at the road ahead less than 25 percent of the time under average conditions.

We know that, if we sample frequently enough, we lose no information because of the sampling process. I do not really care exactly when it starts snowing—the precise moment the first flake hits the ground. I would like to leave for home within a half-hour of the start of the snow. Consequently, if I look out the window every 15 minutes, I certainly will have all the information I can use. There is absolutely no reason to stare unblinking out the window.

How frequently we must sample depends on the rate at which the signal may change *significantly*. I feel ill in mid-morning and take my temperature; if it's normal, I see no reason to take it again 5 minutes or even 2 hours later. On the other hand, when driving my car, I may have to hold my eyes riveted on the road

Figure 7.4
A small segment of the sound signal.

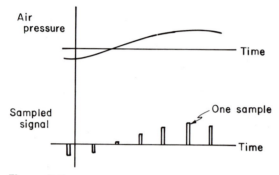

Figure 7.5
Samples of the sound signal. The sample height is the size of the air-pressure signal at the instant of sampling.

ahead if I am following a car driven by an alcoholic, or if there are major potholes or heavy fog. In these cases, the signal (or the situation) may change rapidly, so I must sample frequently.

How often we need to sample can be discussed in intuitive terms. Figure 7.6 shows an analog signal: the long-term record of the body temperature of an individual from the time we start measuring (time 0) for the following 4 hours. Inspection of this curve reveals that the most rapid change occurs in the first 45 minutes of the second hour.

Even in this rapidly changing portion, however, nothing significant happens in less than 15 minutes. Thus, a measurement every 15 minutes provides enough data to keep the physician fully informed of the patient's condition. Instead of the curve of figure 7.6, representing the temperature at *every* instant of time, we might sample and obtain the data of table 7.2. Either this table or the corresponding graph (figure 7.7) is an adequate description of the signal: the way the body temperature changes as time passes.

Thus, we have to sample often enough to be sure that the samples show any important change in the signal. The more frequently we sample, the more complicated the sampling will be, so communication equipment usually samples at close to the minimum rate.

Intuitively we can see that we have to sample often enough so that we do not miss any changes in the signal. In figure 7.8, we do not sample frequently

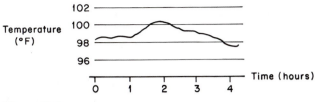

Figure 7.6
Body temperature of a patient.

Table 7.2
Data for the body-temperature signal of figure 7.6.

Time (minutes)	Temperature (°F)
0	98.5
15	98.5
30	98.6
45	98.6
60	98.7
75	99.2
90	99.7
105	100.3
120	100.1
135	99.8
150	99.5
165	99.4
180	98.9
195	98.7
210	98.5
225	97.9
240	97.7

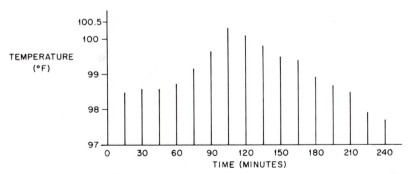

Figure 7.7
Sequence of samples representing the body-temperature signal of figure 7.6. We sample every 15 minutes.

enough—our four samples miss entirely the rapid change between samples 2 and 3. Thus, to find how often we need to sample, we might look at a lengthy graph of the signal, find the interval in which changes are most rapid, and choose the sampling rate accordingly.

There is a mathematical theorem that tells the engineer the smallest allowable sampling rate (the Nyquist sampling theorem, developed in 1933 by Harry Nyquist). We cannot prove or really explain the theorem here, since it requires mathematical background which we don't want to develop, but it can be stated simply: If we sample at an average rate more than twice the highest frequency in the signal spectrum, the sampling process loses no information (that is, the sequence of samples is equivalent to the original signal).

Regular Sampling

In the example of figure 7.7, the samples appear regularly, every 15 minutes. When we sample in our daily activities, we tend to adjust the sampling rate according to the rate at which the signal is changing. In driving my car, I glance in the rear-view mirror occasionally. If there is a police car or an emergency vehicle behind me, I increase the sampling rate enormously since I am now interested in rapid changes in the situation. Similarly, if the patient's body temperature has passed 104°F, the physician wants to know immediately if there is a further rise.

Technological systems usually work with a constant sampling rate. We sample at regular intervals—for example, every 1/8000 of a second for a phone conversation. Even if the speaker pauses for a half-second between words, the sampling rate remains the same. The equipment is enormously simpler if we sample at regular times, even though nothing may be happening during many of the samples.

Final Comment on Sampling

Sampling is the first step in converting a signal to digital form. Sampling gives a signal where the values are known at particular, regular instants of time. We have two more steps before the signal appears as a sequence of zeros and ones (binary digits).

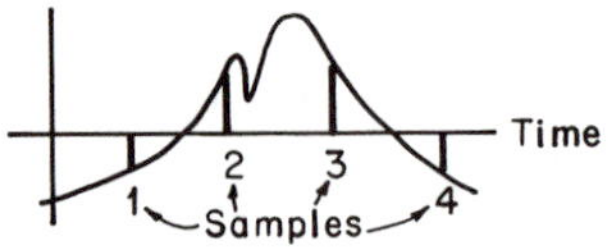

Figure 7.8
Sampling too seldom.

7.4 Quantizing

We are in the middle of converting a signal to *digital* form—that is, representing all the information in the signal by a sequence of binary digits. Figure 7.9 shows the process; we have moved from A to B at this point.

The second step is *quantizing*, which means rounding off the sizes of the samples. For example, if human body temperature is the signal, we might have the following sequence of samples at B in figure 7.9:

97.313
98.219
100.172
101.861
101.873
100.444.

Clearly, these numbers are much more precise than any doctor would want; we should round them off.

We need to decide how precise to be. Suppose we find that half a degree is sufficient for medical purposes. Then we change the numbers to

97.5
98.0
100.0
102.0
102.0
100.5.

This rounding off carries the name "quantizing." (A quantum is a minimum chunk; here any change must be at least 0.5°). Thus, at point C in figure 7.9, the sampled and quantized signal looks, graphically, much the same as the sampled signal at B, before quantizing, but the sizes are all rounded off.

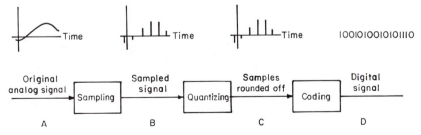

Figure 7.9
Three processes in converting a signal to digital form.

Obviously we introduce some error in this quantizing process. 97.5° is not the same as 97.313°. But even our original set of sample values is quantized, since every thermometer has a maximum number of decimal places that it reads. Although we do discard information in rounding off, no information of significance is lost.

In a sense, this quantizing throws away irrelevant, confusing detail. We do this all the time to allow intelligent thinking. When we say that in the last 20 years the population of New York City has dropped from 8 million to 7 million, we realize that these are only rough numbers—but they are precise enough to describe the important aspect.

7.5 Coding

In figure 7.9, which illustrates our three-step process for changing to a digital signal, we are now at point C—ready to do the coding or conversion to binary numbers. If we continue with our body-temperature example, we have the measurements

97.5   98   100   102   102   100.5.

(Recall that we have rounded off to 0.5°.)

The first question to ask is: With the rounding off we have done, how many different signal values can there be? In this example, we are measuring human body temperature, which in almost every case is between 95° and 107°. There are then only 25 different temperatures we may encounter:

95	97.5	100	102.5	105
95.5	98	100.5	103	105.5
96	98.5	101	103.5	106
96.5	99	101.5	104	106.5
97	99.5	102	104.5	107

We are planning to represent each of these temperatures by a different binary number (for example, 01001). How many digits (zeros or ones) do we need in each binary number to allow at least 25 different possibilities?

In table 7.3 we find that we can have only two temperatures if we use just one binary digit (or *bit* in the terminology of the engineer. The term "binary digit" is abbreviated "bit"; the bi is from "binary", the t from the end of "digit"). Hence, to represent 25 different temperatures, we need five binary digits or bits. (Four digits would give only 16 possibilities.) Now we can choose our *code*, or the rules by which each binary number represents a different temperature (box 7.4).

Table 7.3
The binary system is not efficient in terms of the number of digits required. To represent decimal numbers up to 999, we need ten binary digits.

Number of binary digits	Total number of sample levels	
1	2	
2	4	
3	8	
4	16	
5	32	
6	64	
7	128	
10	1024	(about one thousand)
20	1,048,576	(about one million)

One possible coding scheme. Each temperature is represented by a unique five-digit number.

95	00000	97.5	00101	100	01010	102.5	01111	105	10100
95.5	00001	98	00110	100.5	01011	103	10000	105.5	10101
96	00010	98.5	00111	101	01100	103.5	10001	106	10110
96.5	00011	99	01000	101.5	01101	104	10010	106.5	10111
97	00100	99.5	01001	102	01110	104.5	10011	107	11000

Box 7.4

The sequence of temperatures we measured corresponds to the digital signal as follows:

00101	00110	01010	01110	01110	01011
97.5	98	100	102	102	100.5

We have completed the conversion from the original analog signal to a digital signal.

The three steps (sampling, quantizing, and coding) might be called "digitization"—conversion to digital form. Engineers have a special term: *pulse code modulation*, abbreviated PCM. Modulation means a change in form, here from an analog to a digital signal. The adjective "pulse" means our final signal uses a sequence of pulses (for example, a positive pulse for a 1, and no pulse for a 0). The adjective "code" indicates that we code the signal.

The code shown in box 7.4 is very simple. We just listed the binary numbers in order in the usual way of counting; thus, the successive binary numbers are the representations of 0, 1, 2, 3, ... Then we let these numbers correspond to successive values of temperature, starting with the smallest. This decision was arbitrary. We could have arranged the binary numbers in any order. For example, we might choose the Gray Code (box 7.5), an arrangement that is occasionally advantageous because each entry is only one digit different from the preceding or the following entry. Since the temperature is most likely to stay the same or to change at most 0.5° from one sample to the next, this code may result in simple equipment.

We only want to emphasize here, however, that the code chosen is arbitrary. Problem 7-1 shows another code used for speed control in the BART subway system as a second example of this flexibility.

7.6 Breaking the USPS Code

With the U.S. Postal Service moving toward automation in letter sorting and routing, I find arriving letters now frequently carry the printed bar code shown in figure 7.10. Presumably these 32 symbols represent 11794 (the Stony Brook University zip code). As a problem, we want to break the code. Initially we will work only from this one example; as work progresses, we will use other examples.

One possible reasoning sequence follows.

1. The bars are of two heights, so probably the code is binary. If we let a short bar represent a 0 and a tall bar a 1, then 11794 is

10001100011100011010001001100101.

Gray Code (compare with the code in box 7.4)				
00000	00111	01111	01000	11110
00001	00101	01110	11000	11111
00011	00100	01010	11001	11101
00010	01100	01011	11011	11100
00110	01101	01001	11010	10100

Box 7.5

Figure 7.10
Postal bar code for Stony Brook University

2. Perhaps each decimal digit is represented by its binary equivalent:

0—0000   5—0101
1—0001   6—0110
2—0010   7—0111
3—0011   8—1000
4—0100   9—1001

If so, the two ones starting 11794 should give the binary sequence

00010001.

But this does not appear near the beginning of the envelope code. Our optimistic guess is wrong.

3. There are 32 symbols to represent the five decimal digits. There is no obvious reason to make the code complex—cheating the code does not seem to be a rewarding pastime. Consequently, each decimal digit is probably represented by the same number of bits (binary digits). But 32 is not divisible by 5. Therefore, we might guess the initial and final ones are just "guard rails"— that the 30 interior digits represent the 11794. If so, each six bits represent a decimal digit—for example:

1	000110	001110	001101	000100	110010	1
Start	1	1	7	9	4	End

But this is not attractive. If the code is simple, the bits for a 1 probably are the same, regardless of where the 1 appears in the zip code. Our second guess is wrong.

4. Perhaps there are six bits to start and end (again we assume symmetry), and four bits for each decimal digit:

100011	0001	1100	0110	1000	1001	100101
Start	1	1	7	9	4	End

Again the two ones have different bit representations.

5. Maybe a check digit is used, so there are six decimal digits to be represented. Again, if there is one bit to start and end, each decimal digit is represented by five bits:

1	00011	00011	10001	10100	01001	10010	1
Start	1	1	7	9	4	Check	End

Finally, this looks good: at least both ones have the same five bits.

6. If we assume we are on the right track, we know four representations:

1	00011
7	10001
9	10100
4	01001
Check for 11794	10010

Gazing at these for a while, we notice that all five of these have exactly two ones. Perhaps each decimal digit is represented by a five-bit sequence with two ones:

```
11000  01100  00110  00011
10100  01010  00101
10010  01001
10001
```

How many possibilities are there? Exactly the ten that we need to represent: 1, 2, 3, 4, 5, 6, 7, 8, 9, 0.

7. At this point we need an additional example. My home zip code is 11746, which is represented by figure 7.11, or by the following:

1	00011	00011	10001	01001	01100	00011	1
Start	1	1	7	4	6	Check	End

This tells us that 6 is 01100. In addition, it indicates that the check digit for 11746 is a 1. Probably the rule for finding the check digit is simple. Maybe I just add the five digits of my zip code:

$$1 + 1 + 7 + 4 + 6 = 19.$$

An error in the last digit of the sum would indicate a single error in one of the digits. But my last digit is a 9, and the check digit is 1. Perhaps the check digit is the tens-complement of the last digit of the sum: that is, whatever I must add to the sum to make the last digit 0.

If this is the correct rule, the check digit for 11794 will be 8: the sum is 22, and we need to add 8 to make the total 30. If this is correct, then 8 is 10010.

Figure 7.11
Postal bar code for 11746.

8. We now know

1	00011	7	10001
4	01001	8	10010
6	01100	9	10100

but we still do not know 0, 2, 3, 5. If we look at the above listing, we find that each number is larger than the one above in regular binary numbers. Suppose we list all five-bit numbers with two ones (from paragraph 6) in order of increasing size in standard binary numbers:

00011	1	01100	6
00101		10001	7
00110		10010	8
01001	4	10100	9
01010		11000	

Probably the others are in the order listed (recall we assumed the code is simple):

00101	2
00110	3
01010	5
11000	0

and perhaps we have broken the code.

9. A mailing from *American Scientist* in New Haven arrives with its nine-digit zip code, 06511-9988 (figure 7.12). We are delighted to see this; it seems to confirm our analysis.

This example shows how bar codes can be helpful in automation of both manufacturing and service industries. In the postal system, the post office must add the bar code. When you mail a letter, it goes to the local distribution center. There the letters travel one at a time on a conveyor belt past a clerk who reads the zip code and types in this code so that a machine can print it on the bottom right of the envelope. Thereafter, automatic equipment can sort and route the letter to the recipient's local post office. If the nine-digit code is used, equipment can sort mail for the local carrier.

Figure 7.12
Postal bar code for *American Scientist*.

When the zip code was first introduced, the hope was that equipment would be able to read the printed or typed zip code automatically. This has proved to be extremely difficult to accomplish without a large number of errors. (The same difficulty arises in banking, where people read the amount of each check and control the printing of this number below the signature in machine-readable form.) Thus, automation is still only partial.

7.7 Limits of Human Communication

We can convert any message to digital form. In the compact disc, we store or record music as a long sequence of zeros and ones. Each second of music corresponds to about 700,000 binary digits, or bits. Thus, when we are playing the disc on our home hi-fi system, the equipment is delivering about 700,000 bits per second to our ears through the sound signal.

The human being receives information through the various senses—vision, hearing, touch, taste, and smell, as well as nerves which respond to temperature, pain, muscle movement, and so forth. All these senses deliver information to the brain through the nervous system. As we sense the world around us, there is a flow of electrical pulses or signals through the nervous system to carry the information to the brain, where we make decisions on what to do and then send appropriate signals to specific muscles. In this sense, the brain is the control center accepting incoming signals and generating outgoing commands—in most cases, without conscious action on our part.

The engineer, given such a communication-and-control system, typically asks: How good is the system? What are the limits on what the system can do? In this example, we would ask: How much information can the human brain accept? Notice that here we focus on information coming from outside the person (for example, through vision, hearing, and touch), since we can then make measurements.

Vision
One way to measure information flow is to have an individual read printed material. We know that each letter in our alphabet can be represented by a five-digit binary number; thus, each letter carries perhaps five bits of information. The average word is five letters long, so we have 5×5, or 25 bits per word in English.

As we saw in section 2.1, however, the English language has an enormous amount of redundancy. At least 60 percent is redundant. So printed words carry at most 10 bits per word (40 percent of the 25 above).

A bright college student reads at a rate of about 360 words per minute, or 6 words per second. Thus, in reading we accept information at a rate of about 10×6, or 60, bits per second. Advertisements for speed-reading classes always promise fantastic increases in reading rate, but 360 words per minute seems to be a good maximum figure for reading material that is reasonably unfamiliar (where we cannot guess at the content of the next paragraph or page or easily skip large chunks).

There are other ways we might try to measure the rate at which human vision can receive information. For example, we can flash symbols or objects on a screen for a very short time (a fraction of a second) and test how much information the viewer has received. Such experiments confirm that the maximum information rate for vision is probably less than 100 bits per second. (We obtained the number 60 bits per second from reading, but we made all sorts of assumptions—words per minute reading, bits per word in English, and so on—so we really have no confidence in the figure of 60. Thie number may well be 30 or 100. All we can say confidently is that the rate seems to be less than 100 bits per second). An average person cannot accept information at a rate faster than 100 binary digits per second. If information is sent to the person at a faster rate, the information simply does not register.

Hearing

Perhaps we do much better with hearing. One experiment involves recording speech, then speeding up (or accelerating) the speech electronically. (Cassette players with this capability are now available commercially.) Normally when we read aloud or are talking smoothly, we are speaking at a rate of about 125 words per minute. When speech is accelerated and played back to us, we can understand it only up to a rate of about 300 words per minute; at higher rates, we are lost.

According to our calculations in the subsection on vision, 360 words per minute corresponds to about 60 bits per second. Consequently, the maximum rate for listening to speech (300 words per minute) means that the listener is accepting infromation at about 50 bits per second—certainly under our estimate of 100 bits per second as the maximum human rate.

Touch

Tactile communication seems to give a similar result. We can touch a person briefly in one area for a 1, in another area for a 0, as we discussed in section 7.1. We might also try a different scheme using six different areas and the Braille code, or we might go to even more locations.

As we increase the number of areas, learning becomes more difficult for the person receiving the information. But experiments have indicated that, no matter what scheme we use, we cannot achieve information rates higher than about 50 bits per second.

Combining Senses

The military services have been interested in maximizing human performance, and have conducted experiments using vision and hearing simultaneously. There seems to be no evidence that the maximum information rate can be appreciably raised by such a combination.

Thus, experimental evidence acquired so far seems to indicate that the human being is able to accept information only at a rate of less than 100 bits per second. The experiments mentioned above are, of course, highly restricted in the types of signals given to vision or other senses. Perhaps when we look at a new scene (for example, on a slide) for a second, we do absorb more than 100 bits of information. Even the very exploratory research on vision, however, does seem to confirm that there is a rather severe limit on human capabilities—perhaps a limit near 100 bits per second.

If we accept such a limit, we may then ask why more than 700,000 bits per second are recorded on a compact disc—7000 times as much information as any listener can absorb? The situation is even more extreme in television. It can be shown that a TV video signal is capable of carrying 30,000,000 bits per second of information.

Clearly, when we are communicating with people electronically, our systems are using "technological overkill." The technology is enormously more elaborate than is necessary. The reason is simple: The engineer or designer does not know what particular information the human vision or hearing needs for complete understanding of the message. What do we actually hear as we listen to recorded music, or see as we watch TV? Unable to answer these questions, the engineer simply builds the audio or video technology to transmit everything. Human physiology then can select the parts of the sound or picture it can use.

Perhaps in the next century we will understand human senses and brain operation and then be able to design systems that match our capabilities.

7.8 Digital Audio

Digital audio equipment provides unusually pleasing music, according to many hi-fi enthusiasts, and the CD is rapidly replacing the long-playing 33⅓-rpm record (see box 7.6).

History of Audio Recording

1877	Edison invented a sound-reproducing system: to record, a needle dented tin foil. Edison envisioned the principal use would be recording incoming phone calls (the answering machine).
1855	Chichester Bell and Tainter used a cardboard cylinder coated with wax.
1887	Emile Berliner invented the gramophone, the first flat disc.
1890	Poulsen, Denmark, demonstrated the first magnetic recording of sound along a steel wire. The system was never used commercially.
1925	Electric-motor drive replaced the manual wind-up.
1939	German engineers used plastic tape coated with magnetic material, for the first useful magnetic recording.
1948	Peter Goldmark and CBS Laboratories introduced the long-playing, high-fidelity, 33⅓-rpm disc. A 12" disc held one half hour of music.
1950	Tape replaced records in radio studios.
1955	Stereo tape recorders appeared, along with videotape.
1958	Stereo records appeared, with the monaural signal the radial motion of the pick-up, and the stereo information simultaneous up-and-down motion.

Box 7.6

The compact disc works as follows: When the disc is made, the manufacturer first converts the audio or music signal to digital form—a long sequence of binary digits. These zeros and ones are then recorded on circular paths around the disc. A path consists of occasional raised portions (figure 7.13). In each time interval, a *change* in height means a 1 is recorded, *no change* represents a 0.

Once the music is recorded, how do we recover it? As the disc spins, a laser beam (a sharply focused light) shines on the path moving under the beam. If there is no change in the height during an interval, the laser beam reflects off the disc to a light sensor and the equipment reads a 0. If there is a height change, the light is diffused and reflects in different directions, the sensor receives relatively little light, and the equipment reads a 1 for that interval.

Thus, there is no mechanical contact, no needle riding on the disc as in the older hi-fi systems. The only contact with the disc is by a light beam which exerts essentially no pressure to cause wear or deterioration of the disc with repeated playing. The compact disc has other remarkable advantages over the older 33⅓-rpm disc, as we will see in the following paragraphs.

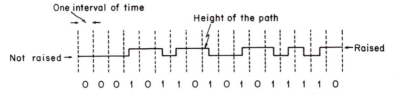

Figure 7.13
Side view of one part of a circular path around a compact disc. Part of the path is raised, part is not. In each interval, no change represents a 0; change up or down represents a 1. Each change is only one-sixth of a millionth of a meter.

Complexity of the Digital Signal

The best hi-fi systems reproduce all frequencies from about 20 hertz (cycles per second) to 18,000 hertz—from 3½ octaves below middle C to 6 octaves above middle C. This is roughly the range of human hearing (figure 7.14); hi-fi or high fidelity means we must reproduce faithfully all the sounds people can hear. Thus, there is really no reason for an audio system to record orchestra sounds at frequencies higher than about 20,000 Hz, even though a violin (for example) does give sounds up to 60,000 Hz.

In recording music on a compact disc, the recording company must sample the sound signal on the way to generating the digital signal. This first step in going to a digital signal is done with 44,000 samples per second. By the Nyquist sampling theorem, the digital signal can therefore preserve all sound frequencies up to 22,000 Hz (half the sampling rate), well beyond the limit of human hearing.

The size of each of these samples then must be described by a binary number (the quantizing and coding steps we discussed previously). How many binary digits should be used? In section 7.5 we used five bits (binary digits) to describe body temperature. This is nowhere near enough for high-quality music, however. The compact disc uses sixteen binary digits for each sample.

Now we begin to have a picture of the digital signal. We have 44,000 samples every second; each sample is described by sixteen binary digits. Thus, we have

44,000 × 16, or 700,000 bits per second

in the digital signal that represents the music. Each second of sound has to be represented by more than 700,000 zeros or ones.

The usual disc holds 74 minutes of music. If we perform the simple multiplications, we find that each disc holds more than 3,100,000,000 bits.

This number is so large that it really has very little meaning for most of us. Figure 7.15 illustrates how densely the information is packed. The large circle represents a typical disc. Within the small circle, there are 900,000 binary digits

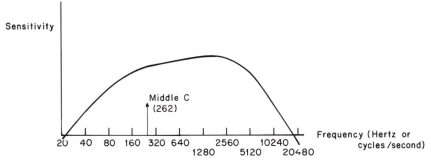

Figure 7.14
Sensitivity of the hearing of a healthy young person. Hearing is most sensitive (that is, can detect the weakest signal) when the frequency is about 2000 hertz. 18,000 hertz is about the maximum frequency, although infants and a few adults go to higher frequencies.

stored. In this region, the system must decide 900,000 times whether there has been a change in level or not. Obviously the laser beam must be aimed at precisely the correct spot on the disc. This technological accomplishment is even more astonishing when we realize that the system works in an automobile moving over bumpy streets.

Significance of This Complexity

The choices of 44,000 samples per second and 16 bits per sample mean that the CD gives major improvements in the performance of hi-fi systems. Indeed, these numbers are so large, we might ask why were they chosen. Both numbers exceed the capability of human hearing. Since hardly anyone can hear frequencies above 16,000 hertz, why not sample at 32,000 times per second rather than 44,000? Similarly, 12 bits per sample are about as much detail as human hearing can distinguish, so why go to 16? If the manufacturers had used 32,000 and 12, the recording and playback equipment would have been much simpler.

There are arguments for the higher performance of the CD. First, these digital recordings will last forever and hence represent permanent records of today's music. We should anticipate future demands and then design technology, when possible, to meet those needs. For the first time, we have the technology to do a superb job of recording sound; if we do not make the best equipment possible now, will it be obsolete in 60 years?

There is also a strictly commercial argument if one assumes that industry is motivated only by the "bottom line." To convince customers to discard their conventional turntables and 33⅓-rpm discs in favor of digital audio, the manufacturers must offer a product that is unquestionably better. Around

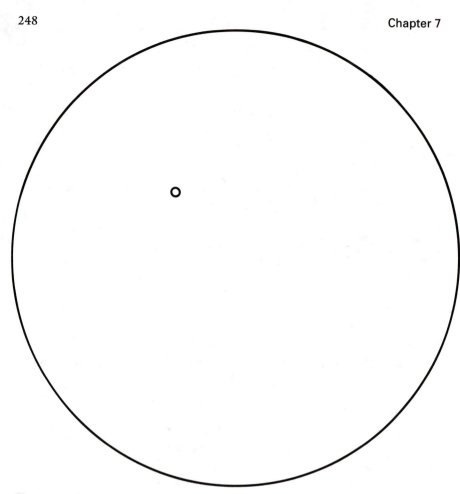

Figure 7.15
The large circle represents the size of a compact disc. The small circle holds about
900,000 bits of information.

1950, when CBS introduced the 33⅓-rpm record, audio enthusiasts did discard the obviously inferior 78-rpm equipment and make the major investment required for the changeover. Quadraphonic sound (three-dimensional instead of the two-dimensional stereo) was, in contrast, a marketplace failure, as the public never considered the music quality significantly better.

Advantages of the CD system

Is the CD (compact disc) system really better than the older 33⅓-rpm system? Some years ago, when CD equipment first appeared, engineers at the California Institute of Technology carried out an experiment to answer this question. They invited manufacturers of both analog (33⅓-rpm) and digital (CD) equipment to set up systems, then asked trained musicians to compare the performances without being aware of which system they were listening to at any time. The results were inconclusive: neither system was significantly better in the opinion of these musicians.

Such an experiment is interesting, but not really too meaningful in anticipating customer acceptance. Most hi-fi enthusiasts do not have unlimited money to spend on equipment, acoustically ideal rooms in which to locate speakers, or the resources to use only new discs. Consumer acceptance of digital equipment indicates that many buyers *do* find the new equipment significantly more pleasurable.

What are the principal advantages of digital audio? We can group these in two categories.

First, we have the potential capabilities for accurate reproduction of sound.

1. As noted above, the digital system can handle audio frequencies out to 22,000 hertz. This is a slight improvement in fidelity over the best analog system. (Some manufacturers are considering audio discs that record all frequencies out to 60,000 hertz or more.) Furthermore, the high-frequency performance of the 33⅓-rpm disc deteriorates rapidly as the pickup moves in toward the center. The first song recorded may carry frequencies out to 18,000 Hz, but the last song has less than half this frequency range. The problem is that the disc turns at a constant speed; near the end of the recording, the distance the needle travels in one revolution is small. Since the signal is the speed of the stylus, the grooves must have wider excursions to offset their lower speed in order to maintain signal fidelity. The digital system avoids this problem by increasing the rotational speed of the turntable as the laser pickup moves inward, so that the number of bits per inch is about the same throughout the recording. Every song appears with the same fidelity.

2. The digital system uses sixteen bits to describe each sample. Sixteen doublings of size are possible as we go from the weakest to the strongest signal.

In terms used by audio engineers, each doubling corresponds to an increase in sound amplitude of 6 deciBels. (This is really the definition of deciBels.) Thus, using sixteen bits means that the strongest signal can be 16×6 or 96 dB louder than the weakest signal. In the terminology of the hi-fi enthusiast, the "dynamic range" is 96 dB for digital audio. This capability contrasts markedly with the performance of analog systems. The 33⅓-rpm record gives a dynamic range of about 66 dB, limited by the maximum allowable radial motion of the pickup because of its mechanical nature (in particular, its inertia). Audio tape has a slightly larger dynamic range of about 76 dB, still much less than the CD's 96 dB. Furthermore, in both mechanical and magnetic analog systems, there is a certain amount of noise present, even with no signal. In the mechanical system, the needle has a slight radial movement because of its natural oscillation and because of imperfections in the circular groove. In the magnetic (cassette) system, there is always some residual magnetism. As a consequence of these features, the digital system is remarkably quiet during pauses in the music, then can move from very soft to unusually loud sound.

The second group of advantages of the digital system arise from the flexibility of digital signals and the nature of the playback mechanism:

1. There is essentially no contact with the disc, so there is no wear. Hi-fi enthusiasts often find that the quality of an LP deteriorates seriously after a few playings.

2. Having the signals in digital form (a sequence of zeros and ones) keeps minor imperfections of the disc from affecting the sound: the pickup needs only to be able to determine in any interval whether there is a change in height or not.

3. The disc will play properly even if there is a small hole at one point (even a hole the size of the small circle in figure 7.15). Automatic correction for these errors comes from two techniques: (a) Successive binary digits are recorded on different parts of a rotation, rather than together. Consequently, a hole or defect in the disc affects a set of numbers drawn from many *different* samplings of the original sound signal. (b) After the special-purpose computer in the playback system restores the binary digits to their proper sequence, redundancy is used for automatic error checking and correcting.

Thus, the playback computer automatically corrects any errors introduced by the small defect.

To conclude this section on digital audio, we should emphasize that the CD system possesses its various advantages because it uses digital signals. Once we convert the sound signal to a sequence of zeros and ones, we can use all the power of electronic digital techniques (including special-purpose computers) to process the signal—to record, to pickup, and to ensure fidelity. Even though the number of bits required each second seems overwhelming, we gain all the important advantages inherent in digital signals.

Review Questions

R7-1. In PCM we might quantize into 64, 128, 256, 512, or 1024 levels. Explain why only these numbers are used.

R7-2. Why are almost all new communication systems now PCM?

R7-3. The human being apparently can receive information at no greater a rate than about 100 bits per second. What does "100 bits per second" mean?

R7-4. In digital telephony, the equipment typically quantizes to 128 levels. Why was this number, 128, chosen?

R7-5. In digital telephony, the equipment samples 8000 times per second. Why was this number chosen?

R7-6. Where in the conversion of an analog signal to digital form do we introduce error?

R7-7. A physiological signal has a spectrum with a maximum frequency of 200 Hz. How many periodic samples are required to represent all the information in the original signal?

R7-8. "A compact disc can play perfect music even if there is a small defect." Explain briefly.

R7-9. What does the Nyquist sampling theorem state?

R7-10. "The dynamic range with a compact disc (CD) is 20 dB greater than with an LP." Explain briefly.

R7-11. My home audio system throws away all components over 10,000 Hz. How many samples per second are required if I want to put this signal in digital form?

R7-12. What lobbying group opposes the sale of DAT (digital audio tape) equipment in the United States? Explain briefly. (See problem 7-8.)

R7-13. The dynamic range of the compact disc is 96 dB. How is this achieved?

R7-14. Why was the sampling rate for digital audio tape chosen to be different from the rate for the compact disc? (See problem 7-8.)

R7-15. What are the advantages of digital audio tape over the compact disc? (See problem 7-8.)

R7-16. The compact disc maintains fidelity as the player moves toward the center. How?

R7-17. Why are successive samples scattered around the compact disc?

R7-18. What is meant by the quantization step in digitization?

R7-19. How can we determine the maximum rate (bits per second) at which human beings can receive information?

R7-20. What are the three steps in converting a signal to digital form?

Problems

P7-1. The BART mass transportation (subway) system in the San Francisco area has been beclouded by arguments and public criticism because of large cost overruns, unexpected delays, early safety problems and difficulties with the automated train-control system, low ridership, and failure to alleviate traffic problems. Now that several years of experience are available, there is still a strong feeling that the project was foolish.

Much of the technology is interesting. As one very small example, the central computer sends out electrical signals to each train to indicate the desired speed. Eight different speeds can be ordered, each represented by a six-digit binary signal:

130Km/h	101111
113	100111
80	101011
58	100011
44	100101
29	101001
10	100001
0	100000

Each order can be sent in $1/3$ second, each bit of information (a zero or a one) in $1/18$ second. The order is repeated continually.

a. To send eight different speed commands requires only three bits, or binary digits. When we choose a signal of six bits, we obviously have available an enormous amount of redundancy. Recognizing that the receiver of this signal may not know *when a particular signal begins and ends*, describe briefly how this redundancy is used.

b. Can the same successful communication without a synchronizing signal be obtained with five-digit signals—in other words, are six digits needed?

Hint: Although we might look for a general formula for the number of digits needed, it is easier to look at each case. For example, if we use a signal of four binary digits, the possibilities are the following:

A	0000	I	1000
B	0001	J	1001
C	0010	K	1010
D	0011	K	1010
E	0100	L	1011
F	0101	M	1100
G	0110	M	1101
H	0111	O	1110
		P	1111.

But signals with only one 1 are indistinguishable when a repeated signal is sent. For example,

BBBB   0001000100010001
CCCC   0010001000100010.

If we started observing at an unknown time within this sequence, we could not tell which signal we were picking up. Hence, if we use B, we can eliminate C, E, and I. We are left with

A	0000	J	1001
B	0001	K	1010
D	0011	L	1011
F	0101	M	1100
G	0110	N	1101
H	0111	O	1110
		P	1111.

Similarly, only one of the signals with two ones in a row and two zeros can be used. If we use D, we eliminate G, J, and M. Three ones in a row uses H but eliminates L, N, and O. We now have

A	0000	H	0111
B	0001	K	1010
D	0011	P	1111.
F	0101		

Finally, if F is used, K cannot be, and we have only six possibilities:

A	0000	F	0101
B	0001	H	0111
D	0011	P	1111.

Four digits are clearly not enough to send eight speeds if we insist that each speed is sent several times and reception can begin at any time in the sequence.

P7-2. The Gray Code is shown in given in box 7.5. This code has the interesting property that only one digit changes as we go from one number to the next larger (or smaller). By inspection of the example given in section 7.5, determine the rule or algorithm for generating the sequence of binary numbers. Apply this rule to list in sequence the five-digit binary numbers representing the decimal numbers 0 through 31.

P7-3. In comparison with the eye, the ear is exceedingly poor at detecting the direction from which a signal comes, but much better at noticing every short change in sound. For example, the ear can detect a sound break only $1/500$ of a second long. In this sense of determining brief signal changes, the sense of touch performs between hearing and vision. The human being is able to detect an interruption of only $1/100$ second in a steady pressure applied to the skin.

Thus, we might communicate with a human being by attaching to his skin buzzers or pressure devices at perhaps a dozen points around the body (points well separated and where the skin is sensitive to pressure). By applying different signals at the various locations, we can develop a complex code for sending information to the human being.

a. We desire to calculate the rate at which information can be communicated to a person through a system of vibrators attached to the body at six different locations. Each signal is a pulse lasting $1/10$ second. How many different symbols do we have if we can vibrate any one point, any pair of points, any triplet, and so forth, up to and including all six at once? (Note the similarity between this system and Braille.) Actually, we have to choose the sites with some care. They must be far apart, not connected to the ear (otherwise you "hear" the vibration), and not on corresponding points on the two halves of the body (why?).

b. We might increase the number of different signals by making each signal one of two possible intensities (e.g., soft or strong). Actually one can detect more than a dozen different intensities of pressure or vibration at a single point, but in rapid communication we want to use only signals which can be easily and reliably detected. With this greater flexibility, how many different signals are now available? In question c, we call this number N.

c. There are now N different signals which we can deliver to the man in any tenth of a second. The maximum amount of information that can be conveyed in $1/10$ second is then given by the equation

$$2^x = N,$$

where x is the amount of information in bits. The equation says that the number 2 raised to the x power is equal to N. We can find this amount of information without using the equation at all if we are satisfied with an approximate answer. Look at Table 7.4. If N is 400, the value of x lies somewhere between 8 and 9 (since 8 corresponds to N = 256 and 9 to N = 512). Hence, if there are 400 different signals, we can send a little more than eight bits of information. How many bits are represented by each of our N signals?

d. For our value of N, how much information can be sent every $1/10$ second? How much information per second? How does this compare with information sent through the eye in reading? To build a system such as this, we would have to train a person to recognize or understand the incoming signals. Does such a scheme seem feasible?

Actually, this idea of communicating through the sense of touch is hardly new; it was suggested by Jean-Jacques Rousseau in 1762 in his treatise "Emile." It is only in the last few years, however, that we have begun to understand scientifically the types of touch signals that can be understood by the human,

Table 7.4

x bits	2^x
1	2
2	4
3	8
4	16
5	32
6	64
7	128
8	256
9	512
10	1024
11	2048
12	4096

the structure of communication signals, and the ways in which signals might be coded and presented to a person for easy and reliable understanding. Experimental systems have been built that give rates of communication appreciably above those of telegraph transmission, but we still are a distance from matching the rate of communication that can be achieved by speech. Interest in this research comes from the military, anxious to communicate in dark and noisy environments, and from the problems of communicating with blind or with blind and deaf people.

Optional supplement: We might also try to obtain some measure of the human ability to receive information through the nerves leading from the hand to the brain by considering the activities of a good pianist. If each of the ten fingers can hit any one of three notes, how many different combinations are there (in other words, how many different signals)? Actually, nowhere near all these combinations are equally likely, so we might estimate a much smaller number as the number of different signals. If the pianist plays at a rate of 300 notes per minute, what is the corresponding ability of the nervous system to carry information, measured in bits per second?

P7-4. In April 1986, Bloomingdale's department store chain announced it would start using the UPC bar code on all items. (The UPC, or Universal Product Code, is discussed in chapter 2). There is still a question whether department stores will generally adopt the system. Will clothing manufacturers be willing to add the label to their products regardless of the increase in cost? Why is there a question about clothing manufacturers when food-product manufacturers comply?

Extra problem: With a black pen it is easy to change a UPC 5 to an 8 on the left side: we only need blacken bars 5 and 6. Is it possible to find a change such as the above where the check digit can easily be changed also to be correct?

P7-5. For automatic routing of mail, the Russians have an excellent system. On the bottom left of the envelope, there are guidelines for inserting the "zip code" (figure 7.16). For each digit, light guidelines are printed to show nine possible line segments (numbered above). Each decimal digit is represented by the code of Table 7.5.

Thus, the digit 0 is represented by the nine-digit binary number 111001101. The back of the envelope shows the code to be used—that is, how to form each digit (figure 7.17).

The code described above is really not ideal. With nine possible line segments, there are 512 possible binary numbers. We need only ten, one for each decimal digit. We certainly should be able to pick these ten so that each one differs from all others in at least two or three binary digits. But here, 0

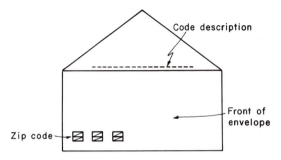

Code description

Front of envelope

Zip code

Figure 7.16

Table 7.5

Segment	Digit									
	0	1	2	3	4	5	6	7	8	9
1	X				X	X			X	X
2	X		X	X		X		X	X	X
3	X	X	X		X				X	X
4		X		X			X	X		
5				X	X	X	X		X	X
6	X						X	X	X	
7	X	X			X	X	X		X	
8			X	X						X
9	X		X			X	X		X	

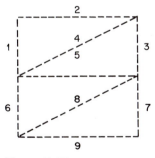

Figure 7.17

(111001101) and 8 (111011101) differ in only one digit, the fifth. It is relatively common for the reading equipment to mistake a 0 for an 8, or vice versa. (A careless pencil mark or dirt along segment 5 could cause the error.)

Unfortunately, the Russian engineers felt the above code was the best they could do. Explain why.

Postscript: Figure 7.18 shows a scheme where every symbol differs by at least three segments from every other.

P7-6. An entirely different scheme leads to the check digit for the ISBN (International Standard Book Number) code. A particular book might have the number

0-07-925140-4.

Here the initial zero indicates publication in the United States (other nations have different initial digits), 07 indicates the publisher (in this case McGraw-Hill), 925140 are the digits are assigned by the publisher to the specific book, and 4 is the check digit. If the ten successive digits are a, b, c, d, . . . , j, the check digit j is determined by the fact that

10a + 9b + 8c + 7d + 6e + 5f + 4g + 3h +2i + j

must be divisible by 11 with no remainder.

a. Show that the check digit for the ISBN number above is actually 4.

b. Why would such a complex scheme be used for finding the check digit?

P7-7. In section 7.4 we used the example of body temperature as a signal to be converted to digital form. We found that there were 25 different temperatures (95, 95.5, 96, . . . , 106.5, 107), so we needed five bits for each value.

We can get by with fewer bits. Suppose we send the first temperature (98.5) in the usual way , using five bits. Thereafter, we send only the *change since the last sample*. In our example in section 7.5, the temperatures and changes were

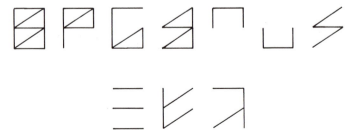

Figure 7.18

97.5

+0.5

98.0

+2

100.0

+2

102.0

0

102.0

-1.5

100.5.

Now we might find that there is never a rise of more than 2° or a drop of more than 1.5°. Hence, we need only eight different changes:

+2.0   0
+1.5   -0.5
+1.0   -1.0
+0.5   -1.5

These eight values can be represented by only three bits; our digital signal is simpler.

This concept of communicating the *change* rather than the total value of a signal is called delta modulation (the Greek letter delta is used in mathematics to represent change).

In telephony, delta modulation allows three bits per sample instead of seven. Explain why such a large saving is possible.

P7-8. In the mid-1980s, Japanese firms completed the development of Digital Audio Tape (DAT) equipment. This allows audio recording and playback, just as with conventional audio cassettes (although the DAT cassettes are slightly smaller), but with the sound recorded in digital form. The equipment has all the advantages of the CD, but also allows recording and is much less sensitive to vibration (e.g., in an automobile installation). Although the initial cost is about twice that of CD equipment, mass production will undoubtedly bring it down to a comparable level.

The American CD manufacturers and record companies reacted strongly to this threat. On February 5, 1987, Senator Albert Gore and colleagues introduced S.506, a bill requiring copy-code scanners in digital audio recorders. The same bill was introduced in the House of Representatives. It reads, in part, as follows:

(2) A "copy-code scanner" is an electronic circuit or comparable system of circuitry (A) which is built into the recording mechanism of an audio recording device; (B) which, if removed, bypassed, or deactivated, would render inoperative the recording capability of the audio recording device; (C) which continually detects, within the audio frequency range of 3,500 to 4,100 hertz, a notch in an encoded phonorecord; and (D) which, upon detecting a notch, prevents the audio recording device from recording the sounds embodied in the encoded phonorecord by causing the recording mechanism of the device to stop recording for at least 25 seconds.

(3) a "digital audio recording device" is any machine or device, now known or hereafter developed, which can be used for making audio recordings in a digital format. The term "digital audio recording device" includes any machine or device which incorporates a digital audio recording device as part thereof.

(4) An "encoded phonorecord" is a phonorecord which has a notch within the audio frequency range of 3,700 to 3,900 hertz.

(5) A "notch" is an absence of sound resulting from the removal of sound signals at a certain frequency.

(6) A "person" includes any individual, corporation, company, association, firm, partnership, society, joint stock company, or any other entity.

(7) A "phonorecord" is a material object in which sounds, other than those accompanying a motion picture or other audiovisual work, are fixed by any method now known or later developed, and from which the sounds can be perceived, reproduced, or otherwise communicated, either directly or with the aid of a machine or device. The term "phonorecord" includes the material object in which the sounds are first fixed.

After committee hearings, Congress asked the National Bureau of Standards to determine whether the proposed "notch" would seriously impair the music quality. Early in March 1988, the report responded affirmatively and the legislation was not sent by the committee to the full Senate.

The Japanese firms still, at the beginning of 1989, hesitated to market their DAT equipment in the United States.

a. The proposed legislation is remarkable. If it were passed, what music would have poorer quality? Explain briefly.

b. In order to discourage direct transfer of the CD digital signal to the DAT equipment, the DAT sampling rate is 48,000 per second. As a result, how can CD recordings be taped on DAT equipment?

Chapter 8
Signals through Space

Most of us have seen photographs taken by an infrared camera—bizarre colors in odd shapes that remind us of abstract art. Editors love to use these pictures on the covers of their magazines because they are eye-catching and at the same time look "scientific."

The pictures taken by infrared camera measure the *temperature* at each point in the scene. The process is called thermography—the pictorial measurement of heat. The normal camera measures the amount of light coming to the camera.

After you have had a few beers, thermographs of your body show the rise in the temperature of your liver. After a few puffs on a cigarette, the poorer circulation causes a noticeable drop in the temperature of the ends of your fingers. Applications abound for this technology:

1. Doctors locate tumors, which are hotter than the surrounding tissue.

2. Doctors treat severely burned patients by determining which skin is dead (the dead skin is 2 or 3 degrees cooler).

3. Coast Guard rescue helicopters locate boats lost on the ocean.

4. Firefighters pinpoint the hottest spots in a forest fire, even through intense smoke.

5. Rangers find lost hikers in the mountains.

6. Building managers locate areas where heat is leaking out of the building on cold winter days.

7. Wildlife managers count elk grazing at night.

8. Ranchers determine which cattle have fevers.

9. Military personnel detect the enemy in the darkness of the jungle.

This technology is an example of a system originally developed under Department of Defense funding, but later applied to a wide range of important civilian problems.

The camera equipment is expensive (perhaps $50,000 for a complete system), but remarkably flexible. The desired range of temperatures can be set by the user.

Furthermore, the picture can be displayed in either black and white or color. In black and white, the hotter the region, the whiter the image. For color pictures, distinct colors are arbitrarily chosen to represent each separate temperature. Vivid, clashing colors are generally used so the resulting picture is easier to interpret.

What is the camera actually measuring? The popular literature commonly says "heat waves" are given off by the object being observed. Before we can explain what this means, we first need to understand the properties of a more familiar signal: visible light.

8.1 Light

On a sunny afternoon at the beach, you gaze at your arm to see how sunburned you are. What is actually happening when you see your arm? What passes from your arm to your eyes? Light from the Sun hits your arm, then reflects off to your eyes. But what is light?

Light is an amazing phenomenon: *the ability to do work at a distance.* Electrically charged particles in the Sun are excited; then millions of miles away charged particles on your arm are excited in exactly the same way. This is light. Nothing travels from the Sun to your arm. Nothing passes from your arm to your eyes. In chapter 4 we learned that sound results from pressure variations in the air, but with light there is nothing happening to the air or in the space between the Sun and the Earth.

We can draw an analogy to the gravitational pull of the Earth. If you jump from an airplane, you fall toward the Earth. Nothing passes between you and the Earth, yet you are pulled and accelerated downward.

All atomic and molecular particles are continually in motion; the higher the temperature, the faster the motion. In the Sun, charged particles (electrons and ions) move rapidly because of the extremely high temperature. This movement of charged particles exerts forces on other charged particles, even those far away (like charges repel one another, opposite attract, and moving charges result in magnetic forces). So we can describe light as electric and magnetic forces at a distance.

The electric and magnetic *effects* of the charges moving in the sun travel outward at the speed of light (186,000 miles per second). Five hundred seconds after the motion of the charged particles in the Sun, the *effects* reach the Earth. The electrons and ions in your arm move. This action in turn causes electrical activity in the retina of your eye.

Thus, there is a sequence of electric and magnetic effects at a distance. Nothing material actually travels from the Sun to your arm or from your arm to your eyes. There is no domino effect of one electron causing motion in the next electron, causing motion in the next electron, all the way from the Sun to the Earth. In fact, the space between the Sun and the Earth is almost free of any particles at all.

This concept of an ability to do work at a distance is not an idea familiar to us from everyday experience. Until the end of the nineteenth century, many scientists still argued that there must be some substance filling space that light could travel through; they called this substance the "ether." Scientists love to think in terms of analogies, and they were familiar with waves traveling through water and sound waves traveling through air or other substances. The concept of a reaction at some distant place, with nothing in between, was too strange.

Electromagnetic Waves
In order to understand the phenomenon involved in light traveling from the Sun to your arm to your eyes, we introduce the idea of an *electromagnetic wave*. An electromagnetic wave is an *imaginary concept* that helps us describe the behavior of light, radio, x rays and ultraviolet light.

As the electrons move in the Sun (figure 8.1), we say an electromagnetic wave travels out from the Sun in all directions, with a very small part directed toward the Earth. The resulting *effects* of the electron motion appear first at the planet Mercury, then at Venus, and then at the Earth. This electromagnetic "wave" moves outward from the Sun at the speed of light (186,000 miles per second). Thus, the effects can be understood if we imagine a wave moving outward from the source. We can also talk about the velocity of the wave, the frequency, and the wavelength—just as we did for sound signals in chapter 4.

But what is the light "wave" made of? In a sound wave, we can measure the variation of pressure at a point as the wave passes by. In a water wave, we can observe the crests and troughs. In our light wave, two quantities "travel" with the wave: an electric force and a magnetic force; hence the term *electromagnetic wave*. When light strikes your arm, these forces cause the electrons and molecules to move very slightly. Indeed, if your arm stays in sunlight for awhile, it starts to heat up (the higher temperature meaning that the particles are

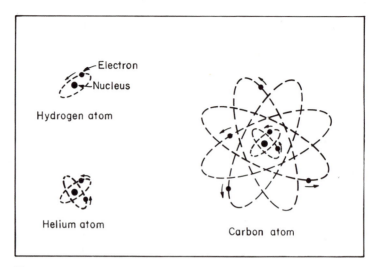

Figure 8.1
Simplified pictures of atoms of various elements.

moving more rapidly). When we say light is reflected off your arm to your eyes, we really mean that this motion of charged particles near the surface of your arm causes a new light wave to be emitted by your arm. But it is simpler to think in terms of our wave picture and just talk about reflection.

This is also the reason that light can pass through a windowpane but not through your arm. In a windowpane, there are very few free electrons roaming around to absorb energy from the incoming signal. Furthermore, the glass molecules cannot absorb energy at the frequency of the light signal, so the light passes through. In contrast, your arm is opaque, meaning that its molecules do absorb the light energy. Thus, when light hits a solid object, three things may happen (figure 8.2):

reflection (surface particles are excited, then reradiate the light backward)

transmission (no particles are excited, the light passes through)

absorption (interior particles are excited, little light either goes through or is reflected).

Often, of course, we find a mixture of all three.

In summary, we can explain many of the phenomena observed with light by visualizing light as an *electromagnetic signal or wave* traveling through space.

Velocity of Light
The velocity of light in space is usually given the symbol c (rather than v). The value of c is 186,000 miles per second, or 300 million meters per second ($3 \times$

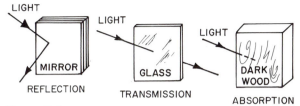

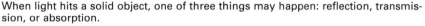

Figure 8.2
When light hits a solid object, one of three things may happen: reflection, transmission, or absorption.

10^8 m/sec). This is the maximum possible velocity; the value is less when light is moving through a liquid or solid substance.

Frequency of Light

Our eyes respond to electromagnetic signals at any frequency between 430×10^{12} Hz (430 trillion cycles per second) and 750×10^{12} Hz (750 trillion cycles per second). Hence, this is the range of frequencies corresponding to *visible* light (light that we can see). Only frequencies in this range stimulate the retina of the eye to generate electrical signals, which then travel through the optic nerve to the brain.

The different frequencies within this range correspond to the different colors of the rainbow (red, orange, yellow, green, blue, violet). Color vision is discussed in more detail in chapter 11; here we need only note that the lowest frequency corresponds to a deep red, the highest to a violet (figure 8.3).

8.2 Other Electromagnetic Signals

Electromagnetic signals can have frequencies anywhere from below 1 Hz to far above 10^{20} Hz. As is shown in figure 8.4, signals that represent visible light cover only a very small fraction of this range.

Other frequencies represent waves with different properties, so scientists have given them specific names. As we go up in frequency (figure 8.5), we have radio, microwaves, infrared, visible light, ultraviolet, x rays, and so on.

All these signals are electromagnetic waves, similar to light except in frequency. They all travel through space or air at the same velocity (about 186,000 miles per second), and they all show the characteristics of a wave, even though the basic phenomenon is the ability to do work at a distance.

Why are signals visible only in a very narrow frequency range? To answer this question, we have to use the picture of matter. An atom consists of a nucleus (neutrons and protons) around which electrons rotate in orbits. In the simplest model, there can be two electrons in the first orbit out from the nucleus, eight

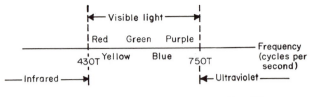

Figure 8.3
Visible spectrum, with colors indicated.

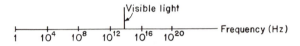

Figure 8.4
Range of frequencies for electromagnetic signals. Each scale division division is 10^4 (or 10,000) times the preceding one.

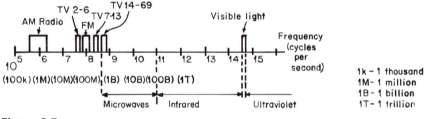

Figure 8.5
Electromagnetic spectrum.

in the second, and so on. The number of electrons is different for each element (hydrogen has one, helium two, and so on). The number of protons in the nucleus is equal to the number of electrons in the atom.

One way for an element or material to absorb energy from the incoming electromagnetic wave is for an electron to be excited and thus jump from its normal orbit to a more distant one. The energy required for this must be equal to the energy in a packet (photon) of incoming light at a frequency in the visible-light range. Thus, electromagnetic signals at these visible frequencies can deliver their energy to electrons in atoms or molecules. When such an electron falls back to its normal orbit, it emits an electromagnetic signal (light) again.

The detailed physics is much more complex than our description would indicate. But we can say that electromagnetic signals stimulate the retina only when they have just the right frequency (or energy per signal packet). This happens when the frequency is around 600×10^{12} Hz, the middle of the visible-light range.

At lower frequencies (such as radio waves), the signals pass right through wood or glass and are stopped only by a metal, in which there are a large number of free electrons moving around, unbound to any particular molecule. These free electrons can absorb any small amount of energy, so the frequency can be much lower than the visible range. Thus, radio waves pass easily through the walls of a wooden house, and your TV antenna can be located in your attic as well as on the roof.

At frequencies higher than the visible range, the electromagnetic signal carries so much energy that it can ionize atoms (that is, completely separate the electrons from the nucleus) or damage molecules.

Infrared Signals

Now we can return to the example that opened this chapter: the infrared camera. The term *infrared* means *below the red*, so we are talking about electromagnetic signals at frequencies less than the red end of the visible range. Actually the term applies to an enormous range of frequencies, from about 1×10^{11} Hz to 430×10^{12} Hz; that is, the highest infrared frequency is about 4300 times the lowest.

Any object at room temperature contains electrons and other particles which are moving randomly. This is the meaning of temperature: the higher the temperature, the faster this random motion. This motion of charged particles results in the radiation of electromagnetic signals. A resting or seated person radiates at a rate of about 100 watts—a phenomenon we are familiar with in a crowded room on a hot summer day, when the air conditioning system cannot pump all this heat energy outside.

Most of this energy is infrared radiation; there is no visible light (people do not glow in a completely dark room). The temperature is so low, the velocity of the charged particles so small, that any oscillations are at frequencies below the visible range. There is also radiation at radio frequencies, but the energy is so small that this does not account for much of the heat radiated.

When we light a charcoal fire, the fuel first is heated by using flammable lighter fluid or paper and wood. Before the color changes at all, we can feel the heat radiated—the infrared signals. As heating continues, we develop a "red-hot" fire: the temperature is now high enough to give some radiation in the red end of the visible range. Further heating gives a "white-hot" fire, with electro-magnetic signals covering the entire visible range. By far the greatest part of the energy radiated is still in the infrared region: we have much more heat than light.

Similarly, an incandescent light bulb is just hot enough to radiate white light (that is, light over the full visible range of frequencies). If the light bulb were slightly cooler, all the energy radiated would be infrared or heat, since the electrons in the filament are not moving fast enough to generate electromagnetic signals at a frequency high enough to be visible. (In problem 8-5, we see that a 6 percent drop in light-bulb voltage reduces the light output by a much higher percentage. When the voltage drops, the filament temperature falls and soon we find no visible light at all, just infrared or heat.)

Now let's return to our infrared camera. A person is radiating electromagnetic signals at infrared frequencies (at a power of 100 watts). These infrared waves travel outward from the person exactly like light waves if the person is standing in sunlight, but the infrared signals are too low in frequency to stimulate the retinas of our eyes.

Ordinary photographic film is sensitive to the same frequencies as the human eye. Indeed, the photograph should reproduce the scene just as we would see it. Infrared film, on the other hand, changes chemically in response to electromagnetic signals at infrared frequencies.

The infrared signals depend critically on the temperature of the object the camera is *looking at*. When the temperature rises as little as a part of one degree, the infrared radiation changes. How much this special film is exposed (that is, how white that part of the picture is) depends on the temperature of that spot in the picture.

Thus, in each of the applications mentioned at the beginning of this chapter, the infrared camera simply measures differences in temperature among parts of the scene being *viewed*.

Uses of Electromagnetic Signals

Figure 8.5 shows that electromagnetic signals at different frequencies are used for AM radio, FM radio, and TV. Other frequencies are reserved for police radio, amateur radio, Citizen's band radio, navigation, mobile telephones, radio between pilots and flight controllers, microwave relay, radar, and satellite communications.

Each of these applications is assigned its own group of frequencies so that we avoid interference. For example, when we turn our TV to channel 9, we don't want to hear a police radio message.

All the frequencies from the very low to the infrared are assigned in the United States by the Federal Communications Commission (FCC). Once we get into the infrared and visible-light ranges, the natural signals are so strong that these frequencies cannot be used for broadcasting, so the FCC worries only about frequencies below the infrared range.

Microwave Ovens

Percy L. Spencer was standing near an operating radar set one day when he discovered that a chocolate bar in his pocket had melted. This gave him the idea to use the heat generated by microwaves for cooking. In 1945 he obtained the basic patent for the microwave oven.

As we saw in figure 8.5, microwaves are electromagnetic signals at frequencies from about 500 million Hz to about 100 billion Hz. In a microwave oven, a signal at 2450 MHz is generated in a device called a magnetron. This signal travels down a metal tube to the cooking chamber. The microwave signals bounce or reflect off the walls, and pass back and forth within the oven chamber.

The frequency has been carefully chosen. This is a frequency at which water molecules absorb energy from the electromagnetic signal—a type of resonance phenomenon. Since all foods contain water, when the microwave signal hits this moisture the water molecules vibrate. This energy from the vibration of the molecules causes heat, which cooks the food. The microwaves pass directly through paper or plastic dishes, which contain no water. The efficiency is exceptionally high, since the energy goes only into the moist food (a microwave oven uses as little as ¼ of the energy used by a regular oven).

There is a risk in cooking pork in a microwave oven. To kill the trichinosis microorganisms, a temperature of 170°F must be reached throughout the pork. Water is not evenly distributed through pork, however, so some small, particularly dry regions may not be heated enough to kill the microorganisms. In a 1981 bulletin, the U.S. Department of Agriculture suggested that users rotate pork during cooking and check the temperature in several locations with a meat thermometer.

Other frequencies could be used: 5800 and 10,600 MHz are also possibilities. Litton Industries requested FCC permission to sell ovens with a 10,600-MHz option to improve the external browning of meat, but this frequency was allocated to Xerox for a business communication system.

There are over 10 million microwave ovens in use in the United States. The ease and speed of cooking make them particularly attractive. Microwave cooking also preserves more of the nutrients in food, since they are not dissolved in the water or broken down by the long cooking time of a conventional oven.

The question most often asked about microwave ovens is "Are they safe?" This cannot be answered with a firm *yes* or *no*. In section 8.3, we will see why.

Electromagnetic Interference

With all the electromagnetic signals now being generated, it is not surprising when the signal from one device affects the operation of an entirely different device. Many examples of this have already been reported, and as we become more and more surrounded by electronics, new problems of electromagnetic interference will continually arise.

In 1975, the National Highway Traffic Safety Administration required that all new trucks have anti-skid braking systems. Manufacturers decided to use electronic controls. Some time later, it was discovered that a Citizen's Band radio operated near one of these trucks would actuate the brakes; 18,000 trucks had to be recalled.

Many home ovens have electronic timing controls; before leaving home, you can set the timer so the oven turns on at a desired time. Unfortunately, if a neighbor opens a garage door by remote control or a police radio is used nearby, the electromagnetic signal may turn on your oven.

Citizen's Band radio can interfere seriously with channel 2 on television. When an AM radio station sends out signals at an authorized frequency, great care is taken so that the signals are only within the allowed range of frequencies. In CB radio, where cheaper, less elaborate transmitters are used, the signal includes harmonics of the desired frequency (just as we saw in chapter 4 that a musical instrument gives harmonics). The second harmonic of the CB frequency falls in the band set aside for TV channel 2.

A very expensive sports car with electronic fuel injection stalled each time it attempted to pass another car in which the driver was using his CB radio.

A newly installed hospital paging system interfered with medical electronic equipment in the hospital's intensive care unit. Fortunately, the problem was corrected before any patients were affected.

One person operating a hand-held two-way radio knocked out an entire oil refinery for an afternoon because the refinery was using electronically based automated equipment. It cost the company hundreds of thousands of dollars to get the plant back into production.

How do we prevent such problems? Electromagnetic signals do not pass through metal, so we need to shield (enclose in metal) all critical electronic systems. Next, each transmitter (for example, a CB radio) must not radiate signals outside its allotted frequency band. Unfortunately, both solutions require expensive equipment and demand government policing action to enforce the regulations.

All these phenomena are effects of electronic equipment on other electronic systems. Even more interesting is the possible effect of electromagnetic signals on people.

8.3 Biological Effects of High-Frequency Electromagnetic Signals

What are the effects of electromagnetic signals on human beings? Are dental x rays risky? Is a microwave oven dangerous? If you work or live near a TV broadcasting station, will your health be adversely affected?

These are very difficult questions for which science often has no simple answers. We do know the problem can be broken into two parts (figure 8.6). At frequencies above the range of visible light, the signals are *ionizing radiation*. Here the signal has enough energy to break up molecules and atoms: electrons are pulled completely away from the atom, which is left with a positive charge (that is, it is a positive ion). At frequencies below the range of visible light (the frequencies of radio and radar), the energy is too low to pull apart atoms. The primary effects are on free electrons or ions—the free electrons in a metal or conductor, or the charges already flowing through the nervous system (when the effects are essentially electromagnetic interference).

We know that gamma rays (from a nuclear explosion, for example) can have disastrous biological effects when exposure is strong. Body cells are destroyed and chromosomes are split when gamma rays enter the body, as scientists found after the explosions at Hiroshima and Nagasaki.

X rays and ultraviolet signals can also have serious effects. Excessive ultraviolet light leads to skin cancer, and x rays can cause genetic changes and lead to the death of body cells. The human body is such an adaptive, self-correcting system, and the effects vary so much by chance, that we cannot say that ten chest x-rays every 20 years are OK and more are dangerous. All we can say is that the more chest x-rays you have, the more likely it is that there will be adverse consequences.

8.4 Biological Effects of Non-Ionizing Radiation

Electromagnetic radiation in the lower frequencies (visible light and below) is an entirely different matter. This radiation is called *non-ionizing*: the energy is

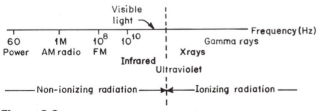

Figure 8.6
Range of electromagnetic frequencies.

not sufficient to break up the atoms or molecules. Do these electromagnetic signals (radio, microwave, infrared, and visible light) have any negative effects on people? The question is important because the number of electronic devices emitting low-level radiation is growing explosively (figure 8.7).

Engineers and scientists do not know the answer. Most scientists working in radio or radar think not. Scientists always tend to underrate the risks in their own field. Some of this reaction is due to the fact that familiarity breeds contempt; some of it certainly arises from the feeling that "I have been working with radar for 20 years, and I'm still healthy." On the other hand, a few vocal scientists have been as extreme in the opposite direction. They claim that Americans are endangered by the electromagnetic signals from the 11,000 broadcasting transmitters, the 30 million CB radios, and the 40,000 miles of overhead high-power transmission lines.

As with so many environmental problems, the truth probably lies somewhere between the two extremes. Locating the truth requires much more careful scientific research than has been done so far. Yet even with our very inadequate knowledge, society has to make a decision. Do the possible risks involved in the technology outweigh the benefits?

The effects of non-ionizing electromagnetic signals on human beings is representative of an entire class of environmental problems:

1. We know that massive amounts of the "pollution" are harmful. As the electromagnetic signals are steadily increased in intensity, we reach a point at which the body cannot dissipate the heat.

2. We are continually subjected to a small amount of the "pollution" from nature—electromagnetic signals from the Sun and Earth.

3. We do not know whether there is an exposure threshold—that is, a value of signal strength below which there is no effect at all. If we could do carefully

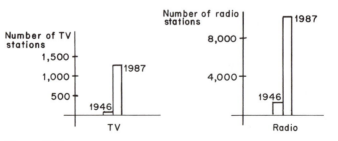

Figure 8.7
Growth in numbers of radio and TV stations between 1946 and 1987. These stations contribute only a fraction of the electromagnetic pollution that surrounds us. CB radios, garage-door openers, TV games, calculators, auto ignition systems, and many more electronic devices also cause low-level radiation.

controlled experiments with many people over a long period of time, which of the graphs in figure 8.8 would accurately describe the situation?

4. We do not understand the electrical and magnetic operation of our central nervous system or other parts of the body well enough to predict the effects of electromagnetic signals.

5. Studies on animals (mice or primates) may not be directly relevant to human beings.

6. Experiments on people are generally not possible within ethical and moral standards. No one would seriously suggest testing the effects of electromagnetic radiation by subjecting 100 children to specific doses of radiation for 10 years.

7. We probably need experiments over a very long period of time. Just as cancer tends to be 20 years in developing, we would not be surprised if the effects of electromagnetic signals did not show up until years after the initial exposure.

8. There may well be synergistic effects. In other words, electromagnetic signals may influence certain biological mechanisms and change the effects of other external factors. Then whether the electromagnetic signal has an effect or not depends on whether the other agent (perhaps a virus) is present. Possibly electromagnetic fields and saccharin together are harmful, but each alone is harmless. (This is a ridiculous conjecture, but it is illustrative of synergistic effects.) Unfortunately, scientists cannot test every possible combination of pollutants.

9. To understand the problem, we listen to the *experts*. Unfortunately, speakers on both sides frequently exaggerate more and more as they seek to influence the public and, often, to enhance their own reputations.

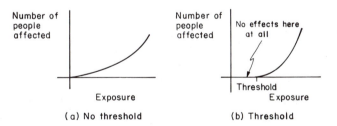

Figure 8.8
Two possible results of complete scientific studies. (a) Even with extremely small exposures, there is a very small probability of bad effect. (b) For all exposures below the threshold, there is no measurable effect.

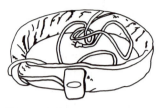

Figure 8.9
The I-ON-A-CO or Wilshire Belt. In 1926, a highly successful media expert and land developer, Gaylord Wilshire, announced the discovery of "a simple and effective method of using magnetism for the cure of human ailments." In newspaper ads, he promised that the I-ON-A-CO belt not only cured illness but also beautified the wearer. When plugged into a wall socket, the coils of wire conducting current sent a magnetic field through the wearer. So many of these belts were sold that both the American Medical Association and the Better Business Bureau tried to protect the public by announcing that there were no curative or beautifying effects.

8.5 Standards for Exposure

The extensive use of radar during World War II created an interest in the possible human effects of electromagnetic fields. This early radar equipment often broke down, and it was not uncommon for technicians to spend hours standing beside the operating radar to make manual adjustments.

There were some early reports of male sterility, presumably as a result of radiation. Some years later, there were reports of eye cataracts developing rapidly in individuals who worked intensively with high-power radar equipment designed to detect enemy missiles at long range.

In the late 1950s, a committee was established by the American Standards Association (now the American National Standards Institute). People were assembled from industry, universities, and throughout the profession to establish a standard for safe exposure to electromagnetic fields.

Problems in Setting a Standard

The committee faced almost insurmountable problems. When you assemble such a group, you naturally want knowledgeable people—preferably individuals who have already worked extensively in the area. The trouble is that these people are likely to be working or consulting for the industries manufacturing or using the equipment in question. While they may try to avoid personal biases, individuals working in an area tend to underrate the risks of that field. Furthermore, a standard formulated by such a committee can be attacked by individuals seeking stricter regulation just on the basis of the conflicts of interest of committee members. On the other hand, we certainly do not want regulations formulated by people who know nothing about the subject.

A second problem in the United States is the inevitable pressure from industry to set the allowable exposure level at the highest possible value. We are a litigious society, starting lawsuits over issues that would never reach the courts in other advanced nations.

A popular story takes place during a war between two small nations, one supported by the U.S. and the other by the USSR. There is a collision of two tanks. The Russian driver of one tank jumps out waving a white flag and yells "I surrender." The American driver of the other tank hobbles out moaning "Whiplash."

This love of lawsuits, and the plentiful supply of lawyers, means that an unreasonably low national standard of electromagnetic exposure would encourage product-liability suits against the manufacturers and distributors. To avoid such suits, the manufacturers would have to go to considerable expense to keep exposure low, and the national economy would suffer needlessly. Thus, there is pressure to set the standard as high as possible while still protecting the public.

U.S. Standard

The committee to establish the standard for electromagnetic exposure deliberated almost 10 years before announcing a standard in 1966. It had the following facts to work from:

1. We are all exposed to some electromagnetic fields from nature—for example, the radiation from warm objects all around us. This exposure (below the infrared frequencies) is about $1/10$ microwatt per square centimeter, written as $1/10\ \mu W/cm^2$. This sounds like a small amount of power—one ten-millionth of a watt—and indeed it is. But electromagnetic power is often very small. For example, the human eye responds to light as weak as $10^{-17}\ W/cm^2$. The electromagnetic signals thus are measured by the power (watts) they deliver to a given area of your body. Into each square centimeter, the natural signals transfer $1/10$ of a microwatt, or one-tenth of a millionth of a watt. In this section, we will always measure signal strength in microwatts per square centimeter.

2. Calculations had shown that a person can get rid of an extra $10,000\ \mu W/cm^2$ of heat transferred into the body. The normal physiological processes of perspiration, metabolic changes, and so forth allow the person to maintain the desired body temperature even when this much heat power is being delivered to the skin. The body loses 100 watts normally, and its surface area is about 20,000 square centimeters, so the healthy body is dissipating about $5000\ \mu W/cm^2$. Twice this amount can easily be dissipated, even by a conservative estimate.

3. The only known effect of electromagnetic signals on human beings was the heating of the body.

4. Experiments on small animals indicated that lengthy exposure to 500,000 μW/cm² caused cataracts and inhibited reproduction.

Thousands of hours of committee work went into these considerations, but it must be emphasized that there really was not much information on which to base a decision. Yet a standard was clearly necessary. We could not subject people to obvious risk for the many years required to establish scientific facts based on carefully controlled experiments.

The committee decided on a standard for worker exposure of 10,000 μW/cm²—an amount of heat that seemed to be easy for the body to get rid of without any question. This was a standard to protect workers using or near electronic equipment; it was not intended as a guide for allowable public exposure for short periods of time. (The length of time you are exposed is obviously important, since brief exposure to intense heat is not harmful.)

The Soviet Union set its standard 1/1000 times as great: only 10 μW/cm² per work week. (Defending the U.S. standard, one engineer pointed out that, if an equally low level were required for infrared radiation in the USSR, the Sun would be banned.)

Such a great difference between the two countries is startling. There were many reasons for the difference (see page 277):

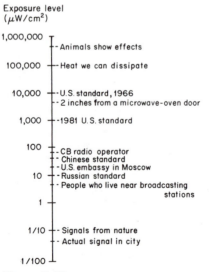

Exposure level
(μW/cm²)

1,000,000 — Animals show effects

100,000 — Heat we can dissipate

10,000 — U.S. standard, 1966
 — 2 inches from a microwave-oven door

1,000 — 1981 U.S. standard

100 — CB radio operator
 — Chinese standard
 — U.S. embassy in Moscow
10 — Russian standard
 — People who live near broadcasting stations

1

1/10 — Signals from nature
 — Actual signal in city

1/100

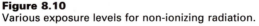

Figure 8.10
Various exposure levels for non-ionizing radiation.

1. The Americans were much more experienced in electronics and the development of radar equipment.

2. There are no product-liability lawsuits in the Soviet Union, and enforcement is at the discretion of the government, which is also the manufacturer. Thus, enforcement occurs only when it is convenient.

3. The Soviets believed that exposure caused neurological and psychological effects, although scientists in other countries were unable to repeat results of Soviet studies and questioned the validity of the reports.

Developments during the 1970s

In 1972, the columnist Jack Anderson revealed that for years the Soviets had been beaming electromagnetic signals into the U.S. embassy in Moscow, and that there had been a secret study in 1965 to determine whether there were any adverse health effects. Neither this study nor a later one by Johns Hopkins University was able to detect any health effects on the embassy personnel.

The Soviets apparently did believe there were ill effects from electromagnetic radiation. When the American Bobby Fischer soundly defeated Boris Spassky in a chess match in Reykjavik, some Soviets claimed that Fischer had had microwave equipment hidden in his chair and had debilitated Spassky with electromagnetic signals.

The U.S. government also established a safety standard for microwave ovens: 5000 µW/cm² at a distance of 5 centimeters (about 2 inches) from the oven door. (Here again, the time of exposure is important. This is the standard to cover people working in restaurants where the oven has heavy use. The homeowner is exposed so little of the time, that there probably is no risk of any significance.)

In the late 1970s, scientists discovered that electromagnetic signals could influence brain waves. When an electromagnetic signal varies in amplitude at a frequency close to a brain-wave frequency, the external signal can entrain or capture the brain wave—that is, the external signal causes the brain wave to change its frequency to that of the outside signal, so the two are in step. This discovery that electromagnetic signals could influence brain waves raised important issues. First, it showed that heating is not the *only* effect of electromagnetic signals on people; it raised the possibility there may be other effects on the central nervous system, which operates with its own electrical signals. Second, it was disturbing since it is not clear what the significance of changing brain-wave frequencies may be on the behavior of the person.

There were, at various times, other suggestions that electromagnetic signals might have important biological effects other than heating. Headaches and

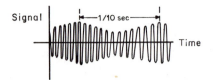
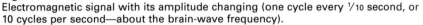

Figure 8.11
Electromagnetic signal with its amplitude changing (one cycle every ¹⁄₁₀ second, or 10 cycles per second—about the brain-wave frequency).

blood disorders among people working with radar or radio were occasionally blamed on exposure. Life scientists discovered that electric currents could accelerate the healing of fractured bones, that electromagnetic signals could alter biological rhythms, and that current could reduce pain when appropriately applied. Potassium transfer across cell boundaries is modified by electromagnetic fields. There still was no clear evidence that electromagnetic signals below 10,000 $\mu W/cm^2$ had any harmful effect on people; on the other hand, science can never prove that a particular environment is completely safe.

In 1977 the journalist Paul Brodeur published a book, *The Zapping of America: Microwaves, Their Deadly Risk and the Cover Up*, in which he charged that everyone in the United States is living in an electromagnetic environment hazardous to health. He accused the government, the military, and industry of overt attempts to keep this information from the public. After the appearance of this book, and other articles by scientists who argued that there were significant dangers, the increased public awareness led to court actions trying to stop construction of radio and radar transmitters, and to protect people living or working in areas where electromagnetic signals are strong.

One important result of this open, public debate was the reduction of the U.S. exposure standard by a factor of ten. Possibly of more importance is the federal government's support of a large number of research projects to study the effects of frequently encountered low-level electromagnetic signals on animals and human beings.

8.6 Project Sanguine-Seafarer-ELF

In the 1950s, the Cold War dominated American military planning. Both the United States and the Soviet Union had nuclear weapons, intercontinental ballistic missiles, and nuclear-powered submarines that could run submerged for weeks at a time. By the end of the decade, long-range missiles that could be fired without surfacing were added to the nuclear subs. If attacked, we wanted to be able to retaliate with the certainty of catastrophic damage to the aggressor. Knowing this, no country would consider being an aggressor.

The missile-firing nuclear submarines appeared to be the answer to this military goal. If we have a large number of submarines cruising continuously, no other country can hope to know where every submarine is located. Each sub would use its precision inertial-navigation equipment to determine its position and, hence, how to aim its missiles to hit pre-specified enemy targets.

There is one problem with this "ideal" solution: if we are attacked, how do we get the word to all those submarines submerged throughout the oceans of the world? How do we order them to retaliate?

Possible Ways to Communicate

Unfortunately, the usual radio signals disappear rapidly as they travel through water. A signal at 25,000 Hz travels only about 6 feet below the ocean surface. Furthermore, high-frequency radio signals do not bend around the surface of the Earth, so we need many transmitters to reach all parts of the world. An answer to both these problems is to use *extremely low* frequencies for the radio signal—as low as 76 Hz. These signals *do* travel a few hundred meters through water, so the submarine need not risk exposure by raising an antenna to the surface; and they do bend around the Earth, so one transmitting antenna is all that is needed.

The complete extremely-low-frequency system has not yet been built, even though the Navy has long argued that it is essential for national security. How do we now communicate with the submarines?

The primary answer is through airplanes transmitting signals at very low frequencies between 14,000 and 40,000 Hz. This TACAMO (for TAke Charge And Move Out) system depends on aircraft flying over both the Atlantic and Pacific Oceans. To radio, the plane extends an antenna nearly 5 miles long. Even so, the submarine has to rise near the surface and extend its own receiving antenna. Finally, there is the possibility the system would fail during war because of the vulnerability of the airplanes, the EMP effects (see the appendix of this chapter), and the susceptibility to jamming.

A second possibility currently being studied is a blue laser beam sent from an orbiting satellite. Light of this color (frequency) penetrates several hundred feet through the sea. The limited power available in the satellite (possibly 400 watts) means that the beam must be sharply focused, so the beam has to sweep back and forth until contact is made with the submarine.

Richard Garwin (an IBM scientist who has contributed various imaginative approaches to defense planning) has suggested a RAGU system (Radio receiving And Generally Useful). A "fish" (a torpedo-like device) would move just below the ocean surface, receive radio signals from a satellite, and re-transmit them to the submarine by sound or sonar signals.

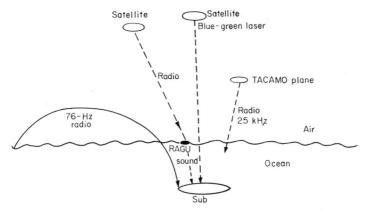

Figure 8.12
Submarines can travel at tens of knots, hundreds of feet underwater. But radio
signals broadcast by ground stations and TACAMO aircraft penetrate no more than
30 or 40 feet in seawater. To receive a message, the sub must slowly tow a wire or
buoy—keeping it on, or slightly beneath, the surface—or deploy a dish antenna to
monitor satellite transmissions. ELF, the blue laser, and the proposed fish RAGU
allow subs to run in deep waters, at any speed, without breaking contact. RAGU
would relay satellite messages to subs via an acoustical link. The sub's sonar would
pick it up; yet the signal would dissipate quickly in the water, so as not to be heard at
long range. (From *Popular Science*, April 1987, p. 48, drawing by Eliot Bergman.)

The 76-Hz System

The most promising way to communicate with submarines is a radio signal at
76 Hz. To transmit a signal at this very low frequency, we need an exceptionally
long antenna—one about 120 miles in length. (The higher the frequency, the
shorter the antenna.) Clearly a vertical antenna over 120 miles high was out of
the question, so the original Navy plan was to build a horizontal antenna that
covered an area 150 miles by 150 miles (the size of Connecticut, New
Hampshire, and Massachusetts).

But size is not the only problem. The ground under the antenna must be a
poor electrical conductor, so that the return current (figure 8.13) flows back
to its source deep under the ground. If the current flows back close to the
antenna wire, there is almost no energy radiated, since the magnetic fields from
the two currents nearly cancel. This requirement ruled out such obvious
locations as the atomic test site in Nevada. Only three locations seem to be
feasible and not too densely populated: northern Wisconsin, central Texas, and
northern Michigan.

History

The Navy started research on this communication system in 1958 under the
name Project Pangloss. By the time of the public announcement 11 years later,

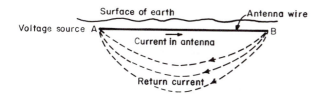

(a) Current flow in the horizontal, underground antenna.

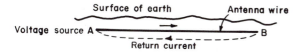

(b) Unsatisfactory operation -- the earth is too good a
     conductor, and very little power is radiated or broadcast.

Figure 8.13
Power radiated depends on electrical conductivity of ground.

the name had been changed to Project Sanguine, and a location had been
selected in northern Wisconsin. A public-relations film, "A New Voice in the
Northwoods," explained the project, which was to cost over $1 billion and
cover 41 percent of the state.

Reaction from the Wisconsin public was so vehement that a few years later
the Navy announced a shift to a site in Texas, close to the L. B. Johnson ranch
and in a region where public sentiment supported strong defense measures.

During the next year, public objections mounted steadily in Texas, so the
Navy moved the site to northern Michigan (Gerald Ford's state). Again, the
citizens of the state objected so strongly that in 1974 the Navy announced
temporary suspension of all work on Project Sanguine. By that time, $73
million had been spent without any start on actual construction.

During the next fiscal year the research work on the project continued. The
presidential campaign of 1976 brought Jimmy Carter to northern Michigan,
where he assured the residents that the system would not be located there if he
were elected. The budget presented to Congress in 1977 again included funds
for the program, then renamed Project Seafarer.

During the next four years, research and testing of a small model in northern
Wisconsin continued, with occasional interruptions as the government debated
whether to go ahead or not. In the presidential campaign of 1980, Ronald
Reagan again promised Michigan the project would not be pursued, but in
1981 $35 million was included in the budget for a much smaller version ($1/20$

the original area, but still covering over 1000 square miles), renamed ELF (for Extremely Low Frequency).

With continuing objections from the public, the Navy is now operating Project Mini-ELF. In northern Michigan there will be 56 miles of cable above ground, using telephone poles in the shape of an F. The northern Wisconsin transmitter (28 miles in an X shape) is already in operation. The hope is that this smaller system will demonstrate the importance of the system to national security and the safety to people in the vicinity; then the Navy can move toward the full-scale system necessary to reach all parts of the world reliably.

The sequence of names (Pangloss, Sanguine, Seafarer, ELF, and mini-ELF) is a commentary on technological public relations. Who doesn't love elves? Mini-elves are even better. Whoever coined "Sanguine" apparently thought the word meant only confident and optimistic and overlooked the other meaning: bloody.

Signals to Be Broadcast
The plan is to broadcast continually at either of two frequencies, 72 and 80 Hz, with the possibility of shifting from one frequency to the other 16 times every second. In other words, if 72 Hz is represented by a 0 and 80 Hz by a 1, the system will be able to transmit 16 binary digits a second. The one-second message

1 0 1 1 0 1 0 0 1 1 1 1 0 1 0 0

would be sent by broadcasting sine signals at frequencies of 80, 72, 80, 80, 72, 80, 72, 72, 80, 80, 80, 80, 72, 80, 72, and 72 Hz. Each signal would be sent for 1/16 second. During the first 1/16 second, the system would broadcast exactly five cycles of an 80-Hz sinusoid; during the next 1/16 second, 4.5 cycles of a 72-Hz sinusoid (figure 8.14). The information about an attack would be sent by a pre-arranged secret code using the binary digits.

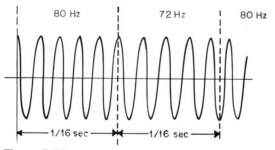

Figure 8.14
First 2/16 second of the message in the text.

The average frequency is 76 Hz, so a very long antenna is necessary. The antenna planned for the full system is a grid of wires in two directions: north-south and east-west. (This ensures radiation in all directions and complete coverage of the Earth.) The north-south array consists of 25 wires, each between 19 and 96 miles in length and spaced 3 to 5 miles apart. Thus, the north-south antenna might have the appearance of figure 8.15. This arrangement is used to obtain the effect of a much longer single antenna. The cables are not of equal length and not parallel in order to avoid hazards such as ponds and to take advantage of government rights-of-way along highways. The east-west array is in the same region and approximately perpendicular to the north-south arrangement.

In order to radiate enough power to give a detectable signal at the receiving antenna of the underwater submarine, the power fed to the cables must be very large. A voltage of 5000 volts results in a cable current of 100 amps; the total array absorbs 14 million watts, about the same as 14,000 homes.

Feasibility

Opponents of Project Seafarer frequently claim the system will not work in actual wartime conditions. After a nuclear attack, radio propagation is seriously disturbed by atmospheric ionization (see the appendix of this chapter). Furthermore, at the low frequencies used here, the noise level is high and an enormous amount of redundancy will be necessary to ensure reception of the true signal. The system described above can send only 16 binary digits a second. If we add redundancy (for example, repeating each message eight times), it takes as long as five minutes to send one coded message.

Furthermore, since the one antenna will cover the world, it will be relatively easy for the enemy to build its own antenna before it attacks the United States. Simultaneously with the attack, the enemy could start transmitting meaningless or confusing signals which would "jam" our transmissions.

The grid of antenna wires means that a bomb hit on one part of the array would still permit broadcasting; there is, however, the possibility that an enemy could destroy the electrical power generating station.

Figure 8.15
North-south antenna array.

Environmental Effects

The environmental effects are always very difficult to anticipate in a major project such as Seafarer. The Navy has operated its single test antenna, which is a few miles long, in northern Wisconsin with no significant environmental effects observed, but it is not clear that the results would be the same with a larger system.

The Navy and a committee of the National Academy of Sciences have considered a variety of possible environmental effects and in each case have debated whether existing scientific knowledge would indicate a reason for concern. The biological topics that have been considered include the following:

1. cell growth and division

2. genetics

3. fertility, growth, and development

4. triglyceride levels in human beings

5. circadian rhythms

6. electrosensitive fish

7. insect behavior

8. magnetotactic bacteria (these bacteria line up along magnetic fields and then swim in that direction)

9. bird orientation and navigation

10. plant development

11. mammalian neurophysiology and behavior

12. soil organisms

13. small mammals.

The National Academy of Sciences study, completed in 1977, found no clear indication of any harmful effects, although it did emphasize that research should continue in several of these areas. For example, the committee found no real evidence of an increase in serum triglycerides in people exposed to low-frequency electromagnetic fields, and no indication that ELF fields are a genetic hazard. In other areas, the report recognized that there might be effects on magnetotactic bacteria and electrosensitive fish, but it was not clear that the effects would be harmful.

Thus, the study stated strongly that environmental and biological changes resulting from Project Sanguine-Seafarer-ELF were likely to be minor and not necessarily harmful. This conclusion was reached in spite of a number of reports by scientists of significant adverse effects.

The Navy has continued this research with one unexpected result. Thirty rhesus monkeys were exposed for 22 hours a day for 4 years, with a control group of 30 not exposed to electromagnetic signals. After several years, it was discovered that the exposed males had a 10 percent *higher* growth rate than those not exposed, although there was no difference among the females. The reason for the phenomenon is not clear. One possible explanation is that at the start of the experiment the males were just entering puberty, while the females were already well into that developmental phase. However, the effect may be related to an anatomical structure unique to the males.

Social and Human Impact
The principal reasons for the local protest against the project in Wisconsin, Texas, and Michigan were the fears of the impact on individuals living and working in the area. These worries include the following:

1. Declining property values. Citizens owning property in the affected region worried that they could never sell their house if the antennas were on their property. If the system worked properly, the region would be the primary target for a missile attack.

2. Danger to people. Because the underground cables carrying large currents cause strong electric and magnetic fields at the surface (these are exactly the fields radiated into space), there is the question of the danger of electric shock to people in the area. Near the ground end of the cable, the fields are strongest, possibly as much as 15 volts per meter (still much smaller than can be found under an electric blanket). This means that the "step potential" or step voltage (the voltage between the two feet as one takes a step) is close to 15 volts— enough to feel if the ground is moist and the skin resistance is low. Such electric fields can also occur near cable faults that develop over years of continuous operation. The danger would arise if someone dragged a long metal ladder along the ground (figure 8.16), trailered a boat, or operated a plow (cases where large voltages can be transmitted to the person).

3. Long-term effects. Are there any long-term effects of living in the region with its ac electric and magnetic fields? Unfortunately, there has been no real epidemiological study of this question. In the late 1980s, there were studies of people living near high-voltage power lines, with indications that birth defects and child leukemia may be higher than normal.

4. Other effects. What would be the effects on the telephone system (one report conjectured that phones would ring continuously in some houses), and on radio and television reception? Would metal gutters become charged to

Figure 8.16
If the man is standing in a puddle of water and his shoulder clothing is wet, ELF can apply as much as 90 volts to his body in this situation—enough to give him an annoying shock.

dangerous voltages? Barbed wire fences? The perturbing fact is that we really don't know the answers.

Summary

The history of Project Sanguine-Seafarer-ELF encompasses many of the factors that make intelligent control of technological change so difficult.

In evaluating any technological development, we first have to estimate the need for the project. Is Project Seafarer really essential if the submarine deterrent is to be useful? Will it work as promised? These are technical and strategic questions which the public is not able to answer. Unfortunately, often the only knowledgeable people are closely associated with the project sponsor—in this case, the Navy—and irrational in their support.

Next, the benefits must be weighed against the risks, but here there is very little known (until the project is actually built). Furthermore, opponents tend to be irrational in their exaggerations of potential effects. One way to "wake up the public" is by scare tactics: the more gruesome the possibilities, the better.

Under such circumstances, thoughtful attitudes by the public and intelligent decisions by political representatives demand that we wend our way carefully through the maze of claims and counter-claims.

Related Civilian Issues

Project Sanguine-Seafarer-ELF is especially interesting because the average frequency of the signal is 76 Hz—remarkably close to the 60 Hz in use for the distribution of electric energy. If there are significant effects from the ELF broadcasting, they probably will also be found in people living near high-voltage transmission lines, in people who regularly sleep under an electric blanket, and in employees of the electric utilities who work on "live" equipment. At the present time, we have only suggestions that such exposures lead to harmful effects, but further research is certainly needed.

8.7 A Natural Resource Gone

A large group of demonstrators are walking back and forth in front of the White House carrying signs which read "Save the Spectrum." Thinking you have misread the slogans, you pause for a second look; it does not say "Save the Seals," it says "Save the Spectrum."

Why are you so amazed? Is the electromagnetic spectrum a limited natural resource, similar to our supply of fossil fuels, our ocean beaches, our beautiful forests? If it is, then what must we do to make sure all space on the spectrum is wisely allocated?

If we consider the limited ocean coastline of the United States, we find that only a fraction has beautiful beaches suitable for recreation. Unfortunately, many states have allowed individuals to purchase ocean-front property and then limit public access. In other cases, towns forbid parking near the beaches, thus excluding outsiders. As a nation, we have not utilized this resource (the beaches) for the maximum benefit of all the people. Fortunately, in some areas far-sighted government officials have ensured that the state or local government took title to the beachfront property before private development started.

In many ways, the beaches and undeveloped woodlands are our most limited natural resources. Politicians and public figures talk at great length about the world's bounded supply of oil or natural gas, but these limitations are strongly economic. There is an enormous quantity of oil in the western shale and undoubtedly in unexplored parts of the world; the limitation is that extraction is only possible at a cost significantly above even the current OPEC prices. And if the price rises enough, synthetic fuels become attractive.

Thus, in the energy situation the problem is dominantly economic. A switch away from Saudi Arabian oil would have traumatic effects on our total economy, especially if the change had to be made in a few years.

Beaches and parks are much more strongly limited. As the U.S. population grows and more and more people seek vacations at these sites of natural beauty, there are essentially no options even if costs are not considered. Artificial islands in the off-shore areas are perhaps possible, but at such enormous expense that they are not at all likely. Recognition of these fundamental limitations led to the founding of such influential organizations as the Sierra Club.

The federal government has the ultimate responsibility for the protection of such public assets, and our national park and forest systems are impressive responses. Unfortunately, there is often a severe conflict between the needs of American industry and the long-term recreational interests of the public. Asking that all recreational land be converted to parks is a simplistic approach: if there are too few jobs, people cannot afford vacations anyway. On a small scale, the problem is even more poignant. If a group of families make their living from timber in an area, should the government take over that woodland for the public good, even at the cost of severe hardship for the small group?

The Electromagnetic Resource

The electromagnetic spectrum is also a natural resource. Here we refer to the frequencies available for radio communication. There is only one space around us through which radio signals can travel. Once a certain band of frequencies is used for FM broadcasting, these same frequencies cannot be used for other purposes—exactly as our beaches have limited space (once 2 million people are on Coney Island in Brooklyn on a hot summer afternoon, no normal person wants to join the throng).

The federal government (since 1934, through the Federal Communications Commission or FCC) has allocated the frequencies from 88 MHz to 108 MHz for FM broadcasting. Once this decision is made, these frequencies are not available for other purposes. For example, if we decided to use the frequencies around 95 MHz for radios allowing communication among firefighters at the scene of a major conflagration, the firemen would hear music from a local station; nearby people trying to listen to the FM station would find their program interrupted by the firemen's reports.

Thus, the electromagnetic spectrum (that is, the frequencies available for radio communication) is a severely limited public resource. We might consider the range of frequencies from 500 kHz to 1000 MHz. These are roughly the frequencies of primary importance for public uses of radio. Below 500 kHz the antennas have to be too large; above 1000 MHz the electronics for transmission and reception become complex and costly. Once all these frequencies are assigned, there is no room for a novel use of radio—unless the potential user can convince the FCC to terminate some other allocation.

Uses of Radio

To appreciate the severity of the limited spectrum space, we need to consider the wide range of uses of radio in today's society. Radio is now accepted as a means of both mass communication (from a broadcasting station) and person-to-person communication (when at least one of the parties is in a changing location, so that ordinary telephone wires are not useful).

1. In the frequency range of interest, we have available a total of about 1000 MHz. Over 40 percent of that is allocated for broadcast television (box 8.1). Thus, the 68 possible TV channels represent the major commitment of this limited resource, and reflect the great importance that the government and the public place on this medium of mass communication. We are a TV-oriented society

2. AM and FM radio occupy about 21 MHz, or another 2 percent of the total available spectrum.

3. The federal government requires a variety of allocations for such operations as air traffic control and communication with pilots, navigation, broadcast of precise time and disaster information, and communications within such agencies as Defense, Agriculture, and Parks.

4. Local governments require allocations for police, fire, and highway departments.

5. Taxi and limousine fleets and dial-a-bus transportation systems offering individual pickup use radio for dispatching and routing. Other business uses include communication with trains, maintenance crews along pipelines, and traveling sales representatives.

6. In the last few years, personal paging systems have become common. A medical center can reach a staff doctor within a 50-mile radius, even in a metropolitan region.

7. Amateur radio is an important hobby, and CB radios are commonplace.

8. Mobile telephone service is available. When you pick up your car phone, the electronic equipment automatically searches for a free channel, then establishes radio communication with the telephone-company receiving station where the signal is clearest. Once the link is set up, you receive a dial tone and you are tied into the regular phone system.

Channels	Frequencies (MHz)
2–4	54–72
5–6	76–88
7–13	174–216
14–69	470–806

Total TV band is 408 Mhz. (Here VHF stands for Very High Frequency, UHF for Ultra High Frequency).

Box 8.1

9. Remote pickups of TV and radio signals are sent back to the broadcast station.

This list only touches the surface, but it does illustrate the ways in which radio has become a necessity in government, industry, and our daily lives. Fortunately, over the last 50 years as the applications of radio have grown, electronic technology has developed in parallel so that we could use a broader and broader range of frequencies. When AM radio appeared in the 1920s, we could build inexpensive receivers only up to 1 or 2 MHz. By the arrival of UHF television in the 1960s, equipment was available to 900 MHz. The recreational-beach parallel would be the opening up of new beaches as the size of the vacationing population grows.

But now we are nearing the end of spectrum growth. We are close to the infrared frequencies, where significant amounts of energy are radiated from objects just because of their temperature. The only promising hope is that eventually television may go entirely to cable, at least in the metropolitan areas where spectrum congestion is most severe. If television broadcasting disappears in the next 25 years, an enormous amount of the spectrum will be freed for other applications.

Such a development is not obviously beneficial to the public, since the costs of receiving TV will certainly rise with the switch from broadcast to cable. Furthermore, such an evolutionary development will be fought by the existing broadcast stations and the major networks. Finally, in many parts of the country, cable TV is provided by companies serving quite small population groups, and the quality of service varies enormously. Once one company has a franchise in a town, there is little incentive for a competitive system.

Thus, for at least the next few decades we can anticipate growing problems with our limited spectrum space and rising pressures for decisions on national priorities.

FCC Problems

The task of the FCC in allocating portions of the spectrum for specific radio purposes is often horrendously difficult. When frequencies above 800 Mhz were chosen for cellular phone service a few years ago, the FCC then had the problem of which companies should be authorized to provide the service.

For the 90 largest markets, the FCC received 1200 applications to be one of the two companies in each market. The FCC then had the task of evaluating these applications—a procedure which required several years and cost the applicants large amounts of money.

The FCC then received congressional approval for a lottery to simplify the process. For the next group of markets, 100,000 applications were received!

Entrepreneurs put in applications with no intention of actually supplying service; if they won the lottery, then they would sell their authorization to the highest bidder.

Now the FCC has proposed auctioning off the licenses, the way the Department of Interior auctions offshore oil leases. Certain public groups oppose this policy because the licenses will end up with only the richest firms.

International Aspects

The spectrum problem is much more difficult than that of recreational beaches because of the international aspect. This country's beaches are our problem, and probably the people of Guatemala couldn't care less how we decide to use that natural resource. But Guatemalans have to be concerned with our use of the electromagnetic spectrum.

The allocation of frequencies by the U.S. government affects directly the situation in neighboring Mexico, since radio waves recognize no national boundaries. Likewise, Mexico's policies, determined in part by ours, affect Mexico's neighbor, Guatemala—and so on through the hemisphere. The situation is much more complex in Europe, where radio signals from Liechtenstein reach into a dozen or more countries.

This problem is even more acute because only certain frequency bands are available for satellite and international communication. The advanced countries of the world are already utilizing most of this part of the spectrum for their governmental and business purposes. Officials in the developing nations recognize that no spectrum space will be available by the time their countries are ready to start international communications.

Every 20 years, representatives of all nations meet in Geneva to decide on new spectrum allocations. The 1980 meeting witnessed bitter arguments between the developed and developing nations, with the latter trying to reserve certain frequency bands for their future needs. The very natural differences seem irresolvable when we are dealing with a severely limited natural resource.

Appendix 8.1
EMP (Electromagnetic Pulse)

Switzerland has historically been a neutral country. And yet, fearing a nuclear war, the Swiss have built a computer center buried 1800 feet under a mountain to house their banking records. They undertook this expensive construction not in fear of being attacked, but to avoid the effects of high-altitude nuclear explosions over the USSR or Western Europe. The effects the Swiss worry about are not explosion, heat, or radiation, but EMPs—electromagnetic pulses.

If a large nuclear bomb exploded 250 miles above Nebraska, a very small instant of time later a very short, intense pulse of an electromagnetic signal would hit all 48 contiguous states and much of Canada and Mexico. With power and telephone lines acting as receiving antennas, electronic equipment could be subjected to pulses of 3 million volts, 10,000 amperes, or 30 billion watts—a condition far more serious than multiple lightning strikes.

Although no tests have ever been done on a large scale, many engineers suspect that almost the entire power and communication systems of the United States would be put out of service, and that computers would be seriously damaged. There is a question whether the national defense system would be able to operate—that is, whether the president could determine if an attack was underway and, if so, order appropriate strikes at enemy military targets.

The EMP would be so brief that people would not be affected by it any more than they would be by the effect of a distant lightning stroke. Electronic equipment, however, could be destroyed.

What Causes an EMP?

In the explosion of a nuclear bomb at high altitude (over 20 miles), the gamma rays emitted travel outward in all directions. Those rays moving upward have to travel long distances before colliding with and ionizing air particles. Those rays traveling toward the earth, however, soon encounter particles, and electrons are freed. These electrons are deflected into spiral motion by the earth's magnetic field, and this current (motion of electrons) causes the downward and outward radiation of an electromagnetic pulse.

The pulse occurs very rapidly and briefly. In 1/100 of a microsecond (millionth of a second), the pulse reaches its peak, and it dies out in less than a microsecond (figure 8.17). The electric force reaches a maximum value of 50,000 volts per meter—a force much greater than that found directly under very high-voltage transmission lines.

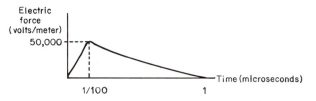

Figure 8.17
An EMP. The pulse reaches its peak in 1/100 millionth of a second, then dies out in less than a microsecond. A lightning flash is much slower, reaching its peak of 1000 volts per meter after about 5 microseconds.

Area Hit by an EMP

If a nuclear explosion occurs 250 miles above the Earth, the resulting EMP starts at the same altitude. In figure 8.18, the signal is radiated outward and covers a portion of the Earth from A to B—the area determined by the curvature of the earth. Looking at the surface (figure 8.19), we see a circle of coverage with a radius the same as distance d in figure 8.18 (the distance from C to A).

Discovery of EMP

The U.S. discovery of EMP dates back to the last air testing of nuclear weapons, in 1962. The history just before that time is important in any assessment of the military threat now posed by EMP.

1958   First high-altitude (27 and 48 miles) U.S. tests over Johnson Island in the Pacific. These tests created very serious disturbances in the ionosphere and played havoc with radio and radar.

Late 1958   U.S. and USSR. agreed to a moratorium on all nuclear testing.

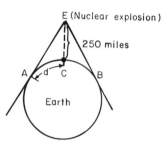

Figure 8.18
Coverage of an EMP formed when a nuclear explosion occurs 250 miles above the Earth.

Figure 8.19
Area covered by an EMP formed when a nuclear bomb is exploded at an altitude 250 miles above point C.

1961   USSR broke the agreement.

July 8, 1962   1.4-megaton hydrogen bomb was exploded by the U.S. 248
                miles above Johnson Island. This had very little effect on radio
                and radar, much to everyone's surprise, so the test at 500
                miles was canceled.

1962   Four U.S. tests in the 25–50 mile range were conducted to
                study radio and radar effects.

1963   Partial test ban treaty stopped atmospheric testing. Senate
                ratified the treaty, with the "Jackson safeguards" passed
                separately (statements of U.S. policy authored by Senator
                Henry Jackson). One of these "safeguards" requires the U.S.
                to "maintain an atmospheric test readiness capacity." Because
                of this, we still have 165 people living on a small Pacific atoll,
                waiting for the go-ahead to resume atmospheric testing.

The discovery of EMP came from the single high-altitude test in 1962.
Although the test caused no trouble to military communications, there were
strange effects: 800 miles away in Hawaii, 30 strings of street lights went out,
power lines were opened, and hundreds of burglar alarms went off. A year later,
scientists from the Rand Corporation explained these effects through the
concept of EMP.

The USSR may be further along than the United States in the measurement
and understanding of EMP phenomena. The Soviet atmospheric testing was
over central Asia, so that EMP effects could be measured much more easily than
with the American tests over the open Pacific. Furthermore, the Soviets made
more tests at higher altitudes.

The MIG-25 airplane flown to Japan in 1976 by a Soviet defector was
surprising in that the technology seemed very advanced, but the electronics
used vacuum tubes exclusively. (Vacuum tubes are insensitive to EMP—the
reason the military communication equipment worked after the 1962 U.S.
test—whereas transistors and integrated circuits are very sensitive.) Some
experts have attributed the "outdatedness" of the Soviet plane's electronics to
a purposeful choice as a protection against EMP.

Current U.S. Activities

Now that the EMP phenomenon is recognized, the United States faces a series
of decisions on how to protect military and civilian systems against the EMP
threat. There are over 40 parallel, redundant communications systems for the
president and military commanders to use if we are attacked— different ways
to give instructions to our strategic nuclear forces. But in 1980, the Air Force
Secretary testified before Congress and asked for yet another system (a

dedicated group of satellites) and stated that *none* of the first systems is certain to survive an initial nuclear attack.

Under these circumstances, the U.S. can decide to "harden" the systems—for example, to protect all electronic equipment by enclosing it in metal containers. Alternatively, we can try to develop new systems which are inherently protected from EMP. For example, fiber optics is to be used in the MX missile system, since light traveling through glass fibers is not affected by the electromagnetic pulse. There is an enormous, totally wood building in New Mexico where EMPs can be generated to test a 747 airplane.

Concluding Comment

The fascinating aspect of EMP is that, despite our elaborate defense system, only recently have we begun to design equipment specifically to operate even if EMPs occur. The entire era of electromagnetic signals is so new that we are still groping with many aspects of it where our understanding is insufficient to permit prediction of phenomena before they occur. Little wonder, then, that we yet know so very little about the effects of electromagnetic signals on a truly complex system, the human being.

Review Questions

R8-1. What does an infrared camera measure?

R8-2. In Project ELF, why must the radio signal have an extremely low frequency (about 76 Hz)?

R8-3. What is meant by the term "an electromagnetic field"?

R8-4. In Project Sanguine/ELF, the rate at which information can be sent is very small. Explain briefly.

R8-5. The threshold question is a major problem in evaluating the effects of an electromagnetic field on human health. Explain briefly what we mean by "threshold".

R8-6. Why are only two specific frequencies used for microwave ovens?

R8-7. What is the principal objection of the people of northern Michigan to the location there of the Navy's system for submarine communication?

R8-8. On what basis has the government established present-day standards for human exposure to non-ionizing electromagnetic fields?

R8-9. In a microwave oven, where does the energy go? What actually is heated?

R8-10. What is meant by the term "non-ionizing radiation"?

R8-11. Why are there only three possible sites for the Project Sanguine/ELF antenna in the U.S.?

R8-12. Opponents of Project Sanguine/ELF have argued that the system very possibly will not work when needed. Explain briefly the reasons they give.

R8-13. Why do submarines need to surface occasionally, even with their INS (inertial navigation systems)?

R8-14. What system is now in place to communicate with U.S. nuclear submarines if the country is attacked?

R8-15. Why did Project Sanguine/ELF go to a radio broadcast frequency as low as 76 Hz?

R8-16. What is meant by the term "ionizing radiation"?

R8-17. Explain briefly why a microwave oven can use only a few specific frequencies.

R8-18. Explain briefly why science finds it so difficult to determine the human health effects of using an electric blanket.

R8-19. Why is it so very difficult to do experiments measuring the health effects of low-frequency electromagnetic fields?

R8-20. Why is it necessary for the Federal Communications Commission (FCC) to allocate specific frequencies on the electromagnetic spectrum for various uses?

R8-21. The American National Standards Institute establishes standards for the electromagnetic field strength for safe exposure. What are some of the arguments for setting the standards too high? For setting the standards too low?

R8-22. What is the primary difference between sound waves and electromagnetic waves?

Problems

P8-1. The early history of x rays (figure 8.20) is an example of how trusting people can be about a technology they don't understand. It also illustrates how rapidly a new technology can be adopted.

On November 8, 1885, Wilhelm Roentgen, at the University of Würzburg in Bavaria, discovered x rays. (He used this name because he didn't understand what the rays were.) He was amazed to find that these rays passed through paper, wool, rubber and many other substances.

On December 28 of that same year, he reported his findings to the Physico-Medical Society of Würzburg. At the same time, he sent copies of his paper and an x-ray of the bones in his wife's hand to various physicists in Europe and the United States.

Within eight weeks, the picture had been printed in newspapers around the world, and public interest in the new discovery skyrocketed.

X-ray studios appeared in all major cities, and people flocked to obtain pictures of their hands, keys hidden in purses, their feet, and so on. Lovers had pictures taken of their locked hands, and society matrons proudly showed x-rays of their spinal columns.

An author, C. H. T. Crosthwaite, published a short story, "Roentgen's Curse," about a man who had x-ray vision (long before Superman).

In his New Jersey laboratory, Thomas Edison tried in vain to obtain pictures of the brain of a living person (the x rays were too weak to penetrate the skull).

The medical profession reacted with equal enthusiasm. They began to take x-rays for every conceivable reason. The invention of the fluoroscope (which displayed the x-ray picture on a screen) enabled the doctor to watch organs in motion and eliminated the time it took to have x-ray pictures developed. Medical journals soon carried numerous articles on applications of x rays. Less than a year after the discovery, Walter B. Cannon, then a Harvard student but later a famous physiologist, used the fluoroscope to study the digestive tract by having his patients swallow a bismuth compound. (He found that the stomach is normally vertical. Anatomy books all showed the stomach horizontal, since this is the position after death and knowledge then was based solely on autopsies.)

After a few years, scientists and research physicians began to realize that x rays could be harmful, that they perhaps should not be used indiscriminately. These early warnings were largely disregarded until in 1905 it was discovered that three men who had worked with x rays for several years were sterile. Even today, however, we are uncertain about the risks involved. To what extent should dentists and doctors be allowed to request routine x-rays of patients with no symptoms of disease?

Why was this scientific discovery converted so rapidly to commercial and professional use? A physicist in Germany discovers a new scientific phenomenon; a few months later you can walk into a studio in New York City and get a picture based on this discovery. At the same time, physicians are using the pictures to locate bullets buried in patients, metal objects swallowed by children, or bone breaks of accident victims.

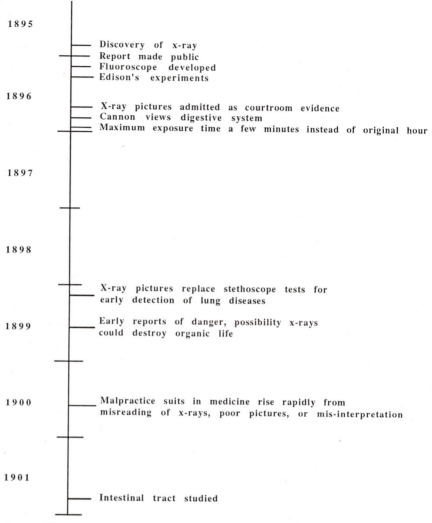

Figure 8.20
Early history of x-ray development.

Several factors led to this amazingly rapid transition from research to use:

1. At the end of the nineteenth century, the public was enthralled by science and technology, especially in the U.S. The Philadelphia Centennial Exposition in 1876 featured a host of new inventions and discoveries; by the end of the century electrical energy was being distributed in the cities, telephones were becoming common, and the first automobiles were appearing on the streets. Thomas Edison was a national hero.

2. Medicine was becoming a science. The stethoscope had gained general acceptance for diagnosis, physiology was emerging as a legitimate discipline, and the surgeon was moving out of his traditional role as a technician and physician's assistant. Only a decade later, the Flexner Report established the first scientific standards for medical schools.

Thus, both the public and the professionals were unusually receptive to new technology. In addition, there were several special features of x-ray machines: the equipment was inexpensive (about $50), so it could be purchased by sidewalk entrepreneurs; The equipment was widely available in science laboratories; relatively untrained people could quickly learn to take pictures. The public enthusiasm also stemmed partly from the fact that x-ray machines were "toys." The average person is entranced by new technological toys—as we see today in the case of elaborate microcomputer games.

Do you think that today we are more cautions about accepting new technology? Discuss with a few examples.

P8-2. The discussion of microwave ovens indicates that the microwave signal transfers energy to the water molecules; the temperature thus rises where there is water, and heat is transferred by conduction to neighboring regions.

a. Why should frozen foods be thawed at a low power level or using intermittent operation? (When a frozen item thaws, small pockets within the material thaw first.)

b. Since in ice the water molecules are locked in position, melting ice in a microwave oven works from the exterior inward. Why?

c. Why does salt in the food increase the heating rate? (Salt is readily separated into positively and negatively charged ions.)

d. In a conventional oven, the surface temperature of a roast reaches $170°$ while the interior is rising to perhaps $75°C$. In a microwave oven, the surface temperature never exceeds $100°C$, the boiling point of water. What differences in appearance would you anticipate when a roast is cooked the two ways?

e. Metal in the microwave oven may reflect the microwave signals back to the generating magnetron and damage that device. Metal may result in sparks to the bottom or side walls of the oven. If an aluminum foil must be used, what precautions are essential?

P8-3. The following article depicts the Electronic Communications Privacy Act of 1986 as irrational. Is such a "technologically illiterate" piece of legislation dangerous? Explain why, both in terms of the arguments given by the author, Robert Jesse, and in terms of the precedents established. How does this compare with the action by several states to make radar detectors illegal?

Forbidden frequencies (reprinted with permission from *IEEE Spectrum* 24, February 1987, p. 17)
It has long been the Commission's view that the initial responsibility for signal protection should be on the signal originator, who is in the best position to protect the signal against unauthorized reception and use—Federal Communications Commission, 89 FCC 2d 455 (1982).

The right of unrestricted access to the radio airwaves enjoyed in the United States since the birth of radio has been struck a death blow by the passage of the Electronic Communications Privacy Act of 1986. Under previous U. S. policy, first codified in the Radio Act of 1912 and affirmed many times since, it was lawful to receive any radio signal so long as the contents of private communications were not divulged or used beneficially—for commercial profit, for example.

As of Jan. 19, the new Privacy Act makes mere reception of specified radio signals illegal, shifting the responsibility for a radio communication away from the one person who transmits it to the millions of people who might receive it. This arrangement is unworkable, and serves mostly to promote a few special commercial interests.

The Privacy Act is not without merit in some other respects. The legal privacy of digital video, electronic mail, and other new forms of communication was left uncertain under the 1968 Federal Wiretap Act, which governed the "aural acquisition" of "oral or wire Communications." The new law fills the gap by prohibiting the interception of "wire, oral, or electronic communications," terms broadly defined to cover any conceivable modulation technique applied to any communications medium. The law then exempts from penalty the reception or interception or electronic communications that are "readily accessible to the general public."

This would appear to be a reasonable policy formulation. Wire and similar point-to-point communications are inherently private; that is, they are hard to get at except by physical intrusion. Not being "readily accessible to the general public," they warrant Federal protection from interception. Other media, notably radio signals, behave differently. Without special technology, radio emissions blanket wide geographic areas and they can be received using commonplace, unsophisticated equipment. What could be more "readily accessible" than signals that enter our homes and pass through our bodies?

It might be supposed that since radio waves are readily accessible there should be no expectation of privacy when using them, and the Government should not attempt to assure it. But the Privacy Act circumvents this straightforward conclusion by including definitions that abrogate the ordinary meanings of the terms defined. Cellular radiotelephone calls, for example, are declared by legislative fiat to be "wire communications" and thus not readily accessible.

The statute also contains a complex, five-part definition of "readily accessible" that has little basis in physical reality. Without regard to band, power, modulation technique, or other engineering criteria, it ordains that certain radio services are not readily accessible to the public—though in fact most are—and makes unauthorized reception of them a criminal act. The law mysteriously permits reception of technically similar services a few megahertz away.

The same logic, were it applied to print media, might grant to certain newspaper pages the same legal privacy given to first-class mail, while allowing the general public unrestricted access to the other pages. The classification of a newspaper page as private or public would depend simply on whether a readership of one or of many was wished. This "logic" is plainly absurd and contrary to decades of reasonable legislative and judicial precedent.

Instead, the law should contain a technically sound and relevant definition of "readily accessible," and protect only communications that are inherently private. The 1968 law achieved nearly the same effect for oral communications using a slightly different test—it protected only oral communications "uttered by a person exhibiting an expectation that such communication is not subject to interception under circumstances justifying such expectation." To illustrate, a quiet chat in one's parlor would likely be protected. Substitute for the parlor a crowded restaurant or the stage of a packed auditorium, and the expectation of privacy is no longer justified. The law would not grant it. Too bad the Privacy Act prescribes neither a realistic "accessibility" test nor a "justifiable expectation" test for electronic communications.

How can a law of the U.S. Congress declare that some forms of radio are inaccessible and private, when the laws of physics dictate otherwise? It would be charitable to answer that this misguidance is a product of technological ignorance or wishful thinking in Washington, DC. However, internal inconsistencies in the Privacy Act suggest that it is more a sham than an honest, if puerile, effort to deal with new technology. One example is the protection extended to cellular radiotelephony under the law. This profits cellular service companies by stemming the loss of revenue from customers who might use the service less if they understood its vulnerability. On the other hand, there is no interdiction whatsoever against the interception of "cordless" telephone conversations, even though the distinction between cellular and "cordless" cannot be supported on technical grounds.

Protection or no, people will not be stopped from receiving radio signals. Even U.S. Representative Robert W. Kastenmeier (D-Wis.), who championed the Privacy Act as a bill in the House, acknowledges that its radio provisions are essentially unenforceable. They will thus have no deterrent effect, and they will not increase the actual privacy of cellular radio calls or other broadcasts. All they will do is engender and perpetuate an illusion of privacy where none exists.

Life in the United States is no safer on account of the Electronic Communications Privacy Act, but is considerably less free—the act gives us nothing for something. Congress ought to scrap the notion of "forbidden frequencies" and begin anew, basing the use and regulation of technology on an accurate assessment of its true properties. Are those properties judged inadequate or unsavory? If so, relief will come only from research and advances in technology—not from wishful legislation.

(Robert Jesse, a consultant living in Baltimore, is interested in operating systems, telecom, and security. He received a BES-EE from the Johns Hopkins University in 1981, and was a member of the senior staff there through April 1984. The opinions expressed here are his own.)

P8-4. The following article is reprinted with permission from *Science News*, the weekly newsmagazine of science (copyright 1987 by Science Service, Inc.).

EMP: Fallout over a naval EMPRESS

Since the Navy first announced its intent to build and operate an electromagnetic pulse (EMP) simulator in the Chesapeake Bay—one of the most productive estuarine systems in the world—there has been growing concern about the project's potential environmental impact. The most recent concerns appear in responses to a new environmental evaluation of the project, in strongly worded comments in a joint resolution by the Maryland legislature and in a lawsuit filed last week.

EMP is the rain of "Compton electrons" produced when gamma rays emitted by the detonation of high explosives—such as nuclear weapons—collide with air molecules. This electronic fallout will induce current or voltage surges through any electrically conducting material (SN:5/9/81, p. 300). While electrical equipment based on the old vacuum-tube technology is relatively immune to it, an EMP could literally fry sensitive electronic devices like those contained in computers, modern consumer electronics and communications systems.

The U.S. military's concern about EMP's possible incapacitating effects on weapons during a nuclear war launched a massive campaign to electronically shield all potentially vulnerable equipment (SN: 5/16/81, p. 314). The Navy's proposed Electromagnetic Pulse Radiation Environment Simulator for Ships (EMPRESS-II)—an antenna system emitting simulated EMPs from atop a barge—would generate more realistic ("threat level") pulses than are now possible, to test how well shipboard electronics have been shielded.

Though in general EMP has been viewed as a problem only for electronics, a number of organizations are coming to question whether it is, in fact, biologically benign. In 1984, the Navy issued a draft "environmental impact statement" (EIS) on EMPRESS-II, as required by law for projects considered highly controversial or with the potential to "significantly affect the quality of the human environment." (There is a much smaller EMPRESS-I facility, for which an environmental assessment has not been done.) But the paucity of biological-effects data on EMP described in the EIS only generated more public concern.

So the Navy commissioned additional studies on potential short-term effects to aquatic life or waterfowl, and published these in a supplemental draft EIS, issued last December. Although the report does say there is evidence "to assure us that EMP has no effect on humans," official comments on this document, filed over the past six weeks, indicate significant public objections to EMPRESS-II still remain.

For example, the Environmental Protection Agency (EPA) reports that "we do not agree with the supplemental draft EIS that EMPRESS-II will cause no impact to organisms of the Chesapeake Bay." According to EPA's Feb. 27 letter, many questions EPA raised earlier about potential impacts of the project remain unanswered, and "statistics presented in the report do not clearly support the conclusions that were drawn."

EPA says that studies involving birds "were too limited . . . to allow definite conclusions," and that too few tests on oysters and crabs were conducted "to allow for any conclusions." Some of the reports of tests on fish not only are confusing and contain discrepancies, according to the agency, but also "lack sufficient data points for reliable statistical analysis." And it says it is possible that some boaters in the bay during EMP-simulation tests could experience a "brief painful shock."

Both Maryland and Virginia, states bordering the bay, strongly oppose siting the EMPRESS-II facility in the Chesapeake. Among Maryland's objections are complaints that: EMP effects on marine electronics have not been adequately assessed, "the Navy has prematurely discounted the effects of [EMPRESS-II's] operation on the Calvert Cliffs Nuclear Power Station" 20 miles away, and the EIS fails to project chronic or long-term impacts of zapping estuarine life with EMPs. Among Virginia's concerns are potential hazards to humans, including cardiac-pacemaker failures and electrical shocks.

Last week Jeremy Rifkin and his Washington, DC-based Foundation on Economic Trends joined the fray with the filing of a lawsuit asking the Defense Department to prepare a programmatic EIS on its entire EMP-simulation program. As a precedent, Rifkin cited a similar suit he won asking for an EIS on the Defense Department's biological weapons program (SN: 2/28/87, p. 132). But in this suit, unlike the biological weapons suit, Rifkin is seeking to halt the EMP program until a program-wide EIS is completed.

The Navy says it is "inappropriate" to comment on the lawsuit prior to its resolution, but hopes to decide whether to proceed with EMPRESS-II by late summer.

This is another example of the familiar public attitude that a facility is necessary, but don't locate it near me! When two government agencies disagree (e.g., the Navy and the EPA), how might intelligent public decisions be reached? Public dissenters tend to turn to the courts, as indicated; is the judiciary the optimal place for the final decision?

P8-5. The normal incandescent light bulb gives only 5 percent of its energy in light; the rest is radiated as heat. Significant energy conservation is possible if we have light bulbs that increase the percentage of energy in light.

For example, if the light output were 10 percent, we could use a 50-watt bulb instead of the present 100 watts. If the bulb lasts 5000 hours, we save 50 watts

× 5,000 hours, or 250 kilowatts-hours (kWh)

At a cost to the consumer of $.10/kWh, the saving is $25 over the life of the light bulb. Widespread conversion throughout the U.S. could save a few percent of our total electrical energy consumption.

Such a light bulb is possible. The electrical energy consumed heats the filament of the bulb; most of this energy then radiates outward as infrared signals. If the light bulb is coated with a material that reflects the infrared, but transmits the visible light, most of the heat is returned back to help heat the filament. Thus, the light radiated is larger compared to the wasteful heat radiated.

Such a light bulb is now on the market. The cost of one bulb is about $15. Will the public be willing to pay this price, even though the life cost of the bulb may be less? Explain.

P8-6. A few years ago, the U.S. Department of Defense announced plans to construct two large radar transmitters to detect and track enemy ballistic missiles launched up to 3000 miles away. One radar site is in California, the other on Cape Cod.

The system is called PAVE-PAWS, an acronym standing for *P*recision *A*cquisition of *V*ehicle *E*ntry *P*hased *A*rray *W*arning *S*ystem. The adjective "phased array" means that the antenna does not rotate; instead, signals fed to different parts of the antenna are continuously controlled by a computer, so that the beam sweeps across the horizon.

During planning and construction, citizen groups on Cape Cod strongly opposed the project because of the possible exposure of citizens to harmful microwave radiation. When the system was actually operational, public measurements showed the following:

1. At the fence surrounding the system, the maximum signal strength was 5 μW/cm². (This was 1000 feet from the antenna.)

2. A mile from the antenna (the nearest normal public approach), the strength was less than 0.1 μW/cm².

3. The most likely spot for public exposure was on Route 6, the mid-Cape highway, where the maximum signal strength was 0.06 μW/cm².

4. There is always the possibility a private airplane will fly through the center of the radar beam, in spite of extensive warnings distributed and posted by the Air Force. A plane a half-mile from the antenna may be exposed to a power of as much as 10,000 μW/cm².

Since the measurements were made on the actual, operating radar, is there any reason for the residents of Cape Cod to be concerned? Discuss.

Chapter 9
Radio

Flying through heavy clouds, the pilot of an airplane searches for the airport. He has essentially no visibility. Fortunately, both the airport and the plane have Radio Direction Finding (RDF) equipment. The pilot turns on the receiver, and shortly thereafter the dial on the instrument panel tells him the direction of the airport.

When someone quietly speaks to you, you turn toward the sound. Unconsciously you adjust the position of your head until the sound signals coming to both ears are about the same. This will happen when you are directly facing the person speaking to you; that is, your ears will be on a line perpendicular to the direction of the sound source (figure 9.1).

A simple RDF system works in basically the same way. At the airport, the transmitter broadcasts a radio signal (an electromagnetic signal) continually. The antenna sends out this signal in all directions.

On the airplane there are two vertical wires that act as receiving antennas. These wires are connected by plastic to form a square "loop" which can rotate freely (figure 9.2). The two receiving antennas pick up the signal being radiated

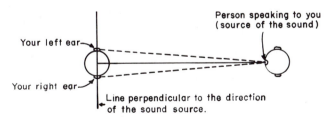

Figure 9.1
Overhead view showing your ears on a line perpendicular to the direction of a sound source. The distance from your left ear to the source and the distance from your right ear to the source are the same.

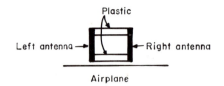

Figure 9.2
"Loop" consisting of two antennas. This "loop," which is attached to an airplane, can rotate freely.

from the airport. Then the receiver measures the difference between the signal coming from the airport to the left antenna and the signal coming from the airport to the right antenna (figure 9.3). It measures signal A minus signal B.

When the "loop" is perpendicular to the direction of the radio signal coming from the airport, signal A and signal B are identical—the difference is zero (figure 9.4). When the antenna loop is at a different angle (part c of the figure), the incoming signal reaches B before A. Now the two signals are not identical—that at A is a little later than the signal at B (part d of the figure).

When the net received signal (signal A minus signal B) is not zero, a motor automatically turns the loop antenna in the direction that decreases the signal. This rotation continues until there is no net signal; then the angular position of the loop tells the pilot exactly the direction of the airport transmitter.

There are some problems with this simple system, as figure 9.5 shows, but the basic principle underlies radio direction-finding systems for airplanes and for ships at sea.

In this RDF system, the radio signal carries no information other than the direction of the source of the signal. In a sense, then, this system is an especially simple use of radio. Usually radio is used to send more complicated messages, such as speech or music. If we tried to make a list of all the uses of radio, we would have to include any situation in which we want to send information to a distant location: that is, radio is a means of telecommunication. The following are a few applications.

1. In a location far from any doctors, a man has severe chest pains. A medical technician hooks up electrocardiograph equipment, and the EKG is sent by radio to a medical center, where a cardiologist diagnoses the condition and prescribes treatment by return radio.

2. In Boulder, Colorado, the National Bureau of Standards has a precision clock setting the time standard for the world. Radio broadcasts carry this time to all points.

3. The federal government operates an emergency radio system to warn people of imminent disasters, such as tornadoes.

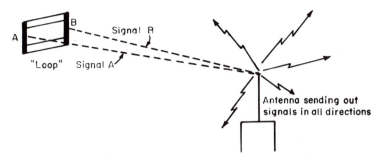

Figure 9.3
The receiver measures the difference between the signal coming from the airport to the left antenna and the signal coming to the right antenna (signal A minus signal B).

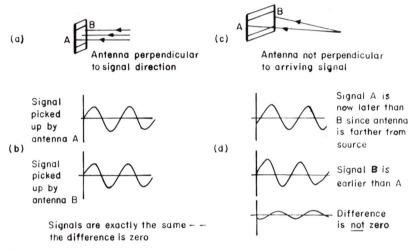

Figure 9.4
Operation of airplane antenna and receiver.

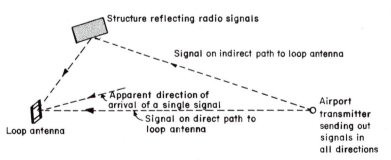

Figure 9.5
Possibility of an error in the simple RDF system. The signal from the airport arrives at the loop antenna by two different routes: one direct, the other bouncing off a nearby structure. The loop antenna assumes that the signal is arriving from only one direction.

4. More and more cars now carry mobile telephones; the driver's voice is sent by radio to the nearest telephone-company receiver, where it is switched into the telephone system.

5. Airplanes and ships use radio navigation systems to determine their exact location (not just the direction of a port, as in the RDF system).

6. Radio signals from planes and satellites are used to map unexplored parts of the world.

7. In auto racing, the pit manager communicates with the driver.

9.1 Radio Signals

How are radio signals broadcast, and how are they received? We recall that radio signals are the same phenomenon as light. When charged particles in the Sun move because of the high temperatures, electromagnetic waves "travel outward" in all directions. The electric and magnetic forces move outward at the velocity of light. When they reach your arm as you lie on the beach, they cause charged particles in your arm to vibrate in synchronism with the motion of the charged particles in the Sun. These moving particles in your arm, in turn, cause a similar motion in your eyes, which you interpret as light. The rapid motion of these particles produces heat; hence the temperature of your arm rises. The original source of these effects is the motion of the charged particles in the Sun.

Radio Broadcasting

Most radio signals, in contrast, have an artificial origin—that is, they are purposely generated. The radio transmitter is an electronic oscillator giving a voltage which varies according to the particular frequency desired (figure 9.6). This voltage is applied at the bottom of a vertical metallic rod—the antenna.

When the voltage is positive, electrons in the antenna are attracted to the voltage at A, the end of the wire. These electrons move downward in the antenna. When the voltage is negative at A, the electrons are repelled. The electrons move upward on the antenna. Thus, the transmitter voltage causes an

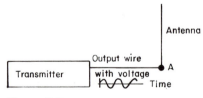

Figure 9.6
Simplest radio transmitter.

oscillation back and forth of the electrons in the antenna, at the same frequency as the sinusoidal voltage of the transmitter.

These oscillating electrons in the antenna cause corresponding forces on charged particles all around the antenna, even miles away—just as the moving particles in the Sun affect your arm, 93 million miles away. We describe this "force at a distance" by saying that the antenna radiates an electromagnetic or radio signal outward in all directions.

Thus, broadcasting (or radio transmission) is accomplished simply by forcing the electrons in the antenna to oscillate at a desired frequency and amplitude.

Radio Reception

As these radio waves "travel outward" from the transmitting antenna, they influence any charged particles they encounter. Every piece of metal has a large number of free electrons moving randomly because of the temperature, but also ready to respond to an arriving electromagnetic signal. Thus, when the RDF system broadcasts its signal from the airport, all the electrons in metal within perhaps a 100-mile radius move in synchronism with the transmitted signal: electrons in railroad tracks, in metal lamp posts, in gutters around the roof of a house, and so on. The electromagnetic wave from the RDF transmitter appears all over the region.

Simultaneously, there are electromagnetic signals generated by many, many different sources. Power lines and telephone lines have moving charges; even a barbed-wire fence has free electrons moving randomly because of the temperature and, hence, generating electromagnetic signals. We saw previously that moving particles in nature cause small radio signals even if you are in the wilderness, far from any artificial sources. In addition, all the radio and TV stations in the region generate signals.

When we want to pick up these transmitted signals at our receiver, we simply use a metal rod—the receiving antenna (figure 9.7). The free electrons in this antenna now move back and forth in response to the radio signals arriving from all directions and all sources. This motion of the electrons causes a voltage at

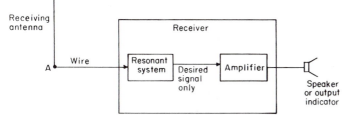

Figure 9.7
Simple radio receiving system.

A: when electrons move downward in the antenna, the negative charges cause the voltage at A to be negative (to repel other negative charges). Thus, this voltage on the wire leading from the antenna into the receiver varies as the total of all the radio signals arriving at the antenna.

In the airplane using the RDF system, the receiver should respond only to the radio signal at the frequency of the airport transmitter. To select this one signal from the multitude of arriving radio signals, the receiver includes a resonant system (see chapter 5)—an electric device that throws out all the unwanted signals. The resonant circuit behaves exactly like a filter for a camera that only allows red light (the light at the frequencies of red) to pass through. Light at the unwanted frequencies of green, blue, etc., never gets through; it is "discarded."

9.2 Frequencies for Radio

The Fourier Theorem says that speech and music signals are made up of components at many different frequencies, from 30 Hz to 18,000 Hz. This is also the range over which the human ear responds to sound waves. (We call frequencies in this range the *audio* frequencies.) To broadcast speech and music over a radio station, we should then generate and radiate electromagnetic signals at these same frequencies.

Such an approach is totally impractical for two reasons. If an AM radio station did broadcast in the range 30–18,000 Hz, there could be only one station in any geographical region. If two or more stations broadcast at the same frequencies, there is no way for the receiver to select one station and not the others.

To permit many stations to broadcast simultaneously, we insist that each station use only a band of frequencies assigned to it by the Federal Communications Commission. For example, a Boston newspaper lists 25 AM radio stations in its region (figure 9.8). The table tells us that WBZ transmits on a frequency of 1030 kHz (1,030,000 Hz). The speech or music spectrum is moved up in frequency to the vicinity of 1030 kHz before the signal is broadcast. When your set is tuned to 1030 kHz, the receiver selects that *one* radio signal by an appropriate resonant circuit, then moves the speech or music spectrum back down to the normal, audible frequencies before it goes to the loudspeaker.

Thus, the broadcast frequency of an AM radio station can be chosen arbitrarily. By requiring the shift of the information to a high frequency, the FCC can provide for many radio stations operating at the same time in the same area.

	kHz		kHz
WEEI	590	WKOX	1190
WRKO	680	WNEB	1230
WCAS	740	WEZE	1260
WCCM	800	WJDA	1300
WHDH	850	WDLW	1330
WROL	950	WLYN	1360
WCAP	980	WPLM	1390
WBZ	1030	WXKS	1430
WGTR	1060	WBET	1460
WILD	1090	WSRO	1470
WSNY	1150	WITS	1510
WJMQ	1170	WNTN	1550
		WUNR	1600

Figure 9.8
AM radio stations listed in *Boston Globe*.

There is a second compelling reason to broadcast at a high frequency. A transmitting antenna radiates a significant amount of power only if the antenna length is a reasonable fraction of the wavelength of the signals being transmitted (figure 9.9). The length of the antenna should come close to ¼ of the wavelength. If the antenna is smaller than ¹⁄₂₀ of the wavelength, very little power actually travels out into space.

This relationship between the efficiency and the size of an antenna appears whenever power is radiated—in sound as well as in radio signals. In the case of sound, the human mouth (a transmitter) and ear (a receiving antenna) are both too small for good efficiency except at the high audio frequencies (figure 9.10). The relation indicates why the loudspeaker to boost the low frequencies in a hi-fi system (the woofer) has to be large, whereas the speaker for high frequencies (the tweeter) is small.

For radio signals, figure 9.10 shows that a station cannot broadcast at audio frequencies—even at 1000 Hz, the minimum antenna length is 9 miles. The table also shows why a television antenna for VHF (Very High Frequency) channels 2–13 is much larger than one for UHF (Ultra High Frequency) channels 14–69. When you use "rabbit ears," they should be extended fully for channel 2 and decreased in size for channel 9.

Thus, in an AM radio station, the speech in the studio is converted to an electrical signal by the microphone (figure 9.11). This signal consists of many different frequency components, covering the range from 50 Hz to about 5000 Hz. Boston's WBZ first moves this information up in frequency to the vicinity of 1030 kHz. The signal is then broadcast and picked up by all the antennas in the region (and by every strip of metal or wire). If you live near Boston, the antenna of your AM transistor radio picks up all the stations broadcasting in the

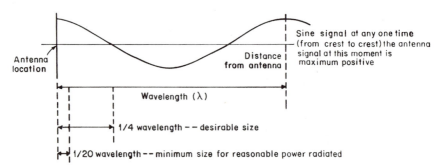

Figure 9.9
The length of an antenna must be a reasonable fraction of the wavelength to radiate
a significant amount of power.

	Use of signal	Typical frequency (Hz)	Wavelength	1/20 wavelength or antenna size
SOUND SIGNALS	Low-frequency speech	100	11 feet	7 inches
(velocity 1120 feet/sec)	High-frequency music	12,000	1 inch	1/20 inch
	Bat sounds for finding food	120,000	1/10 inch	1/120 inch
	Broadcasting at audio frequencies	1,000	180 miles	9 miles
RADIO SIGNALS	AM	1,030 k	950 feet	48 feet
(velocity 300 M meters/sec or 186,000 miles/sec)	TV VHF Channel 2	58 M	17 feet	1 foot
	FM	100 M	9.8 feet	6 inches
	TV VHF Channel 9	190 M	5 feet	3 inches
	TV UHF Channel 30	570 M	1.7 feet	1 inch

(k = thousand, M = million)

Figure 9.10
Minimum antenna size for reasonable efficiency of radiation and reception for
various sound and radio signals. The wavelength of a signal is the velocity divided
by the frequency.

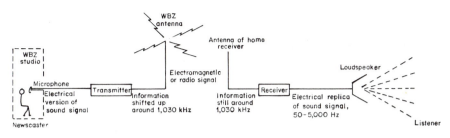

Figure 9.11
Essential parts of an AM radio system. The diagram does not show that, in both the transmitter and receiver, there must be amplifiers to increase the size of the signal. For example, the electrical current in the antenna of a home receiver is so small that it must be multiplied by 1 million or more before it can drive the loudspeaker.

area. You tune a resonant circuit in your receiver to 1030 kHz and select just the WBZ signal. The electronic devices then move this signal down in frequency to the audio band, 50–5000 Hz. The resulting electrical signal at speech frequencies drives the loudspeaker to generate a sound signal that is almost a replica of the sound that originated in the WBZ studio.

The frequency must be shifted upward for two reasons: to allow simultaneous broadcasting by many stations in the same area, and to allow the use of an antenna of reasonable size that will generate enough power in the radiated signal.

9.3 Modulation

We have an information signal (for example, speech) that has only *very low* frequencies. "Very low" here means below 8000 Hz. We want to send this information, but we need to transmit at a much higher frequency. How do we move the information up in frequency?

Let's use an analogy. I am sitting with a pencil at a wooden table, while you are across the room with your eyes closed. I want to send you a message about the way I inhale and exhale—in other words, the way I normally breathe. I tap my pencil on the table at a regular rate (and reasonably fast); you can hear these distinct taps. How do I change the tapping to show you my breathing pattern?

(This is obviously a ridiculous example, but we are interested in illustrating communications at a distance, generally termed *telecommunications.*)

First let us consider my tapping of the pencil on the table at a regular rate and with a steady pressure so the loudness of the sound does not change. When you hear this tapping, you are alerted that there is a signal. It conveys no more information to you. We will call this the *carrier* signal (figure 9.12).

Now I want to send you second-by-second information on how I am breathing. To do this, I can increase the pressure on my pencil so it makes a

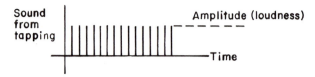

Figure 9.12
Carrier signal. I tap my pencil on the table at a regular rate and with a steady pressure so the loudness of the sound does not change.

louder sound than the carrier signal, or I can decrease the pressure on my pencil so it makes a softer sound than the carrier signal. Thus, I can change how loudly I am tapping according to the expansion of my lungs. As I inhale, I increase the loudness; during exhaling, I tap more and more softly. In other words, how loudly I am tapping at any moment tells you how far my lungs are expanded (figure 9.13).

The second way I can send you this same information is by changing the rate (or speed) at which I tap. If I gradually increase the speed of my tapping, you know I am inhaling; if I decrease the speed of my tapping, you know I am exhaling. The loudness (or amplitude of the signal) remains the same. The rate of tapping (or frequency) changes to give you the information. We call this frequency modulation, or FM (figure 9.14).

Both these techniques are called *modulation*: I am modulating or changing the carrier signal according to the value of the slowly changing information signal. You, as the listener or receiver, must know what scheme I am using, so that you can properly interpret the signal you receive.

As you have probably guessed, this example is described because it illustrates the two common forms of commercial radio broadcasting: AM and FM. In radio, our "slowly changing" information signal is the speech or music signal (with a maximum frequency of 18,000 Hz). The carrier is a high-frequency sine signal (typically 1 MHz for AM, 100 MHz for FM).

9.4 Some Radio History

Heinrich Hertz (after whom the unit meaning cycles per second is named) first demonstrated the existence of radio waves in 1886. He generated a signal of 75 MHz, which was picked up a few feet from the transmitter. Although James Clerk Maxwell had shown that such waves should exist and were like light but at a different frequency, the Hertz experiments confirmed the theory and showed that radio signals travel through many opaque objects but are stopped by metal screens. Twenty years after these experiments, radio was exciting the public.

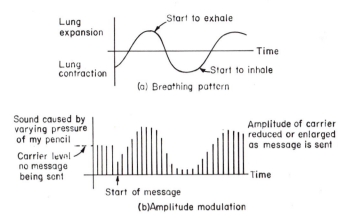

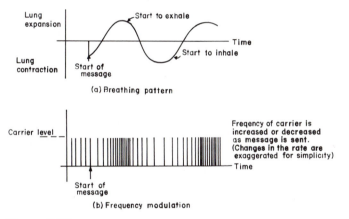

Figure 9.13
Part a shows how my lungs expand and contract as I breathe. Part b shows the
varying sound level caused by my pencil hitting the table. As I inhale, I tap a bit
louder each time to show my lung expansion. Then, as I exhale I gradually decrease
the sound level of my tapping. In other words, I vary the *amplitude* of the sound
signal.

Figure 9.14
Part a shows how my lungs expaned and contract as I breathe. Part b shows how
the frequency of the carrier (which is a regular series of pulses) varies as the
message is sent. This is called frequency modulation.

In those early days there was no thought of broadcasting speech or music. Just getting a radio transmitter to turn on and off was an accomplishment. Thus, radio telegraphy was developed: the transmitter was turned on for a short period of time to send a dot, and was left on three times as long to send a dash.

The Italian entrepreneur Guglielmo Marconi recognized the commercial possibility of sending telegraph messages without wires. But by that time there were telegraph wires into all the towns of the major countries of the world, and there was no apparent market for radio telegraphy over land.

The one obvious place for radio was in communication to and from ships at sea. To sell his ideas, Marconi went to England (then the dominant maritime and naval power, with its far-flung empire), and also to the United States (then emerging from the "century of invention"). In 1899 Marconi first demonstrated his wireless telegraphy by reporting to shore on the America's Cup yacht races off Newport.

On December 15, 1901, Marconi radioed the letter S from England to Newfoundland. Within a few years, newspapers and magazines were certain about the potential of this fantastic way to communicate. *The North American Review* proclaimed "Our whole human existence is being transformed by electricity."

The sonnet "Wireless Telegraphy," by John Hall Ingham, published in the *Atlantic Monthly*, ended with these lines:

Somewhere beyond the league-long silences,
Somewhere across the spaces of the years,
A heart will thrill to thee, a voice will bless,
Love will awake and life be perfected!

In this era when utopian novels were popular, the press promised that everyone would be able to communicate confidentially with anyone else anywhere in the world. Frank Merriwell and Tom Swift books quickly capitalized on the public enthusiasm for radio.

Western Union and American Telephone and Telegraph were more knowledgeable and recognized the limitation of spectrum space. By 1912 there were several hundred thousand amateur operators, and the federal government had to start regulation (the Radio Act of 1912). Public excitement was repeatedly stimulated. In 1919 Marconi reported receiving signals coming from beyond the Earth; Nikola Tesla argued they came from an advanced civilization on Mars.

By 1912 there was regular radio telegraph service from California to Hawaii. As early as 1904, ships carried radio transmitters, and the telegraph signal CQD was internationally accepted for emergencies. (CQ was standard for "calling all stations," and D stood for danger.) The simpler SOS came later, along with the voice signal "Mayday" (from the French "m'aidez," meaning "help me").

Voice communication was much more difficult than telegraphy and really had to wait until the invention of vacuum tubes by Lee DeForest in 1906. The first time the human voice was sent by radio is a subject for debate. Claims to that distinction range from the "Hello Rainey" spoken by Nathan B. Stubblefield to a partner in a test near Murray, Kentucky, in 1892, to an experimental program of talk and music by Reginald A. Fessenden of Brant Rock, Massachusetts, in 1906, which was heard by radio-equipped ships within several hundred miles.

In 1915 speech was first transmitted across the continent (from New York City to San Francisco) and across the Atlantic Ocean (from Naval radio station NAA at Arlington, Virginia, to the Eiffel Tower in Paris). There was some experimental military radiotelephony in World War I between the ground and aircraft.

The first commercial radio broadcast of speech and music in the United States occurred in 1920 at Westinghouse station KDKA in Pittsburgh. Within a decade, hundreds of stations were broadcasting, and an entirely new form of home entertainment and news dissemination had profoundly changed American life.

Until the late 1930s, all radio stations were AM.

Today over 50 million radios a year are sold in the United States, and 99 percent of U.S. households have a radio receiver (the average is six operating sets per household). There are almost 5000 AM stations and almost as many FM broadcasters.

The first automobile radio appeared in 1929. The receiver was hidden behind the instrument panel, under the hood. In 1930 the receiver was on the running board (with 45-volt batteries), and the antenna ran from axle to axle under the car. By 1932 a 6-volt battery was adequate, and the auto companies built the antenna into the car. By that time, there were 200,000 auto radios in use (each at a cost of about $220 in today's money).

From the very first appearance of the car radio, there were heated arguments as to whether this technology should be legal. Auto accidents were becoming a recognized national problem, and there was strong sentiment that the radio would distract the driver. Today there is a similar debate over car phones.

Commercial radiotelephony linking North America with Europe was opened in 1927, and with South America three years later. In 1935 the first telephone call was made around the world, using both wire and radio circuits.

Until 1936, all American transatlantic telephone communication had to be routed through England. In that year a direct radiotelephone circuit was opened to Paris. Systems to other countries followed. Telephone connection by radio and cable is now possible with more than 180 foreign points.

Microwave telephone transmission was first sent across the English Channel in 1930. A microwave telephone system, between Boston and New York, went into operation in 1947. The first overseas telephone call from a moving automobile was made from St. Louis to Honolulu in 1946.

It was not until after World War I that regular broadcasting began. The first system used was AM (amplitude modulation).

Licensing of broadcast stations on a regular basis began in 1921 with WBZ of Springfield, Massachusetts. By the mid-1920s, government control of the radio spectrum was clearly essential to avoid mutual interference of competing stations.

Experimental network operation over telephone lines existed as early as 1922. President Coolidge's message to Congress was broadcast by six stations in 1923. In 1926 the National Broadcasting Company started the first regular network with 24 stations. Its first coast-to-coast hookup was in 1927. In that year the Columbia Broadcasting System was organized. The first round-the-world broadcast occurred in 1930.

Though a patent on frequency modulation (FM) was issued in 1902, the principle of FM had been known previously. However, its advantages for broadcasting were not developed until shortly before World War II. Largely as a result of developmental work by Edwin H. Armstrong in the 1930s, the Federal Communications Commission in 1940 authorized commercial FM broadcasting to start January 1, 1941.

On October 31, 1940, the FCC granted construction permits to fifteen stations simultaneously. The first licensed commercial FM station was WSM-FM of Nashville (May 29, 1941), which operated until 1951.

To enable FM broadcasters to obtain additional revenue, the FCC in 1955 authorized them to provide a supplemental "background music" service to subscribers. The signal is, in effect, "piggy-backed" on regular programs for reception on special sets in stores, factories, etc.

In 1961 the Commission authorized FM stations to broadcast in stereo. This involves dual transmission and reception to give a more realistic effect to music and other sound.

9.5 Amplitude Modulation, or AM

As we saw in section 9.2, the Federal Communications Commission assigns a specific band of frequencies to each radio station. This permits many radio stations in one area to broadcast simultaneously. '

For example, Boston station WBZ must change the frequencies carrying information to the vicinity of 1030 kHz before it broadcasts. This sinusoid at 1030 kHz is the carrier signal for the station. Figure 9.15 shows the audio or speech signal and the carrier signal assigned to WBZ.

One way to change the frequencies from the audio or speech band to the vicinity of 1030 kHz is to let the amplitude of the high-frequency carrier signal vary exactly as the speech signal varies (figure 9.16). Because the amplitude is "modulated" or changed according to the information signal, this process is called *amplitude modulation*, or *AM*.

Thus, WBZ broadcasts the 1030-kHz signal continuously, 24 hours a day. When the newscaster pauses for breath or there is a break before a song or a commercial, the signal has the average amplitude and is just a pure sinusoid at 1030 kHz. When speech or music is present, the amplitude of this high-frequency carrier is changed exactly in synchronism with the information signal.

Spectrum of an AM Signal

A Fourier decomposition of the AM signal of figure 9.16 would show the spectrum of figure 9.17. The spectrum of the speech signal contains frequencies from about 50 Hz to 8000 Hz.

When this speech-signal amplitude modulates a sinusoid at 1030 kHz, the spectrum of the resulting broadcast signal (figure 9.16) consists of three parts:

1. A single-frequency component at 1030 kHz (the carrier).

2. An "upper sideband," from 1030 to 1038 kHz, which is the original spectrum shifted upward in frequency.

3. The "lower sideband," the mirror image of the upper sideband.

Thus, the AM signal covers a band of frequencies twice as wide as the speech signal: figure 9.17b covers 16,000 Hz, while figure 9.17a covers only 8000 Hz.

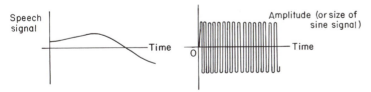

Figure 9.15
Signals that radio station WBZ works with. In contrast to the last section, where the carrier was a series of regular pulses, in broadcast radio the carrier is always a sine signal at one frequency. Left: Speech signal. This varies slowly with time, since the frequencies are lower than those at right. Right: A sinusoidal carrier signal at 1030 kHz. (Many more cycles should be shown to be an accurate picture.) The amplitude of the sine signal does not change.

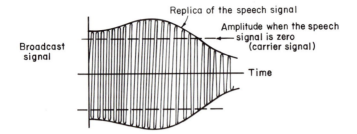

Figure 9.16
Signal broadcast by WBZ.

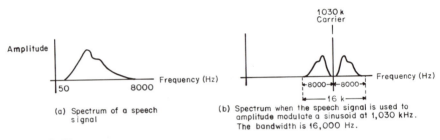

(a) Spectrum of a speech signal

(b) Spectrum when the speech signal is used to amplitude modulate a sinusoid at 1,030 kHz. The bandwidth is 16,000 Hz.

Figure 9.17
Effect of AM on the spectrum.

The lower sideband is really redundant—all the original signal information exists in just the upper sideband.

Unfortunately, by the time engineers realized that both sidebands were unnecessary, millions of receivers were in the hands of the public, and it was too late to change the technology. Consequently, even today AM radio stations broadcast the simple AM signal, which includes both sidebands.

Normal AM signals
Figure 9.17 shows that a single AM radio station needs a bandwidth (the width of the spectrum) of 16,000 Hz for speech. To broadcast high-fidelity music, the bandwidth would have to be 36,000 Hz, since the music signal has frequencies up to 18,000 Hz. Thus, if we wanted high fidelity music on AM radio, each station would have to be allocated 36,000 Hz. WBZ might be given exclusive rights to the frequencies from 1012 kHz (18,000 below the center frequency of 1030 kHz) to 1048 kHz (figure 9.18). Stations in the same geographical region would have to be at least 36 kHz apart.

Figure 9.8, listing the stations in the Boston area, indicates that this separation does not exist. Actually, two stations reaching the same listeners (such as stations in New York and Boston that have overlapping coverage) are

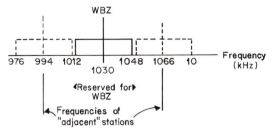

Figure 9.18
Use of frequencies if AM were high fidelity. The presence of WBZ at 1030 means that other stations can be at 994 and 1066; the separation between stations must be at least 36 kHz.

separated by at least 10 kHz. The highest audio frequency is only 5000 Hz. Obviously, AM is not high fidelity. Why did the United States adopt these regulations which doomed AM radio to music of poor quality?

The AM frequency band is

535 kHz to 1605 kHz.

Your radio receives all AM stations by tuning over this range (box 9.1). Within this band, there are 1070 kHz available for various AM stations.

If each radio station were allocated 36 kHz, we could only have 1070/36, or 29, radio stations operating with overlapping coverages—far too few to satisfy our needs. So the FCC decreed that every radio station must first take the speech or music signal and remove *all* components at frequencies over 5000 Hz. Then each station is given exclusive regional rights to only a band of 10,000 Hz—5000 above the base frequency, 5000 below. Overlapping stations can then be separated by only 10,000 Hz, and we have room for 107 stations rather than 29.

AM radio cannot broadcast any signal spectrum beyond 5 kHz, so AM inevitably has poor fidelity (though speech is completely intelligible). When this decision was made, in the late 1920s, there were no serious objections. One reason for this is that radio was a wondrous novelty, and most people were delighted to have moderate-quality sound. Another is that music records at that time were 78 rpm, with poor fidelity.

Since each AM station is given a total frequency band of 10 kHz, each is assigned a center frequency between 535 and 1605 kHz with a number ending in zero. Thus, every frequency listed in figure 9.8 ends in zero.

Band of 9000 Hz
The allowable number of AM stations in any region is severely limited. Each station needs 10 kHz—5000 Hz for the upper sideband and 5000 for the

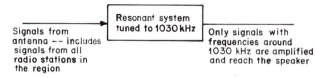

Figure 9.19
A resonant system in the receiver selects just one station.

AM Frequencies

Your AM radio receiver allows tuning within the range of frequencies from 535 kHz to 1605 kHz. Each AM station is assigned a frequency within this band. Why were these particular frequencies chosen for AM when broadcasting started in the 1920s?

When you tune your radio, you are adjusting the resonant frequency of an electrical system. This resonant system lets through only the signal from the one radio station you are tuned to. Thus, the resonant system allows you to listen to one station at a time.

In 1920, a single electrical resonant system could be tuned over a 3:1 frequency range; that is, the highest frequency could be no more than 3 times the lowest. Thus, to keep the receiver simple and inexpensive, broadcasters in the 1920s wanted to operate within a 3:1 frequency range. 1605 is three times 535.

But why these particular frequencies? The choice might have been any of the following 3:1 ranges:

100–300 kHz   (total spread: 200 kHz)
535–1605 kHz   (total spread: 1070 kHz)
3000–9000 kHz   (total spread: 6000 kHz)

The higher we go in frequency, the greater the spread—and the more stations we have room for.

The 535–1605 kHz range covered the highest frequencies at which reliable, inexpensive receivers could be built in the 1920s, so this range was selected.

Box 9.1

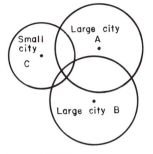

Figure 9.20
The problem of allocating frequency bands is difficult. This picture shows only a simple situation of three cities. Small city C overlaps both large cities, A and B; hence, all the radio stations in the three regions must be assigned non-interfering frequencies.

lower. The number of stations could be doubled if the technology of receivers and transmitters could be changed so that only one sideband was sent (as is actually done in police, CB, and amateur radio). However, transmitting only one sideband would require junking all the existing receivers—not a feasible solution.

A slight increase is possible without loss of quality if broadcast stations discard 1 kHz at the end of either sideband (figure 9.21). Existing receivers will still work—the components from 4000 to 5000 Hz in the audio spectrum are not very large anyway, so we are not throwing away very much.

This 9-kHz band for each station is actually the system used in most of the rest of the world. In the mid-1980s, the FCC proposed introducing such allocations in the United States in order to increase the number of radio stations. There were strong objections from broadcasters, equipment manufacturers, and the public. A major problem would occur with digitally tuned radios: many car radios search automatically every 10 kHz and stop on the first signal; the electronics jumps the tuning in 10-kHz steps. With the 9-kHz band, the allowable carrier frequencies would be 539, 548, 557, 566, 575 kHz and so on. Again we find that once a particular technology is in place (in the hands of the customer), change is very difficult.

Still pressed to expand the number of allowable AM radio stations (especially to accommodate public radio and stations with targeted audiences, such as minority groups), the FCC responded by raising the top of the AM band from 1605 kHz to 1705 kHz (effective in 1990). There are arguments about allocation of these new channels: which should be dedicated to public service, which to minority groups, and so forth One proposal is for one channel to be allocated nationwide for local traffic information.

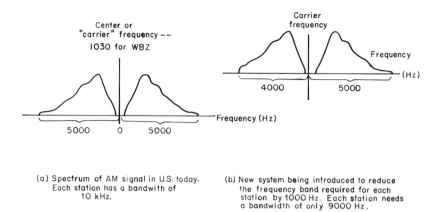

(a) Spectrum of AM signal in U.S. today. Each station has a bandwith of 10 kHz.

(b) New system being introduced to reduce the frequency band required for each station by 1000 Hz. Each station needs a bandwidth of only 9000 Hz.

Figure 9.21
Current and alternative systems for AM.

9.6 Geographical Coverage of a Radio Station

Two radio stations on the same frequency must be far enough apart to avoid interference in receivers located between the two stations. The separation required depends on the power radiated by each station, the heights of the antennas, the topography between the two, and other factors. We can make an estimate of the area covered by a station from the engineering formula for the line of sight.

As we stand on a boat riding in a calm ocean, how far we can see is determined by the curvature of the Earth (figure 9.22). If your eyes are a height h above the surface of the Earth, and if the Earth is a perfect sphere, the distance R you can see is given by the relation

$$R = \sqrt{1.5h}$$

with R in miles and h in feet.

If I stand on the shore of a bay and can just see the low land on the other side, my eyes are 6 feet above the water.

$$R = \sqrt{1.5 \times 6}$$

$$R = \sqrt{9}$$

$$R = 3$$

So it is 3 miles across the bay.

Our interest in the formula stems from the fact that high-frequency radio waves (well above 1 MHz) do not bend appreciably around the Earth. Consequently, if h is the antenna height, R is the distance from the antenna

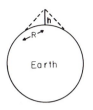

Figure 9.22
Line of sight. At a height h above the surface of a perfectly spherical Earth, you can see a distance R in any direction. If h is extremely large (as in the example of the EMP in chapter 8) and we want to measure h in miles, the formula is $R = 90 \sqrt{h}$, with R and h in miles.

that the radio station can be picked up. For example, if the antenna is atop a 1000-foot building, 1.5h is 1500, and R is approximately 40 miles. (The formula is even more accurate for FM and TV signals, since these waves do not bend around the Earth at all.)

The formula indicates whether you can expect good television reception in your home a known distance from the TV station. There are two cases in which we have to be careful in using the formula, as shown in figure 9.23. Also, since the Earth is not a perfect sphere, the formula is only approximate.

Total Reach of AM Stations

The line-of-sight formula for the range of a radio station works well for FM and TV, but AM stations often have appreciably greater range for two different reasons.

1. Signals in the AM frequency range bend somewhat around the surface of the Earth. The added range depends on weather conditions; with certain variations of temperature and humidity, even TV and radar signals can be channeled to hug the Earth and propagate distances appreciably longer than the line of sight.

2. The region from 30 to 250 miles above the Earth is called the ionosphere. Primarily because of ultraviolet and x-ray radiation from the Sun, there are significant numbers of positive ions and free electrons in the ionosphere. Radio waves reflect from this region and thus "skip" to exceptionally long ranges (figure 9.24). The ionospheric reflection is especially noticeable after sundown. When the sun sets, the ionospheric layers at about 120 miles and 200 miles merge together and on some evenings provide an excellent reflecting region. Consequently, this phenomenon makes it possible on certain evenings to pick up radio stations from across the country. It also lets you receive short-wave broadcasts from Europe or Australia. This is also the reason many local, low-power radio stations are allowed to broadcast only from sunrise to sunset.

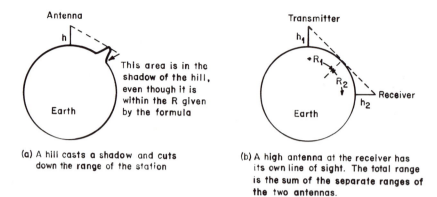

(a) A hill casts a shadow and cuts down the range of the station

(b) A high antenna at the receiver has its own line of sight. The total range is the sum of the separate ranges of the two antennas.

Figure 9.23
Cases in which the line-of-sight formula has to be used with care. (In all figures, the heights of antennas are exaggerated in comparison with the radius of the Earth.)

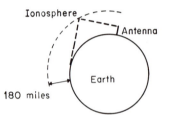

Figure 9.24
Reflection of radio waves from the ionosphere.

During the day their broadcasts reach a very small area, but in the evening they could interfere with major stations located many miles away.

The ionospheric reflection is the reason Marconi was able to broadcast across the Atlantic Ocean in 1901. This is another example in which technology drove science: Marconi succeeded, and then the scientists found the explanation.

The ionospheric reflection is also the basis of our long-range radar monitoring of enemy missile and plane activity thousands of miles away with over-the-horizon radar. Here the equipment automatically changes frequency to optimize ionospheric reflection.

Final Comment on AM

In 1920, the appearance of the first commercial AM radio station ushered in the modern era of electronic mass communication. Today, in the United States, we are so accustomed to listening to radio and TV that we rarely stop to marvel at this fascinating use of the electromagnetic spectrum. In less developed countries, however, radios and TVs are prized possessions. This was poignantly illustrated in 1967 by the strong response when the Indian family-planning minister announced that a transistor radio would be given to each person undergoing voluntary sterilization.

9.7 Speech Scramblers

Once a radio signal is broadcast, anyone with a receiver can listen in. This simple fact is apparently not obvious to some in the federal government. The Communications Privacy Act of 1986 decreed that conversations carried by cordless telephones are not confidential. That is, it is legal for you to listen in on your neighbor using a cordless phone. This makes sense; there is no way to enforce a law that forbids you to listen in. The same legislation decrees, however, that it is illegal to listen in on a conversation on a cellular phone. The two technologies are identical, and enforcement of privacy is impossible. Apparently the law was written at the behest of cellular phone companies to try to assure the customers that their conversations would be private.

This openness is great for commercial broadcasting, but the lack of privacy is a serious handicap in police or business use when the conversation is confidential. Under such circumstances, speech scramblers must be used: before it is transmitted, the speech must be mixed up in a way known only to the intended listener.

The basic system is illustrated in figure 9.25. The scrambler and the unscrambler are bought from the same manufacturer; the unscrambler simply undoes what the scrambler has done and restores the speech to normal form.

The most common scramblers electronically manipulate the spectrum of the signal from the microphone-amplifier. The speech signal arriving at the scrambler in figure 9.25 has the spectrum shown in figure 9.26. The scrambler first discards everything above 4000 Hz, since it is not necessary for good intelligibility (figure 9.27). From here on what is done depends on the complexity and cost of the scrambler.

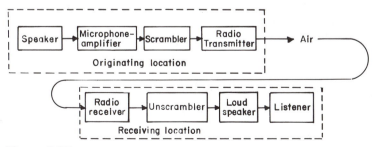

Figure 9.25
Radio system for use when confidentiality is important.

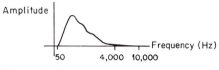

Figure 9.26
Spectrum of signal from a microphone.

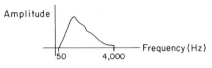

Figure 9.27
The high frequencies unnecessary for intelligibility are removed. Now we know the highest frequency of the spectrum. Here we use 4000 Hz to preserve reasonable speech quality. Police radios often use 3000 Hz.

Simple Scrambler

A common way to scramble a signal is just to turn around the spectrum (figure 9.28). Electronically, this is especially easy now that we know what AM does to the spectrum. Figure 9.29 shows that we use the original speech signal to amplitude-modulate a sinusoidal carrier at 4000 Hz. This process gives us an AM signal with a spectrum from 0 to 8000 Hz; the portion from 0 to 4000 Hz is just what we want. Consequently, we can obtain the scrambled speech simply by passing the AM signal through a system that removes all components at or above 4000 Hz.

Although this type of simple scrambler is often used, it does have two drawbacks:

1. If you listen carefully, you can sometimes understand the scrambled speech, although engineers do not know why. One would think that the scrambled speech would be completely unintelligible, but surprisingly it is not—perhaps because of the way the ear and the auditory portion of the brain operate.

2. It turns out that the radio signal can often be heard unscrambled if we simply tune our receiver slightly off or away from the frequency of the radio transmitter sending the scrambled speech.

Complex Scrambler

A more complex scrambler might divide the spectrum of the original speech signal into the following ranges of Hz (see figure 9.30)

0 to 1000	1000 to 2000	2000 to 3000	3000 to 4000
A	B	C	D

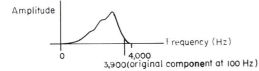

Figure 9.28
The scrambled speech has a spectrum which is reversed from the normal. The
original component at 100 Hz is now 4000 minus 100, or 3900.

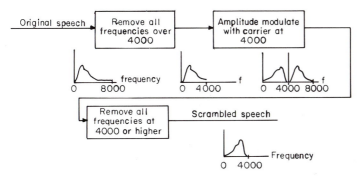

Figure 9.29
Operation of the simple speech scrambler. The spectrum is shown at each step of
the process.

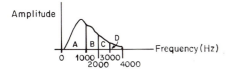

Figure 9.30
The spectrum of the original speech signal is divided into four parts.

and then mix up these ranges according to a code known to the unscrambler. (The code can be changed at arranged times.) Furthermore, we can turn around any portion we wish (that is, reverse its direction along the frequency axis).

For example, today's code might be

Reverse A
Reverse B
Put C into D's slot
Put A into C's slot
Put D into B's slot
Put B into A's slot.

Then the scrambled speech spectrum would have the shape shown in figure 9.31. Now the scrambled signal is unintelligible.

The cost of this more complex scrambler is naturally greater than the cost of the simpler one—one reason the simpler, less effective scrambler is still used.

There are much more complex scramblers available. If the speech is converted to digital form, the speech signal is represented by a long sequence of zeros and ones. We can shuffle up this sequence of binary digits in many different ways, add noise or a confusing signal, and so on. The federal government is now in the process of requiring "secure telephones" for all its defense contractors and its internal communications—a multi-billion-dollar investment.

9.8 Frequency Modulation, or FM

Commercial AM broadcasting has two serious shortcomings:

1. The fidelity is poor for music. This feature is not inherent in AM, but rather is a consequence of its history.

2. Noise (that is, an unwanted signal) adds directly to the AM signal. The AM receiver measures the *amplitude* of the signals near the carrier frequency. When an unwanted signal at about the carrier frequency is present, the interference

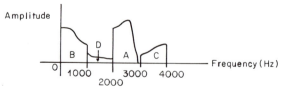

Figure 9.31
Unintelligible scrambled speech.

adds directly to the radio signal. This feature, causing the static and noise in AM, is an inevitable result of the amplitude modulation.

Frequency-modulation or FM radio avoids both of these problems, as will be explained below. First, however, we will consider what is actually broadcast in FM.

The FM Signal

In FM, the sinusoidal carrier conveys the information (the speech or music) by changes in frequency. When the speech signal is positive, the broadcast frequency is slightly higher than the carrier; when the speech signal is negative, the frequency is slightly lower (figure 9.32). The information is communicated by the changes in *frequency* of the received signal.

An FM station broadcasts a signal that is approximately sinusoidal, but the frequency changes according to the speech or music. The amplitude stays the same at all times.

Spectrum of an FM Signal

In AM, the original speech spectrum is shifted upward in frequency and appears as two sidebands, above and below the carrier. Thus, the AM signal covers a range of frequencies twice as large as the original speech signal (figure 9.33).

In FM, the situation is more complicated. Instead of two sidebands, there are typically about fourteen—seven above the carrier and seven below. *Each* sideband is a replica of the spectrum of the original audio signal (figure 9.34).

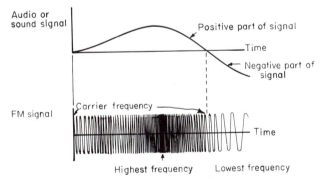

Figure 9.32
An exaggerated picture of the frequency change of an FM signal as the information signal goes positive, then negative. In commercial FM, the carrier frequencies are in the vicinity of 100 MHz. The FCC allows the station to change its frequency (around the carrier) by no more than 75 kHz. Thus the percentage frequency change is very small.

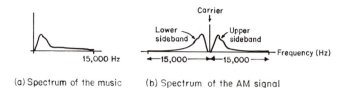

(a) Spectrum of the music   (b) Spectrum of the AM signal
    or information signal

Figure 9.33
Amplitude modulation gives two sidebands; each has all the information in the
original audio signal. Here we show the spectrum if we had high-fidelity AM, so that
all audio frequencies up to 15,000 Hz are communicated.

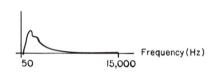

(a) Spectrum of the music or
    information signal

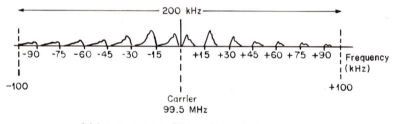

(b) Spectrum of the FM broadcast signal

Figure 9.34
In FM, there are six or seven sidebands on either side of the carrier, each with the
form of the spectrum of the music signal.

The FM spectrum has an enormous amount of redundancy—we really are sending the message 14 times.

Fidelity of FM

Commercial FM broadcasting is high in fidelity simply because the FCC allows FM stations enough bandwidth (a wide enough range of frequencies) so they can transmit all the audio frequencies of the music signal up to 15 kHz. AM stations must throw away all sound components above 5000 Hz before broadcasting, so AM is low in fidelity because of government regulation (figure 9.35). FM did not appear until the late 1930s; by that time, the public was becoming interested in better fidelity, since the novelty of radio was wearing off.

Furthermore, by the end of the 1930s, electronic technology had advanced so that inexpensive receivers could be built around 100 MHz (instead of the 1 MHz limit of 1920, when AM started). Hence, FM stations are given the band from 88 MHz to 108 MHz, high frequencies where more spectrum space is available.

Each FM station is allocated a band of 200 kHz around its carrier frequency. Thus, the lowest frequency of a station is 88.1 MHz, and the highest is 107.9 MHz (figures 9.36 and 9.37).

In summary, the high fidelity of FM stations came about principally because FM arose 20 years after AM, at a time when government policy responded to the public interest in the accurate reproduction of music and when the technology was more advanced. There is no scientific reason why AM should have poorer fidelity than FM.

Noise Rejection by FM

There are fundamental reasons why FM rejects noise much more effectively than AM. First, what is noise? When we transmit a signal, we want to receive *only* that signal. However, since there is so much electromagnetic radiation of signals all around us (from auto ignitions, from lightning in the area, from other radio or TV stations, etc.), many of these signals are picked up by the receiver.

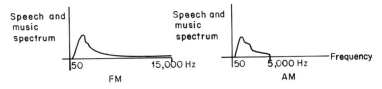

Figure 9.35
FM has high fidelity because it retains the full 15,000 Hz needed for music. AM has low fidelity because the high frequencies are clipped.

	mHz		mHz
WXKS	107.9	WATD	95.9
WBZ	106.7	WHRB	95.3
WVBF	105.7	WCOZ	94.5
WBCN	104.1	WCGY	93.7
WEEI	103.3	WSNE	93.3
WCRB	102.5	WBOS	92.9
WLYN	101.7	WMFO	91.5
WHUE	100.7	WBUR	90.9
WSSH	99.5	WZBC	90.3
WPLM	99.1	WGBH	89.7
WROR	98.5	WERS	88.9
WCAV	97.7	WMBR	88.1
WJIR	96.9	WAAF	107.3

Figure 9.36
The 26 stations covering the region served by the *Boston Globe* newspaper.

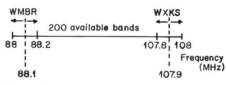

Figure 9.37
Frequencies for FM broadcasting.

What we hear is the message transmitted plus all these other unwanted signals (noise).

There are two ways to explain why FM is more noise-free than to AM:

1. The noise or unwanted signal arrives at the receiver and just adds to the desired signal (figure 9.38). Around the peaks, the desired sine signal is changing very slowly; then the noise adds directly. As the sine signal passes through zero, it is changing very rapidly; an added signal shifts the time of zero crossing by only a very small amount.

An AM receiver measures the amplitude of the total incoming signal: the wanted signal plus noise. So in AM, noise is just added to the desired signal. An FM receiver, however, measures frequency—the time between zero crossings. Thus, noise has much less effect in FM.

2. An even more convincing argument for FM's being almost noise-free can be made from the spectrum. In FM we have fourteen sidebands. Each of these bands of frequency (15,000 Hz wide) carries all the audio information. FM radio communication is like having fourteen separate telephone wires from a talker to a listener. At the listener, the receiver adds up these fourteen incoming signals. Each of the fourteen is corrupted by noise, but the fourteen different noise signals are unrelated: when one is positive, another may be negative and partly cancel the former. All fourteen conversations are the same and add

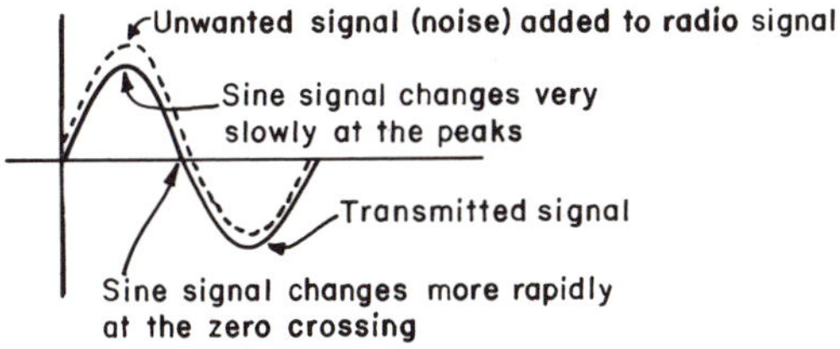

Figure 9.38
When noise is added to the desired radio signal, the change is most noticeable near the peaks.

directly. Thus, the receiver output has very little noise, in comparison with the desired signal.

In these terms, FM achieves its ability to reject noise by the very large bandwidth.

Another Feature of FM

When two interfering signals are received simultaneously in FM, the receiver largely rejects the weaker of the two. Thus, the weaker signal is treated like noise. This is why your FM receiver tends to give a clear audio output even when there is another station at a nearby frequency, and why, as you tune the FM dial, you lose one station and then immediately lock in on the next station.

9.9 Radio Navigation

By using the combination of radio and satellites, one of the classical problems of mathematics and science has been solved: determination of where you are on the Earth or in the air. Radio navigation systems have been widely used since the 1940s, but the most exciting new development is the Navstar GPS (Global Positioning System).

By 1992, eighteen satellites will be constantly in orbit about 12,000 miles from the surface of the Earth (one orbit every 12 hours). Each satellite will broadcast data on precisely where it is. Each broadcast starts on a precise, pre-arranged time schedule. Six satellites are already operating, and others will be put into orbit as soon as the Space Shuttle permits. (Originally the system was to be operational by 1987, but the *Challenger* disaster stopped shuttle flights for a lengthy period.) The system is being developed by the Department of Defense, but will also be available for civilian use. Planes, ships, and even hikers in the wilderness will be able to determine their position by using the Navstar GPS.

The accuracy of the system is amazing. It can give your location within 50 feet and your velocity within 8 feet per second. Very much better accuracy can

---

FM History

1913	Edwin H. Armstrong invented superregenerative receiver, an important development in radio, while he was a Columbia University student.
1917	With Lucien Levy (of France), Armstrong invented the superheterodyne radio receiver, still used today. Armstrong was to devote an inordinate share of his life to court battles over patents; this battle he lost.
1920	Armstrong conceived FM. He thought the bandwidth would be much less than that of AM. If the carrier frequency varied only $\pm$100 Hz around its normal value, the bandwidth should be 200 Hz (not the 10,000 Hz of AM).
1922	John R. Carson showed that the above premise about bandwidth was wrong, and that the FM bandwidth is always at least that of AM. The world lost interest in FM.
1933	Armstrong demonstrated wideband, low-noise FM to David Sarnoff of RCA.
1938	Armstrong's FM station in Alpine, New Jersey, went on the air.
1940	FCC licensed first fifteen FM stations.
1949	Armstrong sued RCA and NBC for patent infringement. The suit dragged on for 5 years; Armstrong himself was on the witness stand a year.
Dec., 1953	Armstrong's wife left him.
Jan. 31, 1954	Armstrong committed suicide by jumping from the window of his high-rise apartment.
1954	Court decided in favor of Armstrong in the patent suit.

Box 9.2

even be realized with more expensive equipment and careful correction for regular errors. Simpler equipment that might be carried easily by backpackers gives location within 150 feet. Your position is displayed in terms of latitude, longitude, and altitude, but this information can easily be converted to the distance and direction of a predetermined spot—such as a ranger station for hikers.

Principle of Operation

Each satellite sends out two radio signals (one at 1227.60 MHz and the other at 1572.42 MHz) consisting of a coded message describing its own location. The user equipment (owned by people wanting to determine their location) has a precise clock and knows the times the message starts from the satellite and is received by the user; hence it knows the length of time it took the radio signal to reach the user. Since the velocity of radio signals is 186,000 miles per second, the receiving equipment can determine the distance from the satellite to the user.

At this point in our explanation, the user has received the signal from one satellite (A in figure 9.39) and calculated the distance from that satellite. The user then must be located somewhere on a sphere with this radius and centered at A.

When the user equipment receives signals from two satellites and determines the distance from each, there are two spheres, A and B. The user must be on both. In solid geometry we learn that when two spheres intersect, the points at which they meet form a circle on either sphere. Therefore, if the receiving equipment knows two spheres, it can calculate the circle on sphere A which is also on sphere B.

Receiving signals from a third satellite, C, the user equipment finds a second circle on sphere A—the circle common to spheres A and C. These two circles now intersect at two points, P and Q in figure 9.40. We can tell by observation that one of these points is clearly the wrong answer (a ship's position must be in the ocean, not far out in space); the other point is the position of the user. The mathematical equations describing the two spheres can be solved in the computer of the receiving equipment to give the user's location in terms of latitude, longitude, and altitude.

Other Features

Since the system should be as accurate as possible within the limitation of reasonable cost, there are several refinements which are interesting because they illustrate the detail that can be considered when we try for extreme precision.

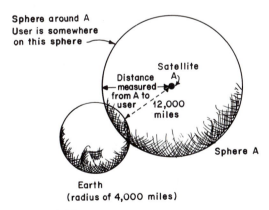

Figure 9.39
Receiving only a signal from satellite A, the user is located somewhere on the sphere surrounding the satellite's position.

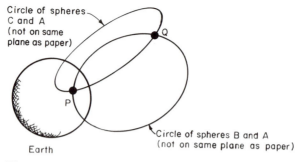

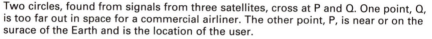

Figure 9.40
Two circles, found from signals from three satellites, cross at P and Q. One point, Q, is too far out in space for a commercial airliner. The other point, P, is near or on the surace of the Earth and is the location of the user.

The system described above requires that the user equipment include a precise clock so the delay of the received message after it was transmitted can be accurately measured. Precise clocks measuring time to a fraction of a billionth of a second are so expensive that the user equipment then becomes costly. If the user receives signals from a *fourth* satellite, the precise time can be calculated, because there is only one time which allows coincidence of the locations determined from satellites A, B, C and satellites A, B, D.

Each satellite must know its own location precisely. Because a satellite even at 12,000 miles encounters some forces from solar radiation and occasional particles, the precise prediction of its orbit is not possible. To regularly correct the satellite's information on its own position, tracking stations in Guam, Alaska, Hawaii, and California continuously detect corrections for the orbits of all the satellites and radio these corrections to the satellites overhead.

The radio signals from the satellites to the user travel through the ionosphere, the region 30 to 250 miles up where the Sun's radiation causes ionization. Radio waves travel through this region with a slightly reduced velocity because of the charged particles. The number of particles varies appreciably from hour to hour and day to day as the ultraviolet, x rays, and gamma rays from the Sun vary. To correct automatically for these slight changes in the speed of light, each satellite broadcasts on two different frequencies (the higher the frequency, the less the signal is slowed by the ionosphere). Comparison of these two signals allows the user equipment to correct automatically for ionospheric effects.

Finally, the satellites broadcast a signal which engineers call "spread spectrum." A much wider spectrum is used than is actually needed for the information. The data giving satellite position can be sent with a spectrum only

50 Hz wide; however, the system spreads this over 20 MHz, for the same reason an FM signal uses a broad spectrum: the redundancy in the spectrum allows the radio transmission to be noise-free.

Major American and Japanese automobile manufacturers are studying the use of GPS equipment in cars. A video disc system would store maps, display the appropriate map on a dashboard screen, and indicate the car's location and heading on this map by a dot and and arrow. Other potential applications are to allow accurate tracking of radio-controlled vehicles (ambulances, taxis, etc.), to track icebergs by dropping GPS receivers and radio transmitters on them, to land aircraft (by measuring position of the plane relative to a receiver permanently located at the end of the runway), and to control trains.

Loran

There are electronic navigation systems already in full operation. The Loran system (an acronym for LOng RAnge Navigation) is already in use by ships and airplanes. The basic principles of its operation are as follows.

Two stations (let's call them A and B) are located at known sites along the east coast of the United States. You are in a ship in the North Atlantic, you can receive radio signals from both stations, and you want to determine your location.

The two stations send out different signals starting at precisely the same time. If you are closer to A than to B, you receive the signal from A first. Your equipment measures precisely the difference in time. Since the speed of radio signals is known, the time difference tells how much farther you are from B than from A (figure 9.41).

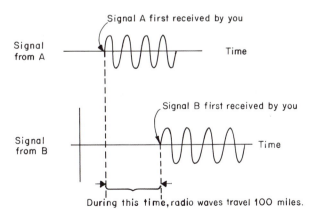

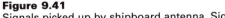

Figure 9.41
Signals picked up by shipboard antenna. Signal A arrives before signal B.

Suppose you are 100 miles farther from B than from A. In figure 9.42, you might be located at M—150 miles from A and 250 miles from B. But there are other points that are exactly 100 miles farther from B than from A—for example, points N and O in figure 9.43. You may also be at one of these points, since all you know is how much farther away B is than A.

If you find *all* points 100 miles farther from B than A, you determine the curve shown in figure 9.44. In geometry this curve is called a *hyperbola*—indeed, this is the definition of a hyperbola in mathematics.

Thus, when your Loran receiver picks up signals from two Loran transmitting stations, the equipment measures the relative time delays of the two signals and thereby determines a hyperbola; your ship is somewhere on this hyperbola.

Your receiver now picks up a third Loran station (C in figure 9.45). The signals from B and C determine a second hyperbola. Since you are located on

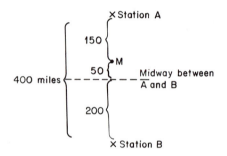

Figure 9.42
Two stations, A and B, send out radio signals to your ship at sea. From the time difference between the two signals, you know you are 100 miles farther from B than from A. You might be located at point M.

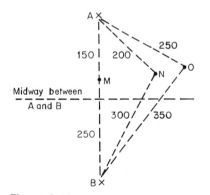

Figure 9.43
Point N is 100 miles farther from B than from A. Point O is also 100 miles farther from B than A.

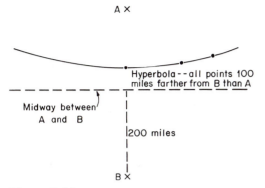

Figure 9.44
All points on the hyperbola are 100 miles farther from B than from A.

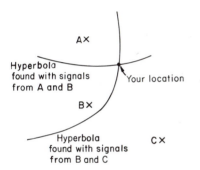

Figure 9.45
The first hyperbola is found by marking all points that are 100 miles farther from B than from A. For the second curve, we find the *difference* between the distances from B and C to our location. We then plot all the points (as we did to find the first hyperbola) and form another curve. Since you are located somewhere on both hyperbolas, you must be at the intersection of the two.

both of these hyperbolas, you must be at the point where the two hyperbolas intersect.

The actual Loran system operates a little differently from the description above. Our receiver picks up signals from three stations (A, B, and C above). One of these is the master station, the other two are slaves; the master controls the time it and each slave station start broadcasting a pulse at 100 kHz. The three broadcasts must not overlap, since we must be able to receive the three and recognize each. Consequently, the master transmits first—say, 80 cycles of the 100-kHz signal. A known amount of time later, B transmits its pulse (maybe 96 cycles, so we can recognize that this signal comes from B). Later C transmits, then even later A again, and so on.

This Loran system, called a *hyperbolic navigation system*, requires a large number of transmitters, so that, wherever you may be, your receiver can pick up three signals. A relatively low frequency (100 kHz) is used so that the radio signals do bend somewhat around the Earth. Since the radio signals are traveling for long distances near the Earth's surface, their velocity does change with atmospheric conditions, and there is some uncertainly about the relative distances of the stations; in the Navstar system, travel through the dense atmosphere is minimized, with the signals coming from space.

9.10 Radar

Peter's success as a Little League pitcher came from a radar gun—the same type device used by police to catch speeding motorists. With his father clocking his pitching speed, Peter was continually challenged to beat his previous speed.

The magazine advertisement from which this story was taken goes on to explain that a similar radar gun is available for "only" $149.95 (without batteries), so even middle-class fathers can now bring their sons to Little League stardom. Since the typical Little League game seems to have at most two hits and twenty or more walks, it is not clear that the primary problem is the speed of the pitcher's fastball. But regardless of what we think of such an ad, it does represent a predictable event in the history of radar.

Radar was first developed in the late 1930s. At the time of the Japanese attack on Pearl Harbor, there were radar stations in Hawaii. Radar operators saw and reported the approach of the planes, but the information was disregarded because the early radar sets were not very reliable. Furthermore, no one believed the Japanese would ever attack a U.S. base.

During the battles in the Pacific that followed, it became clear that U.S. ships needed more sophisticated ranging equipment, so the government awarded contracts to the most prestigious electronics laboratories in the country for the development of radar systems.

The resulting radar could not only spot enemy ships; it could also spot the splash of an off-target shell. This made it possible to correct the aim of the gun rapidly and precisely. Since the Japanese Navy did not have this advantage, radar was a key element in the U.S. victory over Japan in the Pacific.

In the years since World War II, radar has found a wide range of civilian uses, from air traffic control to detailed mapping of the Amazon River basin and the unexplored jungles of South America.

The word *radar* itself emphasizes that this technology is another application of radio: it is an acronym for RAdio Detection And Ranging. This origin of the word also emphasizes the basic uses: detection of an object or target, and determination of the range or the distance away of that target.

Elementary Pulse Radar

The simplest radar system transmits a radio signal for a brief instant, then waits for that signal to travel out to a target, reflect off that target, and return to the set, where the echo is received. This radar behaves exactly like a man yelling in a valley (figure 9.46). To find the distance to the far wall, he yells briefly, then measures the time until the sound echo comes back. Since sound travels 1120 feet per second, an echo 2 seconds after the yell means that the sound has traveled 2×1120 feet; hence, the distant wall is 1120 feet away (the sound has to travel both out and back). Since radio waves and light travel much faster than sound, the time in radar is often measured in microseconds (millionths of a second), but the principle is the same.

If we sent low-frequency pulses, we would need an enormous antenna. Therefore, high-frequency pulses are used. These "pulses" are short bursts of the high-frequency oscillation; typically there are about 1000 full cycles during each pulse. The return, or echo pulse, is *much* smaller in amplitude, but with the same frequency (figure 9.48).

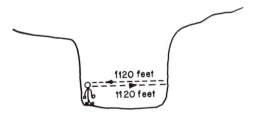

Figure 9.46
Echo ranging by sound in a valley. A person yells briefly. The sound travels to the distant wall and back at 1120 feet per second. If the person hears the echo after 2 seconds, the distant wall is 1120 feet away.

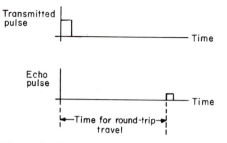

Figure 9.47
Radar measurement of range. Radio waves travel at 186,000 miles per second; thus it takes 5.4 microseconds (millionths of a second) for a radio signal to go one mile. Thus, for a round trip, we need 10.8 microseconds for each mile of distance. A target 10 miles away gives an echo pulse 108 microseconds after the transmitted pulse.

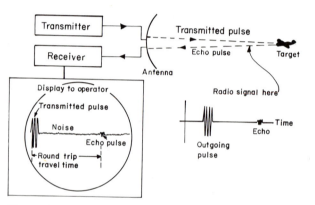

Figure 9.48
Basic operation of a radar system for target detection and ranging.

Finding Target Angle or Bearing

An AM broadcasting station usually radiates signals in all directions in order to reach listeners throughout the region. There are three reasons why a radar set cannot operate in this same, non-directional way:

1. The receiver would pick up echoes from reflectors or targets in all directions simultaneously. In many cases, we would have echoes on top of echoes, resulting in total confusion. (Within 50 miles of a busy airport there may be hundreds of planes at one time.)

2. In broadcast radio, we are transmitting in only one direction, from the transmitter to the receiver. In radar, we have two-way transmission, the signal going to the target and the echo signal coming back from the target. Furthermore, the target radiates (that is, the echo leaves the target) in all directions, so only a *very small* part of the energy reflected from the target heads

toward the radar antenna. The echo is very much smaller than the transmitted pulse. To obtain a measurable echo, we need to focus as much of the transmitted energy as possible on the target.

3. If the radar were transmitted in all directions at once, when we detected an echo we would have no idea where the target was.

To avoid these difficulties, the radar transmits only in a narrow beam (figure 9.49); to cover the region, the antenna rotates slowly, just as you would scan the area around you at night with a flashlight. When an echo returns from the airplane, we know the angle of the target by the direction in which the antenna is then pointing. The range of the target is found from the time lapse between transmitted and echo pulses.

The desired narrow beam of the radar radiation places stringent requirements on the antenna size. If a "dish" antenna is used (figure 9.50), a narrow, well-focused beam is possible only if the diameter of the dish is perhaps 50 times the wavelength. Thus, a radar accurate in measuring the angle of the target must use a very high frequency (in the microwave range, or typically 1000 MHz or more), and must be large.

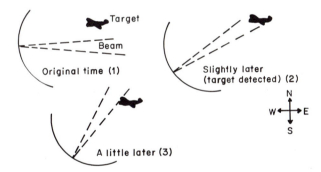

Figure 9.49
Radar transmits in a beam, with the antenna rotating to "sweep" over the region. These are top views, showing the target airplane northeast of the radar.

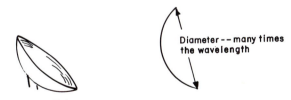

Antenna dish

Figure 9.50
A narrow focused beam is possible only if the diameter of the dish is many times the wavelength.

Digital electronics makes it no longer necessary to rotate the antenna mechanically. When a large dish or antenna (perhaps 80 feet in diameter) is rotated to scan the skies, there are mechanical problems: the drive system does not run smoothly, and in certain positions the antenna sags and bends. The scanning is slow.

Today the tendency is to use electronic scanning. The antenna actually consists of perhaps 2000 small antennas, each driven independently. By delaying the signal to some of these antennas, we can turn the beam. In the simple diagram in figure 9.51, delay of the signal from A means that the A and B signals add only when B has traveled farther than A—hence the beam points somewhat upward.

This system is called a *phased array* radar. The two antennas (one on Cape Cod, one near Sacramento) scanning the oceans for missiles fired from enemy submarines are PAVE PAWS radars (for Perimeter Acquisition Vehicle Entry Phased Array Warning Systems). Such an antenna can scan a 240° sector horizontally and from 3° to 85° elevation in microseconds, since there are no moving parts, and can track hundreds of missiles simultaneously. The accuracy is so high that the Cape Cod system could track a metal basketball over St. Louis if it were aimed in that direction.

"Brightness" of Targets

So far in this section we have learned that a radar transmits a very short pulse of a high-frequency radio signal, then waits for echoes to return. The radio energy is sent out over a narrow beam, so any one pulse detects targets only in a single direction.

The sinusoidal frequency and the pulse duration are chosen according to the particular application. Figure 9.52 shows one possible transmitted pulse. Here the radio signal is at a frequency of 10,000 MHz. The corresponding wavelength is 3 centimeters, or just over 1 inch, so the antenna is a dish about 4 feet in diameter.

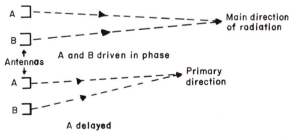

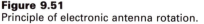

Figure 9.51
Principle of electronic antenna rotation.

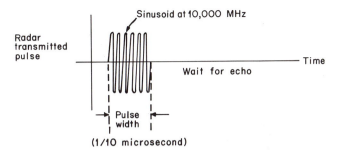

Figure 9.52
Typical transmitted pulse. In this example, the pulse lasts for ¹⁄₁₀ microsecond. The sinusoidal frequency during this pulse is 10,000 MHz; thus the period is ¹⁄₁₀,₀₀₀ microsecond. Consequently, there are 1000 full cycles of the sinusoid during the pulse (even though the picture shows only six).

What objects reflect such a radio signal and generate an echo? In other words, what kind of objects are "visible" to such a radar system? This question is exceedingly difficult scientifically, but the discussion of electromagnetic signals in chapter 8 allows us to give some general answers.

First, any metallic object reflects. If the object is smooth, the strength of the echo back to the radar depends critically on the shape of the target (figure 9.53). Most real objects (such as airplanes) present many different shapes, so the echo returning toward the radar varies as the object turns.

When the surface is rough (figure 9.54), echoes are radiated in all directions, including back toward the radar. A surface is rough if the undulations are of the order of a wavelength, smooth if the variations are much less than a wavelength. Thus, as the frequency increases (and the wavelength therefore becomes smaller), more surfaces seem rough.

Echoes are also generated by turbulent air, such as around an airplane's engine exhaust. If we select the frequency properly, echoes can come from water (as we saw in the case of the microwave oven). Weather radar detects rain by a careful choice of frequency.

The strongest echoes come back from a target called a *corner reflector* (figure 9.55). A corner reflector consists of three flat surfaces at right angles to each other (like the bottom and two adjoining sides of a box). Because the smooth surfaces perfectly reflect the incoming signal, a very strong echo heads directly for the radar receiver.

There is an interesting application of such a corner reflector. In earthquake-prone California, geoscientists want to measure accurately the changing elevation of the ground to try to predict earthquakes. When the astronauts were on the Moon, they left a corner reflector there. A transmitter is located at the

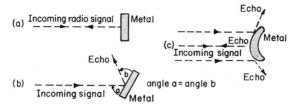

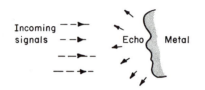

Figure 9.53
Reflections from smooth metal surfaces. The angle at which a radio signal leaves a smooth surface is equal to the angle at which it hits the surface.

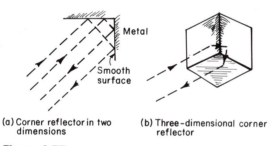

Figure 9.54
When the target surface is rough, echoes go out in all directions, including back to the radar receiver.

(a) Corner reflector in two   (b) Three-dimensional corner
    dimensions   reflector

Figure 9.55
A corner reflector sends all the echo directly back to the source.

critical site in California; an electromagnetic signal travels to the Moon and back. Even though the total round-trip distance is about 440,000 miles, scientists can measure a change as small as one inch to determine how much the ground has risen since the previous measurement.

Corner reflectors also appear quite accidentally. For example, when equipment in airplanes is taking radar pictures of a city region, a tall building towering over a paved highway is a two-sided corner reflector and gives a very strong echo.

Corner reflectors are often useful in other applications. The cover of an auto taillight consists of corner reflectors to reflect the headlights of a trailing car back to the driver of that vehicle.

Side-Looking Radar

A very long antenna is needed to give detailed resolution of targets (or to give a very narrow beam). A long antenna works as shown in figure 9.57: the signals from segments A through G are combined to yield a total signal which has the detailed resolution. In "side-looking" radar, an airplane has a short antenna (the length of segment A). The airplane flies from O to L, so first it measures the response of segment A, later B, later still C, and so on.

A computer takes all these images from A through G and combines them to give the image that would have been obtained from a single antenna of length O to L. In other words, the computer substitutes for the long antenna—or the computer makes the short antenna on a moving airplane equivalent to a long antenna fixed in the sky. Furthermore, the computer does this same operation all along the flight path.

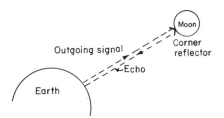

Figure 9.56
Scheme for measuring the amount the ground rises or falls (for earthquake prediction).

Figure 9.57
Principles of side-looking radar.

This technique has been used to generate topographic maps of the entire region of the upper Amazon River in South America—a region previously inaccessible. The detailed radar mapping is possible because of the ability to construct complex computers cheaply and easily.

9.11 Radar Countermeasures

The appearance of radar to detect enemy planes and ships and aim guns in World War II initiated a "war" between radar technology and technology to counteract radar. The first anti-radar tactic was the release from the airplane of hundreds of aluminum-coated strips to give the radar operators a multitude of false targets. The Japanese first used this technique (which they called *gunan-shi*, or deceiving paper) in May 1943 in the Battle of the Solomon Islands, but the U.S. and Britain quickly followed in the European theater (with the names "chaff" and "window," respectively). With this development, the field of ECM or electronic countermeasures was born.

The Germans quickly responded with ECCM (electronic counter-counter-measures): their ground radars looking for Allied bombers used the Doppler effect to pick only targets moving at airplane speed. The chaff tended to slow down quickly as it floated downward. The British then put into play the Moonshine jammer: fast-moving fighter planes received the German radar signal, then retransmitted a large signal giving the appearance of a major target so that the actual Allied bombers were left alone.

The radar-ECM "war" subsided until the mid-1960s in Vietnam. Then Soviet-supplied surface-to-air missiles (SAMs), guided by radar, began down-ing U.S. planes at an alarming rate (one in seven on a mission). The U.S. quickly added transmitters to jam enemy radar receivers, receivers to tell a pilot when enemy radar had locked on him, and missiles to home on enemy radar. By the air strike on Libya in 1986, the anti-radar missiles contained computers to remember and guide even when the enemy only operated the radar for short intervals of time.

The back-and-forth ECM-radar battle continues. One side develops radar or detection devices that can change frequency rapidly and randomly, or that operate at visible-light frequencies. To thwart infrared detectors, burning flares are ejected instead of chaff; the other side compares signals from infrared detectors at two different frequencies to distinguish a jet engine from a flare. The enemy uses aircraft flying very low to hide behind the earth's curvature; we counter with AWACS (Airborne Warning And Control System) aircraft searching over a wide region and automatically evaluating the seriousness of each threat.

This continuing war between radar and ECM emphasizes that the value of each new weapon is strongly influenced by the ease with which countermeasures can be deployed. German radar was initially rendered useless by chaff—an expensive, complex electronic system was counteracted by strips of paper. Today much of the argument against the feasibility of the Strategic Defense Initiative states that thousands of inexpensive decoys could be released during an attack on the U.S., and the defensive system would be rendered ineffective.

9.12 Police Radar

Radar can operate on an entirely different principle from the one we have just discussed. Instead of transmitting a pulse and waiting for an echo, we transmit continuously. The echo from a stationary target comes back at the same frequency at which it was transmitted. If the target is moving toward or away from the radar set, however, the echo frequency differs from the transmitted frequency. This makes it possible for the receiver to pick out the moving echo only. Police radar operates in this way.

Police radar for catching speeders first appeared right after World War II. For 25 years, however, use of the equipment was rare. Even though auto safety gained national attention in the 1960s, speed limits were liberal and enforcement spotty.

Then, after the Arab oil embargo, Congress passed the 55-mph national speed limit—primarily to conserve oil. The federal government began to pressure states to enforce the limit, and the National Highway Traffic Safety Administration gave grants for the purchase of police radar. Motorists began to find radar patrols along major freeways and interstate highways.

The transmitter of a police radar unit is a cylinder that is placed just outside the window of the police car. A radio signal at a frequency of 10.5×10^9 Hz is generated (a second possible frequency was added a few years ago).

This radio signal is sent out in a beam, as shown in figure 9.58. A metal car is an excellent reflector; any car in the beam gives an echo. This echo allows the radar to measure the car's speed, as explained below.

Several problems are obvious. For example, echoes come back from every car that happens to be in the beam. The radar equipment automatically uses only the strongest echo. The equipment in the police car then reads the speed of the car causing that echo and displays it on a numerical indicator.

The policeman has to decide which car on the road is having its speed measured. Unfortunately, the strongest echo does not necessarily come from the nearest vehicle. A compact car can only be detected about ⅓ mile away, but a tractor-trailer may be picked up almost a mile away.

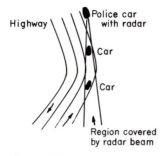

Figure 9.58
Coverage of police radar.

Furthermore, the radar equipment must avoid the problem of first measuring one car, then another well ahead of the former. To prevent this, the radar takes five readings quickly and in a row and averages the five speeds. If these five are not very close together, no speed appears on the indicator.

To understand police radar and the operation of detectors, we need to know how the radar equipment uses the echo to measure the target's speed. This is accomplished by using a phenomenon called the *Doppler shift*. The frequency of the echo signal differs from the original frequency transmitted by an amount called the *shift* (in frequency), which is proportional to the target's speed toward the radar set.

Doppler Shift

Let us first look at a radio wave traveling through space, hitting a *stationary* reflecting target, and coming back to the starting point. For simplicity, let us look at the first two cycles of the electric field variation when the signal leaves the transmitter starting at $t = 0$ (figure 9.59). At the transmitter the signal changes as time progresses as shown in the figure.

As we move away from the transmitter toward the target, the signal becomes slightly weaker (the beam sent out by the antenna is spreading out just as the beam from a flashlight spreads as it moves away). More important for us, the wave travels with a constant velocity, the speed of light. Thus, the wave at A is later than the wave at the transmitter, at B later still, and so on.

Figure 9.60 shows a sketch of the signal at each of the points of figure 9.59. When the signal hits the target, the signal is reflected and starts back, but it also spreads out in all directions, so only a very small echo reaches the radar set.

If we look at one point on the radio signal (for example, point a, the first peak), we see this occurs later and later in time as we go toward the target and back. At D, this peak arrives at t_1. The next peak (b) arrives one period later,

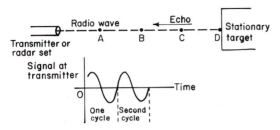

Figure 9.59
Region from radar set to target.

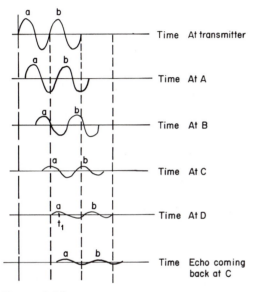

Figure 9.60
Radio signal at various points in figure 9.59. The signal actually decreases in size much more rapidly than is indicated here.

since it left the transmitter a period later. The echo traveling backward has the same frequency as the original transmitted signal.

Now we come to the crucial point. Consider what happens if the target is moving toward the radar set. The first signal peak (a) travels to the target. The second peak (b), coming later, finds the target closer—hence, it doesn't have to travel as far *or as long.* The echo from b starts back sooner than we would expect. *In the echo,* the peaks (a and b) are closer together in time; thus, the echo seems to have a higher frequency (a shorter period) than the original transmitted radio signal.

The faster the target is moving toward the transmitter, the more the echo frequency is shifted upward from the original frequency. The speed of the target is always much less than the velocity of the radio signal (the velocity of light), so the target never moves very far in one cycle of the arriving radio signal. The shift upward in frequency is always a small fraction of the original frequency. (For the standard frequency, the shift is only 31 Hz for each mile per hour of target velocity.)

Electronic Changes

Shortly after the national speed limit was set and widespread enforcement activities began, a number of small companies began selling radar detectors for motorists to warn them of the presence of police radar. As detectors became better, radar manufacturers modified their products; companies making detectors responded with improvements; and the technological advantage oscillated back and forth. The following is a brief history of this electronic warfare.

1. In 1975 radars began to work on a second frequency (24.1×10^9 Hz).

2. The small electronics companies responded with detectors that measured signals at both possible frequencies (This was naturally more expensive, but the cost of electronic parts was falling).

3. Several states passed legislation forbidding possession of a radar detector. In Virginia, police confiscated thousands of detectors.

4. Manufacturers responded by making detectors whose listening antennas could be concealed (for example, behind the car's grille), and whose alarms could be hidden and shut off.

5. Police learned to choose better positions—for example, where a car coming around a curve would be within radar range almost as soon as the detector was activated. (Microwaves do not travel around curves and hills.)

6. Detector manufacturers improved sensitivity and cut down false alarms (for example, from CB radios or auto ignition systems) by making receivers that would electronically reject all signals except police radar signals.

7. Police radar was developed to allow on-off operation. The policeman waits to press the "on" button until your car is in range; detection is now impossible unless the policeman happens to be checking a car in front of you. This on-off system never gained much acceptance, however, because of the need for the policeman to participate actively in the operation.

8. At the end of the 1970s, radar was developed that could work from a moving police car. Echoes are picked up from the ground or fixed objects to allow Doppler measurement of the police car's speed, which then can be subtracted from the measured speed of an oncoming vehicle. Drivers don't see the parked police car, and the driver of the target car has much less time to decelerate (since the two cars are approaching one another at a relative speed of over 100 mph).

9. In the 1980s, police started to deploy unmanned radar transmitters along major highways. Drivers with detectors or those alerted by CB broadcasts slowed down, and the basic purpose of holding traffic within the speed limit was accomplished inexpensively (since these dummy transmitters need have no speed-measuring equipment and no policeman operating the equipment). The Federal Communications Commission, which controls radio transmission in the United States, has objected to these dummy transmitters. (The FCC would not allow Washington state to use solar-powered ones.)

10. In 1989 manufacturers announced laser "guns" to measure auto speed.

Thus a type of electronic warfare is going on. The local and national law enforcement agencies are attempting to enforce the national speed limit and to cut the large number of deaths and serious injuries from auto accidents. Some manufacturers, concerned only with profit, make sure new devices are always available to that segment of the public that wants to outwit the law.

Review Questions

R9-1. What do we mean by a radio signal?

R9-2. On an airplane, we pick up the radio signals transmitted from the airport on a loop antenna. What measurements might we want to make with these signals?

R9-3. Why would an object (somewhere in the vicinity of an airplane) that reflects radio signals cause a problem for the pilot trying to locate the airport?

R9-4. What do we mean by the term "telecommunications"?

R9-5. When we want to "pick up" a particular signal that was transmitted, our receiving antenna also "picks up" numerous other radio signals from many different sources. What are some of these sources that are emitting radio signals (that is, electromagnetic signals)?

R9-6. In AM radio, what are the advantages of broadcasting at a high carrier frequency?

R9-7. What is the relationship between the size of an antenna and the wavelength of the frequencies transmitted?

R9-8. Each AM radio station is assigned a particular frequency. This frequency is the "carrier" signal. How is the carrier signal changed as a message is transmitted? Each FM radio station is also assigned a carrier frequency. What changes are made to the carrier signal as a message is transmitted?

R9-9. In AM broadcasting, there is redundancy in the sidebands. Explain. With our improved technology, AM broadcasting could throw out one of the sidebands. Why isn't this done?

R9-10. Why don't we get high-fidelity music from an AM radio broadcast?

R9-11. If I am on the top of an 80-foot building and look out over a level plain, how far can I see?

R9-12. Why were there so many objections when the FCC recently proposed to change the U.S. AM bandwidth from 10,000 to 9000 Hz?

R9-13. What is the principal advantage of FM over AM?

R9-14. A radar transmits a high-frequency pulse. Is the echo the same frequency? Why?

R9-15. Most police radars transmit continuously rather than in pulses. Why?

R9-16. In commercial FM, there are typically about how many sidebands?

R9-17. In radar, we want the antenna dimension *much* larger than the wavelength. Why?

R9-18. Why is the Department of Defense eager to purposely degrade the performance of the GPS system?

R9-19. The GPS system yields your latitude, longitude, and altitude. With only three quantities to be determined, why do we need to have four satellites in view?

R9-20. Synthetic-aperture (side-looking) radar uses an airplane flying across the target to obtain the characteristics of what kind of antenna?

R9-21. In a pulsed radar, we would like to send out pulses as frequently as possible to have large number of echoes. What limits the rate at which pulses are transmitted?

R9-22. What is meant by the term "synthetic-aperture radar," or "side-looking radar"?

R9-23. Why is an inertial navigation system used rather than Loran for airplanes flying from Anchorage to Tokyo?

R9-24. In an FM altimeter for an airplane, what signal is transmitted? (See problem 9-6.)

R9-25. What are the principal advantages of GPS navigation over Loran?

R9-26. Our air-traffic-control system uses radar to measure only the azimuth and the range of a plane; altitude is measured in the plane and radioed to the ground. Why not use the radar to measure altitude?

R9-27. Loran was possible in 1945, but GPS had to wait until computers were developed to their current state. Explain briefly.

R9-28. The carrier frequency of an FM radio station is 98.1 MHz. Sketch the spectrum of the signal broadcast by that station.

R9-29. Why do certain AM radio stations have to shut down from sunset to sunrise?

R9-30. The Loran broadcasts were changed to 100,000 Hz from a frequency around 2,000,000 Hz. What advantages are there at the lower frequency?

Problems

P9-1. The Loran navigation system is used in many ways in addition to normal ship and airplane navigation: New England lobster fishermen avoid a submerged wreck. Planes drop fire fighters and chemicals to fight a forest fire. Philadelphia centrally dispatches and routes its ambulances. New York fixes the site of an auto accident. Safety officials track a truck carrying nuclear waste. Tankers save $5000 by following the current on the return to Louisiana. This system is operated by the government since it is used extensively by government agencies. Discuss whether the U.S. should charge a fee for non-federal use of the radio broadcasts.

P9-2. At the high frequencies (above 54 MHz) at which television stations broadcast, radio signals travel in straight lines; they do not bend around the surface of the Earth. Thus, even if a station broadcasts a very strong signal, receivers can pick up this signal only at a range determined by the Earth's curvature. To find this range we use the engineering formula for the line of sight:

$$R = \sqrt{1.5h}$$

where R is the range in miles and h is the antenna's height in feet.

The tallest TV antenna in the U.S. (at Fargo, North Dakota) has a height of about 2400 feet. One and a half times this is 3600, with a square root of 60. So this antenna can cover a circular area out to 60 miles in all directions.

If you live 80 miles from Fargo, how high must your home antenna be to pick up the signal?

P9-3 Draw the spectrum of a flute playing middle A at 440 Hz with the following harmonics and amplitudes:

	Frequency	Amplitude
Fundamental	440 Hz	4
Second harmonic	880 Hz	3
Third harmonic	1320 Hz	2
Fourth harmonic	1760 Hz	1
Fifth harmonic	2200 Hz	0.6
Eighth harmonic	3520 Hz	0.1

Show the spectrum of the scrambled sound signal for the complex scrambler using the code described by figure 9.31.

P9-4 If you dial 303-499-7111 in Boulder, Colorado, you can hear the time signal broadcast by the National Bureau of Standards in Fort Collins, Colorado by short-wave radio station WWV. (Fort Collins is 80 miles north of Boulder.) The signal is broadcast at several short-wave frequencies and also at 60 kHz (a low radio frequency). The broadcast sends the following information: time signal, both in a voice announcement and a time code; standard musical pitch; standard time interval; broadcast conditions; major storms in the Atlantic and the Pacific (the Pacific is covered by station WWVH in the Hawaiian Islands).

If we include other nations, there are over 30 radio stations broadcasting accurate time signals throughout the world; in addition, several radio navigation systems can be used for time measurement.

The radio stations give the listener an indication of time accurate to about $\frac{1}{1000}$ second (the telephone pickup is likely to be good only to within $\frac{1}{30}$ second). If we need greater accuracy, we can use feedback to cut the error.

I install equipment that receives the time signal from Fort Collins, then immediately transmits back a signal. In Colorado, the signal received from me is timed with respect to their originally transmitted signal to measure the two-way delay. Half of this is the delay with which I received the original signal. In this way, I can correct my determination of time to within an error of about one millionth of a second.

Pigeon racers use the broadcasts of WWV to ensure simultaneous release of pigeons at a number of different locations. Discuss briefly a few other (more serious) applications of the accurate WWV time information.

P9-5 The television pictures of Jupiter received from the Voyager spacecraft in 1979 were a remarkable communication achievement. The transmitter was 700 million kilometers from the Earth. The radio signal carrying the picture information was picked up by antennas in Spain, Australia, and California, then relayed to the Jet Propulsion Laboratory in Pasadena, California. These Earth-based antennas are about 100 million times more sensitive than your home TV antenna; they can pick up a signal of only 10^{-21} watt.

a. Why did NASA build three receiving antennas rather than one?

b. While the spacecraft is in the vicinity of Jupiter, we need to measure accurately its range or distance from the earth-based antenna. To do this, we send out a special coded signal, which is picked up by the spacecraft and immediately sent back to Earth. We measure the time for the two-way communication, and hence we can determine the range. (1) What is the time, approximately? (2) With this system we can measure range within 10 meters. How much time corresponds to an error of 10 meters? (3) Why is it impossible to obtain a more accurate range measurement?

c. We can measure the spacecraft's radial velocity by using the Doppler shift of the signal frequency. The spacecraft velocity can be found to an accuracy of 0.5 mm per sec. If the radio frequency is 8.4×10^9 Hz, how accurately are we measuring the frequency?

P9-6 In one type of altimeter for airplanes, a radio signal is transmitted downward. The frequency changes as shown in figure 9.61. That is, the frequency steadily decreases from f_2 to f_1, then jumps up to f_2 and starts decreasing again. The echo signal from the surface of the Earth occurs later by a time equal to the *round-trip* travel from the plane to the ground (figure 9.62). The equipment in the airplane takes a small fraction of the transmitted signal and all of the echo, then compares these two signals to find the difference in

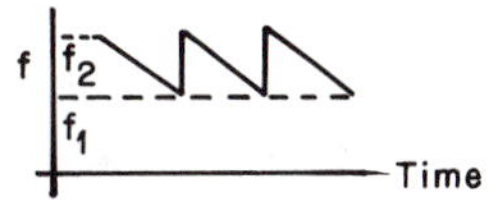

Figure 9.61

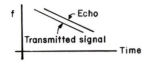

Figure 9.62

frequency. This difference in frequency then measures the altitude of the plane above the ground.

a. There are two times: the round-trip travel time (call this T_r) and the time during which the frequency decreases from f_2 to f_1 (call this T_d). Explain why T_d must be appreciably larger than T_r.

b. To avoid echoes from nearby mountains, the transmitted signal should be in a narrow beam—that is, sharply focused downward. Why does this cause difficulty?

c. Bats use sound waves with similar frequency changes to avoid collisions and to locate food (insects). What factors influence the choice of frequencies? Discuss briefly.

P9-7 The article below by Dr. Heinz M. Schlicke, entitled "Injustice through RFI," is reprinted, with permission, from *IEEE Spectrum* 21 (August 1984), p. 9. After reading this article, prepare a 200-word digest to convey to the typical college graduate the problems associated with the breath-tester technology.

Conviction for drunken driving in many states leads to severe punishment, including a possible jail sentence. One would therefore expect instruments used to determine drunkenness to be reliable beyond any reasonable doubt. Unfortunately, certain breath analyzers still widely used by the police are quite susceptible to radio-frequency interference (RFI). These breath analyzers are mentioned in the National Highway and Traffic Safety Administration's report DOT HS-806-400 entitled "Limited Electromagnetic Interference Testing of Evidential Breath Testers." Among the analyzers most susceptible to RFI was the Smith & Wesson type 900A.

RFI may result from proximity to hand-held or mobile transmitters used by the police, ham-radio operators, and truck and taxi drivers. Other radio services operating in the crowded range from 25 to 470 megahertz and above may also contribute to the interference.

Because of this, lawsuits are, in many states, challenging the admissibility of evidence from the type 900A breath analyzer. The courtroom atmosphere is certainly not conducive to comprehensive, scientifically sound assessment of RFI sensitivity.

I recently was an expert witness in a breath analyzer case in Milwaukee, Wis., and had access to many legal depositions by other experts, some smart and some not so smart. For lack of clear, professionally established guidelines, a strange mix of sense and nonsense can be found in these depositions. In separating the wheat from the chaff, I found considerable irrelevancies, oversimplifications, and contradictions, indicating a complete lack of understanding of the subject. In some presentations distortions were so pronounced that one could not help but suspect intent to mislead.

For example, in a monumental example of oversimplification, the State of Wisconsin contended that experts had measured RFI susceptibility of a breath analyzer at four different frequencies. They did not lie, but their four frequencies were less than 0.4 MHz apart, whereas the actual frequency range of RFI is more than 400 MHz.

I also found in reports submitted some measurements and observations that, taken together, shed a revealing light on the seemingly confusing situation. Three pieces of evidence are particularly demonstrative of the model 900A breath analyzer's sensitivity to RFI.

First is a fine National Bureau of Standards report confirming the 900A's great sensitivity. This report was done for the National Highway and Traffic Safety Administration (the same report mentioned above). It showed that out of 16 breath analyzers tested, 9 were in some way sensitive to RFI. The 900A was shown to be the most sensitive of all.

Second are the open-field measurements of the critical distance at which the 900A's reading becomes affected by RFI of a given power and frequency. These readings were taken by Smith & Wesson, the manufacturer of the breath analyzer.

The company tested 20 of the breath analyzers to determine the distance at which the blood-alcohol content indication was noticeably affected by RFI. An open-field test implies an idealized infinite plane without obstructions that would generate extraneous signals or cause reflections. To simulate this the measurements were made in a large parking lot. An antenna was mounted on top of a car containing a radio transmitter. The breath analyzer was mounted on a wood pedestal (to minimize any field-change reflections that might be caused by a metal object) and rotated in 90° steps (to determine the effect of different orientations on RFI sensitivity). The tests were conducted at four widely separated frequencies; unfortunately, only vertical polarization was used.

The most critical frequency is apparently around 50 MHz, where 10 percent of the units gave false readings within 52 feet of a 10-watt transmitter or 160 feet of a 100-W transmitter (these are typical of the power of police transmitters).

Although open-field measurements are a good starting point, they are gross idealizations that do not take into account field changes imparted by nearby metal objects. These objects can either act as shielding to reduce the strength of the RFI, or as resonators to increase it. To be sure, concrete buildings with welded steel reinforcing bars may reduce unwanted radiation by 90 percent or more. On the other hand, nearby resonators, such as any metal object approximately one-half a wavelength long or multiples thereof (about 1 to 15 feet), will greatly enhance the local field strength. Even power cords may act as antennas. What this all means is that the critical distance can vary widely from the results of Smith & Wesson's open-field test.

The third piece of evidence is that R.E. Jensen, assistant director of forensic science for the State of Minnesota, observed that readings taken on the 900A were very sensitive to the surroundings of the device, indicating either very little or very poor RFI hardening. The 900A is particularly susceptible to RFI picked up by the power cord acting as an antenna. This indicates poor RF filtering on the power cord (feed-through filtering). The instrument itself is housed in a metal box with unshielded openings and slots. These openings could easily be protected by placing wire mesh over them.

The 900A breath analyzer is a simple optical bridge consisting of two photocells facing each other less than a foot apart. In front of each cell is an ampul containing an alcohol-sensitive liquid. Between the photocells is a light source; the light passes to each cell through the ampul.

If one ampul's liquid is exposed to breath containing alcohol, its light transmission changes and the bridge becomes unbalanced. The position of the light source can then be shifted to rebalance the bridge. The displacement of the light source is a measure of the alcohol content of the breath.

The sensitivity of the bridge is increased with an amplifier, the key factor producing RFI sensitivity. The transistors that make up the amplifier act like back-to-back diodes to rectify any stray RF signal and throw off the otherwise reliable bridge.

In this context, it is interesting to note that Smith & Wesson issued a Customer Advisory, dated Sept. 2, 1982. To quote from page 12, "The safe operating distance for the breath analyzer is 75 feet from a five watt transmitter and 450 feet from a 100 watt transmitter."

From a technical point of view, one comes to the uncomfortable conclusion that the test results obtained with the 900A must be taken not with a grain but with a lump of salt. It strikes me, an engineer, as unconscionable that decisions are made, at least in part, on readings from instruments that are poorly designed to reject RFI, yet unavoidably have to operate in an RFI-filled environment. This is particularly disturbing in view of the fact that the RFI susceptibility of the instruments in question can easily be remedied (by feed-through filters and shielding continuity) and that RFI-safe instruments are now on the market.

More important, from a legal point of view, judges are making their decisions based on the readings of a potentially inaccurate instrument. The present system sometimes uses mediocre and prejudiced expert witnesses who are, after all, in the pay of lawyers who are biased by their commitments to their clients. The IEEE might, perhaps, provide small committees of unbiased experts to assist the judge on all types of purely technical matters. This seems to be a chance for the IEEE to have some social impact.

P9-8 An adequate water supply in the western and mountain states is critical for agriculture, mining, manufacturing, and public health. Agricultural needs are especially important, since this region (figure 9.63) is vital for feeding not only the United States but also many other parts of the world. The Department of Agriculture must maintain a continuous assessment of the water resources throughout much of the western U.S. in order to establish logical policies and

Figure 9.63
The Colorado River provides a major part of the water throughout much of the southwest. This map shows just the main river, not the many feeders.

advise farmers. Changes in total water availability demand constraints on use of distribution (through dams) well in advance of periods of possible severe shortage.

To fulfill this responsibility, Agriculture measures the daily precipitation, accumulated snowfall, and temperatures (minimum, maximum, and average) at 1000 remote locations, many deep in the mountains of eleven western states.

These measurement stations are far from towns or highways or telephone lines. The stations are unmanned—it would be prohibitively expensive to hire people to work in such isolation, to build housing, and to provide supplies, and so on. So each station consists simply of measuring devices and a radio transmitter, all powered by solar energy. Once a day, or regularly as desired, the radio transmitter sends the desired information out to a centrally located master station, where a computer develops a model of the water resources in the entire region.

So far, the system seems simple; all we need are 1000 radio transmitters and measurement instruments. Unfortunately, such a system won't work, because radio signals travel through the air only in straight lines. To a good approximation, radio waves travel only to receivers visible with a telescope from the transmitter.

Two basic factors limit the range of the remote-station radio transmitters:

Curvature of the Earth. As figure 9.64 shows, the higher the antenna, the greater the range. Engineers use a formula devised from simple trigonometry:

$$d = \sqrt{1.5h} ,$$

Figure 9.64
An antenna of height h sends a radio signal a total distance d. Points on the surface
of the Earth beyond d cannot be reached.

where h is antenna height in feet and d is range in miles. Thus, even if the
antenna is on a mountain 400 feet high, the radio signal reaches less than 80
miles.

Uneven terrain. The situation is even worse for our system, since many of the
1000 remote stations are on mountains and in valleys. The radio signal may
reach only the nearby mountainside, with everything beyond the mountain in
the shadow. This location is especially likely for precipitation measurement,
since we need to know the rainfall as the clouds move toward the mountains.

Consequently, ordinary radio transmitters are useless. Stringing telephone
lines to each remote station would be prohibitively expensive. We might try
radio transmitters sending signals to satellites passing overhead, but we want
the remote-station equipment to be inexpensive and to use very little energy.
There is a better solution.

The SNOTEL (SNOwpack TELemetry) system uses radio waves reflecting
off the ionized trails left by meteors as they enter the Earth's atmosphere.

More than a billion meteors a day burn up in the atmosphere, releasing
enough energy to produce trails that reflect radio waves. Indeed, more than
200 million meteors a day leave trails visible to the human eye, so when you see
a "shooting star" the event is not really unusual. The number reaching the
Earth's surface is small; indeed, on the average only once in 180 years will
someone be hit by a meteor.

A meteor enters the air at a speed up to 160,000 miles per hour (higher
speeds mean that the meteor originated outside our solar system); as it is
slowed, the energy is converted to heat, light, and a trail of ionized particles
(positive ions and electrons). The trail consists of perhaps 10 billion electrons
in each foot at an altitude of 50 miles; the trail may be as long as 100 miles. These
free electrons are excited by an arriving radio signal, just as electrons at the
surface of a reflecting metal would be. The trail reflects the radio wave back to
earth at a distance as much as 1500 miles from the transmitting station. Within
less than a second, the trail electrons diffuse, and radio transmission stops.

The SNOTEL system operates as follows: The 1000 remote stations are divided into groups, about 60 in each group. The master station first decides to poll or interrogate group A. The master sends out a continuous radio signal coded to ask all stations in group A to respond.

Within a few seconds, a meteor trail appears which allows communication with *one* of the 60 remote stations in group A—let's say station A17. Station A17 receives the signal, immediately turns on its transmitter, and sends to the master the data on the previous day's weather. The transmission must be completed within about ⅒ second, since the meteor trail then fades away. For the next hour, while the other remote stations in A are being interrogated, A17 is turned off.

The master station continues (perhaps 40 minutes) until responses have been received from all remote stations in group A, then turns to group B, and so forth. The remote stations within group A are reasonably separated from one another, so that a single meteor trail allows communication between the master and only one other station at a time.

In engineering, SNOTEL is called a "meteor burst communication system"—the adjective "burst" refers to the requirement that the information be sent in a short burst, or all at once in a very short period of time. A similar system can also be used to communicate with airplanes in flight or ships at sea, or to track icebergs. Television signals (particularly for channels 2–4) also may reflect off meteor trails.

The system operates successfully because the meteor trails appear *randomly.* The altitude is always about 50 miles, but the exact location and time of each trail can only be estimated in terms of probability. Fortunately, there are enough meteors (about 12,000 every second) so that the master station can quickly establish communication with one of the remote radios in the group being interrogated.

Indeed, there are so many meteors that the master can communicate with all 60 stations in group A within an hour—indeed, normally in much less than an hour. Before building such a system, an engineer would make probability studies to be sure of success, calculating the area through which the meteor trail must appear to allow communication to each remote radio and then the probability of a meteor trail's actually appearing within a few seconds.

a. In 1954 the Canadian Defence Research Board began using the first meteor-burst communication (MBC) system. Why was Canada a logical starting place?

b. Shortly after 1960 interest in MBC dropped sharply, largely because of what new technology?

c. By the late 1970s the development of inexpensive microprocessors made MBC attractive again. Explain.

d. The Federal Emergency Management Agency (FEMA) has a system for communication to each state capital in case of war or a national emergency. Why is the MBC system attractive for this application? (The Alaskan MBC system is used to provide statewide communications even in times of disruption by auroral displays.)

P9-9 Car theft is a major crime problem, with more than a million cars stolen each year and only half ever found. Massachusetts is the number one state, with a 1/87 probability that a given car will be stolen.

To fight car theft, a Massachusetts company introduced equipment called Lo-Jack. A miniaturized FM radio transmitter and receiver are hidden in the car. When the car is reported as stolen, the police radio a call signal, which is received at the car. This coded signal turns on the car's transmitter, which allows the police to home in on the stolen vehicle.

An organization now advertises a similar system for protection from kidnapping. They will make the receiver-transmitter in many shapes—for example, "as a pen that you keep in your desk, or a watch to be worn by a child, even in a pack of cigarettes or a micro-miniature hearing aid."

a. As an investor, would you bet on the potential market for such a technology?

b. Does this technology represent a positive innovation?

c. The same technology allows police to track an object by hiding the transceiver in the object. Does this represent invasion of privacy and a serious threat? (Courts have ruled that the transceiver in a vehicle is not illegal, since in any vehicle there is a reasonable expectation that you could be followed. If the tracking continues after you enter your home, however, the authorities do violate the fourth amendment. You can legitimately expect privacy in your home.)

Chapter 10
Medical Ultrasonic Imaging

Figure 10.1 is a picture of twin fetuses in the uterus. A sound source was applied to the mother's abdomen to send sound signals into the body; the electronic equipment then waited for echoes to appear after the sound signal bounced off various parts of the fetus.

This picture is an example of *non-invasive* testing. There was no need to operate to look at the fetuses; the mother did not have to ingest any dyes or marker substances. The physician simply used technology to generate sounds, then measured the echoes received.

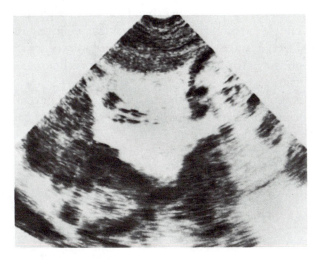

Figure 10.1
An ultrasound picture of twins in the uterus. One is seen on the right side facing left; the other, less clear, is on the left side with the head down.

Ultrasound imaging in medicine is an impressive example of what can be done with modern communications technology. It is also an example of a modern technology that comes directly from military work—in this case, from sonar, which was developed for locating of enemy submarines. Today, ultrasound pictures are an important tool allowing the physician to look into the human body—a totally non-military application.

In this chapter, the goal is to explain the technology of ultrasound pictures, the current status of the field, and the possible health effects.

A hundred years ago, the physician had no way of looking into the human body. At the very end of the nineteenth century, x rays were discovered and bones could be viewed. Today the physician has a variety of ways to obtain pictures without surgery: x rays, magnetic resonance imaging (MRI), nuclear medicine (in which radioactive materials are administered into the body), positive emission, and ultrasound. Among these, ultrasound is the only one that uses sound waves rather than electromagnetic waves; thus, ultrasound imaging is a natural extension of a phenomenon with which we are already familiar.

10.1 Echolocation

Ultrasound pictures such as figure 10.1 are based on the technique of *echolocation*—finding a target by sending out a signal and waiting for an echo to return. If you are standing on one side of a valley and want to know how far it is to a distant mountain, you let out a brief yell and measure the time until you hear the echo (figure 10.2). You know that sound travels through air at about 1100 feet per second. If the echo returns 4 seconds after your yell, the sound has traveled 4400 feet; thus the mountain is 2200 feet away (since the sound must make the round trip). You have used echo-ranging or echolocation of the target (the mountain).

Bats use sound echolocation to navigate in the dark. During the eighteenth century, Lazaro Spallanzini and Charles Jurine found that blindfolded bats

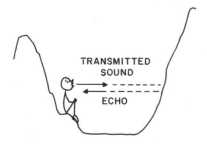

Figure 10.2
Familiar echolocation.

could avoid obstacles while flying at high speed, but that bats with their ears blocked collided with obstacles. Since the flight of bats made no noise, the experiments were completely inexplicable at the time.

It was not until 1938 that Pierce and Griffin showed that bats send out ultrasound signals (the explanation had to wait until electronic ultrasound receivers were available to detect the presence of the signals). Within a few years, experimenters had found that bats use sound signals from 30 kHz to 100 kHz (well above human hearing) not only for navigation around barriers, but also to find insects for food.

To create these sounds at a much higher frequency than the human voice, a bat has a very small and light larynx. The hearing sense of the bat obviously has to extend out to these high frequencies. (The prey can also hear the bat's sounds and thus can take evasive maneuvers).

Porpoises also use echolocation, with frequencies from the audible range up to 170 kHz, to avoid obstacles and to find food.

Thus, echolocation using sound signals is a phenomenon we find in nature. When sonar was developed for the detection of submarines, these natural examples were not known.

10.2 Sonar for Submarine Detection

The first submarine to sink a ship in battle was the *Hunley*, a Confederate submarine built during the Civil War. This submarine had a very short life— since the explosive was on a long pole protruding from the nose of the submarine, the *Hunley* sank along with its victim.

By World War I, submarines ran on diesel engines, were equipped with periscopes so surfacing was not necessary to spot targets, and used torpedoes. The German Unterseebooten ("U-boats") sank hundreds of Allied ships (including the liner *Lusitania* with 2000 people on board). To counter this destruction, the Allied Submarine Detection Investigation Committee (ASDIC) developed a sound system for locating submerged submarines (a system called asdic in Britain, but sonar—for SOund Navigation And Ranging—in the United States).

In the basic sonar system, a sound source sends out a short pulse of sound (figure 10.3). This sound travels through the water until it hits a target (a submarine's shell). Then the reflected sound or echo travels back to the original source, where a receiver detects it. The distance of the target is determined by the time it takes for the sound to travel the round trip, since we know the velocity of sound in sea water. The direction of the target is measured by the direction in which the transmitter is pointing when the echo appears.

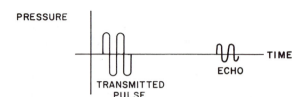

Figure 10.3
Signals in sonar.

In World War II, American ships crossing the Atlantic traveled in convoys—groups of ships surrounded by destroyers equipped with sonar and depth charges. Although the sonar equipment was still crude by today's standards, with a one-mile range whereas a range of 10 miles is possible today, the United States was able to deliver men and supplies safely to Europe.

Frequency of Sonar

What frequency is appropriate for sonar? In order to determine the direction of the echo, we want to use as high a frequency as possible, so that the transmitter will be highly directional—a narrow beam. The transmitter antenna should be larger than the wavelength of the sound signal in order to achieve this directionality.

The velocity of sound in sea water is about 1530 meters per second, or 5000 feet per second. If the wavelength is to be 3 inches ($\frac{1}{4}$ foot), the frequency is given by the relation for any wave:

$$v = \lambda f,$$

$$5000 = \tfrac{1}{4} f,$$

Velocity = wavelength × frequency.

Thus, to obtain reasonable direction-finding capability, we have to use a frequency of at least 20,000 Hz; the higher the frequency, the more directionality we can achieve.

As the sound wave travels through the water, the wave gives up some of its energy (the water is compressed and expanded from the pressure changes, and the local temperature rises). This loss of energy or attenuation of the sound wave increases as the frequency increases—faster changes of pressure result in more energy removed from the wave. Thus, to obtain the strongest echoes and the longest useful range, we would like to operate at as low a frequency as possible.

As so often happens in the design of technology, the engineers had to compromise between two conflicting desires: high frequency (for directionality) and low frequency (for range). The compromise in sonar was just above the range of human hearing (that is, just above 20,000 Hz). Because these sound signals are beyond the hearing frequencies, we give them the name *ultrasound* ("ultra" meaning "beyond").

Thus, the choice of the frequency for sonar represented a compromise—the frequency is in the window permitting both directionality and low attenuation. The basic principle of sonar is echolocation. Measurement of the range of a target is possible only because the velocity of sound in sea water is quite small: 1530 meters per second (3420 miles per hour). Consequently, a target 500 meters away gives an echo about ⅔ second after the transmitted pulse—a time duration that is easily measured electronically.

Transmitter-Receiver
The sonar system requires a transducer to generate the sound pulse and then detect the later sound echo. Fortunately, in 1880 the brothers Pierre and Jacques Curie discovered the piezoelectric effect ("piezo" comes from the Greek for "press"). Certain crystals (quartz, barium titanate, etc.) generate electric charge or voltage when under pressure that changes their shape (or, conversely, change shape when a voltage is applied). Thus, these devices make the conversion either way between electrical and mechanical energy. They can act as a sonar transducer: a transmitter that generates a sound signal from an electrical 20-kHz oscillator, and a receiver that gives an electrical voltage when the echo arrives.

These sonar transmitter-receiver devices can also be used for communication from a surface ship to unmanned submarines exploring the ocean botton, making scientific measurements, searching for sunken ships, and so forth. To communicate, oceanographers and the Navy use one-way sound systems. Again the desired range determines the necessary frequency: for ranges up to 5 miles, 8000 Hz is necessary; for short ranges, frequencies can go up to 200,000 Hz. Higher frequency permits simpler transmitting equipment.

10.3 Echoes from the Body

Obtaining ultrasound pictures from objects within the human body required significant modifications of the sonar technology.

Frequency
First, the appropriate frequency is quite different. We saw that in sonar the frequency was chosen as a compromise between directionality and range considerations. In sonar, we are searching for large targets: an enemy ship, a

large school of fish, or the ocean bottom. In every case, the target is sufficiently large to reflect the arriving sound signal.

In medical examination of the eye, an internal organ, a heart valve, or a fetus, we are looking for relatively small targets. We want a resolution of 1 centimeter. A sound wave (or any wave) passes by objects that are appreciably smaller than a wavelength. A sound wave carrying speech, for example, is not affected by a dime in its path, and the echo from this dime is negligible.

In medical applications, we want a *resolution* of 1 centimeter. That is, we want to see an echo from an object 1 centimeter in size, or to notice an echo change when the target object changes shape or density in a distance of 1 centimeter. Consequently, we need a wavelength of less than 1 cm for the sound signal.

What does this mean about the frequency? Again we return to the basic equation for any wave:

$$v = \lambda f.$$

The velocity of sound in human tissue is about 1540 meters per second, or 154,000 centimeters per sec. Hence a wavelength of 1 cm gives a frequency of

$$154,000 = 1 \times f$$

$$f = 154 \text{ kHz.}$$

Shorter wavelengths (or higher frequencies) are even better.

Thus, for the resolution we need in medical imaging, the ultrasound frequency must be over 150 kHz.

As we saw with sonar, the attenuation or loss of energy increases with frequency. In medical ultrasonics, however, where we are interested in ranges of only a few centimeters, attenuation is less important and frequencies can be much higher than in sonar. In examination of the eye or near-surface parts of the body, we can use frequencies as high as 20 MHz; in abdominal studies when the target is farther away, we use 1–3 MHz.

At these very high frequencies, the sound wave attenuates severely in air or in a gas (the high compressibility means that large amounts of energy are taken from the sound wave). This is the reason that ultrasound cannot be used to examine the lungs; indeed, sound waves cannot pass through the lungs to study the thoracic or chest cavity except through the cardiac notch, a window in the front part of the left lung which allows sound signals to reach the heart.

Pulse Duration
Having decided to use a frequency between 2 and 10 MHz, we next consider the duration of the transmitted pulse. The longer the pulse, the more energy

in each pulse and the stronger the echo. A long pulse, however, tends to give poor resolution in the depth direction (figure 10.4).

How is the pulse duration related to the depth resolution? If the echo were a sharp on-off pulse like that transmitted, the answer would be easy. The time to travel round-trip 1 centimeter is

$$\frac{\text{distance}}{\text{velocity}} = \frac{2 \text{ cm}}{154,000 \text{ cm/sec}} = 13 \text{ microseconds.}$$

Actually the echo pulse is spread out somewhat, so we need a shorter pulse to avoid interference; also, we would like a resolution slightly better than 1 centimeter. The compromise normally used is a pulse duration of 1–2 microseconds. If we use 1 microsecond as an example, the transmitter pulse has the form shown in figure 10.5.

Reflection

When a sonar signal hits a submarine shell, which is much larger than the wavelength, ordinary reflection occurs (figure 10.6). There is essentially total reflection; the reflected wave comes off the target at an angle equal to the incident angle. At the sound source, we pick up the echo from the part of the

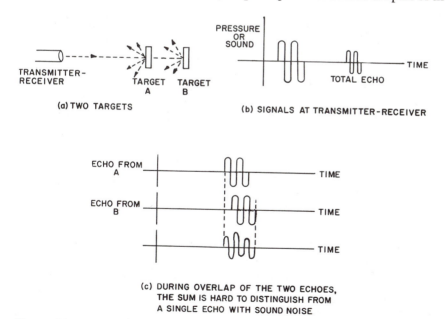

(a) TWO TARGETS

(b) SIGNALS AT TRANSMITTER-RECEIVER

(c) DURING OVERLAP OF THE TWO ECHOES,
THE SUM IS HARD TO DISTINGUISH FROM
A SINGLE ECHO WITH SOUND NOISE

Figure 10.4
Long pulses make depth resolution difficult. The echo from target B arrives before the echo from target A ends.

Figure 10.5
Transmitted pulse with duration of 1 microsecond (μsec) and with two different sound frequencies.

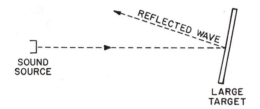

Figure 10.6
Reflection when wavelength is much less than size of target.

target perpendicular to the sending wave, so that the reflected wave goes back to the source. This type of reflection is called "specular"; the word is based on the Greek word for mirror.

In ultrasound pictures of the human body, reflection is much more complex. Now the wavelength and the target are of roughly the same size. As a result, echoes leave the target in all "backward" directions (figure 10.7). We now have what is called *diffuse reflection*.

Figure 10.6 shows only a very small fraction of the outgoing sound energy reflected back toward the receiver. There are two reasons this echo energy is so small:

1. the diffuse reflection—much of the reflected energy does not go to the receiver

2. the weakness of the totality of the refections—much of the energy passes through and by the target, rather than being reflected.

The second feature arises because the target (particular body tissue or an internal organ) does not differ much in acoustical properties from the surrounding medium. The shell of a submarine is made of steel, the acoustical characteristics of which are very different from those of water: steel has a much higher density, and the velocity of sound in steel is much greater. As a result, almost none of the sound energy travels into the steel; almost all is reflected. In engineering terms, we say there is a major acoustical or sound mismatch

Figure 10.7
Diffuse reflection. The echoes leave the target in a wide range of directions.

between water and steel. In contrast, body tissues and organs are primarily water, and there is only a relatively small change in acoustical impedance when the sound wave reaches, for example, the front edge of the liver. Most of the energy travels right on into the liver; only a small fraction is reflected.

Furthermore, as the sound wave passes a lesion or a small target, the wave continues on because of diffraction. (When I shout to you, you can hear me even around the corner of a building because at the corner each point on the wave acts as a source of a new small wave going out in all directions.) This diffraction is most evident when the target is something like a wavelength in size, not as pronounced when the target is very large, as in sonar.

In this section, we have seen that echolocation in the human body differs in major ways from its military progenitor, sonar. In medical ultrasound imaging, we are working with very short distances, and with targets that reflect only a small fraction of the sound wave and thus do not block our inspection of other targets farther away in the same direction. A rowboat can hide behind a destroyer and escape sonar detection, but a medical ultrasound picture can show both front and back boundaries of the liver.

10.4 Basic Equipment

Medical ultrasound equipment employs a piezoelectric transducer (transmitter-receiver). For an abdominal picture, this transducer is held against the abdomen of the patient. A gel is rubbed on the abdomen first so that there is no air between the piezoelectric crystal and the skin. Air has an acoustical impedance very different from that of tissue or the piezoelectric crystal, so air causes serious reflections (figure 10.8).

In the transmitter, an electronic oscillator generates an electrical voltage at 2 MHz. This voltage is applied to the crystal, which then mechanically pumps (expands and contracts) at 2 MHz. We then have a sound wave which travels outward from the transducer; if the transducer is much larger than the wavelength, there is excellent focusing and the sound wave goes out in the shape of the transducer (figure 10.9).

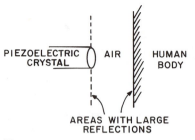

Figure 10.8
The acoustic impedances of the crystal and the human body are about the same;
that of air is very different. An air space causes large reflections at two surfaces.

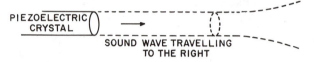

Figure 10.9
Very little spreading of the sound beam occurs if the crystal face is much longer than
a wavelength. If the frequency is 2 MHz and the crystal is 2 cm in diameter, the beam
does not spread appreciably for 50 cm, long enough to cover most medical targets.
If we need greater range, an acoustic lens can be used to focus the beam more
sharply.

The transmitter is turned off after 1 μsec, and the crystal now acts as a
receiver, converting the echo sound signal to a varying voltage, which is
electronically amplified. The gain of this amplifier automatically increases as
time elapses after the transmitter pulse so that distant echoes, inevitably weak,
are amplified more.

There are several ways to display the target information to the operator.

The A Scan

The A scan is the basic technique for portraying echoes on an oscilloscope
screen. Starting at the end of the transmitter pulse, the spot is moved at a
constant speed across the screen from left to right. The receiver measures the
amplitude of the echo oscillation and uses this signal to deflect the beam
vertically. Thus, a single echo would give an A-scan display as shown in figure
10.10. A more typical display is shown in figure 10.11.

The A scan shows the targets on a single line through the body; it is a one-
dimensional image, with the horizontal axis representing time after the
transmitter pulse (or, equivalently, the distance into the body). The vertical axis
shows the amplitude or size of the echo.

The A scan was useful in assessing a head injury—for example, by determining a change in the midline of the brain—before the common availability of x-

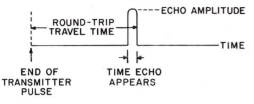

Figure 10.10
A scan showing a single echo. (Usually the transmitted pulse is not shown on the screen.)

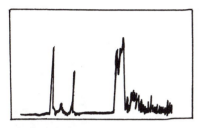

Figure 10.11
An A scan for an eye. As we move rightward on the diagram (corresponding to going deeper into the eye), a series of echoes represent the cornea, the lens, and the back of the eye.

ray scans. A shift in this midline indicates bleeding and the urgent need for surgery.

This A scan was an early portrayal of echolocation information in both radar and sonar. In sonar, a pulse would be sent out in one direction; the operator then waited until all possible echoes were back before rotating the transmitter slightly to scan a different direction in the ocean. Actually, in the very early sonar sets the receiver gave an audible sound output (a "ping") when an echo appeared at the receiver.

The M-Mode Scan

When we are interested in the study of the motion of a part of the body (for example, the mitral valve of the heart), we can use a more complex presentation (figure 10.12). Here we plot time horizontally, over a period of many pulses and echoes. Vertically we plot the depth into the body or the time since the last transmitted pulse. The presence of an echo is indicated by a darker region in the picture.

To understand figure 10.12, consider a simpler case: an ultrasound system picking up an echo from an object which is moving steadily away from the transmitter. The M-mode scan is illustrated in figure 10.13.

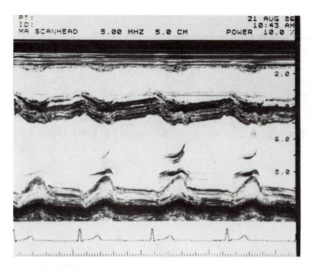

Figure 10.12
An M-mode trace displays echoes from a single sound beam against a moving
background. Motion of the cardiac mitral valve is depicted in this M-mode trace.
(Courtesy Advanced Technology Laboratories, Bothell, Washington)

The B Scan

The most common visual display in ultrasound imaging is the B scan, which
shows a two-dimensional slice through the anatomy. The simplest way to
obtain this is to move the transducer in a straight line across, for example, the
abdomen. The echoes are recorded at each location. Then the oscilloscope
display is a plot of depth vertically against transducer position horizontally
(figure 10.14). The brightness of the spot indicates the strength of the echo at
that location.

The manual scanning can be replaced by mechanical drive of the transducer.

Actually we can also use electronic scanning if we have an array or a set of
different transmitters. The basic idea is illustrated in figure 10.15 for the simple
case of two transmitters, A and B. When transmitters A and B are driven in
synchronism, the two signals add together along line L. The two signals arrive
at the same time at point R or (later) at point S. This simple array has its
strongest radiation to the right along line L.

If we delay slightly the signal driving transmitter A and leave the B signal
alone, the effect is the same as if A were farther away (figure 10.16). Then the
two signals add together directly along line M. The delay of the electrical signal
driving A results in a change in the direction of strongest radiation.

If we vary the delay of the signal driving A, we can sweep the beam across the
area in front of the array. No mechanical motion is necessary, as we obtain the

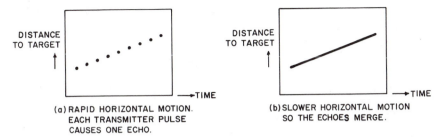

(a) RAPID HORIZONTAL MOTION.
    EACH TRANSMITTER PULSE
    CAUSES ONE ECHO.

(b) SLOWER HORIZONTAL MOTION
    SO THE ECHOES MERGE.

Figure 10.13
M-mode scan for a single, receding target.

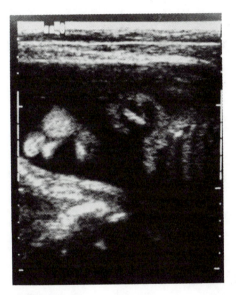

Figure 10.14
B scan for obstetrical imaging. Note the fetal nose, lips, and cheek. (Courtesy Advanced Technology Laboratories, Bothell, Washington)

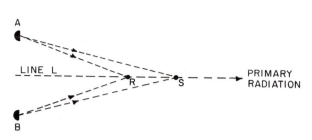

Figure 10.15
Two transmitters driven in synchronism.

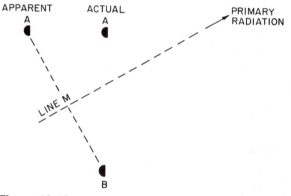

Figure 10.16
Rotation when signal driving transmitter A is delayed.

sweeping electronically. A large number of transmitters (not just the two used above for illustration) permits a narrow beam which changes direction to cover the region where we want pictures.

This is the scheme now used for radar antennas so large that mechanical rotation is impractical: the small separate elements of the antenna are driven electronically by currents which are changed in relative phases (that is, starting times of each cycle). The antenna beam sweeps across the sky to detect the launching of enemy missiles from far away. This is called a "phased-array" radar. We can use the same technique in ultrasound imaging (figure 10.17).

10.5 Health Effects

The impressive results achieved in ultrasonic imaging naturally raise the question whether there are any health hazards. The question is especially important for prospective mothers and their obstetricians, since the doctors frequently take pictures to determine fetal age and the position, or whether

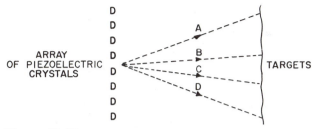

Figure 10.17
Phased array. All eight transmitters are driven by 1-MHz voltages. When the phase of the signal to each transmitter is properly adjusted, the resulting sound beam can be made to rotate from A to B to C to D. The result is echoes returned from a sweep of the target, just as though a single transmitter were moved from top to bottom of the figure.

there are anomalies or anatomical defects. In these cases there may be no outward signs of medical problems, but the imaging is done to assure the mother and the obstetrician. If there were a significant risk, this would clearly argue against unmotivated ultrasound imaging.

The problem is that, although there is no clear evidence of risk associated with ultrasound imaging at the low power levels used by obstetricians, it is impossible to prove that the procedure is completely risk-free. Research has shown that there are hazards in applying ultrasound at higher power levels than are used in imaging. The following things must be considered:

1. A machine called a lithotripter destroys kidney stones and gallstones with intense sound signals directed at the stones.

2. Acoustic cavitation can occur. This means that very small gas bubbles in the fluid expand and contract as the sound wave passes. These changes may cause pressure waves and also raise the local temperature enough to cause chemical changes. The effects here are so localized that they are difficult to detect, and there is no evidence of any harm to a fetus.

3. Some research has indicated that there might be genetic consequences with exposure to strong sound signals (800 times the energy in normal imaging). Specifically, sister chromatid exchanges were observed—crossover between the two chromatids in a chromosome, with the possibility of mutation.

4. The sound wave does cause heating. Again, the energy level must be many times higher than that used in imaging to have an effect of any apparent significance.

The difficulties are typical of what happens when we try to assess the human health risk of any technology that changes the environment.

1. We cannot ethically do extensive experiments on human beings—experiments which may require surgery to determine effects.

2. We can do experiments on animals, but the extrapolation to human effects is very uncertain. Because animals are expensive and we want results in a short time, experimenters have to use excessive doses.

3. Health effects with large doses may not mean there is any effect with small doses. Figure 10.18 shows the problem. We make measurements A and B, both at very large doses. Is there any effect at the dose of human exposure? The answer depends on whether there is a threshold below which there are no effects. The data at A and B cannot tell whether there is a threshold or not (cannot indicate which curve applies).

4. Even if we can prove biological effects (changes in the biology), we do not know there are health effects. When we exercise violently, our heart rate rises (a biological effect), but there may be no effect on health. Or the health effect may be beneficial, rather than harmful.

Thus, there is really no evidence that ultrasonic imaging carries any risk. Nevertheless, our scientific knowledge is still very incomplete. In February 1984, a Consensus Development Conference on the Use of Diagnostic Ultrasound in Pregnancy was held because of the great interest of the medical profession and the general public. The conference included people from the National Institutes of Health and the National Center for Devices and Radiological Health of the Food and Drug Administration. "After consideration of scientific evidence and opinion, the panel concluded that although the relevance to the human in vivo situation is unknown, the existence of some studies showing absolute biological effects together with inadequate evidence of its efficacy contributed to their decision that ultrasound screening of pregnancy should not be recommended at this time." This committee felt that ultrasound examinations should be performed for a specific medical need, not just because parents would like to see the fetus or because they want to know

Figure 10.18
Importance of a threshold.

the sex of the fetus. Of course, this "specific medical need" might well be the assurance of the parents about the normality of the prospective child.

10.6 Conclusion

The goal in this chapter was to emphasize how medical ultrasound imaging, first used in Sweden in 1953, developed from the military work on sonar during World War II—military work which gave engineers the piezoelectric transducers, the electronic circuitry, and the understanding to develop medical instrumentation with characteristics quite different from those of sonar. From the military work has come an application of major importance to human health care. Whether military research and development is the optimum, or even an appropriate, way to generate new technology is open to argument. Clearly, however, the unmatched intensity of the engineering work during wartime leads to broadly significant technological innovation.

Review Questions

R10-1. Why is it important in sonar to use the highest possible frequency?

R10-2. In sonar, what phenomenon argues for the lowest possible frequency?

R10-3. In sonar, what determines the maximum allowable pulse width?

R10-4. In medical ultrasonics the frequency is typically two orders of magnitude higher than in sonar. Explain briefly why.

R10-5. What is meant by the adjective "piezoelectric"?

R10-6. In medical ultrasonics, to look at the fetus, a gel is used between the probe and abdomen. Why is this necessary?

R10-7. Figure 10.1 would be described as what type of scan (A, or M, or B)?

R10-8. What is meant by the term "phased-array antenna"?

R10-9. What are the advantages of a phased-array antenna in comparison with a rotating or moving antenna?

R10-10. The government has urged obstetricians to use ultrasonic fetal imaging only when justified medically. Explain briefly.

Problems

P10-1. The following paragraphs describe briefly the recent history of the study of the safety of the sugar substitute saccharin. Discuss the parallels and differences between this history and the study of the safety of ultrasonic medical scanning.

In 1957, the Federal Food, Drug, and Cosmetic Act included the Delaney clause: "no (food) additive shall be deemed to be safe if it is found to induce cancer when ingested by man or animal. . . ." Congress naturally likes clear-cut protocols and rules, so nothing at all was said about the allowable amounts of additives. An additive is safe or it must be banned.

During the decade 1965–1975, a few scientific studies suggested a relation between saccharin use and cancer. In 1974, a Canadian study definitely reported bladder cancer in rats that had ingested large amounts of saccharin. Following the Delaney clause, in March 1977, the Commissioner of the FDA proposed banning the sale of saccharin; the rule was published in the *Federal Register*, with comments invited until April 15. Extrapolation of data from the scientific studies led to the estimate that one saccharin soda per day consumed by the entire population would result in 1200 cases of bladder cancer per year.

The media, the public, and politicians reacted. Polls showed that the public placed little confidence in the evidence. The argument was made that "rats should not drink 1000 Diet Cokes a day"—an argument resulting from the heavy doses given the rats. There are five problems with such science:

1. In animal testing, primates are too costly. The life span of a rat is only 2 years, so the scientists use very high doses. Then there is always a question whether these results can be extrapolated downward, or whether there is a threshold below which there is no effect.

2. In human beings, one cancer in 1000 or even 10,000 is important, but we typically test only 50–100 rats (including the control group).

3. Epidemiological studies of human populations typically find that the "signal is lost in the noise"—the effect we are looking for is lost in many uncontrollable, larger influences and may appear only over very long periods of time.

4. We have no idea of synergistic effects, which may be positive or negative, and usually little hope of finding them.

5. If the public understood what is known, saccharin use could be a voluntarily assumed risk, but the task of public education seems hopeless.

Several risk-benefit analyses were undertaken. The primary benefits of saccharin are these:

1. Diabetics can more easily hold to a sugar-free diet. This situation might be handled by allowing saccharin as a prescription drug, but it is not clear whether that would work.

2. Normal people more readily keep their weight down. Each pound of extra weight lost adds 29 days to life expectancy. (One legislator proposed that everyone be required to drink two diet sodas a day *in place* of regular drinks— life expectancy would increase by one year, if there were no other change in eating.)

After this public discussion, the Congress approved an exception to the Delaney clause.

Chapter 11
Television

You are driving at 65 miles per hour along a parkway where trees have been planted in a row every 10 feet. The sunlight coming from behind these trees is interrupted regularly. Suddenly, you lose your orientation—the scene in front of you seems to be spinning. What's wrong?

Answer: The trees are blocking the light at about the frequency of your principal brain wave (about 10 times a second), and your normal brain activity is disrupted.

This example illustrates beautifully the difficulties that arise when engineers do not give careful consideration to the characteristics of the people with whom a system interacts. The trouble described above came about because the engineers who designed the landscaping did not anticipate the human effects—resonance with the brain waves.

Television is an interesting technology because it is one of the very few modern devices to have been designed on the basis of a *very careful study of human characteristics*—in this case, the characteristics of vision. Modern television is possible because the engineers designing the original system determined which features of a scene can be perceived by a human being; the technology then carefully preserves these features, so that the TV viewer feels that he or she is watching an accurate picture.

We cannot see very small objects (for example, a virus); accordingly, the TV picture need not carry such detail. We cannot see clearly an object moving at high speed across our field of view. Likewise, we do not see very clearly when a scene is brightly illuminated with blue light in comparison with red light.

These are fundamental limitations of human vision. There is no reason why a television system should communicate from the studio to the viewers any characteristics that the viewers would not see if they were in the studio. Consequently, the camera, the broadcast, and the reception can be simplified and still retain the viewer's perception of a good picture.

Engineers say that in such design *the technology is matched to the relevant characteristics of the human user*. The concept of matching is the central theme of this chapter. Modern television is a superb example of success in this goal of matching.

A few years ago, such engineering to match human characteristics carried the name "human factors engineering" or "man-machine systems engineering." Today the subject is commonly called *ergonomics*. This is a term derived from the Greek *ergo* and *nomics*, meaning work and management, respectively. Originally the term referred to technology designed to maximize the work people could perform; now the interpretation is broader, encompassing the matching of a technology to all relevant characteristics of the people with whom the technology interacts.

Relevant Characteristics

In the italicized clause above, we say "matched to the relevant characteristics." What is meant by the term "relevant characteristics"? If we use television as an example, we evaluate the technology on the basis of how well it satisfies our capabilities in vision. We would have no interest in what force a human can exert, for example, since this is not relevant to TV. The purpose of television is to recreate at your set the visual scene in the studio, so we are interested *only* in characteristics of human vision.

These vision capabilities are both physiological and psychological. Our vision system consists of the eyes, the optic nerve carrying electrical information to the brain, and the processing of these data in the brain. As long as the viewer thinks he or she is seeing an accurate picture, the television system is working properly.

This critical role of viewer perception makes it very difficult to evaluate a technology such as television. As one example, the color in U.S. television is not as true or good as the color in French television. Is this a significant weakness of the U.S. TV system? To determine whether viewers desire high-quality color, one study purposely distorted TV color badly but made available a simple remote control that would restore true colors. The great majority of viewers did not bother to use the remote control. Even if faces had a green tint, the viewers seemed not to object. If the color was lost entirely, viewers would take action. Do we then conclude that color is critically important, but color quality is irrelevant? If this is true for 90 percent of the population, should we design for the 10 percent who are interested in quality color?

Thus, the matching criterion for evaluation of technology is not easy to use. We certainly can state, however, that there is no justification for complicating the TV technology to communicate information that no human viewer can see.

11.1 Telecommunication of a Picture

The television camera photographs the scene; the TV system now must communicate this picture to the home screen of the viewer. Transmission of the information in the picture may be by broadcast, cable, distribution of tape, or radio through a satellite. In the next chapter, we consider these communication options; in this chapter, we focus on the way in which picture details can be reproduced on the home screen. Furthermore, in this first part of the chapter, we simplify by studying only black-and-white television.

A picture includes a large amount of information. The familiar saying that a picture is worth a thousand words is probably an understatement. Since every picture we want to communicate may well show very different objects and actions, we must find a method of describing the picture in a way independent of the subject content.

The standard engineering procedure is to break down the picture into a very large number of small picture elements, called *pixels*. Figure 11.1 shows one such decomposition with 432 pixels (as we shall see, not enough to give a good picture, but enough to explain the procedure). The original picture is described by the brightness of each of the 432 dots. We move from black (no light at all) through shades of gray to white (full light) as we describe the brightness of each dot.

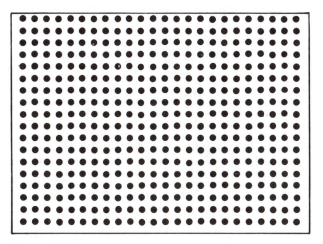

Figure 11.1
A television picture broken down into 24 x 18 or 432 pixels (18 rows, 24 in each row).

In this example, we can represent the original picture by 432 numbers, each indicating the brightness of another dot in turn as we work our way through the picture.

In television we look at successive dots from left to right in the top row, then repeat the left-to-right scanning for the second row, and so on down the picture. In other words, we are reading in the normal pattern. (If television had been invented by the Arabs, we undoubtedly would scan from right to left.)

Thus, the information describing a television picture is carried by a series of numbers indicating the brightness (or *luminance*) of successive dots (or areas) within the picture. Once the designers had settled on this structure for the TV picture or video signal, they had to decide the numerical details: how often must a new picture be sent, how much detail must there be in each picture, and so forth.

11.2 Structure of the Video or Picture Signal

The first television-system designers, facing the task of deciding on how much picture detail was necessary, were confronted with two conflicting requirements:

1. There should be as much detail as possible, so that the viewers would perceive an ideal picture.

2. There should be as little detail as possible, to simplify the technology and hold down the cost.

Realization of a profitable market for television demanded the best compromise between these two goals. The final product had to be a technology that people could both enjoy and afford.

The problem in 1940, when television appeared and the current standards were set, was complicated by the state of the technology at that time. Electronics was still in its infancy: AM radio stations had been broadcasting only 20 years, FM stations only 3 years. The enormous complexity of the TV picture in comparison with the sound of even FM taxed the capabilities of the technology.

From an engineer's viewpoint, the most impressive feature of today's television is the extent to which the designers of 1940 placed emphasis on item 1 above: matching the technology to the characteristics of human vision. These decisions required enormous faith in the future improvement of the technology and a commitment to a technology that would not be considered outdated 20 years later.

The way in which decisions were made in the United States is one of the finest examples of committee activity. In 1939 RCA started production of TV sets, then demonstrated them at the New York World's Fair. Other electronics companies objected that the RCA system did not give a satisfactory picture. Clearly, it was critically important that all broadcasters and set manufacturers agree on a single U.S. standard, so that the same sets could be sold everywhere and the customer could view all programs with a single receiver.

James Fly, the chairman of the Federal Communications Commission (FCC), which regulated broadcasting, joined with GE executive Walter Baker to form a committee to agree on U.S. television standards. Called the National Television Systems Committee (NTSC), this group, with 168 members, worked for 9 months and finally agreed on a single structure for the U.S. television picture.

Picture Renewal

How many pictures must we send each second so that the viewer believes the picture is changing continuously?

Motion of people or objects on the screen should look smooth if we see at least 24 pictures a second (the frame rate for 16-mm movies). For example, in making a cartoon, the artists have to draw a separate picture for the position of the characters every ¼₄ second (that is, a 10-minute cartoon requires 14,400 pictures). Any picture (or frame) rate above 24 per second yields motion that appears smooth.

The numbers given throughout this section for human limitations are normal. For example, 24 pictures per second is enough for almost everyone. Many people think motion is smooth if they see only 20 pictures per second; a rare individual may detect jerkiness at 24.

Thus, television must send at least 24 new pictures every second. The number chosen in 1940 was 30. The precise value of 30 was picked for technical reasons. The home receiver must be synchronized with the broadcast signal—when the camera starts a new picture, the home receiver should be starting also. In the early days there was an advantage in using half the power-system frequency of 60 Hz. (Today the standard is 29.97 pictures per second—very close to the original 30.)

Flicker

If a new picture appears 30 times a second, motion looks continuous, but the human eye sees a flicker. If we have a strobe light (a light that goes on and off at a particular rate) and gradually increase the flashing rate, we find the light appears to be on continually only when the rate is over 45–50 pulses (flashes) per second. This rate (when the light seems continually on), called the *flicker fusion frequency*, varies from person to person. Also, the rate (or frequency of the flicker) has to be higher when the light is brighter (box 11.1).

When the National Television Systems Committee argued about standards for U.S. television in 1940, they recognized that a new picture should be sent at least 25 times a second (so that motion seemed continuous), but that twice this rate was necessary to avoid a flicker. The 16-mm movie projector solves the problem by using 24 frames per second, then showing each frame twice so that the light flashes at 48 times per second.

Television uses a different technique to avoid sending more pictures than necessary. Figure 11.1 shows that the TV picture is made up of horizontal lines. Each horizontal line is formed by a sequence of dots of varying brightness, so that the actual picture consists of a rectangular array of dots. As each line is traced from left to right, the brightness of each dot varies to give the black-and-white picture.

In television, we first trace lines $1, 3, 5, 7, \ldots, 523, 525$ (the odd-numbered ones), then return and construct the even-numbered lines: $2, 4, 6, \ldots, 522, 524$. A complete picture requires two trips over the tube from left to right and from top to bottom (figure 11.2). We trace half the picture every $\frac{1}{60}$ second, or a complete picture in $\frac{1}{30}$ second. There is no flicker because the eye cannot detect flicker in a very small area (that is, between two successive lines). Thus,

---

Experiment with Strobe-Light Frequency

Most discos today use strobe lights to enhance the atmosphere of the room. These strobes are set so that they usually go on and off about 14 times per second—a high enough rate so the patrons are not affected by the flashing lights.

If, however, we were to lower or raise the frequency of the strobe, some amazing things would happen:

At 1 to 2 cycles per second, people in the room would become nauseous.

At 8 to 10 cycles per second (the primary brain wave resonance), patrons would become disoriented. (At this rate, customers with epilepsy might be seriously affected.)

At about 24 cycles per second, the motion in the room would look continuous.

At 45 to 55 cycles per second, the light would look continuous.

If we refer back to the opening paragraphs of this chapter, the disorientation of the driver of the car occurred because the light is flashing at the same frequency as the brain waves. We would guess the light reaching the eyes was varying at about 8-10 cycles per second.

Box 11.1

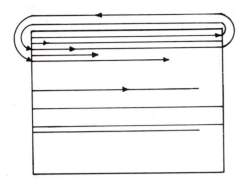

Figure 11.2
Lines traced from left to right.

the picture (or *frame*) rate is 30 per second; for flicker purposes, the eye thinks the picture is being re-created at a rate (called the *field rate*) of 60 per second.

Number of Lines

How much detail do we need in the picture? In other words, how many lines?

Again let's match to the human vision capability. We construct the chart of figure 11.3 and hold this in a well-lit spot in the front of a large classroom. We find that people in the back of the room cannot tell whether there are two dots or a single dot in each row. The vision sense cannot see this much detail.

The human ability to detect that there are two small objects rather than one larger object—that is, the detail we can see at a distance—is limited. We want enough lines in the TV picture so that a viewer sitting a normal distance away does not notice that the picture consists of lines.

If we do an experiment as indicated in figure 11.3, we find that human vision can distinguish objects at a distance less than 2000 times the separation (figure 11.4). At a distance of 2000 feet (0.4 mile), two objects 1 foot apart seem to merge into one. Now we are ready to decide on the number of lines needed in a TV picture so that the normal viewer does not notice the lines. Suppose the viewer sits a distance D from a TV screen which has a height H (figure 11.5).

If there are N lines in the picture, the distance between two successive lines is

$$\frac{H \text{ (height of screen)}}{N \text{ (number of lines in picture)}}.$$

We would like the two lines to merge into one for the viewer. That is, we want

$$D = 2000 \frac{H}{N}.$$

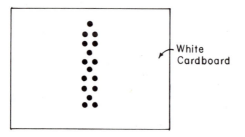

Figure 11.3
Testing with black dots on a white background.

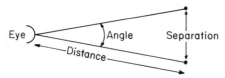

Figure 11.4
Capability of human vision. We can just tell the two dots are separate when the distance is 2000 times the separation. (The angle is then 1/2000 radian.)

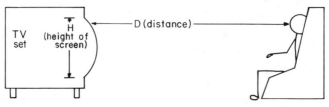

Figure 11.5
Viewer and TV set.

The average viewer (not the young child who parks right at the tube) sits at a distance about 4 times the height of the screen. Hence,

$$4H = 2000 \frac{H}{N}.$$

If we cancel the H terms and rearrange this equation, we find

$$N = 500.$$

The committee decided to use 525 lines for the U.S. television picture.

Aspect Ratio

The next question in standardization is this: how wide should the picture be, compared with the height? People see equally well vertically and horizontally, so a square picture seems sensible. In 1940, however, it was thought that it

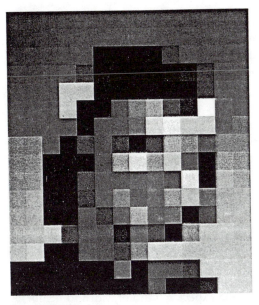

Figure 11.6
Picture obtained with 16 lines and 14 sections per line. When this is viewed from a distance, the form appears.

Figure 11.7
The same picture as in figure 11.6 but with 512 lines and 450 dots per line.

would be many years before enough TV sets would be sold to justify the expense of creating original programs. Consequently, movies would be shown during much of the broadcasting time. Since movies in 1940 had a 4/3 ratio of width to height (because most motion is horizontal rather than vertical), television followed suit. Today's TV screen has the relative dimensions shown in figure 11.8. When a modern wide-screen movie is shown on television, the broadcaster omits sections on the left and right.

This aspect ratio is the one characteristic that was not chosen to match human characteristics: recent tests show that people prefer an aspect ratio of 5/3 or even closer to 2/1, instead of the 4/3 used. Perhaps this preference results from our familiarity with newer wide-screen movies, so that a measurement in 1940 might have resulted in a preference closer to 4/3.

Horizontal Detail

Since the eye discriminates equally well horizontally and vertically, we would assume that the distance between lines is the same as the distance between horizontal dots. Accordingly, we would expect ⁴⁄₃ (ratio of width to height) × 525 (number of horizontal lines), or 700, dots per line.

Recall that when the standards were set in 1940, there was considerable argument and honest uncertainty about how detailed a picture could be used at a cost the public would accept. As a result, the standards compromised on horizontal detail, and the United States now uses 630 dots per line. (In an actual home receiver, we ordinarily do not see 525 lines. The bottom lines are not shown, so we are more likely to see 475, which corresponds roughly to 630 dots per line.)

TV Picture

We have seen that the television picture consists of a sequence of dots of varying brightness. There are 630 dots in each line, there are 525 lines in each picture, and there is a new picture each ¹⁄₃₀ second. In other words, each picture consists of 630 × 525, or 330,000, dots. Each second, we have to know 330,000 × 30, or 10 million, brightness signals to put together a continuous television picture.

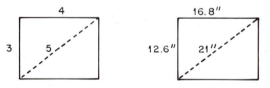

Figure 11.8
Dimensions of TV screen. (Manufacturers describe their TVs by the diagonal distance across the picture. A 21-inch TV has a picture height of about 12 inches, so we should sit 4 feet away from it.)

The television broadcast station, therefore, sends out a signal (the video signal) which consists of a sequence of pulses (figure 11.9)—the height (or amplitude) of each pulse carries the brightness information (the bigger the pulse, the brighter the corresponding spot in the picture). Each pulse is sent in a 10-millionth of a second; then we move to the next spot on the screen.

How many different brightness levels or different pulse heights do we use in a TV picture? Actually, each pulse size directly measures the brightness at that point in the picture. Pulses might have heights of

1.12386, 1.41, 1.444,

and so on. This is what engineers call an "analog signal": each pulse size can have any value.

These pulses are transmitted from the TV studio to the home receiver by broadcast or cable. In this process, the signal picks up noise and the pulse is distorted (that is, the shape changes). Consequently, at the receiver we obtain only an *approximate* measure of the pulse size (figure 11.10).

The pulse need only be sent with enough accuracy that the receiver can determine the size within about eight possible levels. This is enough accuracy to give the viewer a satisfying TV picture.

We now have a description of the TV picture—a grid of dots, with each dot displaying an appropriate shade of gray. The receiver obtains from the broadcast signal a sequence of pulses, and the height of each pulse dictates how bright the corresponding point in the picture should be.

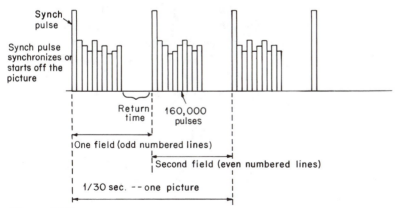

Figure 11.9
Video signal (here all pulses are shown as positive; actually the synch pulses can be negative).

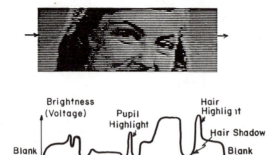

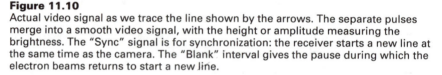

Figure 11.10
Actual video signal as we trace the line shown by the arrows. The separate pulses
merge into a smooth video signal, with the height or amplitude measuring the
brightness. The "Sync" signal is for synchronization: the receiver starts a new line at
the same time as the camera. The "Blank" interval gives the pause during which the
electron beams returns to start a new line.

Creating the Picture

In the home set, the picture is created in the TV tube from the incoming video
signal (the train of pulses). The TV tube contains the parts illustrated in figure
11.11. At the left we see the filament and the cathode. The filament is simply
an electric heater which raises the metal cathode to a high temperature. When
metal is very hot, the free electrons (the electrons free to move in the material)
are moving randomly (high temperature means high velocities of the atomic
particles). These electrons start to "boil off" the surface of the cathode. In other
words, the hot cathode emits electrons.

These electrons (each with a negative charge) are accelerated to the right by
the high positive voltages within the electron gun (positive charge or voltage
attracts electrons). The electron-gun portion also includes plates or magnetic
coils to draw these electrons into a thin beam (the electron beam) moving at
high velocity rightward. The need for very high voltages (thousands of volts)
to obtain this narrow beam is the reason it is so dangerous to work inside the
TV set with the power on.

The video signal changes the density of this electron beam. During a very
bright signal, electron density is high; when the spot is to be black, essentially
no electrons flow.

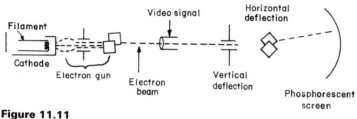

Figure 11.11
TV tube.

The beam is then deflected vertically and horizontally to the appropriate spot on the screen. The screen is made of phosphorescent material: when a small section (a spot) is hit by electrons, that spot phosphoresces, or gives off white light.

Thus, the electron beam needs to be swept across the screen (from left to right, as seen from the front, then returned to the left side, lowered slightly, swept again, and so on). The beam is continually in motion as it retraces again and again the path covering the entire screen. During these travels, the density of electrons in the beam is continually being changed in accord with the video signal.

11.3 Other Video Structures

The European construction of the television picture differs from the American one. As a result, transatlantic broadcasts by satellite from Europe cannot be re-broadcast directly; the picture must be re-photographed and converted to U.S. standards. When colleges set up an antenna to pick up broadcasts from the USSR's orbiting satellites (which cross the northeastern U.S. in order to cover Siberia), a European TV receiver must be used.

How did such an unfortunate situation arise? First, the renewal rate in the U.S. is 30 pictures per second, half the frequency at which electrical energy is distributed. In Europe that power frequency is 50 hertz, so the renewal rate there is 25 pictures per second. From the very outset, then, a major difference existed. Actually, the European rate of 50 fields per second (50 traversals from top to bottom) is very close to the human flicker fusion frequency, so European TV sets are usually not as bright as American sets.

There are other differences. The British were the first to broadcast television (in 1936), and they chose 405 lines. The American standard came into being 4 years later at 525 lines; during those 4 years the technology had improved, and the NTSC recognized that 405 lines required the viewer to sit uncomfortably far from the set.

Just after the U.S. standard of 525 lines was set, United States entered World War II. Scientists and engineers in industry and universities concentrated on the development of electronics for warfare—especially radar. The MIT Radiation Laboratory, for example, brought together thousands of scientists to focus on microwave radar. The technology for transmitting and receiving pulses in radar (where we send out a pulse signal and wait for an echo) proved to be directly applicable to television after the war ended.

By the late 1940s, the TV technology was enormously better and cheaper than in 1941. Just starting their television broadcasting, the French decided on 819 lines per picture; the argument was that French culture could not be represented with a less detailed picture. (This was the era of Charles DeGaulle and France's national determination to excel.)

In 1950 the European nations (other than France and the UK) agreed on a picture structure with 25 pictures per second, interlacing, and 625 lines per picture—more detail than in the U.S., but fewer pictures per second. With satellites not yet feasible, there seemed no strong reason for European and U.S. standards to be the same (and undoubtedly European nations wanted to make it more difficult for U.S. manufacturers to sell in those markets). Ultimately, the U.K. and France gave in, and today the world has two standards for black-and-white television: one for the U.S. and Japan, and another for Europe and much of the rest of the world.

Other Structures

There is certainly nothing sacred about the American or the European TV structure; for purposes other than mass entertainment, quite different structures may be desirable. For example, the Voyager spacecraft sent back to Earth pictures from Jupiter and Saturn by a television system with the characteristics listed in table 11.1. In the Voyager system, there is no hurry, no need to send the pictures for immediate viewing; accordingly, the rate is very slow, to allow accurate measurement on Earth of each of the very weak signals.

Table 11.1

	U.S. commercial TV	Voyager
Time for one picture	$\frac{1}{30}$ second	48 seconds
Aspect Ratio	4/3	1/1
Lines per picture	525	800
Dots per line	630	800
Number of brightness levels	8	256

Mobility Aid for the Blind

A television camera describes a visual scene in terms of a sequence of electrical pulses. For over a decade, engineers have tried to use this information in a mobility aid for the blind. A miniature television camera carried by the blind person would look directly ahead. Information about objects or barriers would be conveyed to the blind person through one of the other senses—hearing or touch.

The first idea was to communicate the information by the sense of touch. The abdomen is quite sensitive, so we can place an array of small, vibrating devices on the abdomen of the blind person. Each little device would vibrate at an amplitude indicating the shade of gray in the corresponding area of the scene ahead. Thus, the customer would receive a sensation in the abdomen depicting the scene. The blind customer would, of course, have to learn how to interpret the various tactile patterns.

Early attempts used 20×20 and 32×32 arrays. Even in the 20×20 case, however, the customer is overwhelmed by the information and unable to interpret as soon as he or she moves from a simple, familiar laboratory setting to the complex scene normally existing outdoors. Then research turned to computer processing of the information from the video camera, so that the customer would receive only information about curbs, obstacles, etc. Also, the tactile information was supplemented by computer-generated speech signals. Such a system, still far from useful to the blind, requires that the computer simplify the television picture enormously, but not overlook anything that might interfere with motion.

Slow Motion

Today we expect to see a slow-motion replay in sports a few seconds after the action. Since 1986 professional football has even allowed the replay official viewing the TV tape to overrule the officials on the field in several specific situations. Fans in the stands are shown slow-motion replays on the scoreboard.

This technological capability for slow-motion television is quite new. In the 1980 Olympics, it was necessary to take motion pictures of the action, then wait 36 hours until the film had been developed and could be transferred to video tape.

In 1984 Sony Corporation made available to the ABC network, for the Kentucky Derby and then the Summer Olympics, a camera that took 90 pictures per second instead of the normal 30. The signal then went to a special-purpose computer, which converted the video signal to the regular U.S. standards (in particular, 30 pictures per second). Playback resulted in a reduction in speed to ⅓ of the original value—slow motion. The normal picture was available by using only every third picture.

HDTV

A final example of different TV picture structure is the high-definition television (HDTV) developed by NHK Research Laboratories in Japan. As of early 1989 there was still no international agreement on the standards for the HDTV picture, but the existing Japanese system uses 30 pictures per second, 60 fields per second, an aspect ratio of 16/9, and 1125 lines/picture. The result is a picture detail superior to that of commercial motion-picture film.

There are two major impediments to introduction of HDTV for a mass audience. First, existing systems are not compatible with today's TV equipment; customers would have to buy new, expensive sets. Second, each picture in HDTV is represented by about 5 times as many brightness pulses as in conventional TV. (There are more than twice as many lines—1125 instead of 525—and an even larger multiplication of the dots per line, since the picture is wider.) As will be pointed out in the next chapter, each TV channel can send the pulses required for the regular TV picture; with 5 times as many pulses, we would need five channels for a single HDTV broadcast. Thus, the only feasible delivery systems would be from satellites or over cable.

Consequently, the next few years will probably see HDTV restricted to special uses—for example, taping rather than filming of movies to permit immediate replay of a scene and greatly simplified editing.

Furthermore, in 1988 the FCC proposed that high-definition TV broadcast in the U.S. should be compatible with existing receivers and should have characteristics different from those of the existing Japanese model. Again, we see an example where political policy is used in an attempt to give an advantage to one nation's manufacturers.

In this section, we have looked briefly at TV picture structures differing from the ordinary broadcast television (the NTSC standard). Special applications (slow motion, for example) may make it economical to build a very different TV system (90 pictures every second instead of 30). All these special television systems, however, involve the same principle: to represent a picture, we scan across the scene and use a pulse to represent the brightness of each spot.

11.4 History of Television

Television is characteristic of modern technology in that we can attribute the invention to no single individual. Some books credit Vladimir Zworykin as its inventor; however, the contributions of many groups of engineers over a long period of time made this technology possible. New products come about because engineers build on the ideas and experimentation of many people that precede them. Similar to the development of communication satellites, fiber optics or computers, television is the result of a complex evolutionary process.

In 1843, Alexander Bain (of Scotland) suggested today's scanning concept and the use of telegraphy to communicate shapes and figures.

In 1873, Willoughby Smith and Joseph May found that the element selenium changes electrical resistance when exposed to light. This discovery gave a basis for obtaining an electrical signal indicating the light level at each point in a scene being photographed.

In 1879, K. Ferdinand Braun (of Germany) invented the cathode-ray tube (today's TV picture tube).

In 1884, Paul Nipkow (of Germany) invented a mechanical system to measure the light in a scene point by point (figure 11.12). Small holes (A, B, . . .) are drilled in a disk. As the disk rotates, hole A first moves across the top of the picture aperture. Light from the top row across the picture falls on a light-sensitive material (selenium), producing a current proportional to the light. When A finishes its scan across, B moves across a little lower in the picture aperture. At the receiver this current flows through an element giving light proportional to the current and sent through a synchronized disc onto a screen.

In 1889, Julius Elster and Hans Geitel (both of Germany) discovered the photoelectric effect, explained by Einstein in 1905. The surfaces of sodium, potassium, and other metals emit electrons when light is present.

In 1907, Boris Rosing (of Russia) and A. A. Campbell-Swinton (of England) suggested the cathode-ray tube as a TV receiver.

In 1911, Campbell-Swinton invented an electronic camera with small photoelectric cells. Electronics technology was still too poor to build a useful system, however.

In 1925, John Baird (of England) demonstrated his mechanical system, the Nipkow disk, in Selfridge's department store in London. He used only eight

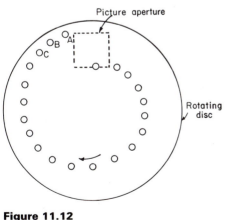

Figure 11.12
Nipkow disk.

lines for the picture. (By 1929 the BBC was broadcasting with 30 lines per picture.)

In 1925, Vladimir Zworykin (a Russian immigrant working at Westinghouse) invented the iconoscope, the first electronic camera to embody the ideas suggested by Campbell-Swinton in 1911. Zworykin first demonstrated the device in 1923, but a working model was not ready until 1933. The patent, tied up in litigation, was issued in 1938. In 1930, Zworykin transferred to RCA when that company became independent of GE, Westinghouse, and ATT under pressure from the federal government's anti-trust division. (RCA had been established right after World War I by the three corporations in response to the government's desire to have radio broadcasting under U.S. rather than Marconi control.)

In 1928, Philo T. Farnsworth (of the United States) patented the image dissector he had discovered 6 years earlier at age 16. This device allowed the photoelectric current to be measured one point at a time by the scanning camera. RCA needed the patent but had a corporate policy never to buy a patent license. Finally, however, RCA was forced to buy the patent in order to broadcast by 1939.

In 1935, the BBC made the first commercial broadcast, using 240 lines and 24 pictures per second. Later that year an improvement in picture quality was made by broadcasting with 405 lines and 25 pictures per second.

In 1939, RCA demonstrated television at the New York World's Fair.

In 1940, the U.S. National Television Systems Committee completed a four-year study with the recommendation for the standards still in use in the United States today.

In 1941, the FCC approved the standards, and broadcasting began in the United States.

All television broadcasting was stopped 6 months later, when Pearl Harbor was attacked. For the duration of World War II, no civilian production of radios or TVs was allowed. At the end of the war the government destroyed all excess military electronic equipment so it would not flood the civilian market. Then RCA and the other electronic companies found a tremendous market for their products.

Thus, the history of television up to the regular commercial broadcasts of 1941 consists of a long series of technological innovations. Its origin took place during the golden age of invention—the last third of the nineteenth century. This was the time when Edison became a national hero, when the telephone and electric lighting appeared, when the first automobiles were made, and when the Philadelphia Centennial Exposition in 1876 attracted crowds by featuring amazing new technology.

Americans tend to be very proud of their country's tradition of experimentation and invention. Although we cite the number of American Nobel laureates, science and engineering are essentially non-national. As the brief history above shows, men from Scotland, England, Germany, and Russia contributed. This is typical of most new technological developments. It is often argued that the United States has not been a leader in science and technology except in the few decades after World War II, when we capitalized on the astonishingly successful war research in electronics (radar) and nuclear energy.

When television first appeared in the late 1930s, Gilbert Seldes, a leading critic, wrote in *The Atlantic* that television would emphasize "a programme of information and ideas. . . . Here is a blackboard for the mathematician, a laboratory for the chemist, a picture gallery for the art critic, and possibly a stage upon which the historian can reenact the events of the past . . . many of the significant interests of intelligent human beings have been stuffed away into the dark corners of radio programmes; it would be a pleasant irony if television brought them to light."

Although television's intellectual level may not fulfill these expectations, its popularity has exceeded even the most optimistic predictions. Television broadcasting resumed immediately after the end of World War II. In 1946, there were only six stations, by 1965 there were 560, and by 1983 there were more than 1000.

Ninety-eight percent of U.S. homes now have TV sets, and 87 percent have color sets. Worldwide there are nearly 700 million television sets in use. These figures alone attest to the awesome influence technology can have on our lives.

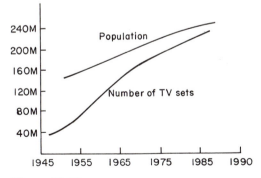

Figure 11.13
In the U.S., we are approaching one TV set per person. This growth has occurred while the cost of a TV set has dropped from 12 percent to 1 percent of the average annual family income.

11.5 Chromaticity Diagram

We now turn to color television and focus on how it differs from the black-and-white system we have considered so far in this chapter.

The way in which humans see color is very complex, and it is not completely understood by scientists and physiologists. When engineers try to design a television system for sending color pictures to a home receiver, they fortunately do not need a complete understanding of human color vision. They are interested only in such problems as how to create a picture which the viewer perceives as having the correct color.

For example, we shall see shortly that a banana looks yellow to you because (1) the light coming from that banana to your eyes consists of many different colors, or (2) the light consists of only a few colors appropriately chosen, or (3) the light is only yellow. You cannot distinguish among these different cases. Thus, the engineer, anxious to create a yellow object, may use whichever approach leads to the simplest technology.

To portray the different colors, the engineer uses a chromaticity diagram. (The prefix *chroma* comes from the Greek word for color.) The chromaticity diagram (figure 11.14) shows all the different colors of light that we can have. To explain this statement, let's take a more detailed look at the diagram.

First, consider the outside, curved portion of the boundary. Here, as we travel from red to orange to yellow and finally to violet, we find the sequence

Red - Orange - Yellow - Green - Cyan - Blue - Violet.

These are the colors of the rainbow—the separate colors we get when we break down sunlight into its components with a prism. Each point along the solid line in figure 11.14 represents a different frequency, from the lowest (red) to the highest (violet). Frequencies below red are not visible to humans and are called infrared (below the red); frequencies above violet, likewise not visible, are called ultraviolet.

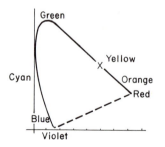

Figure 11.14
Chromaticity diagram showing the component colors of sunlight (the solid line).

Thus, each point on the solid curve represents a pure light of a particular color. The electronic device called a laser generates light of a single color or frequency. A yellow laser, for example, gives pure yellow light corresponding to the point x in figure 11.14.

Mixing or Adding Two Colors of Light

We can obtain various colors of light by combining or adding together different pure colors. For example, we can obtain yellow by adding green and red. I have two slide projectors illuminating the same screen. One projector has a red filter, so only red light goes to the screen; the second projector, with a green filter, has a brightness dial I can turn to gradually increase the amount of green light added to the constant red.

At the start I have pure red. I gradually add a little green, then a little more, and so on. The color resulting from this addition moves along the straight line from A to B in the chromaticity diagram (figure 11.15). When I reach point C, the total light is essentially pure yellow. Thus, I have obtained yellow light by adding red and green.

When we add any two light colors, we find the resulting combination by the same procedure; we draw a line between the two colors to be mixed, and move along this line according to the relative amounts of the two lights. We can mix red and violet also, to move across the dashed boundary of the chromaticity diagram. At the midpoint the combination gives magenta, which cannot be obtained as a pure color. Magenta is always a combination of red and violet and does not appear in a rainbow or as a component of sunlight.

Adding Three Colors of Light

So far we have been working on or very close to the edge of the chromaticity diagram. When we combine lights of three different colors, we move into the central portion of the diagram. One particularly interesting combination is

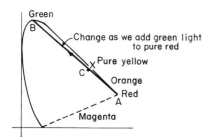

Figure 11.15
Effect of slowly increasing the amount of green light added to red.

green 59%
red 30%
blue 11%.

We first combine red and blue (the dashed line AB in figure 11.16). If the red is brighter than the blue by the ratio 30/11, we are at point C (near magenta). Adding the green moves us along line CD; if the green brightness is 59/41 that of the magenta, we end up at E. The light is then white. Thus, we can make white light by combining red, blue, and green in the percentages listed above.

There are many different ways to obtain white light (figure 11.17). Figure 11.16 indicates that we can almost reach E by combining cyan with red or yellow with blue. Sunlight combines all the colors around the curved boundary of the chromaticity diagram.

In this section, we have introduced the chromaticity diagram—basically a map of ways to reach any desired color of light by combining lights of different colors. The chromaticity diagram also shows that red, green, and violet are fundamental colors. Pure red can be obtained in only one way: by starting with red light.

Portions of the Chromaticity Diagram Used in Color TV

The color TV signal uses only a portion of the chromaticity diagram (figure 11.18). On a color TV screen, we never see pure violet, red, or green. The three basic colors used are red, green, and blue, corresponding to the three vertices of the TV chromaticity triangle.

11.6 Human Color Vision

We have seen that light of any color in the interior of the chromaticity diagram can be generated in many ways, by many different combinations. To understand the engineering of color television, however, we need to know certain capabilities and characteristics of human color vision. We need the answers to the following questions:

Is a person satisfied with a limited range of colors? (We have already learned that color TV works fine within a chromaticity triangle that does not include the very pure colors.)

Can a person distinguish rapidly changing colors within a scene?

How much can colors deviate from the real world before the human viewer begins to find the errors annoying?

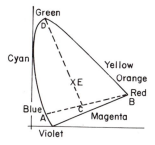

Figure 11.16
Obtaining white light from red, green, and blue.

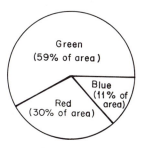

Figure 11.17
Color wheel showing how white light can be generated from the fundamental colors. This wheel, mounted on the shaft of a motor, turns at high speed. When a bright white light shines on it, the wheel looks white even though your eye receives only the green, red, and blue reflected from those surfaces. How do we define "white"? That is, why do we call this particular combination "white"? The answer is that these amounts of green, red, and blue combine to give a light essentially the same as daylight, which is itself determined by the radiation from the Sun.

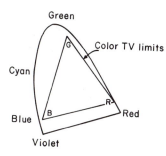

Figure 11.18
The chromaticity diagram shows the colors red, green, and violet at the corners. Color TV uses red, green, and blue as its basic colors. Why not red, green, and violet? The answer comes from the limited range of colors available in a television picture. TV can present only the colors inside the GBR triangle. The corners of this triangle are located approximately at red, green, and blue on the chromaticity diagram. Thus, TV can never give a pure cyan or violet. Either color can be presented when mixed with enough white to move us into the triangle, but the pure hue cyan cannot be presented.

To answer such questions, the designers of color television had to have a basic understanding of the physiology and psychology of human color vision.

Isaac Newton was the first to discover that white light is actually a combination of many colors. He showed that a prism breaks white light into its components, which can then be recombined in a second prism. This, and other work done in his room as a professor at Trinity College of Cambridge University, led to a monumental book, *The Opticks*, completed in 1692 when Newton was 50 years old. Unfortunately, the completed manuscript and the notes were destroyed by a fire while he was attending chapel, and it was 12 years before the book was rewritten.

In 1801, the physicist Thomas Young (who also made basic studies in elasticity and contributed to the translation of the Rosetta Stone) postulated that the eye was sensitive to three primary colors: red, yellow, and blue.

In 1874, the physiologist Ewald Hering argued for the opponent color theory.

In the 1960s, Edward MacNichol, Jr., proved that there are three types of cones, each most strongly receptive to a single one of the primary colors (red, green, blue).

Basics of Color Vision

There are two types of cells (rods and cones) in the back of the retina to respond to light entering the eye. The rods, distributed over the entire retina, respond to dim light but are insensitive to color—that is, they respond regardless of the color. Consequently, in a dimly lit room we perceive no color; everything looks gray.

With stronger intensity, the light energizes the cones, which are primarily located near the fovea (so that we detect color primarily in the center of the scene we are looking at, and objects on the edge of our field of vision are colorless). When a cone is stimulated, chemical changes occur, and an electrical pulse signal is generated. These electrical signals, representing the scene we are viewing, are processed in an electrical system at the front of the retina, then sent along the optic nerve to the brain, where final interpretation occurs.

Thus, the key sensors to measure the color of incoming light are the cones. There are just three types of cones. The red cones are most sensitive to red light, but do respond over a much broader range. Similarly, the green or blue cones respond over a range of frequencies as shown in figure 11.19. When red light arrives at a certain part of the fovea, the red cones respond strongly (many electrical pulses); the blue cones, very weakly (very few pulses). The brain then deduces that it is red light in that part of the image.

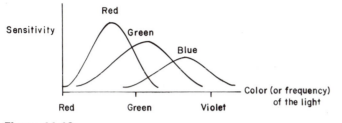

Figure 11.19
Responses of three types of cones.

Then when yellow light appears, at a frequency between red and green, the red and green cones both respond moderately and the blue cones respond very weakly. The combined red and green response—how strong the red is in comparison with the green—allows the person to deduce the shade of yellow or orange actually arriving.

Thus, we see color as a result of the relative responses of the red, green, and blue cones. An object can look yellow for two reasons:

1. It reflects only yellow light.

2. It reflects both red and green in the right proportions to look like yellow.

Even this simplified explanation of color vision is difficult to interpret because of the weak response of a cone even where the color is far from the color to which that cone is tuned. Thus, if we take all the blue out of a picture (by using a camera filter) and we then look at that picture, we do find the blue cones responding, though weakly. The brain has to interpret the responses of all the cones. A viewer who recognizes the scene and who (from experience) expects blue in certain areas will mentally insert that blue even where it does not exist. Thus, color vision is psychological as well as physiological.

There is an even greater complication, however. Scientists now think that when the data from the cones are processed in the front of the retina and the brain, an electrical system measures three characteristics: either red or green (never both), either yellow or blue, and the light level. This "opponent color theory" explains why we never see a color that is a yellowish blue. Even this theory, however, only begins to probe how the brain actually interprets the incoming electrical signals from the retina.

Subsidiary Effects in Color Vision
Surprising things happen in color vision. For example, if we gaze fixedly at a color picture for 30 seconds, then look at a sheet of white paper, we see an

Color Deficiency

Color deficiency (often called color blindness) was first studied scientifically by the color-deficient chemist, John Dalton, early in the 19th century. (The problem is called Daltonism in France.) The problem was understood for the first time in the 1960s, when Dr. Clarence Graham of Columbia University found a woman who was color deficient in one eye, normal in the other, so she was able to describe accurately what a color-deficient person sees.

By far the most common problem is a red-green deficiency; usually the person lacks red cones, but occasionally green. The individual does see shades of red and green (the cones have a broad spectrum of sensitivity), but confusion occurs. Ordinarily the deficiency is not serious; one of the few problems arises with red-green traffic lights. Almost all the U.S. has now standardized on the red light above the green, and Baltimore even goes farther to help by including a vertical stripe through the green light, a horizontal one through the red.

Color deficiency is a genetic "disease", which has been studied for hundreds of years by many of the greatest scientists (Newton, Dalton, Helmholtz, Maxwell, and Schrodinger). The validity of the current theory of color sensors and hence color deficiency has been demonstrated only recently by Jeremy Nathans and his associates in the Stanford University School of Medicine. They used molecular genetics to determine that there are genes on the X chromosome specifying the red and green cones, that the gene for the blue cone is on a different chromosome. They then determined which X-chromosome gene controlled the red cone. Furthermore, their research suggests that our three-color capabilities have evolved from an original two-color system: red or green on the X chromosome, blue on another chromosome. (New World monkeys have a single color on the X chromosome.)

Since the gene for red-green perception is located on the X chromosome, and the normal X is dominant, very few women (0.5 percent) are color-deficient, while 8 percent of the males are. A boy may be born color-deficient if the mother has the recessive trait. A girl must have a color-deficient father and a mother who has at least a recessive trait.

Box 11.2

imaginary image in which red and green, yellow and blue, and black and white are interchanged. Apparently our initial 30-second stare exhausts the cones or color sensors, and only the "opponent" colors respond to white.

The Benham disk (figure 11.20) is less easily explained. If we watch the disk rotating rapidly, we see the colors indicated in the caption. The human being interprets one sequence of black and white as red, another as green, and a third as blue. Intermittent black and white lead us to the totally incorrect interpretation that color is present. Some years ago, a television station in Los Angeles decided to amaze its viewers watching black-and-white sets. Instead of transmitting 30 complete pictures every second, the station broadcast some regular pictures and some pictures with portions blacked out. The blacked-out

Figure 11.20
Benham disk. As we rotate the disk clockwise at an increasing speed, we first see four black or gray rings. At higher speed, the outside circle appears red, the next one yellow, then green and blue. Reversing the direction of rotation reverses the sequence.

portions suddenly assumed color on the black-and-white sets (the particular color depended on the sequence of black and white).

Books on color vision frequently devote major sections to color illusions—techniques for tricking the vision system into believing that false colors are present.

Colors of Objects

Up to this point, we have been discussing the color perceived by the viewer in terms of the colors of the light reaching the eye. We might move in a different direction and ask: What makes a ripe tomato look red in sunlight or when illuminated by white light? Light of all different colors hits the tomato. Only the red light is *reflected back* to our eyes; the other colors are *absorbed* by the tomato.

Actually all colors are reflected a little, but nearly *all* the incoming red light is reflected. The light signal reaching our eyes still has components at all frequencies, but the red parts are much stronger or brighter than the green or blue.

Thus, the color of an object indicates which colors (or frequencies) of light are absorbed and which are reflected.

We can be fooled. If we take a green object and we illuminate this with only red light (not white light), what happens? Then, only red light is present; hence only red light is reflected from the object (even though the object is green, a little of the red is reflected). The object looks red to us.

I have parked my car before dark at a shopping mall. Coming out to look for the car after dark, I find the parking lot illuminated by mercury-vapor arc lamps, which give off bluish light with very little red and yellow. The color of my car is completely strange to me.

A clever supermarket manager uses white light throughout most of the store so that labels on packaged products have familiar colors. Over the meat display, however, he uses bright red fluorescent lights so that the meat looks especially succulent. (Obviously, the customer should look at the meat in white light before deciding to buy.)

A few substances can be fluorescent—that is, can generate light at a different frequency than the incoming light. A fabric brightener (added to a detergent) absorbs invisible ultraviolet light; electrons are stimulated by this ultraviolet. These electrons then fall back to lower energy levels in smaller steps, and in the process emit blue light.

Once we recognize that the color of an object depends on which light is absorbed and which reflected, the chromaticity diagram shows what happens when we mix paints. The simplest paints to mix as primary colors would be yellow, cyan, and magenta. Each absorbs one primary color of light. Yellow reflects red and green, but absorbs blue. Cyan reflects green and blue, but absorbs red. Magenta reflects blue and red, but absorbs green. We can also use red, yellow, and blue (or other combinations) provided that we do not demand that we cover too much of the chromaticity diagram (figure 11.21).

11.7 Color Television

As we see again and again in our study of communications, the technology is vastly easier to understand than the physiology. The principles of color television are much simpler than those of human color vision. The technology was designed by human beings.

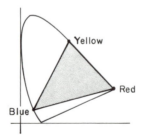

Figure 11.21
Portion of the chromaticity diagram covered by blue, yellow, and red.

Our discussion of the chromaticity diagram and human color vision indicates the challenge faced by the engineers designing a system for color television. We can send a color picture by sending three separate pictures: red, green, and blue. Adding up these three pictures will give a full-color copy of the original scene.

When engineers face a new problem, the first thought is such an approach. The system for black-and-white television exists. With this system we can send the red picture, for example. Thus, the straightforward solution is simply to send color by three separate broadcasts—for example, on channels 4, 5, and 6.

But this is not really a useful solution. The customer has to buy three receivers plus the electronics to combine the three pictures into one. Keeping the three pictures exactly superimposed is likely to be a horrendous problem. Broadcasting will be expensive and the number of different stations very limited.

Then the engineer searches for an alternative that is more attractive economically and technically. We know the problem is solvable; we need an efficient solution. Do we really require three separate pictures, each of the quality of a black-and-white picture?

The answer is no, thanks to the characteristics of human color vision. Once again, we need only match the technology to human characteristics. Fortunately for the designer, human beings do not see color in the same detail in which they see black and white. We know this intuitively from painting: watercolors need not have the fine detail of line drawings.

Consequently, a color television system need send only a limited amount of information about the color of each part of the picture—so limited that, as we shall see below, the color picture can be sent within the same one channel needed for a black-and-white picture. Once again, the idea of *matching* the technology to the human user guides us toward the technological solution.

Early Color System

Color television was demonstrated in 1928 with mechanical scanning, but the first promising work was that of Peter Goldmark of CBS around 1940 (just after black-and-white broadcasts began). The camera was easy: he simply scanned the scene three times—with red, green, and blue filters in turn. The receiver was similar, with three separate pictures created; in front of the picture tube there was a rotating disk with red, green, and blue filters, so the viewer saw in rapid sequence the red, green and blue components of the total picture.

In 1949, Goldmark was ready to go on the air with his equipment. By that time, the FCC had issued licenses for most of the available television channels, and there were several million black-and-white television sets in the homes of customers.

Goldmark was trapped by his technology. To broadcast simultaneously three separate TV pictures (one for each primary color), he would need three channels—at a time when there were very few free channels left. In order to broadcast the three video signals within one channel, he decided to depart from the NTSC standards for black-and-white television (30 pictures per second, 525 lines per picture) and to use 24 pictures of each color per second (a total of 72 pictures per second) and 405 lines per picture. In order to send more pictures, he reduced the number of lines (and also sent each brightness pulse with less sharpness). The system no longer matched human capabilities.

Even worse, the CBS color system did not match the technology that customers already owned: it was *incompatible* with the black-and-white system then in operation. The black-and-white receivers would pick up no picture at all when tuned to a channel with color broadcasts. One would have to buy an entirely new receiver to watch the color programs.

Occasionally the public has been willing to junk existing technology for a new system that held very marked advantages. In the early 1950s, audio enthusiasts bought new systems to play the 33⅓-rpm records of CBS and the 45-rpm records of RCA instead of the older 78-rpm records. In the 1930s, homeowners happily junked coal-burning furnaces for oil burners. In the color TV case, however, CBS was destined to fail: there were few color telecasts, the color pictures were not especially good, and people were still happy with their black-and-white television sets.

The FCC did approve the CBS petition (although RCA protested to the Supreme Court), and on June 21, 1951, CBS began color broadcasts in New York. The experiment ended 4 months later, partly because of the Korean War and the limitations the government placed on the production of TV sets but primarily because of the enormous handicap imposed by incompatibility.

Today's Color System

By 1953, a set of standards for a *compatible* color system was developed by a second NTSC (National Television Systems Committee—not, as someone suggested, Never Twice the Same Color). RCA, the primary developer, started color broadcasting on the NBC stations it controlled. A decade later, color sets became cheap and popular and most stations were broadcasting color signals.

The RCA or NTSC color system was designed from the premise that compatibility is essential. Thus, instead of broadcasting three separate signals (red, green, and blue), we broadcast three signals, one of which is the *sum* of the red, green, and blue signals—that is, just the total brightness signal of the black-and-white set; it is just the video signal described in section 11.2.

In addition, for a color system, we must broadcast two other signals. For example, we might send for each pixel one signal indicating how much red light, and a second signal showing how much green light. The color receiver, knowing the total amount of light, the amount of red and the amount of green, could easily calculate the blue.

Instead, two different measures of the relative amounts of red, blue, and green are used: *hue* and *saturation*. To identify any point in the chromaticity diagram, we draw a line from white through the point to the edge of the diagram. Where this line hits the edge is the *hue*. The *saturation* measures how far toward a pure hue the point is:

$$\text{Saturation} = \frac{\text{white to the color}}{\text{white to the hue}}$$

The trick in compatibility was to broadcast these other two signals (hue and saturation) in such a way that they would not disrupt the normal operation of the black-and-white receiver. Here the designers were saved by an important characteristic of human color vision: we do not clearly distinguish sharp changes in color. The color of a picture can change more slowly across the picture than the brightness. If five consecutive pixels as we move across a line are

red   red   yellow   yellow   yellow,

the viewer is undisturbed by a gradual change, such as

red   red-orange   orange   orange-yellow   yellow.

This limitation of human color vision means that the system can send relatively rough information on color changes. In communication terms, the color signals do not require a full channel. Furthermore, it turns out (as will be explained in chapter 12) that the black-and-white picture does not use the full channel (all the available broadcast frequencies), so that we can broadcast the two color signals simultaneously with the black-and-white signal.

Thus, by taking advantage of the human limitation in color vision, RCA was able to develop today's *compatible* color TV system.

Color Picture Tube

The picture tube for color TV works essentially the same way as that for black-and-white, but with three separate electron guns, one for each color. The screen replaces each phosphorescent spot with three small dots, which fluoresce in red, green, and blue, respectively. Behind the screen is a metal mask to intercept the three beams except where there are one of the 200,000 holes which allow the red beam to strike the red dot, and so on. The phosphorescent dots are so small that the human eye cannot see them, with the result that the three colors are essentially coming from the same spot on the screen.

European Color System

Color television appeared in Europe well after color broadcasts began in the United States. In the early 1960s, the PAL color system was developed in Germany. It was very similar to the U.S. NTSC system except for the inherent differences in pictures per second and lines per picture, which carried over from black-and-white television.

Naturally, the French adopted an entirely different system, called SECAM—to the consternation and expense of Belgians and other neighbors who wanted to watch French broadcasts. The French system sends the two color signals sequentially—one during one horizontal line, the other during the next line.

The Japanese adopted the U.S. system, and have made improvements over the years. For example, Sony Corporation developed a picture tube with only one electron gun, which hits red, green, and blue phosphors in rapid sequence through slots rather than holes in the mask.

Once again we find three incompatible systems emerging. All three are characterized by careful attention to designing the technology to match the related human characteristics.

Appendix 11.1
Human Vision

The human being has dozens of different senses: we can detect hot or cold temperatures, orientation, pressure, sharpness, and so on. The term "sixth sense," meaning intuition, comes from the time when it was thought there were only five senses: sight, touch, taste, smell, and hearing. Even though today we recognize that the body is vastly more complex, we still receive by far the most information from our sight.

Vision is so important that when malignancy exists in both eyes of a patient, the physician will operate on only one eye. The possibility of loss of sight in both eyes would be too traumatic. Conversely, when a person blind since birth has his or her sight restored, the psychological adjustment is overwhelming.

This central role of vision explains the extensive efforts in technology to give both mobility and reading ability to blind people. It also explains the tremendous impact television has had on life styles, attitudes, and activities.

In the normal individual, the eye is a fantastic device. We can focus on objects over a wide range of distances; we can see in very bright light and in near darkness; we can distinguish thousands of different colors. In vision and brain processing of the signals, we find the astonishing pattern-recognition capabilities of the human being: for example, you recognize a friend immediately when you see him totally unexpectedly—a feat we have not been able to match with the most elaborate computers. Scientists really have no understanding of how the eye and the brain accomplish this recognition, or even what parameters of the face we use.

The information we obtain through vision is often important even when other senses dominate. For example, your *orientation* system allows you to sit or stand in a desired position even when you're in motion. This orientation system is primarily run by the information received in the inner ear, where the semicircular canals sense angular acceleration and the otoliths measure linear acceleration. But these acceleration measurements need to be supplemented by visual signals, as is shown by two simple experiments:

1. March in place with your eyes closed. Most people unknowingly start to rotate slowly.

2. Stand with one foot in front of the other and with your arms akimbo (figure 11.22). For most people, this is not too difficult with the eyes open. When you do this with your eyes closed, you'll find that a low-frequency oscillation grows until you lose your balance.

Thus, even with the inner-ear sensors, we need the visual sense for good performance of the total orientation system.

The difficulty in understanding human vision arises from two features:

1. The vision process is extremely complicated. Not only does the eye change incoming light signals to electrical signals for transmission to the brain, but the

Figure 11.22
With your eyes closed, a low-frequency oscillation arises. That is, your body starts to rock from side to side.

retina and the optic nerve are extensions of the brain. The eye does not just measure the camera image of the object you are looking at, then send this image in electrical form to the brain. Instead, the data are partially processed in the eye and coded in some way before they travel to the brain.

2. Often when scientists try to understand how the human body works, the search for knowledge is severely handicapped because we cannot experiment on people. Consequently, we have to deduce how human vision works either by experiments on animals or by trying to reason from observed performance capabilities. In the former case, we are never sure that the animal results can be carried over to humans. In the latter situation, we can measure human ability to adapt to sudden darkness, for example, but then we have to guess how that adaptation is accomplished in the eye and the brain. Thus, the study of vision is a detective story: we have clues provided by observation or limited measurements; from these, we try to deduce how the system works internally. Such understanding is essential not only for medical treatment, but also to design technology which is matched to human characteristics.

In the 1960s, the neurobiologists David Hubel and Torsten Wiesel carried out a remarkable experiment on kittens. They found that placing a patch over one eye for 3–6 months led to amblyopia (a healthy eye that cannot see properly). In other words, if a normal kitten could not use one eye during this critical period just after birth, that eye did not function properly later. Even though the nervous system is fully developed at birth, the normal pathways apparently must be used to develop normal effectiveness.

If this experimental result can be carried over to humans, it means that serious eye defects (such as crossed eyes) should be corrected early in infancy (say, at 6 months). Perhaps it is dangerous to wait a few years for the child to "grow out" of the problem. If so, pediatricians clearly need methods for testing the vision of infants—methods that do not require that the patient understand verbal orders or stay attentive for long periods. This has been the incentive for the development of technology to photograph the light reflected from the back of an infant's eyes in order to measure how well each eye is focusing the incoming image.

A simple experiment may catch serious vision problems when they exist in a very small child. In this test, the child is seated before two large squares: one solid gray and one striped. Infants strongly favor striped patterns to solid gray. If the baby shows no preference, visual problems are suspected, and further tests can be made.

Our understanding of human vision therefore depends on deductions from observed performance and relatively simple experiments, either on animals or on people (if the experiments are non-traumatic and non-destructive). In the

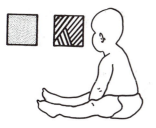

Figure 11.23
Infants strongly favor striped patterns over solid gray.

following pages, we consider some of the measured performance capabilities of the human eye.

Performance Capabilities of the Eye—Brightness

The engineer, looking at human vision, tries to describe the eye in the same terms used for electronic or photographic equipment. Thus, the function of the eye is to measure incoming light signals. If we carry this analogy along, we naturally ask: What are the weakest signals the eye can detect? What are the strongest signals? The answers describe some of the performance capabilities of the human eye.

Sensitivity

How sensitive is the eye? That is, what is the weakest light signal that can be detected?

Experience tells us that we have a remarkable ability to see in very weak light. Even outside on a cloudy night, we can walk down a driveway or through a wooded area once our eyes are accustomed to the darkness. To put this capability of vision in more dramatic terms, we have to understand the dual nature of light: light behaves as a wave, but also like a group of particles.

Light is a form of electromagnetic radiation. The term "visible light" refers to those frequencies that stimulate the retina of the eye. Thus, light "traveling" from an incandescent bulb to your eye is really a concept: nothing material actually moves outward from the bulb. When clear glass is placed between the bulb and your eye, light still "travels" the same path, just as a radio or TV signal moves through the wooden walls of your house.

Thus, light is an electric and magnetic field—the ability to do work at a distance. This electromagnetic field has many of the same properties as a gravitational field. (Think of the Earth attracting an object thrown out of an airplane window, or the Moon attracting a landing lunar vehicle.)

In attempting to understand light, a physicist might notice two characteristics:

1. When a laser light source is pointed at the Moon, the light "travels" outward at a speed of 186,000 miles per second, or 300 million meters per second. Since the Moon is about 220,000 miles away, the laser light reaches the Moon, is reflected, and returns to the Earth in slightly more than 2 seconds.

2. Light signals can be diffracted or bent around a barrier in their path. Furthermore, two light signals of the same frequency will show interference (cancellation when the maximum of one coincides with the minimum of the other).

Both these phenomena mean that light has the properties of a wave traveling through space—an electromagnetic wave.

The physicist Max Planck showed that light *also* behaves like moving particles. Light comes from a source in small packages of energy, each package called a *photon*. In light (or a visible electromagnetic signal), each photon has an energy of about 3×10^{-19} joules. This is a very small amount of energy. A 60-watt light bulb gives off about 3 watts of light, or 3 joules per second. Thus, every second, 10^{19} photons leave the bulb if we adopt this particle concept of light.

The particle "nature" of light tells us that one photon is the least possible amount of light. Obviously, no technology can detect less light than one photon. What is the weakest light signal that the eye can detect? In other words, how many photons are needed to fire a retina receptor and generate an electrical signal to the brain?

Albert Rose, a television engineer at RCA, has shown that the eye responds to a minimum signal of only about three photons, and that a burst of 100 photons is clearly visible. In this remarkable work, Rose made this deduction by determining the number of photons reaching the eye from a black scene with a gray spot just detectable by an observer. This analysis shows that the eye comes close to the ultimate sensitivity: we cannot build technological devices that detect appreciably less light than the eye.

Range of Intensity

What is the brightest light we can see? In other terms, what is the range in light intensities over which the eye will work?

The answer is astonishing: 10^{11}, or 100,000,000,000. That is, the brightest light is 10^{11} times as strong as the dimmest light detectable. This is a range that, again, cannot be readily matched by technology. Human hearing is a remarkable sensing operation, but the range there is only 10^7, or 10 million, from the weakest detectable sound signal to the signal causing pain and damage to the ear. The range of vision is 10,000 times as great.

Dark-Light Adaptation

When you walk from a brightly lit street into a dark theater, at first you cannot even see the aisles. Gradually, your eyes "adapt" to the darkness; after perhaps 30 minutes, you are even identifying familiar faces in the theater. Part of the eye's remarkable range results from this adaptation to large changes in light level.

We do not know exactly how this adaptation occurs. There are apparently several separate changes in the eye. Entering a dark environment causes enlargement of the pupil (the black portion of the eye inside the colored part; this is the window admitting light to the eye). The area of the pupil changes by a factor as large as 16.

In addition, there probably are chemical changes in the eye. Finally, there seems to be a "variable-gain amplifier" between the eye and the brain. In other words, when the light signals are very weak, the electrical signals are amplified more. The same characteristic is built into your car radio: when the received signal is weak, the gain is high so that the sound level is approximately constant even when you drive behind hills or to a hilltop.

Although dark adaptation takes up to 30 minutes, light adaptation takes only a fraction of a second, as you know when you turn on a light after waking up in a dark room. We don't understand how this difference is achieved physiologically, but the very fast light adaptation is necessary to protect the visual system from damage when we are suddenly exposed to bright lights.

More Performance Capabilities of the Eye

How acute is human vision? For example, over what variation of distances can we see an object clearly? The answer depends on many factors, including the amount of light coming to the eye from the object and its environment, the light levels from other directions, and the contrast in color and brightness between the object and its surroundings. From an engineering viewpoint, we can begin to describe the capabilities of human vision in terms of a few simple

Pupil nearly closed   Pupil wide open

Figure 11.24
Dark adaptation.

experiments which give us enough information to determine how to design a
television receiver for a pleasant picture.

Sharpness

On a large piece of white paper, we place two small black dots 1/4 inch apart.
We place the paper on the wall of a large, well-lit area and walk backwards away
from it. At a distance of about 40 feet, we find that the two dots seem to merge
into one.

We can describe the "sharpness" of human vision by the results of this
experiment. The dots are ¼ inch apart, and they can be distinguished at a
maximum distance of 500 inches (about 40 feet). Thus,

$$\frac{\text{Separation}}{\text{Distance}} = \frac{1/4}{500} = \frac{1}{2000}.$$

If the dots were 1 foot apart, we could recognize them to be separate at
distances up to 2000 feet.

Figure 11.25 shows the geometry of our experiment. The angle, called θ, is
just the separation divided by the distance (in the case of our experiment
1/2000 radian).

Visual Field

Gaze steadily at an object directly ahead of you and ask someone to walk in a
circular arc around you (figure 11.26). You will find that you lose sight of your
friend approximately when he passes A, and that you detect his appearance
again about at B. In other words, the visual field covers about 180°. The field
is limited for each eye by the nose on one side and the facial bones on the other,
so the exact angle depends on facial structure.

Accommodation Ability

How successful is the eye in accommodating or adjusting to different object
distances? A reasonably good camera can vary its lens to bring into focus objects
at distances ranging from 3 feet to infinity. Does the eye do as well?

A person with normal vision can focus on objects a long distance away, so
visual performance is measured by how *close* an object we can focus on. If we
hold a pencil in front of one eye and close the other eye, then gradually bring

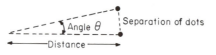

Figure 11.25
Definition of angle θ.

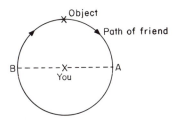

Figure 11.26
Measuring field of vision.

the vertical pencil toward the eye, we reach a point at which the image is no longer sharp. This is called the "near point." The closer this is to the eye, the better the performance capability of the eye.

Figure 11.27 shows that this accommodation ability of the eye (the ability to focus sharply on near objects) normally deteriorates rapidly after the age of about 40. This is the reason most elderly people need glasses for reading. (Glasses were probably invented by Roger Bacon around 1275; bifocals were invented by Benjamin Franklin near the end of the eighteenth century. Glasses did not become commonplace until this century; now they are used by more than 100 million Americans, or almost half the population.)

Other Capabilities

Throughout this discussion of vision we are focusing on the engineer's viewpoint: how vision is comparable to the technology that might be built to substitute for the human eye, or how the characteristics of human vision determine the design of technology to be used to produce images. The physician or ophthalmologist, in contrast, focuses his attention on eye disorders and possible treatment. The psychologist is perhaps interested in mental impressions deduced from the visual image.

To understand other performance capabilities, we want to look at the separate parts of the eye. Before we turn to this, however, we will digress briefly to discuss the simple lens, since basically the eye passes the incoming light signals through a lens to create an image of the object being viewed, just as a camera lens creates an image of the scene at the film surface.

Lens

A camera lens takes the light rays arriving from the scene to be photographed, then bends them in such a way that an image of that scene is created at the film surface. Obviously a lens should have three characteristics:

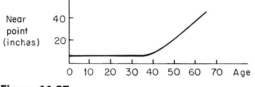

Figure 11.27
Accommodation deteriorates with age.

1. It should be transparent.

2. It should bend the incoming light rays.

3. The bending should be such that an accurate image is created at the desired distance.

All three criteria can be met by a convex glass or plastic material with each surface spherical in shape (figure 11.28).

To understand lens operation, we first consider what happens as a beam of light enters a plastic or glass substance, in which the velocity of the beam of light is less than in air (figure 11.29). A beam of light always has a certain width; consequently we can talk about a beam made up of a number of rays. The incoming beam is made up of parallel rays. Each ray travels through the air at the same speed. When ray 4 hits the surface of the plastic, it slows down because the plastic is denser than air. Ray 1, at this time, is only at point A. During the time ray 1 remains in the air, ray 4 advances only to point B (the velocity of ray 4 has decreased because of the density of the plastic). Thus, in order for the beam of light to continue to move in a parallel formation, the four rays must now move in a different direction.

A light wave entering a denser substance is bent toward the normal at the surface (figure 11.30). The amount of bending depends on the relative velocities of light in the air and in the plastic—that is, how fast the light travels in air as compared to how fast the light travels in plastic. A light wave entering a *less dense* substance thus bends away from the normal (figure 11.31).

Now let us look at what happens to one light ray passing through a lens (figure 11.32). Two bendings now occur, one at each surface (points A and B).

If we carry through this geometry carefully for all rays passing through the lens from the light source, we find that, because of the shape of the lens, they all meet at a single point: the image of the original light source (figure 11.33).

All sources at the same distance from the lens give images at the same distance. Thus, the lens creates a perfect image of the scene to be photographed or viewed (figure 11.34), although the image is inverted and generally not the

Figure 11.28
A lens.

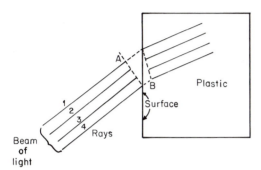

Figure 11.29
Bending of light at surface.

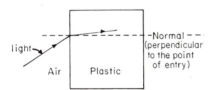

Figure 11.30
Light is bent toward the normal when it enters the plastic.

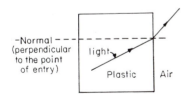

Figure 11.31
Light is bent away from the normal when it leaves the plastic.

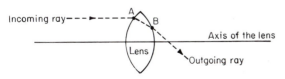

Figure 11.32
Light ray arriving parallel to the axis of the lens.

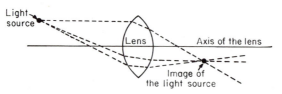

Figure 11.33
All rays from a light source meet at one point.

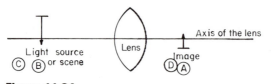

Figure 11.34
Source and image.

same size as the original scene. (In a camera or in vision, we want a smaller image, of course.)

A lens creates an image at one location (A in figure 11.34) from a light source or scene at location B. A light source farther away from the lens, say at C, gives an image slightly closer, at D. When the source or scene is far from the lens, the image doesn't move much as the source moves closer or away. When the source is closer, the image position is more sensitive to the source distance—this is why, with a camera, we must be especially careful to set the distance accurately if we are shooting a close-up.

If we want to keep the image at one particular location (the retina in the eye), we can compensate for different source distances by changing the curvature of a lens: the more curvature, the closer the source can be. When you measured your "near point" in the last section, as you moved the pencil inward, your eye lens became more and more curved until you reached a point at which the muscles could no longer give you the required curvature. Older people are unable to change the curvature of the lens very much.

From this basic concept of a lens creating an image, we can now turn to a consideration of the parts of the eye.

Parts of the Eye
Figure 11.35 shows the important parts of the eye. Light rays from the object being viewed reach the cornea, and are bent so that an image of this object is formed at the retina in the back of the eyeball. There the light signals are converted to electrical pulses, which travel out the optic nerve to the brain.

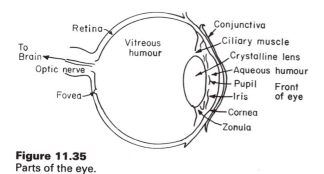

Figure 11.35
Parts of the eye.

Cornea The light waves pass through the conjunctiva, merely a thin protective covering, and reach the cornea. Most of the lens action (the bending of the light rays) occurs at this point, since this is the surface at which there is the greatest change in the velocity of light. With the velocity of light much less in the cornea than in air, the rays are bent toward the normal, or toward the center of the eye (figure 11.36).

The cornea needs to be kept clear at all times for good vision. Every few seconds you blink to clear away any debris from the cornea and to spread tears for cleaning (everyone cries continuously at a low rate). The cornea has no blood vessels (they would ruin the optical properties), so it is nourished from the aqueous humour.

There are two familiar vision difficulties associated with the cornea. First, because the cornea is the principal lens of the eye, it is important that the surface have a constant curvature. Astigmatism is the vision problem in which curvature varies, so that the images are fuzzy. Second, the cornea occasionally becomes opaque, and the individual requires a cornea transplant.

The cornea has one other function: it blocks the transmission of ultraviolet light, to protect the retina. Ultraviolet light is electromagnetic radiation at frequencies just higher than those of visible light; excessive exposure causes sunburn and, when prolonged, skin cancer.

Aqueous Humor The incoming light rays next pass through the aqueous humor. This is a liquid that provides nutrients to the cornea. The liquid is continuously draining and being replaced; normally it is totally replaced every four hours. If the drainage is partially blocked, the pressure in the liquid tends to build up. This is the intra-ocular pressure the ophthalmologist measures in an eye examination to detect glaucoma.

Commonly the aqueous humor contains a few floating particles which block the passage of light; these are the easily moved spots we see when looking at a clear, white scene.

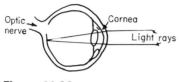

Figure 11.36
Light rays bent by the cornea.

Iris and Pupil   The iris is the colored ring you see as you look at another person's eye. The iris is opaque, so the incoming light must go through the center of the ring (the pupil) to reach the inner eye. Thus, the task of the cornea is to bend the incoming light rays so they pass through the pupil.

As mentioned previously, dark-light adaptation is partially obtained by a change in the size of the iris: when we move from a very bright area to a dark area, the pupil increases in area by a factor of as much as 16 (the radius grows from 2 to 8 millimeters) because of a change in the iris.

The pupil, which is circular in humans (figure 11.37), looks black when you look directly into someone's eye. Actually, the pupil is transparent. Any light reflected from the back of the other person's eye (the retina) would have to come from your own eye, where there is no source. Consequently, as you look directly in the other person's pupil, you see only blackness. The ophthalmoscope allows the physician to look directly through the pupil into the patient's eye (figure 11.38).

Crystalline Lens   The incoming light has now been grossly focused by the cornea, and the light we want to look at has been selected by the pupil. We are ready for the fine focusing by the crystalline lens.

This lens again has no blood vessels, so light is not blocked. The lens has a focal length of about 16 millimeters and behaves like a camera with an f/2 opening at low light levels, f/8 at high.

The lens accommodates (that is, adjusts to objects at different distances) by changing shape under the control of the *zonula* and the *ciliary muscle*. The former is a membrane holding the lens, the latter is a muscle that contracts to make the lens more convex when we look at nearby objects (figure 11.39).

The lens is an unusual organ. Since it draws nutrients from the surrounding liquid, the center dies continuously and more and more rapidly as the lens grows on the outside. In this organ, then, dying starts before the person's birth, but growth never stops. By the time the normal person reaches an age of 40 or 50, the dead material in the center has accumulated so much that it is no longer possible to change the lens curvature enough to focus on nearby objects; thus, the accommodation ability begins to deteriorate rapidly.

Figure 11.37

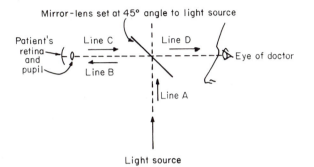

Figure 11.38
The principle of the ophthalmoscope. Light comes up from a light source (line A). It strikes a special kind of mirror-lens combination that reflects half of the incoming light and allows the other half of the light to pass straight through. As the light strikes the mirror-lens, half of the light is reflected toward the pupil of the patient (line B). It enters the pupil, then is reflected off the retina, goes back through the pupil, and back to the mirror-lens (line C). Now, half of this light (which shows the retina) passes straight through the mirror-lens to the eye of the doctor (line D). The first time, the mirror-lens is used as a reflector; the second time, the light passes straight through the mirror-lens.

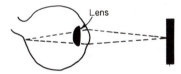

Eye focusing on distant object

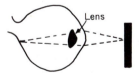

Eye focusing on near object

Figure 11.39
A crystalline lens changes shape when focusing.

The most common eye problem with elderly people is cataracts, in which the lens becomes opaque. In the normal cataract operation, the cornea is pulled back and the crystalline lens is simply removed. Thereafter, the individual can see lightness and darkness, but cannot focus without glasses. In recent years, surgeons have started to insert an artificial, plastic lens clipped to the iris. Almost a quarter of the 400,000 cataract operations a year now involve the artificial lens, even though the lensless person with glasses normally can see well (although there is no side vision beyond the angles covered by the glasses or contact lenses, so that objects tend to pop into and out of view).

Retina   Finally, the incoming light reaches the retina at the back of the eyeball. The retina spans about 240° (⅔ of a complete circle), all the way from the ciliary muscle to the muscle on the other side (figure 11.40). In the *back* of the retina, there are two types of special cells sensitive to light:

240 million rods sensitive to brightness

12 million cones sensitive to color (red, green, or blue).

Thus, the light passes through the maze of blood cells and nerve fibers in the front of the retina to reach the *rods* (the cones will be discussed below). Although Johannes Kepler recognized the important function of the retina in 1604, it was not until the late 1940s that George Wald explained the operation of the rods. He showed that there is a large molecule (rhodopsin) in which incident light causes a chemical change releasing a proton; the electrical charge causes a nerve cell to fire or discharge electrically, and the light signal has been converted to an electrical pulse of voltage.

Most of the back of the retina consists of these rods, which respond to the brightness of the incoming light. The electrical signals generated in the rods (and cones) then move through the nerve-system network toward the optic nerve. The front of the retina (really part of the brain) routes these electrical signals through as many as four different connections and different types of cells. After this analysis of the signals, the modified information is transmitted over a million fibers in the optic nerve to the brain.

The other light-sensitive receptors are cones, most of which are found in or close to the *fovea* (the area of the retina that receives the light from the object

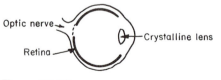

Figure 11.40

we are looking *directly* at). The fovea contains 20,000 densely packed cones and rods, with the central portion almost entirely cones. The fovea covers only 2° and hence primarily receives the incoming light from an angle of 2° surrounding the direction in which we are staring (figure 11.41). Thus, our angular discrimination is best for objects directly ahead (because the rods and cones are so densely packed in the fovea), and our color perception is also best here (because most of the cones are at the fovea).

Just from this very brief explanation, we can understand some characteristics of human vision:

1. If we fix on an object straight ahead, we can see almost no colors far to the right or the left. In figure 11.42, if the eye is fixed on point A, light from B hits the retina at C, far from the foveal region where the cones are most dense. Hence, primarily rods are excited, and we see mostly in black and white. To demonstrate this, you need to view an unfamiliar object (so you don't mentally assume the familiar colors are present) situated near the edge of your visual field—you can't easily tell whether the object is colored or not.

2. The peripheral vision (the cones near the ends of the retina) are useful primarily to detect a moving object, so that we are alerted to move our eye around to have a better look. This is why flashing neon signs along the highway are so much better for advertising than steady lights: the edge of the retina notices the flashing, and we turn our eyes toward the change.

3. In a poorly lit room, we see no color. As the lights are dimmed in a theater, a point is reached at which we lose color. Obviously, the cones require more

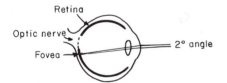

Figure 11.41
The fovea receives light from a 2° angle.

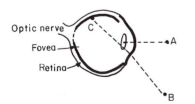

Figure 11.42
Side vision.

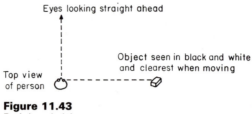

Figure 11.43
Peripheral vision.

light than the rods to generate an electrical signal, just as color film needs brighter lighting.

4. Sailors on night watch at sea are told that, to detect a small ship on the horizon, they should look slightly above or below the horizon. The reason is that the center of the fovea is primarily cones, which are insensitive to low light; the light slightly off the direct line of vision reaches the densely packed rods near the fovea.

5. We have a blind spot for each eye. This spot is the region from which light comes in and hits the optic disc (the end of the optic nerve where there are no retinal sensors).

6. The different sensitivities of the rods and cones is one reason night driving is so dangerous. The rods well away from the fovea give us our spatial orientation; these rods respond to dim light, so at night we feel that our visual capabilities are good. As a result, many drivers do not decrease their speed at night. Unfortunately, the low light means that the cones may not be activated at all, and our ability to detect small objects (such as pedestrians) in the direct line of sight is poor. This night-vision ability can often be markedly improved by using glasses similar to those for myopia (nearsightedness).

The retina is the central element of vision, since here the incoming light signals are transformed to electrical pulses. The retina is also interesting medically because it is the only part of the central nervous system that can be seen without surgery, and because the ophthalmoscope allows the physician to study the arteries, capillaries, and veins. The doctor's examination of the retina gives important information about a wide range of health problems: high blood pressure, diabetes, kidney malfunction, reaction to certain drugs, problems of the central nervous system, and so on.

Improper development of the retina caused blindness in over 10,000 children born in the late 1940s and the early 1950s, when premature infants were put in incubators, typically with air containing 50 percent or more oxygen (in order to avoid brain damage from a lack of oxygen). By the late 1940s, it was clear that an unusual number of these children developed normally except that, about 3 months after birth, the blood vessels in the retina began to grow abnormally, often breaking out from the retina into the vitreous humor and sometimes pulling the entire retina forward.

For several years the cause of this problem was unknown. Many hypotheses were advanced, and various treatments were tried. By the early 1950s, attention focused on the high levels of oxygen in the incubators. In July 1953, the National Institutes of Health began a carefully designed one-year study of 800 infants born in eighteen hospitals. There were serious questions raised as to whether such a study was ethical: if the probable cause was too much oxygen, was it ethical to expose some infants, chosen at random, to a high-oxygen environment? This is a basic problem in the interplay of technology and medicine: there is no point to doing a controlled experiment until there is a reasonable probability of understanding the cause or having confidence in the experimental treatment. Once this "reasonable probability" exists, the experiment then puts the control group of patients at risk.

By 1954, the results of the experiment clearly demonstrated the important role of too much oxygen. Apparently, the excessive oxygen caused the developing blood vessels in the retina to wither. When the infant returned to the normal environment, there was wild and erratic regrowth of the blood vessels, in some cases causing the retina to move out to the lens.

As soon as the test results were publicized, hospital practices were changed, and the disease (called retrolental fibroplasia, or RLF) subsided quickly. Unfortunately, the usual response was simply to cut the oxygen level in incubators. By the 1960s, it was discovered that other problems of premature infants then increased. Indeed, one study 15 years after the experiment indicated that each child saved from blindness cost sixteen deaths. Today it is recognized that the premature infant must be monitored carefully, with the oxygen level regularly adjusted to yield the best compromise among the conflicting requirements. The recent increase in cases of RLF has further complicated medicine's understanding.

The history of this retinal problem is interesting not only for the ethical problem associated with the controlled experiment, but also because it illustrates the general problem so often encountered with a new technology. In this case, the new technology (the incubator with a large amount of oxygen) was introduced to ameliorate a recognized problem (brain damage from too little oxygen). The technology succeeded. Then the side effect appeared (the blindness). The response was to drop the technology completely. Many years had to pass before society arrived at the optimum use of the new technology.

A similar sequence of events occurs again and again as we move into an increasingly technological environment. "Technology assessment" is an attempt to anticipate the side effects of technological change. The Office of Technology Assessment (OTA) of the U.S. Congress was established in the early 1970s solely to carry out such anticipatory studies. Unfortunately, in most cases we don't understand the social system and the human system well enough to be able to predict the effects of a technological innovation.

Review Questions

R11-1. A color TV signal requires the same bandwidth as a black-and-white signal. Why is this possible, in terms of the capabilities of human vision?

R11-2. Show on a sketch of the chromaticity diagram how we move if we start with magenta light, add a little red light, then add green light.

R11-3. Briefly describe how a color TV signal can also be shown on a black-and-white TV set.

R11-4. Why was an aspect ratio of 4/3 chosen by the National Television Systems Committee?

R11-5. What characteristic of human vision leads to the requirement for interlacing in TV-picture construction?

R11-6. In the history of TV, what was the role of the NTSC, the National Television Systems Committee?

R11-7. Which hues never appear in the rainbow or the breakup of sunlight? Explain briefly.

R11-8. Explain briefly how slow motion is achieved in TV broadcasts of athletic events.

R11-9. To see an object in very weak light, you should look just *below* where the object might be. Why?

R11-10. Why did the Europeans use 25 TV pictures per second while the Americans used 30?

R11-11. The French initially used 819 lines per TV picture, arguing that their culture demanded this quality. What were the disadvantages of this system?

R11-12. Why does high-definition TV use a 16/9 aspect ratio rather than the 4/3 ratio used today?

R11-13. The distance the normal viewer sits from the TV set determines what characteristic of the video signal?

R11-14. Many videocassette recorders allow you to stop one picture at a time. This means you are looking at pictures how far apart in time?

R11-15. The U.S. color TV broadcast sends the luminance, hue, and saturation signals. Why are these used instead of red, green, and blue?

R11-16. As you drive down a straight highway at night, why are flashing lights on the side of the road particularly noticeable?

R11-17. Why have manufacturers of TV sets for the U.S. market not been particularly concerned about color quality?

R11-18. "A technology, once in the hands of the public, is very difficult to change or improve." Discuss briefly one example.

R11-19. Why is it impossible to single out one person as the inventor of modern television?

R11-20. High-definition television (HDTV) uses 1050 or 1150 lines per picture. Why have all major companies now decided *not* to start broadcasting HDTV in the near future? That is, what is wrong with the technology?

R11-21. Human *color* perception occurs primarily in the fovea, a small region in the "center" of the retina. What are the implications for the compatibility of color with black-and-white TV?

R11-22. "Newton showed that white light can be broken up into separate colors—red, yellow, green, cyan, violet, and magenta." What is wrong with this statement?

R11-23. American television uses 525 lines per picture. This choice was made because of what behavior characteristic of people?

R11-24. What characteristic of the TV picture is established by the human flicker fusion frequency?

R11-25. Define hue and saturation in terms of the chromaticity diagram.

R11-26. The TV antenna for channels 1–13 is much larger than the antenna for channels 14–69, yet the signals broadcast by channels 1–13 are stronger. Explain.

R11-27. The color of a particular dot (called a pixel or picture element) on the TV screen is described by a hue of yellow and a saturation of 80 percent. Explain what this means.

R11-28. A lover of modern technology buys a 100-inch TV screen (projection type) for his den so he can watch "big pictures." Explain why this is a stupid purchase if he has a normal-size den.

R11-29. Why can the U.S. television picture be brighter than the European picture?

R11-30. Why was the original British TV standard of 405 lines undesirable?

R11-31. In mixing paints, yellow, cyan, and magenta are primary colors. Explain briefly.

R11-32. How many octaves are represented by the visible-light spectrum?

R11-33. When TV pictures are sent from Europe to the U.S. by satellite, why is it necessary to "re-photograph" the picture before broadcasting here?

R11-34. "TV was invented in Russia (England, Germany, the United States)." Explain briefly how each of these four different statements can be true.

R11-35. Explain how the human factor of "persistence of vision" was used to set the standard of 30 pictures per second for the TV picture system.

R11-36. The French color system sends red information on one line, blue on the next, then red again, and so on. Why does this give a color picture that is satisfactory for the viewer?

Problems

P11-1. The story of a technology such as television is fascinating. With each new technology, risks accompany opportunities, and disadvantages go along with advantages. To illustrate this, a few pages from a 1985 report to Congress ("Federal Government Information Technology: Electronic Surveillance and Civil Liberties," OTA-CIT-293, Washington, DC, October 1985, pp. 62–67) follow.

Prepare a two-page letter to your representative urging the selection of whichever one of the five options you favor.

As cameras have become smaller and easier to activate from a distance, they have become more attractive as a tool for watching people and recording their activities. The evidence that can be obtained from electronic visual surveillance, especially if accompanied by audio surveillance, is as complete as investigative authorities could expect. But there are questions about the intrusive nature of electronic visual surveillance, and the circumstances under which its use is appropriate. Electronic visual surveillance, more than any other form of electronic surveillance, reminds people of the specter of Big Brother watching at all times and in all places.

There is presently a great deal of electronic visual surveillance of public places. Banks have cameras running continuously to monitor both the interior teller counters and also the outside automatic teller machine areas. Airports use electronic visual surveillance in a number of places to ensure the security of the passengers and equipment. Many large department stores, as well as all-night convenience stores, use electronic visual surveillance to deter and detect shoplifting and to compile a visual record of activity. Many cities use closed circuit television to survey street corners in high crime areas, subway platforms, and entrances to public buildings. The Federal Government uses electronic visual surveillance at various Federal buildings to monitor people coming and going. Some employers, especially factory owners and those who maintain large clerical pools, use electronic visual surveillance to monitor the activities of workers.

The motivation for this electronic visual surveillance is a heightened concern for security; the result is that people are becoming more and more accustomed to being watched as they carry out their public life. As cameras become smaller, and easier to install and to monitor, their attractiveness as a means of monitoring activities in private places becomes greater. Previously, one could take actions to ensure an expectation of privacy in a private place, e.g., locking the doors and closing the curtains. But, in the absence of legal standards, the only effective barriers against electronic visual surveillance are the limitations of the technology and such limitations are few.

Electronic visual surveillance of public places is not specifically addressed by Federal statutes, although the assumption is that it is legitimate. Electronic visual surveillance of private places is not presently addressed by Federal laws. The Department of Justice has developed policy guidelines on the use of electronic visual surveillance in private places. These guidelines are regarded as requirements for Department of Justice bureaus (FBI, INS, and DEA) and advisory for other Federal investigatory agencies (Bureau of Alcohol, Tobacco and Firearms and Customs). Electronic visual surveillance of private places where one party has consented to the surveillance, even if that party is an undercover agent or informer, is assumed to be legitimate. The Supreme Court has not ruled on the many questions that are raised by using electronic visual surveillance. For example, if Government agents wish to observe private behavior with the assistance of video cameras or closed-circuit TV, must they get a court order as they would for the use of electronic eavesdropping equipment? Can a court, without specific statutory authority, give authorization for new types of searches or does this overstep the legitimate boundaries of judicial policymaking?

No one has accurate data on the extent of the use of visual surveillance, but there is general agreement inside and outside the investigative community that it is increasing. The Department of Justice has indicated that it has used electronic visual surveillance 18 times in the past year for investigative purposes. Other Federal agencies, such as Treasury and Defense, use video surveillance routinely to monitor the traffic at ports of entry or at buildings containing sensitive materials.

The ease with which video surveillance of private places can be used is in dispute. Some argue that the installation and changing of film make its use prohibitive unless there is easy access to the building or room on a regular basis. For example, video surveillance was used successfully in monitoring the activities of the FALN group in Chicago,[12] but the group met in a "safe house" and thus it was easy for law enforcement agents to gain access. Others argue that the miniaturization of cameras and the use of film that is triggered by activity make it easy to install and maintain video equipment. In support, they cite numerous technological developments and an R&D trend that indicates cameras and film will become more attractive for investigative purposes.

Electronic visual surveillance of private places is most often used when one party consents to the surveillance and can either install and monitor the camera or make it possible for others to do so. Under this circumstance, no Title III warrant or judicial intervention is necessary. However, such enhancement of what an undercover agent or informer can witness and testify to may be significantly more intrusive than an agent acting alone, and on that basis might be required to have some form of judicial authorization.

Background

Before analyzing policy issues and policy options, a review of electronic visual surveillance developments will be presented to provide a context for the policy discussion.

The early literature on modern surveillance techniques warned of the great potential offered by hidden television and video cameras.[13] In the 1960s, this was viewed as a threat rather than a reality because the size and sophistication of cameras made it difficult to install, conceal, and maintain them for surveillance purposes. A number of developments have eliminated such problems.[14]

Miniature television cameras equipped with a "charge-coupled device" rather than the traditional bulky television tubes are widely available at reasonable prices. Closed-circuit cameras also make use of this technology and thus can be easily installed. Technological advances have refined the sensor in the charge-coupled device and have made it even smaller and more powerful. It is predicted that miniature cameras will soon be on the market. These cameras could be concealed in anything from a briefcase, to a lamp, to a plant. It would thus be easy for an agent who has even brief access to an area under surveillance to install a miniature camera, leave, and return later to retrieve the film.

Fiber optics also permits the concealment of small cameras with the lens located at the surveillance site and the camera located at a distance. This is possible because of a "light pipe," a bundle of thin, transparent fibers, which conducts light and visual images from a lens to a camera. With these devices, an agent need only enter the premises once, to install the lens; film changing and retrieval can be done at a distance.

Low light level television technology makes it possible to see in the dark. Such devices have been used in several cities to detect street crime. Infrared television cameras also make it possible to see in the dark by detecting infrared radiation and converting it to electrical images. The systems can then produce a detailed black and white picture.

The major advance in the area of visual technology in the 1980s is the development of machine vision systems. Such systems combine video and computer technologies to allow computerized analysis of what is being captured on the camera. Both the computer hardware, which allows the system to rapidly scan and pick up the coordinates that define the outline of images,[15] and the software, which is derived from artificial intelligence research and enables images to be scanned in relation to preprogrammed patterns,[16] are important to the effectiveness of machine vision systems. Such systems have been used primarily in industry to perform a number of labor-intensive inspection tasks, including identifying shapes, measuring distances, gauging sizes, determining orientation, quantifying motion, and detecting surface shading.[17]

Although the major market for machine vision systems is thought to be factories, there are other areas in which labor-intensive analysis of films could be done by these systems.[18] One is in defense for verification of treaties or evaluation of reconnaissance films from satellites.[19] Another is in the investigative area where films that are captured through electronic visual surveillance are then analyzed by machine vision systems to differentiate the segments of the film that are relevant to an investigation from those that are not. Use of machine vision systems would drastically reduce what is presently a very labor-intensive part of electronic visual surveillance, and thus might make it more attractive.

Findings and Policy Implications
1. OTA found that electronic visual surveillance is not currently cover - ed by Title III of the Omnibus Crime Control and Safe Streets Act. The U. S. Department of Justice voluntarily complies with some Title III provisions. Some judges have asked for congressional clarification.

The courts have upheld the use of video surveillance for law enforcement purposes in a number of cases.

In 1981, the Court of Appeals of New York, in People v. Teicher, 439 N.Y.S. 2d 846, upheld the use of video surveillance in a case where a dentist was charged with sexually abusing his patients. The judge ruled that the warrant authorizing video surveillance was valid because probable cause was clearly established by the affidavit, the warrant described the place to be searched and things to be seized, the warrant explicitly provided that surveillance be conducted in such a way as to minimize coverage of activities not related to specified crimes, and the warrant gave evidence that there were no less intrusive means for obtaining needed evidence.

In December 1984, the Seventh Circuit Court of Appeals handed down the major decision to date on the question of video surveillance, United States v. Torres. At issue was the FBI's video surveillance of the Puerto Rican nationalist group FALN for more than 130 hours over 6 months. The Seventh Circuit, in an opinion authored by Judge Richard Posner, held that the courts could authorize electronic video surveillance if they followed the requirements of the fourth amendment's warrant clause, i.e., "no warrants shall issue, but upon probable cause, supported by Oath or affirmation, and particularly describing the place to be searched, and the persons or things to be seized." In this case, the Government asked for the warrants in conjunction with its application for Title III eavesdropping warrants and followed the Title III requirements. The Court held that:

A warrant for video surveillance that complies with those provisions that Congress put into Title III in order to implement the fourth amendment ought to satisfy the fourth amendment's requirement of particularity as applied to such surveillance.[20]

The court went on to state that it did not suggest that compliance with Title III was necessarily required, but said that "we would think it a very good thing if Congress responded to the issues discussed in this opinion by amending Title III to bring television surveillance within its scope."[21] It is important to note that Judge Posner did not include all of the Title III requirements, i.e., the exclusionary rule, the limitations on which Federal officials could make an application, limits on the severity of the crimes that could be involved, and limits on State and local use.[22]

The Department of Justice policy is to require a warrant analogous to a Title III warrant for electronic visual surveillance that is not in a public place or that is conducted in a nonconsensual situation. The policy is the result of a desire to have evidence as clean as possible, and the view that it is better to get a warrant "just in case" rather than have a judge rule the results of electronic visual surveillance inadmissible at a later date. The Department of the Treasury reports that it follows the Department of Justice guidelines for use of electronic visual surveillance.[23]

Although the present Department of Justice guidelines require a warrant analogous to a Title III warrant for electronic visual surveillance, the Attorney General has delegated the authority to authorize television surveillance to a responsible official within the Criminal Division who may authorize the surveillance if he or she:

. . . concludes that the proposed surveillance would not intrude on the subject's justifiable expectation of privacy . . . If such official concludes that the surveillance would infringe on the subject's justifiable expectations of privacy, he shall initiate proceedings to obtain a judicial warrant.[24]

In the case of electronic visual surveillance of public places or places to which the public has unrestricted access, the head of each Department of Justice investigative division has responsibility for issuing guidelines for that division.

In 1984, Representative Robert Kastenmeier introduced the Electronic Surveillance Act of 1984 which, in part, would bring video surveillance under the Title III warrant requirements. In this bill, video surveillance is defined as "the recording of visual images of individuals by television, film, videotape, or other similar method, in a location not open to the general public and without the consent of that individual."[25] In September 1985, Congressman Kastenmeier introduced a separate bill, the Video Surveillance Act of 1985 that deals exclusively with video surveillance.[26] Other electronic surveillance activities are covered in the Electronic Communications Privacy Act of 1985, also introduced in September 1985.[27]

2. Electronic visual surveillance appears to pose a substantial threat to civil liberties, especially if conducted in private places and with audio (as well

as video). The governmental interest varies depending on the stage of the investigation in which electronic visual surveillance is to be used.

Before examining specific policy options, it is useful to examine the policy implications of electronic visual surveillance in light of the principles that appear to have guided surveillance policy to date. Based on the dimensions introduced in chapter 2, electronic visual surveillance, especially when used in conjunction with audio surveillance, poses a great, if not the greatest, threat to civil liberties.

The nature of the information that is gained with electronic visual surveillance is very personal. The information is quite complete, including the content of movements, facial expressions, and nonverbal communications, as well as conversations if audio is used.

Video surveillance can be usefully applied to surveillance of any area. The present controversy is focused on the surveillance of private places. Electronic video surveillance is capable of penetrating the most private places, where curtains are drawn and doors are locked, without leaving a trail.

The scope of a video or closed circuit TV camera is broad. All persons and activities that come in camera range will be filmed. Depending on the area under surveillance, it is likely that a number of people unrelated to the investigation will be covered. In this case, the more private the area to be monitored, the narrower the scope of the surveillance. The scope of the surveillance might be minimized by the use of machine vision systems that could scan the film for the targets of the surveillance or for certain types of motions.

Given the miniaturization of video and TV cameras, it is very difficult for an individual to detect electronic visual surveillance. Again, one would have to suspect that he or she was the target of an investigation and would have to look carefully to locate a hidden camera. Additionally, the present policy of allowing electronic visual surveillance without a warrant if one party has consented raises very serious questions about how the concept of assumption of risk is applied.

The historical analogy would be to undercover agents, although the use of video surveillance is much more powerful in terms of detail and unimpeachability. While the testimony of an agent or informer could always be questioned and needs corroboration, the film would probably be accepted. It is always possible, however, to edit a film to make it more incriminating and some editing may not be detectable.

The governmental interest in using electronic visual surveillance will vary. Video surveillance would be useful in investigations for any purpose, but, given the threats to civil liberties involved, would probably be difficult to justify for investigations to ensure the proper administration of Government programs and investigations of minor felonies and misdemeanors. Given the difficulties of installing and monitoring and the need to have certain basic information, electronic visual surveillance will most likely be used when there is a high level of suspicion. As it is such an intrusive form of surveillance, it would be very hard to justify its use during the early stages of an investigation. Although electronic visual surveillance is more effective and less costly than less technologically sophisticated techniques, the threat to civil liberties involved would seem to require that other techniques be tried first.

The present rules on the accountability of authorities using electronic visual surveillance are not clear. The Department of Justice guidelines appear to leave officials in the Criminal Division some discretion, in that they have to determine if the surveillance would violate an expectation of privacy and hence require a court warrant. Also unclear is the definition of a public place.

3. OTA identified five policy options for addressing electronic visual surveillance—ranging from prohibiting such surveillance as unconstitutional to doing nothing. In formulating policy, the issues of consensual v. nonconsensual visual surveillance and surveillance of public v. private places need to be given careful consideration.

The five policy options are discussed below.

Option A. - The first option is to legislate a prohibition on electronic visual surveillance because Congress considers it an unreasonable search under the fourth amendment. The basis for choosing this policy option might be the assumption or belief that electronic visual surveillance is an inherently unacceptable form of surveillance because: 1) the information it secures is so complete and specific; 2) it can pick up the most private activities in heretofore private places; 3) it captures the activities of people not under investigation; 4) it captures the unrelated activities of the targets; 5) it is very difficult to detect, and 6) its preelectronic analogy, i.e., undercover agents, is also regarded as intrusive.

Option B. - The second policy option is to regard electronic visual surveillance as more intrusive and invasive than eavesdropping, but not unacceptable in all circumstances. The legislative option then would be to subject electronic visual surveillance to higher authorization standards than exist for bugging and wiretapping under Title III. This option would be especially applicable in four areas. First, new minimization standards or a new concept to restrict the scope of the invasion, in terms of both place and content, might be developed. Additionally, the list of crimes and circumstances for which electronic visual surveillance is considered appropriate might be developed independently of the list for wiretapping. Third, the use of video surveillance might be restricted to only very sensitive and important types of investigations. Lastly, documented exhaustion of other techniques might be required.

Option C. - The third policy option would be to treat electronic visual surveillance in the same way as electronic audio surveillance. The advantages of this are that visual surveillance is generally conducted with audio surveillance so that only one warrant would be necessary, and that Title III is a known and tested procedure. The disadvantage is that the use of both audio and video may pose a greater risk to civil liberties.

Option D. - The fourth policy option would be to apply a lower standard to electronic visual surveillance than to eavesdropping. This would be hard to justify, given the principles that appear to govern the use of surveillance. It could only be justified if video surveillance were being used alone.

Option E. - The fifth option would be to do nothing. The disadvantage of this option is that both Judge Posner's request to Congress to deal with the issue and the questions raised with the existing Department of Justice guidelines would remain unanswered in terms of legislated policy.

Notes

[12]See United States v Torres (No. 84-1077, decided Dec. 19. 1984).

[13]See: Alan Westin, Privacy and Freedom (New York Atheneum, 1967) and Samuel Dash, R. F. Schwartz and Robert Knowlton, The Eavesdroppers (New York: Da Capo, 1959).

[14]For a review of the technologies available in the mid-1970s see: David P. Hodges "Electronic Visual Surveillance and the Fourth Amendment: The Arrival of Big Brother?" 3 Hastings Constitutional Law Quarterly 261 (1976).

[15]Marsha Johnston Fisher, "Micro-Based 'Roving' Eye Sifts Motion," MIS Week, Nov. 14, 1984, pp. 1, 42.

[16]Paul Kinnuean, "Machines That See," Technology, April 1983, pp. 30-36.

[17]John Meyer, "Vision Systems: Technology of the Future at Work Today," Computerworld, May 27, 1985, p. 13.

[18]See: Edith Myhers, "Machines That See," Datamation, Nov. 1983, pp. 90-103, and "Machine Vision Merges with Process Imaging," Electronic Market Trends, February 1985, pp. 17-19.

[19]David Hafemeister, "Advances in Verification Technology," Bulletin of the Atomic Scientists, January 1985, pp. 35-40.

[20]United States v. Torres, No. 84-1077, p. 17 (7th Cir., Dec. 19, 1984)

[21]Id. at 19.

[22]Remarks made at OTA Workshop, May 17, 1985.

[23]Remarks made at OTA Workshop, May 17, 1985.

[24]Department of Justice, Order No. 985-82, "Delegation of Authority to Authorize Television Surveillance."

[25]H. R. 6343, sec. 8, 3117, c.

[26]See H. R. 3455, Video Surveillance Act of 1985 and U. S. Congress, House of Representatives, Congressional Record, Extension of Remarks, Sept. 30, 1985, p. E-4269.

[27]See H. R. 3378 and S. 1667, Electronic Communications Privacy Act of 1985; U. S. Congress, House of Representatives, Congressional Record, Extension of Remarks, Sept. 19, 1985, p. E-4128 and U. S. Congress, Senate, Congressional Record, Sept. 29, 2985, p. S-11795.

P11-2. The scanning technique of television is very similar to that used in personal verification systems—technology to test whether an individual is who he or she claims to be. The following article "Biometric Security: What You Are, Not What You Know," by Sam Diamond, describes the current status of personal verification. (Reprinted, with permission, from *High Technology Business* magazine, February 1987. Copyright 1987 by Infotechnology Publishing Corporation.)

Construct a chart of the various systems described, arranged in ascending price, and indicate the claimed percentage of false positives and false negatives. Discuss whether the data verify the argument that "you get what you pay for."

Security-conscious corporations often find their security devices seriously lacking. Keys can be duplicated, identification badges can be forged, and personal identification numbers and combinations can be stolen. To overcome these problems, many companies are turning to "biometric" security systems that identify a person by his or her voice, fingerprint, hand geometry, or retinal pattern.

For example, La Reserve (White Plains, NY), a luxury hotel, recently replaced the lock and key on the hotel's wine room with a fingerprint reader. "The key that gave access to $10,000-$20,000 worth of wines and champagne could be found anyplace at any given time," explains Margaret Schneider, the hotel's vice-president. "So for a rather low investment—about $2000—we went with biometrics."

The system La Reserve installed was th : Ridge Reader from Fingermatrix (North White Plains, NY), which identifies individuals by scanning a person's fingerprint and using proprietary algorithms to compare the configurations of specific points along the print's ridges with those stored in the system for that person. The only other major manufacturer of fingerprint systems is Identix (Palo Alto, CA).

The yardstick by which all biometric systems are measured is the error rate. False negatives, called type I errors, are what prevent authorized users from gaining access because of an inaccurate reading of the biometric parameter. False positives, or type II errors, occur when an impostor gains access. It is generally not possible to have both the lowest type I and type II errors—they must be balanced. For example, if a system is designed to guard stringently against access by anyone whose biometric data fails to match perfectly with the stored system data, it will also reject a greater percentage of authorized people based on slight variations in their data.

Unfortunately, vendors as yet have no standards to ensure that they are using the same criteria to obtain accurate error-rate measurements. In part to generate such standards, a group of biometric system companies formed an industry trade association late last year. Located in Washington, DC, the International Biometrics Association is developing standards in such areas as error-rate measurements and system interfaces, and is also disseminating information about the industry.

In the fingerprint system segment, the lowest type I error rate yet achieved is one in a thousand; type II errors have been reported as low as one in a million. While this appears to be fairly good protection, it may not be adequate for extreme security applications. In these situations, retinal scans are often considered. Like fingerprint patterns, the patterns of blood vessels at the back of the eye differ among individuals. The error rates for false positives and negatives in retinal scans, however, are both less than one in a million. EyeDentify (Beaverton, OR) attributes the difference to the fact that fingerprint readers can be affected by such factors as grease and abrasions, whereas the eye's condition remains essentially constant.

EyeDentify holds a patent on retinal scan systems used for identification, and is currently the only manufacturer of such a system, which sells for $11,000. A marketing obstacle the company has had to face is that some potential users are reluctant to place their eye in the path of what they fear to be a laser. In fact, the scanning light source is a harmless infrared light emitting diode. The system measures the reflected light to determine the pattern of the retinal vasculature.

Some users who do not require the most extreme security are opting for hand-geometry, voice-identification, or signature-verification systems. An advantage of these systems is that they neither carry the stigma of being fingerprinted nor generate the fear of eye damage.

Hand-geometry readers make identifications on the basis of finger length, palm dimensions, and skin translucency, with specific techniques varying among manufacturers. One of the most popular systems, the Identimat sold by Stellar Systems (Santa Clara, CA), reportedly achieves false positive and negative rates of 2.5 percent; the price is $8745 for a complete system.

The Stellar Systems error rate and price are both higher than other biometric systems, but Ben Miller, publisher of Personal Identification News (Washington, DC), an industry newsletter, notes that the company has been in business for more than 10 years and thus has a fairly high profile compared to some newer firms in the market. Nevertheless, he says competitors are entering the hand-geometry field, "and they are starting to pull away some of Stellar's business by offering better error rates and lower prices." Two such firms are Recognition Systems (San Jose, CA), which markets a system called ID-3D and Mitsubishi Electric Sales America (Cypress, CA), with its Palm Recognition System. Esselte Tech (Solna, Sweden) also plans to introduce a system in the U.S.

One reason for the increased competition is the perception among vendors that hand-geometry readers will be easily accepted by users. Because people are used to shaking hands and putting their palms on door knobs, they will not object to placing their hands in a reader.

Another relatively new biometric technology - voice identification, which requires a user to speak a few words into a telephone-like instrument - is also receiving increasing attention because of its perceived user acceptance. Currently, only two companies—Ecco Industries (Danvers, MA) and Voxtron Systems (New Braunfels, TX)—sell voice identifiers commercially. System costs average about $2500 per protected door, error rates are comparable to fingerprint readers.

Each vendor uses its own proprietary techniques to extract voice features for speaker identification. Ecco bases its system on a method called linear predictive coding (LPC) which attempts to characterize each speaker's vocal tract mathematically. "LPC is very speaker-dependent," says Ecco president Heath Paley "because the geometry that produces a certain word for one person is not going to be the same as for another person." Voxtron, on the other hand, employs a technique that uses filter banks to extract and compare the frequency and pitch of each utterance. Either method can easily identify impostors, claims Paley, because people attempting to impersonate others' voices rely largely on duplicating the phrasing and intonation, which would be virtually ignored by the LPC and filter-bank algorithms.

The National Cooperative Bank (Washington, DC) was the first commercial user of Ecco's VoiceKey Access Control Security System. Dennis Opicka, the bank's corporate vice-president, believed that the card readers the bank previously used for controlling access to offices were not providing adequate security, and that the voice-identification system would be readily accepted. "It looks like a telephone, is not intimidating, and is simple to use," he says. An added advantage for the bank was the system's ability—common to many biometric systems—to maintain audit trails of all users automatically without their having to enter personal identification numbers.

The only other biometric systems now available commercially are those that identify people by their signature dynamics—the speed with which they sign their name, the pressure used, and how they dot their i's and cross their t's—which are extremely difficult to forge. Their primary application so far is at point-of-sale terminals where customers are already used to signing their names. Manufacturers include Confirma (Menlo Park, CA), Thomas De La Rue (Herndon, VA), IBM's Information Products Division (Charlotte, NC), Inforite (San Mateo, CA), Signify (Baltimore, MD), Ion Track Instruments (Burlington, MA), and TITN (Grenoble, France). Error rates range from below 1 percent for type I to over 3 percent for type II. This rate is far from negligible, but it is good enough to dissuade most thieves from trying to subvert the systems which are almost always located in public places. System prices are generally below $1000.

Even though the range of technologies is wide and growing wider, "all the biometric systems will find their own niches and will be developed to the point of filling the requirements of that niche," says Russ Maxwell, a staff member at Sandia National Laboratories (Albuquerque, NM), who runs a biometric systems evaluation program for the Department of Energy.

This process is already under way. Manufacturers of signature dynamics identification systems are targeting their products toward retail applications, while vendors of fingerprint readers are focusing on law enforcement. The primary area for retinal scanners seems to be the high security government market and voice identification is penetrating office environments where telephone communication is a way of life.

Even as these systems become refined and drop significantly in cost, new technologies can be expected to surface as developers work to find the most accurate or user-friendly methods for specific applications. Already an identification system based on wrist vein patterns is being developed at the British Technology Group (London, England). Typing rhythms are being explored at Electronic Signature Lock (San Francisco), while hand topography is under study at Onset Venture, Palo Alto, CA. Still in the research stages at Batelle Columbus Laboratories (Columbus, OH) is a method that identifies the unique lipids and fatty acids found in skin oils extracted from forehead sweat.

Increased demand for biometric systems will develop as the needs for security intensify with growing dependence on the computer. Even now, vendors report that computer facilities account for approximately 50 percent of their sales. For example, On-Line Software International (Fort Lee, NJ) recently announced that its Omniguard security package designed to protect IBM mainframe environments now supports Signify's Sign/On signature verification system. Other vendors are proposing systems that will limit access to personal computers.

In 1986, the U. S. market value of all biometric systems sold for computer security applications was projected to reach $4.4 million, according to a market survey prepared by the Business Communications Company (Stamford, CT). By 1991 the report predicts the total value of all biometric systems sold for this purpose alone should increase to at least $24.2 million for a total annualized average growth rate of 41 percent.

Several other application areas could also become important markets for biometric technology. Miller of Personal Identification News predicts that biometrics will complement another emerging technology, smart cards. These microprocessor-equipped credit cards house personal financial and identification data. In the wrong hands they could result in the perpetration of much more serious fraud than is possible with conventional credit cards. To guard against such misuse, Miller suggests smart cards will have to use biometric checking to verify the user's identity. Thanks to its on-board memory, the card itself can contain the user's biometric "print" which could be loaded into a security system for comparison with a reading taken directly from the user.

P11-3 The various picture structures proposed have had the following numbers of lines per picture:

First CBS color	343	$(7 \times 7 \times 7)$
Early British	405	$(3 \times 3 \times 3 \times 3 \times 5)$
NTSC	525	$(3 \times 5 \times 5 \times 7)$
European	625	$(5 \times 5 \times 5 \times 5)$
French	819	$(3 \times 3 \times 7 \times 13)$
HDT	1125	$(3 \times 3 \times 5 \times 5 \times 5)$

These numbers are remarkable in that each is the product of small prime numbers as shown to the right above. This is certainly more than coincidence. Explain.

P11-4 When we mix yellow and blue paint, what possible colors result? We can think in terms of what colors each material absorbs.

Yellow absorbs blue and violet.

Blue absorbs yellow, orange, and red.

Consequently, the green is not absorbed by either, so the mix will have a strongly green tint.

When we paint a color disc ⅓ yellow and ⅔ blue, the rotating disk looks violet.

Explain both of these situations in terms of the chromaticity diagram.

P11-5 Geostationary satellites over the equator at an altitude of 22,500 miles stay in a fixed location with respect to points on the surface of the Earth. Hence such a satellite can be used as a relay station, receiving a signal from an originating Earth station, amplifying the signal, and transmitting it to an Earth receiving station.

Almost half of the capacity of such communication satellites is now used for voice or telephone communication; most of the rest is used for TV relay and distribution. The prediction is that in the future most of the capacity will be used for TV and for data transmission (between computers), and that the voice transmission will switch to cables and fiber optics (both in the ground and underwater).

What is the principal disadvantage of communication satellites in voice transmission? (Note that two people conversing on the phone seem to want to be able to easily interrupt one another.)

P11-6 Telephone usage is very high in the United States, Canada, and Sweden. Telephone service plays a much less important part in the lives of people in other countries. Why these three countries?

As we try to think of an answer, we uncover the following facts:

1. These are the only countries where most of the research, manufacturing, and operation have all been the responsibility of a single telephone system.

2. These three countries do not have the language problems of Switzerland and The Netherlands (teletypewriter service is much more common in business in Europe than in the U.S.).

3. In the U.S. and Canada, the telephone system is run by private companies. When national government runs the system, the budget allocations depend on national priorities and compete against health, education, defense, etc.

With these facts and others in hand, describe briefly the reasons for the high usage in the three countries. Would the same situation hold for other telecommunication technologies (for example, radio and television)?

P11-7 The International Telecommunication Union (ITU), based in Geneva, is the organization responsible for setting standards and establishing policies on radio and television when the technology reaches beyond national boundaries.

May 17, 1865, was the date of the first international agreement on telegraph standards—particularly important in Europe to ensure that telegraph wires could cross borders. Before this agreement, telegrams had to be delivered by hand in printed form across national borders. The ITU, which includes several permanent organizations, including the CCIR, or International Radio Consultative Committee, which is now setting standards for high-definition television.

There are three quite different approaches to HDTV: the Japanese, the American, the European. Why is there a strong unwillingness among Americans and Europeans to accept the Japanese technology, which is in operation?

P11-8 The following article, the text of a talk given by Dr. Hans Mark on March 7, 1979, appeared in *The Bridge*, the journal of the National Academy of Engineering. After reading the article, describe briefly how naval navigation required the development of new technology in the eighteenth century.

It is very interesting for me to see the enormous vitality of our industry and the continuing ability to do new things. This is at the very heart of our national strength.

As a charter member of the "military-industrial complex" I have been on the defensive lately. In spite of all our past achievements, we are held in low esteem today by the public at large, especially by the press and some of the other pubic information media. Most people have forgotten the time and the circumstances that caused President Franklin Roosevelt to refer to us as the "Arsenal of Democracy."

In any event, there is no doubt in my mind that the government-industry structure we have built is still vitally important in establishing a strong basis for our national defense. Rather than bemoan our current low estate, I thought I would try to see how the so-called "military-industrial complex" originated. Maybe there is something in our history and in the traditions that have been established that might be useful in understanding ourselves and how we operate. This, in turn, could be useful in explaining what we do to the public at large. In looking back, what I have found is really quite fascinating and hopefully is of more than passing interest.

Perhaps the most important thing I discovered in my sojourn into the past is that our traditions go back almost 300 years. What was started at that time was the combination that persists to this day - the arrangement by which the government in collaboration with the scientific community and industry creates new technology that is applied to the national defense.

Furthermore, the enterprise which drove the first organization of the "complex" is a most appropriate one for this group, since it was nothing other than the mastery of the art and science of navigation at sea.

In order to see how things happened we need to go back to England in the middle of the 17th Century. When Oliver Cromwell was finally defeated, the monarchy was restored and Charles II was crowned King of England in 1661. This remarkable monarch presided over a "mini-renaissance" in which a number of things were initiated that had very profound, long-term effects.

First and foremost in 1662, Charles II chartered the first of the modern scientific academies, the Royal Society. It is not clear whether he actually had the modern structure in mind since the membership at that time consisted mostly of some intellectuals who happened to be the King's friends as well. Nevertheless, even if Charles did not have the specific model of our current national scientific academies in mind, there is no question that the members saw to it that the Royal Society eventually evolved into a modern academy of science. It was in this sense that, for the first time, they secured some organized influence within the government for the members of the scientific community.

A second important step that Charles took was to establish a Royal Astronomical Observatory in 1675. The creation of such an institution was not a new thing since many other monarchs had such establishments already. What was new and different about the newly established Royal Observatory at

Greenwich is that it developed the first government operated "laboratory" in which new technology was nurtured and then applied to the service of the state.

The first Director of the Observatory (or Astronomer Royal as he was called) was John Flamsteed, a wealthy amateur astronomer who was also a personal friend of the King. In fact, Flamsteed paid for most of the equipment in the Observatory when it was first installed.

The Observatory was built at Greenwich, about 20 miles west of London on a hill overlooking the Thames River. The buildings were designed by Sir Christopher Wren, the same architect who built St. Paul's Cathedral, and they still stand today.

Wren, by the way, was also a member of the Royal Society, and it was perhaps through this connection that the famous power struggle between Flamsteed and the Society developed.

The major issue in this battle was very simple. Who gets the results of the observations made by the Astronomer Royal and how are they used? Flamsteed believed that astronomy must be practiced for its own sake and that he owed nothing to his sponsors. On the other hand, it was already perceived by a few far-sighted naval officers that the astronomical results, especially the ephemeris related measurements, would be exceedingly important in establishing once and for all Britain's supremacy at sea. Thus, the struggle was not over a trivial question of scientific precedence but over something that vitally affected the nation's power.

As you will see, some very weighty personalities were involved in this struggle which illustrates its importance better than anything else. (A full account of the story is given in an article by P. S. Laurie in the April 1971 issue of the Royal Astronomical Society Quarterly Bulletin entitled "The Board of Visitors of the Royal Observatory.")

Matters came to a head in 1710, by which time Queen Anne had succeeded to the throne. Several members of the Queen's government felt that the Observatory would have to be put at the disposal of the national interest and they therefore resolved to get control of the institution. They chose the Royal Society as the instrument for this move since that was the one place within the Court where sufficient technical expertise existed for the job. Accordingly, the Queen's Secretary of State and privy Councilor Henry St. James (later Viscount Bolingbroke) wrote the following letter to the President of the Royal Society:

"To our trusty and well-beloved, the President of the Royal Society for the time being:

"Anne R.

"Trusty and well-beloved, we greet you well. Whereas we have been given to understand that it would contribute very much to the improvement of astronomy and navigation, if we should appoint constant Visitors to our Royal Observatory at Greenwich with sufficient powers for the due execution of that trust, we have therefore thought fit in consideration of the great learning experience and other necessary qualifications of our Royal Society to constitute and appoint you, the President, and in your absence, the Vice President of our Royal Society, for the time being, together with such others as the council of our said Royal Society shall think fit to join with you to be constant visitors of our said Royal Observatory at Greenwich: Authorizing and requiring you to demand of our Astronomer and Keeper of our said Observatory, to make such astronomical observations as you in your judgement shall think proper. And that you do survey and inspect our instruments in our said Observatory as often as you shall find any of them defective, that you do inform the principal officers of our Ordnance thereof that so the said instrument may either be exchanged or repaired.

"And so we bid you farewell

"Given at our Court at St. James the 12th day of December 1710, in the ninth year of our reign."

By Her Majesty's Command

H. St. John.

This letter is exceedingly important. I think a case can be made that it lays the groundwork for the establishment of what we today call the "military-industrial complex." On the surface, it does not seem to look that way, but in effect, that is what it started. The letter charters the President of the Royal Society to exercise supervision over the work at the Royal Observatory.

At the same time, it asks him to look at the quality of the equipment and at the quality of the observations being made with it.

Finally and perhaps most important, it lodges the responsibility for the maintenance and improvement of the equipment with the Master of Ordnance, who was a military official (the closest modern equivalent of the Master of Ordnance is today's Under Secretary of Defense for Research and Engineering).

Most significant of all was the fact that the President of the Royal Society, to whom this letter was addressed, was none other than Sir Isaac Newton. Newton had been elected to the position in 1703 and was well established by 1710. He was ready for the job of taking over the Observatory by the time he received the instructions to do so. As a matter of fact, there were people in the Society who were quite eager to take the step that was now being proposed in order to expand their own influence at Court.

A lengthy and rather amusing bureaucratic battle followed in which Newton proved to be very adroit at bending others to his will. As soon as the Board of Visitors of the Observatory was established, Newton wrote a letter to Flamsteed which went as follows:

"Sir, by virtue of Her Majesty's letter to us, directed, dated the 12th day of December 1710, we do hereby order and direct you to observe the eclipses of the sun and the moon this year and particularly of the sun on July 4th ensuing and we desire you to send such of your observations to us at our meeting of the House of the Royal Society in Crane Court on Fleet Street.

Signed: I. Newton."

This is a blunt and tough instruction which was very clear indeed. Although Flamsteed did not like to be subordinated to the government in this manner, he finally acceded and did send a published version of his observations.

An amusing piece of evidence about his bitterness at the situation survives in a letter he wrote to a friend where, in a fit of scientific jealousy, he disparages the new edition of Newton's Principia Mathematica, "I think his new Principia worse that the old, except in the moon and here he is fuller, but not so positive, and seems to refer much to be determined by observations. The book is really worth seven shillings or eight shillings. It costs four shillings fourpence a piece, printing and paper. Dr. Bentley puts the price at 18 shillings and so much mine cost me." On second thought, maybe he was just angry about the high cost of textbooks!

Flamsteed died in 1719 and the new Astronomer Royal, Sir Edmund Halley, was a member of the Royal Society and was indeed a member of the Board of Visitors that had been used to take over the Observatory for the government.

Thus, the first step in the process of creating the "military-industrial complex" was accomplished, in that advanced technical expertise was put immediately at the disposal of the government. (This is what we would today call "in-house competence.") Furthermore, the institution in which this "competence" resided was funded by the military through the Master of Ordnance. It now remains to explain how the second component, namely industry, was brought in.

As you all know, the most important navigational problem in those days was to develop a method to determine longitude at sea. In order to encourage people to find a solution to this problem, the Government established a special committee called the "Board of Longitude" with a very prestigious and competent membership. The Chairman was the Lord High Admiral, roughly the equivalent of our Chief of Naval Operations today, and among others in the membership were the President of the Royal Society, the Astronomer Royal, the Professors of Mathematics at the Universities of Oxford, Cambridge and London, and a number of serving military officers. This Committee is not unlike, although somewhat more prestigious, a committee that might be chartered today by something like the Defense Science Board to look at important technical problems with great military implications.

A number of ways had been proposed to determine longitude. There were, at the time, several well known astronomical methods for performing the job, but these could not be applied on shipboard where accurate observations from the heaving deck of a sailing ship was impossible. Furthermore, the vagaries of the weather made it difficult to observe the sky on many nights and therefore astronomical methods generally were rejected.

In his statement to the Board in 1714, Newton said, "That for true determining of the longitude at sea, there have been several projects. True in the theory, difficult to execute." He then went on to mention the use of the eclipses of Jupiter's satellites and the observation of the so-called lunars, that is, the relative motion of the moon with respect to the stellar background, but with regard to all of these, he said that they simply would not work. He then went on to discuss some of the more promising methods, and among other things, he said: "One is by a watch to keep time exactly, but by reason of the motion of the ship, the variation of heat and cold, wet and dry, and the difference of gravity in different latitudes, such a watch hath not yet been made."

What Newton was talking about was, of course, the marine chronometer. You all know how the idea works. Longitude is simply determined by comparing the time of a chronometer set to local time on the Greenwich meridian to the local noon at the position of the ship. Since the time difference can be related to a distance difference depending on latitude, the longitude can be determined. The whole trick is to make a clock which keeps time accurately enough to do the job and, of course, Newton recognized this had not yet been achieved. The Board of Longitude then decided to offer a prize for the development of Newton's "watch."

What they did in modern terns was to issue a Request for Proposal. There was even a performance incentive in the RFP which read as follows: "The winner shall receive 10,000 pounds for any method capable of determining a ship's longitude within one degree; 15,000 it if be determined within 40 minutes of arc, and 20,000 if it be determined within half a degree." These were formidable technical requirements for those days. Since ocean voyages were lengthy, the clock had to be accurate to better than one second per day.

The clock-making industry was invited to make proposals and under certain circumstances grants would be issued to the proposers in order to support the work. The British clock-making industry was therefore mobilized to help solve this exceedingly important national problem.

Furthermore, the Royal Observatory, which was now a going concern under government control, would be used for evaluating the results of the competition. This is simply another way of saying that the government had some "in-house competence" for determining whether the contractor knew what he was doing.

I am sure you have all heard these words before and what is interesting here, of course, is that all of what I have said took place in the years between 1710 and 1714.

In developing the chronometer, the Board disbursed over 100,000 pounds in the period from 1714 to the end of the century. This is actually a fairly large amount of money when you remember that a line-of-battle ship, fully equipped, in those days cost approximately 20,000 pounds. I suppose the lesson to be learned from this figure is that research and development is not cheap now and never has been cheap.

The board also was deluged by the usual share of screwball proposals. There was a letter from someone who claimed that: "A Mr. Robert Davidson hath invented a machine that keeps perpetually going and may be completed to work the largest mills or keep a clock constantly going." I am sure that the Board had to hire a staff in order to filter out proposals of this kind and so we had also the beginning of the bureaucracy!

As you all know, the man who finally made the first successful marine chronometer and who won the prize was a private entrepreneur from Yorkshire named John Harrison. Harrison spent some 30 years accomplishing this difficult technical task. The essential invention that he produced to solve the problem was the bi-metallic spring which permitted a clock to operate on a constant tension spring independent of temperature. He also worked on better bearings which would keep their friction constant under all conditions of humidity and temperature. In other words, he solved all of the problems to which Newton had alluded in his testimony before the Board of Longitude.

In the meantime, test facilities were established at the Greenwich Observatory to check out the things that were being submitted to the Board. These 18th century environmental test chambers, if you will, were installed and hundreds of clocks were tested before sea trials of the various survivors of these tests were actually made. These environmental test chambers are still at Greenwich and you can go and see them if you visit the Naval Museum at the site.

In 1765 the Board of Longitude finally agreed that John Harrison had won the prize. As you know, it took him another seven years to get the money. Along with inventing the competitive system of procurement, our 18th century friends also had to learn how to deal with protests and proprietary rights and all the other things that characterize our system.

In a very interesting book on the subject, Commander Ruper Gould ("The Marine Chronometer", Holland Press, London 1960) has written: "Faced with the decisive proof (that Harrison's chronometer worked) the board passed a resolution on February 9th, 1765 to the effect that they were unanimously of the opinion that the said time-keeper has kept its time with sufficient correctness without losing its longitude in the voyage from Portsmouth to Barbados beyond the nearest limit required by the Act 12th of Queen Anne (the original Request for Proposal) but even considerably within the same. However, Harrison had not yet explained to the Board the principles on which the chronometer was constructed. They accordingly resolved to give him half the award as soon as other clocks of his making should perform equally well."

Needless to say, Harrison was infuriated by this response since he felt that he had fully complied with the provisions of the original Request for Proposal. In any event, there followed a long and acrimonious dispute as to how the prize money would be paid. The issue in the dispute, as usual, was not whether the equipment worked, but how it worked and whether it precisely fulfilled the specifications. Finally, Harrison washed his hands of the Board of Longitude entirely and took his appeal to the House of Commons.

Amusingly, this is in precise analogy of our protest structure today in which the General Accounting Office, an arm of our "Parliament," has the decisive voice.

In 1772, Harrison finally succeeded in receiving the rest of the money and he died a respected and honored figure in 1776 at the age of 83.

Thus, a pattern of how we do the business of providing new technology for the government was established by the end of the 18th century. Moreover, the longitude problem and its ultimate solution caused the government-industry alliance which has persisted to the present time.

I am telling you this story in the hope that the next time one of you is accosted for belonging to the "military-industrial complex" you can look the accuser straight in the eye and tell him that it all started a long time ago with Sir Isaac Newton!

Chapter 12
Broadcasting and Narrowcasting

A major social and political concern today in the United States is the deteriorating infrastructure of many cities. One element of the infrastructure is the road system—the streets and bridges; another is the mass transit system of subways and buses; another the school buildings and facilities; another the water-supply system. In many older cities, particularly, the financial problems of recent decades have led to extensive delays in repairs and to postponement of the replacement of old structures with modern facilities.

New York is the most populous of America's cities and, and at the same time, one where the population has not been increasing and the levels of education and training have seemed to leave a population increasingly divided into two segments: those qualified for the increasing number of more demanding jobs, and those out of the economic and social mainstream.

The problems are exacerbated by the changes in the nature of jobs in New York City in recent years. The rapid development of communication and transportation technologies has allowed companies in the garment industry to keep their offices in New York but move dress manufacturing to such locations as Haiti, where labor costs are an order of magnitude lower. Insurance companies can move *back-office operations* (the routine processing of claims, premiums, etc.) to any location in the country. New York Telephone routes New York City directory-assistance calls to remote upstate locations where operators are available at lower wages than would be necessary in the city.

As a result of such developments, New York City has become an *information capital*. Two-thirds of both the jobs and the income comes from such activities as these:

financial services, accounting

banking (including offices of 300 foreign banks)

corporate headquarters (over 12 percent of the largest companies)

advertising

publishing

television and other media

management consulting.

In addition, the primary work of most government operations (federal, state, and local) is the processing of information. The importance of New York City as an information center is illustrated by the specific examples in box 12.1; box 12.2 lists a few of the facilities that make up the telecommunications sector of the infrastructure.

Thus, this particular sector of New York's infrastructure is exceptionally alive and healthy. Indeed, the rapid development of telecommunications is creating a very difficult social problem. While the growth of the information industry is critically important to the economic health of the city, the communication facilities encourage companies to move the less-skilled work to remote locations where labor and living costs are much lower. The number of available jobs grows, but the demand for less-skilled workers falls. When these developments are coupled with the changing nature of the family and the increasingly complex environment within which education, health services, and city services are offered, we begin to comprehend the complexity of the problems of the homeless, crime, drug use, and so on.

In this chapter we consider only one facet of this telecommunications infrastructure: the delivery of television programs to the viewing audience. There are two quite different approaches:

Broadcasting. From its antenna, a television station radiates a signal that can be picked up by anyone with a receiver in the region.

Narrowcasting. A television station (or a cable company) sends a signal to specific customers who are connected to the cable system.

12.1 Video Signal

Before we consider TV broadcasting, we need to reconsider the characteristics of the video signal—the signal carrying the picture information. In chapter 11, we saw that the U.S. video signal has the features shown very roughly in figure 12.1.

The synchronizing (synch) pulse tells your home receiver to move back to the upper left corner of the screen for the start of a new picture. In the picture tube, there is then scanning across line 1 (625 pulses, each showing the

New York City has more than 5 million telephones (as many as East Germany and Poland combined) and more word processors than all of Europe.

New York Telephone will soon be serving over 100,000 cellular phones.

New York Telephone runs two circuits around Manhattan: one for 48,000 phone conversations, the other for video.

Six companies offer communication-satellite facilities to supplement private Earth stations. One-fourth of all U.S. overseas phone calls originate in New York.

Cable companies, microwave systems, and *smart buildings* wired with local area networds are growing rapidly.

Box 12.1

A few telecommunications facilities in New York City.

Satellite access

Teleport on Staten Island (Port Authority, Merrill Lynch, City)
17 antennas to access at least 22 satellites
220-km, 24-strand fiber to Newark, Manhattan, etc.

Glenwook NJ: Blairsat Corp. delivers commercials for 104 stations—less than one week to air time

Spring Creek Satellite Station, East New York, Brooklyn (Hughes)

Hauppauge, Long Island—HBO

Vernon Valley, NJ—RCA, PBS; uplinks for probrams of channels 9, 11

Stamford, Conn.—ABC

Empire City Subway Company, Ltd. (subsidiary of NY Telephne since 1891)
11,000 miles (10,000 manholes) underground in Manhattan and Bronx

Rents its ducts from the city, can add conduit as long as no interference with water and sewage

Securities Industry Automation Corporation (SIAC)
Owned by NYSE, AMEX for communication within financial community, underground fiber cable system

Television
Headquarters for three major networks; main switching in NYC

All large advertising firms, production of most TV commercials

Largest cable companies—HBO, Showtime, Cinemax, Movie Channel

Center for 22 cable TV programming services

Seven VHF, two UHF broadcasters

City Uses
Government services	Police
Education	Fire
Off-track betting	Sanitation
Transit information	

Box 12.2

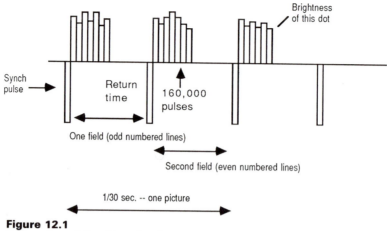

Figure 12.1
Basic nature of the video signal.

brightness of one dot on the screen). The receiver then moves to line 3, then line 5, and so on, until completion of the bottom line—one field, requiring 160,000 pulses.

Actually, within this one field there are other return times and synchronizing pulses as the beam moves from the end of line 1 to the beginning of line 3, and so on, but we omit these to simplify the figure (we certainly do not want to draw 160,000 pulses for each field).

The brightness or luminance information is carried by the size or amplitude of each of the upward pulses in figure 12.1. The larger a pulse, the brighter the corresponding spot on the screen.

Bandwidth Required

The video signal contains about 10 million pulses per second; consequently, each pulse has a duration of $1/10M$ second. The ideal pulse (figure 12.2) is square—rising abruptly to its peak, holding there, then abruptly falling back to zero.

To send such a signal, an extremely large band of frequencies is required. The rapid change represents action in a very short time (much less than $1/10M$ sec), so it requires very high frequencies—billions of hertz. Fortunately, we can send the desired brightness information with a system that yields at the receiver a pulse changing much less rapidly than that illustrated in figure 12.2. Indeed, we find that throwing away the very high frequencies results in a pulse that is a reasonable replica of the ideal, as shown in figure 12.3.

What bandwidth is necessary to obtain a pleasing television picture on the home screen? The answer comes from tests of actual equipment, since it

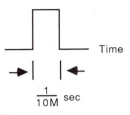

Time

$\frac{1}{10M}$ sec

Figure 12.2
Basic pulse in the video signal.

(a) All frequencies above
    10 MHz discarded

(b) All frequencies about
    4.5 MHz discarded

Figure 12.3
As the band of frequencies is narrowed, the pulse departs more and more from the ideal.

depends not only on the resulting pulse shape but also on the capabilities of human vision. From such studies in the early days of television, developers found that 4.5 MHz is sufficient. Thus, the spectrum of the video signal is that shown in figure 12.4.

This discussion sheds light on the problem associated with the broadcasting of high-definition television (HDTV) mentioned in chapter 11 . The current HDTV in operation in Japan (often used in movie production in the U.S.) has 1125 lines and an aspect ratio of 16/9—hence, it has about 5 times as many dots per picture as the regular U.S. standard. Each video-signal pulse must then be ⅕ the duration of the normal pulse. The required bandwidth would be 5 times as great (5×4.5, or 22.5 MHz).

Newer technology takes advantage of some of the redundancy in the video signal (successive lines tend to be very much alike) and allows a smaller bandwidth, but still much more than the normal 4.5 MHz. Thus, we really cannot hope to see HDTV broadcast on VHF channels, and broadcasting would probably have to be from satellites (where 36 MHz is allotted to each channel already).

12.2 Broadcast Signal

A television station cannot broadcast the video signal directly, for two reasons:

1. Only one station could be on the air at a time, and we would have to shut down all AM radio stations and others using the frequencies from 0 to 4.5 MHz.

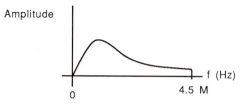

Figure 12.4
Spectrum of the video signal. The band is about 1000 times as much as for tele-phone, so a TV channel costs nearly 1000 times as much as a telephone conversation for long-distance transmission.

2. The smallest significant frequency in the spectrum of figure 12.4 is about 30 Hz. Broadcasting a signal at such a low frequency would require an antenna 200 miles high. (The lower the frequency, the larger the antenna.)

For these two reasons, the video spectrum is shifted up to a much higher frequency before it is broadcast.

If we use channel 2 as a specific example, the spectrum is shifted upward, by ordinary amplitude modulation (AM), by an amount of 55.25 MHz (figure 12.5). As we saw in chapter 9, AM results in two sidebands—one above the carrier, one below. Either one carries the full video information, so there is really no reason to broadcast both. In TV, the transmitter throws away almost all of the lower sideband.

To simplify and reduce the cost of the receiver, the TV station retains a little of the lower sideband—that portion labeled the *vestigial sideband* in figure 12.6. Furthermore, the audio signal to accompany the video is sent by FM in the 0.25 MHz just above the video spectrum.

Figure 12.6 shows the way channel 2 uses the 6-MHz band assigned to it by the FCC—the band from 54 MHz to 60 MHz, which is reserved for channel 2 television stations everywhere in this country.

TV Audio
Early in the history of television, the decision was made to broadcast the audio signal by FM (frequency modulation). The bandwidth is sufficient to allow broadcasting of high-quality, stereo music. Once designers of TV sets learned that most people have little interest in sound quality, however, sets were made with poor sound characteristics in order to keep the price down. There was no incentive for broadcasters to send out a high-quality sound signal. Indeed, viewers wanting to watch an opera or a symphony concert commonly watched on TV and used an FM radio to hear the music (*simulcasting* of the sound).

By the late 1970s the prices of TV sets had fallen markedly in constant dollars, and manufacturers sought changes that would encourage customers to update

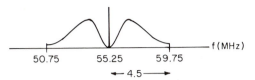

Figure 12.5
TV spectrum after amplitude modulation with a carrier frequency of 55.25 MHz
(channel 2).

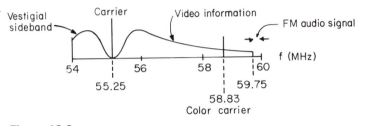

Figure 12.6
Spectrum of broadcast signal from channel 2.

their old equipment. In 1978 Japanese TV stations began broadcasting stereo sound; West Germany followed in 1982, and in 1984 the United States joined the trend. (In the United States, FCC approval was required. Such approval is often delayed by extended debates on standards, lobbying by interests opposed to any change, and the requirement that the regulatory agency invite public comments on any proposed change.)

Thus, the Japanese have much more experience than the Americans with stereo broadcasting. They have also been more imaginative with the use of the second audio channel. Essentially, stereo means that the broadcast includes separate sound information for the left and right speakers. If the stereo effect is not needed, the two signals can carry different sound tracks. For example, in Japan the following uses have emerged:

1. In baseball broadcasts, one announcer is impartial, the other biased.

2. One signal carries detailed commentary, the other much less.

3. Bilingual speech can be broadcast.

4. In foreign movies, one signal is dubbed; the other is not.

5. In educational programs, two different levels of difficulty can be used.

6. In *karaoke* (sing-along), one sound track carries the lyrics and the music, the other the music only (so the viewers can sing).

Color

The color information is broadcast in a band of frequencies around the color carrier frequency shown in figure 12.6. We saw in chapter 11 that human vision cannot detect sharp changes in color, so the bandwidth required for the color signal is much less than the 4.5 MHz needed for the luminance or brightness signal.

The luminance (black-and-white) signal comes close to repeating itself 30 times per second; the picture does not change much from one picture to the next. Hence, the spectrum looks like figure 12.7: the frequencies of the components are close to 30 Hz and all the harmonics of 30 Hz. We have a spectrum, then, that includes only frequencies near multiples of 30 Hz.

The spectrum for the color signal is placed between these *spikes* so that the receiver can separate the color from the luminance. (The French have a different color system: red is transmitted one line, blue in the next, and the receiver includes a short-term memory to portray full color in every line.)

12.3 TV Broadcasting

Each broadcasting television station requires a band of frequencies 6 MHz wide. Channel 2 uses the band from 54 to 60 MHz.

The Federal Communications Commission (FCC) has allocated the following frequencies for the various TV channels:

Channels	MHz
2–4	54–72
5–6	76–88
7–13	174–216
14–69	470–806

Thus, as figure 12.8 shows, television fills more than half the frequencies available out to 800 MHz, with the UHF channels 14–69 the principal *consumer*. (The range from 30 to 300 MHz is called VHF, or Very High

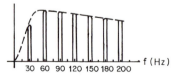

Figure 12.7
Spectrum of the luminance signal.

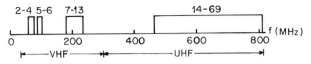

Figure 12.8
TV occupies more than half the available frequencies to 800 MHz.

Frequency; that from 300 to 3000 MHz is called UHF, or Ultra High Frequency. Thus, channels 2–13 are VHF and channels 14–69 are UHF.)

These frequency allocations determine which channels can operate in the same city. To avoid interference, stations on channels adjacent in frequency must be about 75 miles apart. (The actual minimum separation depends on the station's power, the height of the antennas, the nature of the terrain, and other factors determining the chance of interference.) Thus, if channel 2 broadcasts from New York, channel 3 can be located in Philadelphia or Hartford.

This restriction means that a major market, such as Los Angeles, can have at most the following VHF channels:

2   4   5 or 6   7   9   11   13.

There is a frequency separation between channels 4 and 5, and another between 6 and 7. Thus, it is really not surprising that Los Angeles, Chicago, and New York all use channels 2, 4, 5, 7, 9, 11, and 13.

Stations broadcasting on the same channel (for example, channel 4 in Boston, New York, and Washington) must be about 150 miles apart, so that people midway between two stations do not receive two different signals on the same channel. With these two restrictions on channel allocations (adjacent and the same channels), the FCC's problem of awarding broadcasting rights becomes a very complex affair. In much of the United States, all available VHF channels have been assigned.

The preceding discussion suggests a number of other interesting questions:

1. Why are there frequency separations between channels 4 and 5, and between 6 and 7? Why not simply allocate a continuous range of frequencies to channels 2–13? The answer is that important applications of radio were already using the frequencies not given to TV. FM radio occupies the band between 88 and 108 MHz, just above channel 6. Air-traffic-control radio uses some of these frequencies, and the FCC could not easily require all aircraft owners to buy new radio equipment.

2. What happened to channel 1? We do not usually start numbering with 2. Channel 1 (48–54 MHz) was originally used for TV, but the FCC then decided to use this band for other purposes (including police radio).

3. For many years, New Jersey had no broadcasting TV station in the VHF band, and political leaders complained bitterly. Why was a leading industrial state with 8 million people so disadvantaged? The answer is that New York City, bordering northeastern New Jersey, had received channels 2, 4, 5, 7, 9, 11, and 13. Philadelphia, 90 miles away and bordering southwestern New Jersey, received the other channels. Nothing was left for the Garden State. A few years ago, under FCC pressure, channel 9 moved across the Hudson River to broadcast from New Jersey.

12.4 Digital Television

The U.S. consumer market is now beginning to see *digital television* equipment—both television sets and VCRs (videocassette recorders). What signals are actually digital?

The broadcast signal is still as described in the two preceding sections—basically an *analog* (not digital) signal in which the amplitude of each pulse carries the information about the luminance of the corresponding point in the TV picture. In the VCR or the receiver, this video signal is converted to digital form—a sequence of zeros and ones, with each group representing the amplitude of a pulse or the luminance of a particular point.

Advantages of Digital Video

What can we do when the video signal is converted to digital form? Why is it worthwhile to go to the trouble of digitization, then go back to analog form to drive the TV tube? Once the video signal is digital, we can use the power of computer electronics (solid-state devices, chips, and so on) to easily manipulate the signal. For example, digital VCRs and receivers have the potential for the following:

1. Presentation of a picture with an apparent improvement in detail. The broadcast signal contains luminance information for 525 lines. The digital equipment can generate information for 1050 lines: each new line is the average luminance of the lines above and below. The picture then seems to the viewer to have the detail of HDTV—detail close to that of commercial movie film. There is no more information in the digital picture signal, but the viewer perceives much more detail and a more attractive picture.

2. Splitting of the screen. If we digitize incoming signals from more than one channel, the viewer can elect to look at channel 2 in one corner of the screen and channel 4 on the remainder of the screen—with the relative areas under the viewer's remote control. (The sound is associated with only one channel.)

Indeed, one digital receiver now allows dividing the screen into six parts, with a different channel on each. (A cynic about new technology might wonder why anyone would want to watch two or more channels concurrently. Perhaps football enthusiasts want to be sure not to miss an outstanding play on either of two games broadcast at the same time.)

3. Stop action and zoom. When the TV set is showing the output of a VCR tape, we already can stop action and advance one frame at a time (an increment of $\frac{1}{30}$ second), but the picture is often not particularly good. The digital system gives a high-quality picture, and indeed the interpolation technology (filling in between the lines) allows the viewer to stop action, then zoom in on one segment of the picture. This feature is thought to be especially attractive to renters of home-instruction, exercise, and sports tapes—a significant fraction of the rental market.

In other words, once the video signal is in digital form, manipulation of the picture is easy. Whether this technological development really contributes to the enjoyment of television and the quality of life is left as a question for the reader.

Information in the Video Signal

The U.S. video signal consists of 10 million pulses every second. How many binary digits (bits) are required when this signal is digital?

Each video pulse has an amplitude or size indicating the brightness of that spot. How many levels of brightness can the human vision system distinguish? Measurements indicate that we can discern about eight different brightness levels: if each pulse is represented as one of eight possible brightnesses (from black to white), we obtain a satisfactory picture. Thus, 10 million times a second we need to have three binary digits to determine one of the eight levels. This analysis indicates that the digital video signal contains

30M bits per second.

This number is a little low, since eight levels of brightness gives a picture of minimal quality. We can approach the question in a different way. The recently adopted international standard for digital television requires sampling at 13.5 million times per second—higher than is needed in the United States, because European television has a wider bandwidth (more pulses per second). If we quantize to 128 levels, each sample requires seven binary digits, and the information rate is about

100M bits per second.

Neither of these numbers takes into account the enormous redundancy in the picture: two successive dots on one line seldom differ much in brightness; two successive lines are usually very much alike; and two successive pictures typically differ very little. If we take advantage of this redundancy to decrease the number of bits we have to have, we find that it is possible to put a video signal in satisfactory digital form with 3 million bits per second.

At this point, the reader is justified in asking, "What is going on here? How much information is there in a TV picture? Why do we have three different answers in three consecutive paragraphs?"

The answer is that the three numbers represent three different quantities:

30M   This is the information that could be carried by a video signal of average quality.

100M   This is the information available in a signal carrying a high-quality television signal. The international standards for digital TV allow for this greater quality.

3M   This is the decreased amount of information we can easily reach by taking into account very obvious redundancies in the picture signal.

Thus, there is no inherent contradiction; a mediocre broadcast system carries a signal capable of communicating 30M bits per second, but the actual video signal does not change rapidly and hence can easily be sent with 3M bits per second (indeed, even less if we go to more elaborate schemes to take advantage of redundancy).

Human Capability and the Information Rate
Even 3M bits per second is a high information rate. The picture signal contains much more information than a human viewer can absorb.

The human being can receive through the senses only so much information—probably about 100 bits per second, as we learned in chapter 7.

Thus we now have a picture of the TV system sending maybe 3,000,000 bits of information to a viewer who accepts at most 100 bits per second. Even if different viewers want a total of 3000 bits per second, the TV signals carries 1000 times the useful information—enormous technological "overkill." If engineers really understood what information is perceived by viewers, we could have 7000 instead of seven VHF channels.

12.5 Unconventional TV Broadcasting

Section 12.3 described the basic structure of the U.S. television broadcasting system. If we consider only the VHF channels 2–13, we quickly see that the allocation of these channels is an extremely complex affair. As is shown in figure 12.9, once New York City has its seven channels, these are not available for Philadelphia, Binghamton, Albany, New Haven, etc. Then when 3 is assigned to Philadelphia, Wilmington is shut out of the 2, 3, 4 group.

As a result, the required spacing of high-power stations left many regions of the country with at most one or two stations. Harrisburg, for example, has poor reception from New York and mediocre reception from Philadelphia, but is too near each to have a station that would cause interference for people halfway between Harrisburg and New York. The trouble arises because the rules try to protect people living between two cities from receiving interfering signals on the same channel.

In 1980 the FCC allowed low-power television (LPTV) stations to go on the air to service these *underprivileged* regions. These VHF stations are limited to 10 watts power output and typically a range of 10–15 miles; the critical requirement is that there be no interference with the coverage of existing high-power stations. These LPTV stations can originate their own programming or use network offerings.

Current predictions are that there will be 3000 LPTV stations in the United States by the mid-1990s. (The only other country with such technology is Italy, where there are 2000 broadcasters.)

Another way to reach large numbers of people in areas not adequately covered by regular VHF stations is by broadcasting from a geostationary satellite. Satellites were first used by the networks and such organizations as Home Box Office to relay programs to the entire range of recipients—local broadcast stations, regional cable companies, and hotels or motels desiring to offer HBO, ESPN, or other special services to their patrons. The receiving location needed only a receiving antenna (a "dish") aimed at the satellite transmitting the signal—although at these frequencies a line of sight clear even of trees is required.

Three different frequency bands are available:

(a) C-band, 3.7–4.2 GHz.(GHz stands for gigahertz, or billions of hertz.) These channels are used by networks for relaying programs. Low-power transmitters are used; the receiving antenna is 6–10 feet in diameter.

(b) Ku-band, 11.7–12.2 GHz. Similar to (a), but medium power and antenna need be only 3–5 feet. In both (a) and (b), anyone can "listen" if the signal is not scrambled.

(c) Ku-band, 12.2–12.7 GHz. This is the only band allocated for Direct Broadcasting Satellite (DBS) systems; a 2-foot antenna is adequate with the high-power transmitters. The available 500 MHz is divided into "channels," with 36 MHz per channel—enough for high-definition TV.

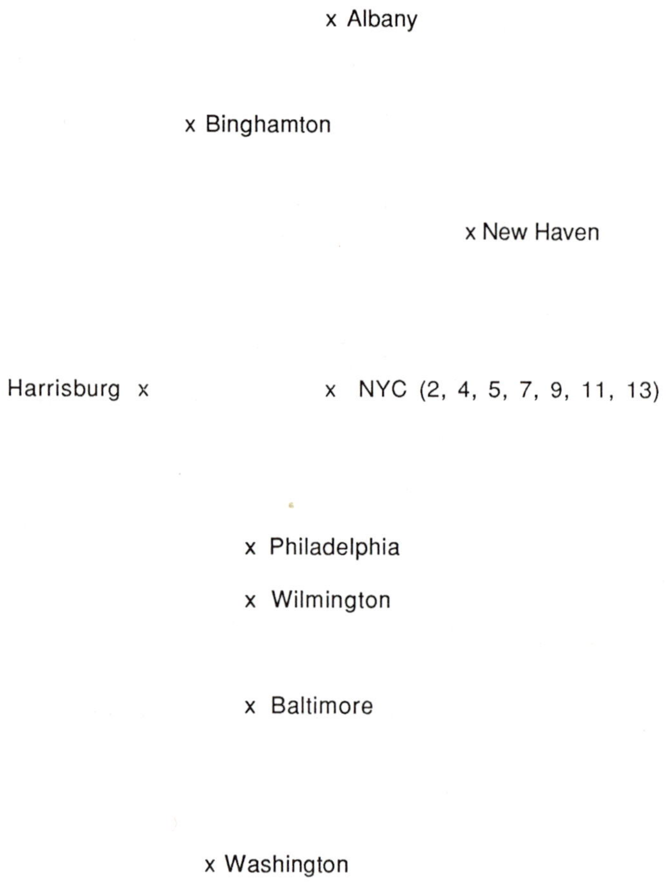

x Albany

x Binghamton

x New Haven

Harrisburg x   x NYC (2, 4, 5, 7, 9, 11, 13)

x Philadelphia

x Wilmington

x Baltimore

x Washington

Figure 12.9
Coverage by cities overlaps.

DBS systems broadcasting to homes now operate in Japan and in the USSR (to reach Siberia).

As the cost of receiving antennas and equipment dropped, networks, HBO, and others using satellites to send programs over the country found that more and more people were picking up the satellite-relayed programs. For this reason they started scrambling the signals, so that potential viewers must obtain a descrambler and pay for an authorization code.

There are various techniques for scrambling a video signal (audio scrambling was discussed in Chapter 9). The simplest technique is inversion (black changed to white, dark gray to light gray, etc.). More complex is the insertion of inversion randomly according to a prearranged code. Synchronization signals can be removed. Finally, we can break up each line and send the segments in a random order (this is analogous to breaking up the spectrum in audio scrambling).

In subscription TV (STV), the broadcast signal is scrambled and viewers pay for the descrambling of each program they view. First introduced in 1950 in New York City, STV has been strongly opposed by broadcasters and theater owners. The FCC finally authorized STV in 1967, but only in areas where at least four VHF stations were broadcasting and only if 28 hours of programs were broadcast unscrambled per week. These restrictions were lifted in 1982, but cable TV has essentially killed STV.

Finally, some regions have Multichannel Multipoint Distribution Service (MMDS). Operating in the 2-GHz frequency range, this microwave system is essentially "wireless cable." Each customer must buy or rent receiving and descrambling equipment.

In this section, we have looked briefly at the various technologies that are used to overcome the severe limitations imposed by the limited spectrum space available for TV (the limited number of channels and the requirement that a new station not interfere with the coverage of existing broadcasters).

12.6 Cable TV

Another way to increase the number of channels available in a home is through *narrowcasting*: sending the video signals directly from a central location through "wires" to the customer. The most common "wiring" is coaxial cable. First introduced in the 1930s, coaxial cable can easily carry a band of frequencies from 0 to 360 MHz (or 60 television channels). The electromagnetic wave is entirely enclosed within the cable, so there is almost no energy lost by radiation. In contrast, a pair of wires radiates at higher frequencies.

The first North American cable TV system began operating in Mahanoy City, Pennsylvania, in 1948 to bring TV broadcasts from major cities to towns too far away or with their line-of-sight transmission blocked by mountains. An antenna on a mountaintop picked up the signal, which then traveled by coaxial cable. These early systems were called Community Antenna TV (CATV), since the primary purpose was to serve a community unable to receive regular broadcasts.

Once CATV systems proved effective, entrepreneurs extended the technology to urban areas where reception was poor because of reflections off tall buildings, and to suburban areas near the limit of the line of sight from broadcasting antennas. By 1950, there were seventy cable TV operations in the U.S.; today about 50 percent of homes receive cable signals.

The growth of cable TV was much faster in Canada. There TV broadcasting did not start until 1952, and major cities were "cabled" early to receive U.S. broadcasts. Today 75 percent of Canada is served by cable. Throughout western Europe, cable systems are growing rapidly.

The simplest cable systems simply bring to the home TV set the basic VHF channels. Most cable systems today feed a converter on top of the home TV set. This device allows tuning to any of the 28 or more cable channels; the selected signal leaving the converter goes to channel 3 of the home set. With so many channels available, cable companies attracted customers by program variety, even in areas where broadcast reception was good.

The technology has improved steadily , so more and more channels have been available:

early CATV systems, 1950s	3 channels
1960s	12 (still common in older cable systems)
late 1970s	35
early 1980s	60
1988	75

Around 1980, it was common to use two cables to offer 120 channels. The shortage of programs led the cable companies to fall back to 75.

In the 1980s, cable TV underwent a change from coaxial cable to fiber optics. Here a pure fiber the size of a human hair carries a light signal (a sequence of light pulses, with the signal in digital form). The light, commonly generated by a laser, stays inside the fiber because of total internal reflection: the fiber is designed so that the light approaching the boundary is bent back into the fiber.

The concept of total internal reflection has been known for a long time, but the technology became feasible only in the 1970s, when fiber manufacturing was developed to control the index of refraction (the speed of light) and to remove nearly all impurities which would scatter the light. (Today's fiber is so pure that a slab half a mile thick would transmit as much light as a clean windowpane.)

The recent history of fiber optics is a superb example of the rate of change of technology. The quality of a transmission system can be measured by the product of two quantities:

distance between repeaters or amplifiers to boost the signal size (in kilometers)

and

information-carrying capability (in bits per second).

The quality available in 1979 was 5 km × 45 M bits per sec, or 225M. In 1988, 40 km × 560M bits per sec, or 22,400M, was available. A quality of 100 km × 3000M bits per sec, or 300,000M, has been demonstrated in the laboratory. Thus, in one decade, this figure of merit has multiplied by 100; another factor of more than 10 has been demonstrated in the laboratory.

Since fiber is cheaper, smaller, and easier to install than coaxial cable, engineers predict that in the future the communication needs of each urban residence will be served by a single fiber.

The evolution of cable TV has an interesting parallel in the transatlantic cable used for communication between the United States and Europe. The first telegraph cable was placed in operation well over a century ago, but a cable to carry telephone conversations had to await the end of World War II and the rapid development of coaxial cable. The first telephone cable was completed in 1956, with 48 channels or simultaneous conversations. In 1963, 140 channels were available. Satellite service started in 1965. In 1970 there were 840 channels; in 1976, 4200. In 1988, with fiber-optic cable, 40,000 channels were available. Now we are able to transmit television signals on the cable.

With satellites available, why bother any more with cable? There are several reasons. First, fiber-optic cable is now competitive with, and perhaps cheaper than, satellite relay. Second, the fiber-optic system is very secure; it is not easy to "listen in" to the messages—a characteristic important in both business and diplomacy. Third, in the case of a nuclear explosion or war, satellite communication will be disrupted.

Fiber-optic cable is ideal for the U.K. and western Europe; the cable branches near Europe, and signals go either to the U.K. or France, where they enter the elaborate national telephone systems. For communication to Africa, satellites are preferable since Africa does not have an efficient local telephone system; satellite transmissions reach all countries separately.

Review Questions

R12-1. Why is it possible to send a color TV signal in a narrower bandwidth than is required by the brightness signal?

R12-2. The TV pulse lasts about 1 microsecond. A radar with this pulse would require a bandwidth of 10 MHz, but TV uses only 4.5 MHz. Why is this possible for TV?

R12-3. What is the velocity of light in space? Does the velocity of light depend on the medium or material it is passing through?

R12-4. Cable TV was originally used in towns too far from stations to get good reception; now cable is being awaited anxiously by many residents of Queens in New York City, even where reception is superb. Why is cable now so attractive?

R12-5. Explain briefly how a TV station (such as channel 2 in New York) can transmit teletext information (written news) at the same time it is transmitting a regular entertainment program.

R12-6. The video bandwidth is 4.5 MHz, but each TV station is allocated 6 MHz. Why?

R12-7. TV audio is sent by FM but is generally low in fidelity. Why has this practice become common?

R12-8. Explain the origin of the acronym CATV

R12-9. Canadians use cable TV much more than Americans. Explain briefly what reasons there might be.

R12-10. Why is the antenna for UHF so much smaller than that for VHF?

R12-11. Why do Soviet communication satellites not sit in geostationary orbits?

R12-12. Geostationary orbit is at 22,300 miles and the satellite orbits the Earth in about 24 hours. At an altitude or range of 220,000 miles (where the Moon is), what would be the orbital period of a satellite?

R12-13. Why is satellite communication (rather than underwater cable or fiber optics) very advantageous for phone calls to Africa from the U.S., but not for calls to Europe?

R12-14. What is the primary responsibility of the FCC (Federal Communications Commission) in regard to radio?

R12-15. South American countries object to all the U.S. satellites in geostationary position to serve the U.S. Why?

R12-16. Why is the bandwidth of a SETI receiver only a few hertz (cycles per second)? (See problem 12-6.)

Problems

P12-1. The following paragraphs briefly describe some of the dangers inherent in an interactive cable TV system. Prepare a letter to the editor of your local newspaper in which you argue for a citizens' committee to monitor the procedures of the local cable company. The letter should be no more than 200 words in length and should emphasize those risks most meaningful to the average, concerned citizen.

The right to privacy has always been traditional in the U.S. We take for granted that no one is spying on us or noting our every move. Now a new technology has arrived by which information on our personal habits is recorded and stored. This information can be compiled to make a personal profile of a particular family or individual. Interactive cable TV has the *capability* of acting as a spy in our home. Let us examine the system and see how this threat is possible.

An interactive cable TV system allows us to send messages (through signals) from our home to the transmitting cable station. This message is sent over the same cable that brings TV programs into our house. Why would anyone want to send messages to the central office of the cable company? A variety of valuable services can be provided:

1. In an emergency, we could call for help by simply pushing a "panic button" on the TV set. Another button would tell the cable company to call the fire department or the police.

2. We could order items advertised on TV simply by punching in the appropriate digits on our set. For example, bookstores could describe new books on TV and then encourage the audience to place their orders immediately. The viewers could punch in their credit card numbers to pay for the books.

3. Viewers could respond immediately to public opinion polls, then the results of the polls could be shown on the TV screen.

4. Courses offered on television could have more of a classroom format, because students could respond to the instructor by means of their interactive system.

5. In an experiment in Japan, viewers were provided with TV cameras and appropriate equipment so they could be televised in their homes. Then in town-meeting discussions, individual viewers appeared on the screen to express their views. Part of the favorable public response in the town resulted because people enjoyed recognizing one another when they subsequently met while doing errands.

Clearly, interactive cable systems add an entirely new dimension to television. In Columbus, Ohio, one football team decided to give the TV audience a chance to play quarterback. The team agreed to let the public call every play through the interactive cable system. The viewers were given a list of plays, and the majority decision was communicated to the bench, then to the quarterback. (The team lost, which perhaps is a commentary on the value of plurality voting on issues.)

As so often happens with technological innovations, however, this interactive feature also has its disadvantages. The very features that make it attractive can infringe on our personal privacy. For example:

1. For billing purposes, all systems must maintain records of the programs watched by each subscriber. Thus, the central computer could generate a detailed profile of the viewing habits of a particular household. Perhaps in a future political campaign, a candidate will announce the pornographic movies watched in his opponent's home.

2. When burglar-alarm service is provided by the cable company, the computer could develop a detailed pattern of the hours when a house is vacant.

3. When viewers record their opinions, this information can be stored in the computer. If viewers were asked to vote on a controversial issue, such as gun control, the computer could retain a list of all those on either side of the question. We can easily visualize the time when the cable company will be able to provide a picture of the attitudes of each subscriber family.

In all of these interactive systems, the viewer is always warned when expressed viewpoints are being stored in the computer memory. Furthermore, enormous care is taken to make sure the computer data is secure and restricted for ethical uses only. However, as we have seen in other systems involving computer data storage, information can be stolen and used illegally.

Let us continue our list of socially significant and risky applications of interactive cable:

4. Once the cable company knows which subscribers favor something (for example, gun control), and which are opposed, a politician can easily tape a campaign speech with two different versions of the particular segment devoted to the gun-control question. The cable company then sends into each home only the particular version of the speech that shows the politician to be in agreement with the views expressed by that household.

5. By consulting the computer memory for records of who watched which advertisements and by encouraging the use of credit cards or other identifiers at the neighborhood supermarket with an automated checkout system, the cable company can evaluate the effectiveness of commercials.

All of this technology is now available. If we look a decade into the future, we can imagine even more questionable infringements of privacy. By then, computer generation of speech will undoubtedly have reached the level at which the computer can copy the particular speech characteristics of an individual. Perhaps in a presidential election you will be subjected to the following scenario: One evening your phone will ring. When you answer, the "voice" of one of the candidates will greet you, exchange pleasantries, ask how you liked a particular movie you saw last night, inquire about the health of your daughter after her recent gymnastic accident, and then go on to discuss your specific views on the election. The "candidate" will show a surprisingly detailed understanding of your opinions.

Just as interactive TV is growing, the U.S. government is withdrawing from its role of protecting the public. In order to understand this, we have to look very briefly at the recent history of government regulation.

The 1960s saw the birth of the idea that the federal government has a strong responsibility to protect the individual and the environment. Rachel Carson's book *Silent Spring*, and then Ralph Nader's book *Unsafe At Any Speed*, stimulated this change. By the mid-1970s, we had regulations on auto safety, pesticides, food additives, water and air pollution, and safety in the workplace. The public accepted the idea that government must protect the individual, particularly when the citizen could not understand the science and even might not be aware of the risk involved.

Problems probably were inevitable. As one government agency after another was established, rules and regulations grew astonishingly. For example, Congress passed the Clean Air Act to try to control air pollution. The act runs on for 185 pages. Then the Environmental Protection Agency had the job of making rules to carry out this act. These rules cover 2500 pages. Any company wanting to abide by the law must find, in the 2500 pages, each rule that applies to it, and then decide how to operate within these regulations.

By the late 1970s, U.S. industrial leaders were publicly arguing that they could not compete with other countries when they had to pay a large staff just to understand and fulfill government regulations. It was not unusual for a manufacturing plant to have to follow rules made by as many as 21 federal agencies, plus state and local regulations. As jobs disappeared, the public questioned the regulatory bureaucracy more and more.

Responding to these arguments, the federal government began to withdraw from its regulatory activity. Both Democrats and Republicans cut back the regulatory agencies. The job of protection of the individual was turned over to the states and local governments. This sort of national change rapidly becomes a bandwagon, so even the regulation of cable TV was left to the city or county.

This situation carries some risk. County governments often do not have the technical expertise to understand the potential for infringement on privacy. If the people really want interactive cable TV, they are likely to allow it in under any conditions.

P12-2. Several cable-TV companies are now bidding for the franchise to offer cable services to your city. One company has submitted a proposal promising 120 channels to every home. The decision is made partly on the basis of factors other than technical capabilities. (Each proposal has to describe the rates that will be charged subscribers, the fees paid to the city for the franchise, the schedule of availability in each district, the number of necessary subscribers.)

a. You work for the company with the proposal for 120 channels. Competitive proposals would offer only 40 channels. Write a brief description of the advantages to the public of the enormously greater capacity your company offers.

b. Fiber-optic systems currently under development would have enough information capacity to provide each residence with 1500 TV channels. There seems to be no technical reason why this capability should not reach a million channels in the future. Approximately how many channels would be necessary to allow the homeowner to select any program broadcast in the last 20 years? (Exclude news programs and consider only the three major networks.)

P12-3. Cable television has grown rather slowly in the U.S. (compared with Canada, where broadcasting did not start until 1952). In 1975, the best cable systems provided 28 channels offering broadcast signals; signals relayed to the cable company by microwave links; programs originated locally; weather, news and sports; business news; and channels for use by schools, local government, and community groups.

a. Today cable systems often provide 60 channels or more. What programs are available today that were not common in 1975?

b. Television studios largely use digital signal processing of camera signals. Home receivers more and more convert the signal into digital form, but the transmission from broadcaster to viewer seems likely to remain with the signal in analog form. Explain.

P12-4. There have been major attempts by the electronics industry to develop picturephones and video teleconferencing. The hopes were that people would want to see the person they were talking to on the phone, and that companies would save travel money and time by holding conferences with participants in different locations.

The communication cost is proportional to the bandwidth needed, so emphasis was placed on reducing the bandwidth far below the 4.5 MHz of normal TV. There are two ways to take advantage of the redundancy in the video signal:

1. We can transmit only the changes from one picture to the next. In ⅟₃₀ second, relatively little changes; indeed, the background of someone talking may be largely unchanged for many pictures.

2. Within each picture, the changes from dot to dot and from line to line are small.

By taking advantage of these characteristics, engineers were able to reduce the required bandwidth to ⅟₆₀ of its normal TV size.

a. The rate of 60 fields per second has not been reduced in this technology, even though such a reduction would decrease the bandwidth proportionally. Why?

b. If you were involved in a video teleconference, what would you as a viewer notice about the picture quality? That is, under what circumstances would the quality be poor?

c. Teleconferencing requires a large screen so everyone in the room can see the picture. One system uses an image 20 feet wide and 15 feet high. To obtain good resolution, 1024 lines and 1024 dots per line are used. How do these characteristics affect the bandwidth needed?

P12-5. To be successful, a new communications technology must satisfy many constraints. Some of these follow (naturally, not all of these apply in each particular case).

1. The technology must be matched to the physiological characteristics of the people with whom it interacts. For example, a television system showing only one new picture per second results in annoying jumpiness.

2. The technology must not demand total discarding of earlier technology unless the improvement is so marked that people are willing to discard old

equipment. The LP record is the most remarkable example; it rapidly displaced the 78-rpm system.

3. The use of the technology must fit in with the ethical standards of our society. For example, it would be easy to implant a radio transmitter in everyone with repeated arrests on criminal charges, then continuously track those individuals at all times. Most people don't seriously consider such an approach to crime control. We don't even like the idea of reading all license plates of cars going through a tunnel or over a bridge, then checking them against a computer master list of scofflaws or wanted individuals and stopping certain drivers at the exit of the bridge or tunnel.

4. The technology should be designed to satisfy the particular interests and desires of an appreciable segment of the potential market. For example, the telephone system is designed for excellent intelligibility; most people don't care about fidelity.

5. The technology should be described as honestly and completely as possible to the public. People will oversell the technology themselves, so engineers must be especially cautious. For example, lie detectors were first presented to the public as being foolproof. Now we know that this is not true.

6. Failure of the technology (and it will occasionally fail) must not cause a disaster far greater than the advantages when everything works. The many attempts to build a device to prevent an intoxicated individual from starting his car have floundered because of the times the devices operate when they shouldn't.

7. The technology should be standardized early so that customers can buy from any manufacturer. This happened with audio cassettes and color TV, but not with video tape recorders and video discs.

8. The cost must be reasonable for the public's perception of the services. The picturephone has never been popular, partly because the cost is too high for the additional advantages it has over a telephone.

9. The technology should have long-term utility. If we make a major financial investment in a TV set, we want to be able to use the set for many years.

Select one specific example of communications technology (where the term *communications* can be interpreted broadly—a machine can be communicating in quite simple terms to a human being).

a. How does the technology meet each of the appropriate constraints listed above? Explain.

b. Are there other important constraints which your technology must satisfy?

P12-6. In the Search for Extra-Terrestrial Intelligence (SETI), we point a very sensitive antenna toward a star that might have a planet with intelligent life, perhaps much more advanced than ours. We "listen" for radio signals broadcast from that distant civilization. The exciting goal is to locate another civilization and prove that we are not unique.

The first question is: At what frequency should we "listen"? If their civilization is similar to ours, the most abundant element is hydrogen, which resonates or emits at 1.420 BHz. Water is essential; the OH hydroxyl radical resonates at 1.67 BHz. Thus, it seems logical that "they" might broadcast in this "water hole" between the two frequencies. This band is also relatively noise-free.

The receiver has to have a bandwidth of only a few hertz to minimize the noise. Since the transmitting and receiving planets are both moving, there is a Doppler shift which we do not know; thus we have to vary the tuning of the receiver over the possible frequency range. To cover all of the sky, we keep the antenna in one direction for only 2 minutes and hope that the other civilization was broadcasting toward us at the corresponding time in the past.

Project META (Megachannel ExtraTerrestrial Assay) is now using an antenna in Harvard, Massachusetts.. Stanford University, NASA, and the Jet Propulsion Laboratory are completing much more elaborate equipment in California. Clearly the odds of success are small, but the potential impact is enormous.

a. There are strong arguments that we should not broadcast signals toward a distant star and thereby reveal our existence. Explain.

b. Funds for SETI will come from the U.S. government. Is this an appropriate use of federal funds?

P12-7. The SONY RDSS (Radio Determination Satellite System) allows the owner of a fleet of trucks to track and communicate with each truck at all times. Each vehicle continually measures its own location through the Loran-C navigation system (chapter 11). Information about this location as well as messages from the truck operator and data on vehicle operation are transmitted to a geosynchronous satellite owned by Geostar Corporation (founded by Gerard K. O'Neill). The satellite sends this information to the ground station in Washington. The fleet headquarters then can access this information over regular telephone lines.

From the standpoint of the truck drivers, is this technology a step forward or backward? Describe the advantages and disadvantages.

P12-8. In recent years, fax or facsimile technology has been one of the fastest growing communication technologies:

	No. of machines	Market
1986	191,000	$712M
1987	475,000	1.2B
1988	910,000	2.1B
1991 (est.)	1.5M	2.8B

The FAX technology allows the free use of graphics in printed messages, where graphics have traditionally been avoided because of the print difficulties. Using the regular telephone system, FAX promises to seriously damage the several overnight mail services.

The concept of facsimile dates back to 1848 and the Scottish clockmaker Alexander Bain. It was 1902, however, before Arthur Korn developed a photoelectric scanning system. Five years later, Korn established a commercial network linking Berlin, London, and Paris.

Facsimile service remained rather crude until the 1970s. A sensor scanned a page line by line (just as in TV), and an electronic signal indicated the black or white pixels. The communication cost was still high, however, since a page required as much as 6 minutes.

In the 1980s, the speed increased, to a rate as high as 20 seconds per page, largely as a result of transmission of the signal in a digital form, which allows simplification (e.g., for a long white space, the equipment need send only the length of the space).

Why is the speed of transmission limited? (Recall that the regular telephone system is used.) Explain, including an estimate of the number of lines scanned across an 8½ × 11-inch page.

Index